Female & Male Voices in
Early Modern England

Female & Male Voices in Early Modern England

An Anthology of Renaissance Writing

EDITED BY

Betty S. Travitsky
and
Anne Lake Prescott

Columbia University Press
New York

Columbia University Press
Publishers Since 1893
New York   Chichester, West Sussex
Copyright © 2000 Columbia University Press
All rights reserved
Library of Congress Cataloging-in-Publication Data
Female and male voices in early modern England : an anthology of Renaissance writing / edit-
ed by Betty S. Travitsky and Anne Lake Prescott.
      p. cm.
     ISBN 0–231–10040–X (cloth) — ISBN 0–231–10041–8 (paper)
     1. English literature—Early modern, 1500–1700. 2. England—Civilization—16th
century—Literary ollections. 3. England—Civilization—17th century—Literary collections.
4. Sex differences (Psychology)—Literary collections. 5. English literature—Women authors.
6. English literature—Men authors. 7. Sex role—Literary collections. I. Travitsky, Betty S.,
1942– II. Prescott, Anne Lake, 1936–
PR1121 .F46 2000
820.8'003—dc21   99–057975

Casebound editions of Columbia University Press books are printed on permanent and
durable acid-free paper.
Printed in the United States of America
c 10 9 8 7 6 5 4 3 2 1
p 10 9 8 7 6 5 4 3 2 1

Contents

Introduction

Studying Gender in the Early Modern Period: Complicating the Picture

This volume was born of the realization that it is still difficult for scholars to teach gender-aware courses on the early modern period, since many traditional anthologies—even fairly recent ones—have almost no selections by women, offering only slight evidence to show that, so to speak, Judith Shakespeare *did* exist in early modern England. There are, of course, inherent difficulties that in part explain this situation. Responsible surveys of early modern English documents must reflect the fact that more early modern English men than women could write (as well as read), and anthologies of early modern English literature, after all, must inevitably be dominated by male authors such as More, Sidney, Spenser, Donne, Bacon, Wyatt, and Herbert. Even admirably edited anthologies of early modern English texts that take pains to include women writers, therefore, cannot escape a certain tokenism: women writers are far outnumbered. How then, we asked ourselves, could one achieve a doubled vision of this record? One solution is to assign a selection of women's writings alone, but such collections unavoidably risk ghettoizing women's voices.

At present, in our opinion, there is probably no wholly satisfactory way of dealing with the unhappy fact that although women made up half the population in early modern England and although all writers perceived the world through categories that include gender, the early modern written record is dominated by men. However, we theorized, if women's texts could be foregrounded without being ghettoized, readers would be more likely to take gender into account when reading the literature of the past. As it is, too many people, we suspect, still think of literature by men as literature and literature by women as women's literature. An anthology that accomplished such a feat, we reasoned, would encourage readers to take gender into account when reading texts by both women and men. *How* they would take it into account—what they would make of similarities and differences, whether they would read difference as inherent or as socially constructed—would be up to them to decide (and an interesting focus for class discussion enabled by such a collection). An anthology that brought women's texts together with texts by men in terms of gender, sex, and eroticism, would, we decided, aid the scholarly world's efforts to recover women's voices, not (and this is our innovation) by adding a few to a male-dominated anthology or by collecting texts in a separate volume but, rather, by juxtaposing a considerable number of those voices to those of men.

We have therefore put together a collection of early modern English writings that without pretending to reflect the statistical reality of the early modern period nevertheless explicitly encourages students to be more aware of gender as a significant category of thought and perception. *Female and Male Voices in Early Modern England* includes works by both women and men—including some new and important recoveries—grouped so as to show authors of both sexes writing in the same generic tradition or dealing with similar topics. It brings the voices of English Marrano women (or secret Jews) such as Sara Lopez into print for the first time and the Miltonic poetry of Jane Lead into print for the first time since the seventeenth century; it fits some recently recovered texts into different grooves, juxtaposing, for example, the country-house poem of Amelia Lanyer with an expression of a different type of nostalgia by Surrey. It includes unconventional voices, as in the homoerotic poems by Richard Barnfield or the possibly lesbian poems by Katherine Philips.

In order to situate these excerpts, we now sketch the altered view of early modern England that would result from a foregrounding of gender in thinking about the period, instancing a portion of the contents of this volume as we do so. We offer the following outline not to recap the history of early modern England but to demonstrate the way in which foregrounding gender in the study of texts refocuses our understanding of several early modern cultural issues (including the issue of periodization itself): communication (including the production of belles lettres), politics, religion, and domestic life and sexuality. Although scholars disagree about details, they do agree that some major changes took place in communicating and in viewing the world in the early modern period. We believe that thinking about gender affects the way we understand these changes.

Periodization

Joan Kelly argued many years ago that "there was no renaissance for women, at least not during the Renaissance" ("Did Women Have a Renaissance?" first printed in *Becoming Visible: Women in European History*, ed. Renate Bridenthal and Claudia Koonz [Boston: Houghton Mifflin, 1977], pp. 137–64, 139). She was referring to the traditional meaning of the term "renaissance" as a rebirth of classical culture after the dormant period of the middle ages, and she was arguing that women were not liberated or reborn during the Renaissance in the same way that we traditionally have said that men were. Now that scholars have shifted to a stress on continuity, rather than rupture, between the middle ages and modern times and have changed their terminology for the 250-year period following the middle ages to the early modern period, the issue of periodization may seem less urgent. After all, we do not associate this very long stretch with a dramatic change in outlook or status as we traditionally did the Renaissance; rather, we see it as a transitional period between medieval and modern times. Therefore, if we cannot say that dramatic changes for women (in, say, legal status) defined the limits of the period, the same would be true for men. Nevertheless, we complicate our understanding of the epoch now called the early modern period when we consider women, because if we try to define this period on the basis of the evolution of the position or status of English women over that of women living in the medieval period, we would probably not choose the dates 1500–1750. More important dates might be much later ones: the year of the passage of the Married Woman's Property Act, the years when safe formulas became available for infants and comfortable, well-concealed sanitary products for women, and the year when contraceptives became legally available. Even so, there are changes in England in the condition of women and in the position of women writers during the period we now call early modern, even if these changes do not always coincide with those in the condition of men. Indeed, some shifts further constricted women.

Communication

During the middle ages, learning tended to be cultivated in the oases constituted by religious houses. Some women in these establishments achieved very high degrees of learning; some became authors. But the masses of laypeople and even most nobles in the general population were illiterate. Along with the revival of commerce that followed the crusades, the development of urban centers and of trades to support them, and the invention of the printing press, European society underwent a transformation from an oral and manuscript to a mixed oral, print, and manuscript culture. The written word became much more widely available; small schools to teach basic skills were opened to boys and girls. The rise of national states, the growth of national languages, the availability of reading material in the vernacular rather than merely in the learned languages, all meant opportunity for less privileged members of society—and we focus on women, in every class less privileged than men—to participate more in the culture of their time. The translation of learned works into the vernacular—Juan Luis Vives's *Instruction of a Christian Woman* (1529) being one important example—encouraged and enabled women to improve themselves. (As we show below, religious and educational theorists would deliberately cultivate varying degrees of learning in women.) Women, traditionally barred from public communication, began to write—slowly and as translators of religious materials at first, in greater numbers, and as authors of original religious and secular materials as the early modern period proceeded. In the seventeenth century, Margaret Cavendish followed the lead of Margary Kempe, the first writer of an autobiography in English, appending her autobiography to her biography of her husband, reflecting on her need to compose and providing an interesting contrast to the reflections on the same subject by Richard Brathwait, an earlier seventeenth-century biographer.

The extent of female literacy is by no means established, and today's scholars also disagree about women as a category of readers, while what women read or should read was a traditional area of dispute, connected in the early modern period to general arguments about the nature of women. Christine de Pisan (1365–1430), an Italian woman living in France, contributed importantly to such debates, and when arguments about the nature of women accelerated during the early modern period, Englishwomen began to add their salvos. Over time the controversy evolved to include medical debate and debate over women's rights to practice such professions as midwifery, a traditionally female profession that was slowly closed to midwives. Before this exclusion occurred, Jane Sharp, a midwife, wrote a gynecological text in plain English for the understanding of unlearned readers; in contrast, the physician John Sadler, purporting to write to women, laced his text with Latin.

Women composed polemical writings concerning gender as well as other topics, despite the traditional conviction that women should remain silent and should not allow themselves a public voice even on the printed page. But over the course of the early modern period, particularly in turbulent times, public speaking and writing by women grew in both quantity and type. Beginning with translation of religious works by Margaret Beaufort, Englishwomen, by the end of our period, were, like Ann Collins, writing poetry; like Aphra Behn, imaginative drama; like Mary Wroth, narratives; like Elizabeth Grey, handbooks on practical subjects; like Mary Carleton, life stories; like Bathsua Makin, essays; like Mary Astell, treatises; like Jane Lead and Sarah Chevers and Katherine Evans, prophetic, mystical, and sometimes learned tracts. They acted as literary patrons and collected literary coteries about themselves. Like Gertrude Dawson, they participated in print culture by becoming printers. In this volume we pair Collins's poetry with Henry Colman's; Wroth's romance with Philip Sidney's; Grey's recipes with Hugh Platt's; Carleton's adventures with Thomas Whythorne's; Jane Lead's religious ecstasy with John Milton's ode on the birth of Christ; the Quaker Chevers and Evans's imprisonment in Malta with the Jesuit William Weston's imprisonment in England. Metaphors about writing were also frequently gendered. Some types of writing came to be considered effeminate, some masculine, with these types varying over time. We find praises of manly wit, of effeminately effete writing, and such tropes as the pregnant pen. Possibly the most remarkable of such tropes has been attributed to the childless Margaret Cavendish, a woman who wrote critically of the energies other women poured into child care and who reportedly would awake at night exclaiming, "I conceive, I conceive" as a new notion struck her.

Family Structure and Sexuality

Since professions and self-employment were severely limited to them, women were deeply affected by the norms of family life. In the England of that much-married monarch, Henry VIII, the domestic arena came under great scrutiny. Writers interrogated male and female authority both inside the home and—it was thought analogously—outside it. They examined woman's place from the standpoint of religious, political, and social codes. Although theorists did not seek women's opinions, two late-sixteenth-century Englishwomen, Jane Anger (or Ongar) and Margaret Tyler, voiced an opinion in print, and others took up the struggle in the early seventeenth century.

If women were not invited to voice their opinions about their status and roles, however, they certainly seem to have been expected to read the opinions of male authorities. And they were also enjoined to educate their children and their servants—each of these duties suggesting that they would be able to read themselves. By the late sixteenth century, we find women keeping diaries and writing manuscript books of advice to children (and grandchildren), and in the early seventeenth century they originated a new subgenre: the mother's advice book, a product of the new literacy and the new responsibilities of women. The late-seventeenth-century "Legacy" of Susanna Bell to her children, printed with an introduction by her minister, Thomas Brooke that is four times the length of her advice, is symptomatic both of the movement of women toward a subject position and of their containment by men. It is also an example of the juxtaposition of the voices of men and women during the early modern period.

As subjects women also wrote on love, both within marriage and outside it, both happily and complainingly, and both realistically and imaginatively. Well-written coronas by a father and daughter, Robert Sidney and Mary Sidney Wroth, are but one interesting pairing included here. The sprightly love poetry of Isabella Whitney pairs interestingly with the complaints of Thomas Campion; the unhappy poems that passed between Margaret Douglas and Thomas Howard are possibly the earliest known love poems to have been exchanged between English aristocratic lovers; the laments of Rachel Russell over her husband, the political martyr, and the pitiful—if shrewish—letters of Elizabeth Stafford all convey aspects of conventional early modern sexuality. Less conventional, if perhaps more remarkable, sentiments are expressed in homoerotic poems by John Donne and Richard Barnfield and the possibly lesbian friendship poems by Katherine Philips.

Religious and Political Changes The hegemony of the Roman Catholic church was broken during the early modern period, and schism, confrontation, and war all resulted in propagandizing that was greatly enhanced by the new printing press. In sixteenth-century England, religious change came hand in glove with political change, as Henry VIII moved England from the papal camp, changing wives and chief ministers as he did so, arousing religious fervor—on the part of both men and women—both in his camp and in opposition to him, and raising questions about the conduct of the home as well as that of church and country. With the accessions of his three legitimate children, the official religion of the country also shifted. Controversy was not stilled, however. And women played a much publicized part in this controversy, including the prophecies of Elizabeth Barton, and the martyrdoms of Anne Askew and Margaret Clitherow—to say nothing of many lesser-known women. As is often the case, women were tolerated—and even encouraged—as partisans in the religious skirmishes, although the effect of their participation was mixed. If laywomen were encouraged to read and conduct their lives and families with increased piety, the convents in England were closed and the opportunity they afforded some women for a life of the mind was lost, as was the empowering model of the female saints. The support of the priest in the confessional enhanced the sense of autonomy of the Roman Catholic woman, and the insistence on justification by faith that of the Protestant woman. Women and men took up their crosses: Sarah Chevers and Katherine Evans, imprisoned in Malta by the Inquisition; the martyred Jesuit William Weston, imprisoned in England. Women and men wrote of their faith: of a number of compelling pairs contained in these pages, one that is particularly striking is formed by the sonnets of Anne Lock, author of what is probably the first sonnet sequence in English, and her son, Henry Lock.

If massive civil disorder was minimized in sixteenth-century England, religious and political dissent were certainly not stilled. Economic disruptions created a disadvantaged underclass, augmented by soldiers returning from the foreign wars that England was spared on her own soil during the sixteenth century and by persons dislocated from closed religious houses. Economic hardship led to what the English authorities perceived as a great deal of unrest and movement by disadvantaged persons, including women. And economic hardships were particularly difficult for women who, when displaced, were unable to support themselves as easily as men. The most common results, prostitution and illegitimacy, were also increasingly criminalized with the building of workhouses and the execution of women for gendered crimes such as infanticide, and with the perceived need to maintain order came the practice of scapegoating women as witches. Men wrote both credulously and questioningly about such criminalization, and we include Henry Goodcole's record of the interrogation of Elizabeth Sawyer, executed as a witch in 1621, and the brilliantly interrogative speech attributed to her by Thomas Dekker, John Ford, and William Rowley in their *Witch of Edmonton.*

When male medical practitioners tried to oust women from their traditional practice of midwifery, some polemic resulted, as well as handbooks such as Sharp's. Ethnicity and class feeling were aroused as the Welsh Tudors brought in new men, undercutting the older aristocracy, and as James VI and I brought in his Scottish supporters and his foreign queen and attempted to create a Great Britain in place of the old England. Foreign craftsmen and members of displaced groups such as the Marranos, who attempted to escape religious wars on the continent and to build new lives in England, were often resented by the native population. Women in these populations suffered the disabilities of these groups as well as the traditional disadvantages of their sex. Roderigo Lopez, a Marrano, was condemned and executed as a traitor, and his widow's goods were confiscated. Sara Lopez's petition to Elizabeth for relief appears in print here for the first time, as well as a number of other petitions testifying to the presence of the Jewish voice—and the Jewish Question—in early modern England.

Unrest brought with it polemic, including polemics on gender to which women—like men—contributed. And when political and religious differences finally culminated in the civil war period of the mid-seventeenth century, writings by women increased dazzlingly in number and vituperativeness. At court wordplay proliferated, exemplified here by the anagrams of Mary Fage and Francis Lenton. In the country at large, petitioning grew to new levels, and the women's mass petitions of the 1640s and 1650s brought reaction in the form of mock petitions by male satirists. Women preachers, petitioners, and prophets sprouted up all over the country, exemplified here in poems by Eleanor Davies and a follower of the radical Gerrard Winstanley. Yet the power of patriarchy was not broken by the end of this period, and as order was restored, the outspokenness of women was less tolerated.

English insularity was somewhat punctured, however, as the period wore on, in terms of interaction with Europe and with the rest of the world. The captivity narrative of Mary Rowlandson with its fascinating comments on Native Americans and the extract from Hakluyt's "Voyages" reflect the results of this interaction. Influences and cross-fertilization included the importation of foreign consorts with their foreign literary tastes and patterns of behavior; the importation, finally, of a foreign ruling house; the involvement (and noninvolvement) in continental wars—even when they touched daughters of the king; proselytizing by women as well as by men both within and beyond the boundaries of the country; settlement and hardships in the colonies, with records and poetry created by women settlers as well as by men; and the display of women natives as captive curiosities.

The exploration of these and other developments is proceeding rapidly in the field of early modern studies as scholars continue to recover lost voices, many by women, and to turn up new matter for study. Even the questions asked tend to mutate and shift as these scholars learn more about the period's complex synergy of cultural or material forces and as they notice and rethink their own assumptions.

We hope that our volume helps make the lesser known of those voices even more audible. We also hope to give all of them more resonance by positioning them near others of the opposite sex who wrote on the same topic but, often, not in the same tones.

A Word on Methodology

In preparing this anthology, we have attempted to make the texts user-friendly, so after some hesitation, and aware that one fruitful field of modern scholarship is the study of how texts display themselves materially on the page, we agreed that for many students the advantages of modernization outweigh the sacrifice of some culturally significant aspects of style and presentation. We have tried to compensate for such loss in our notes. In adopting modern spelling, for example, we have obscured the texts' potential for wordplay (Renaissance English, with its unsettled orthography, was inherently pun-prone), but our notes sometimes alert readers to instances of verbal ambiguity and wit. We have modernized the punctuation, although less often when editing poetry. On occasion we have added paragraphing and broken up run-on sentences. We follow modern convention in capitalizing "God" and His pronouns but also some abstract nouns if the author is clearly indulging in a little personification allegory (emblematic discourse with, often, an implicitly quasi-visual component that some students are likely to miss unless alerted to its presence).

Students should recall, though, that any modernization can subtly change a meaning. When an early modern writer says "my selfe" does she or he mean what we mean by "myself" or the slightly different "my self"? Although we do not include a secondary bibliography, we have indicated the sources for our texts. We hope that students who wish to study this material further will seek out the originals or the modern scholarly editions we cite in our headnotes, as well the rapidly increasing number of relevant web sites on the Internet.

Our notes and glosses define obsolete or obscure words, translate foreign tags, and identify allusions likely to puzzle less experienced readers. For most of the women writers in this volume and for a few lesser-known male authors, this has meant so treating these materials for the first time. We trust that the more experienced will bear with us. When editing verse, which we have modernized more discreetly, we have indicated the pronounced final "ed" with an accent. Finally, for reasons of space we have sometimes—reluctantly—condensed our selections; all omissions are indicated by ellipses or by phrases in brackets indicating what is missing. We do not think we have distorted any writer, but again we encourage interested students to seek the originals.

A word on organization: our arrangement of such a variety of texts written by so broad a range of writers is in some ways arbitrary. We therefore urge readers (and teachers planning assignments) to try the mental exercise of imagining different ways to pair the writings we include. We have in large part organized this anthology by topic (religion, love, politics) but an equally valid arrangement would be by genre. For example, Anne Lock's religious sonnets might be interestingly juxtaposed to secular ones by Wroth or Barnfield: the themes differ profoundly, but the poets all faced challenges peculiar to the form itself. Or one could arrange the whole anthology by generation, or even by class (aristocrats, whatever their sex, have much in common). Finally, we have treated all our writers as women or men but we recognize the current and useful distinction between anatomical sex, a matter of chromosomes, and culturally inflected gender. Since we offer some homoerotic texts (including a "lesbian" poem by a man, John Donne), our division of writers according to sex should not preclude awareness of gender's more complex possibilities.

Acknowledgments

We thank the following persons who have assisted us as we have prepared this volume: Peter Blayney, Mary Chan, The Bishop of London, the Rt. Revd. and Rt. Hon. Dr. Richard Chartres, Ellen Cordes, Alan Farmer, Susan Felch, Patricia Gallagher, Stephen Greenberg, Dr. John Gurney of the Royal Commission on Historical Manuscripts, Margaret Hannay, Samantha Heller, Elaine Hobby, David Kastan, Roger Kuin, Lydia K. Lake, Lisa Ann Libby, Paula Loscocco, Michael Mallick, Ann Mitchell, Lord Salisbury, Edgar Samuel, Lois Schwoerer, James Shapiro, Victor Skretkowicz, Timothy Wales, Robin Harcourt Williams, Susanne Woods, and Georgianna Ziegler. We also thank Barnard College for a research grant to help cover our costs.

DOMESTIC AFFAIRS

1

Margaret Lucas Cavendish,
duchess of Newcastle (1623–1673)

Richard Brathwait *(1588?–1673)*

Margaret Lucas Cavendish, Duchess of Newcastle, Looks Back on her Life

According to her own account, Margaret Lucas Cavendish (1623–1673) was raised rather indulgently by her widowed mother. Sent to attend the exiled queen, Henrietta Maria, she was courted by William Cavendish (later duke of Newcastle), descendant of the redoubtable Bess of Hardwick, and a widower whose daughters were Lucas's own age. Despite the disparity in their ages and their lack of children, the marriage in 1645 of the experienced courtier and the retiring maid-in-waiting proved a great love match. Supported unreservedly by her husband, the duchess became notorious for her eccentric dress and outspokenness in print. Though she was censured by even judicious contemporary readers such as Dorothy Osborne—who wrote that saner persons were to be found in Bedlam—many of the duchess's views would today be called protofeminist. She became one of the most prolific of seventeenth-century women writers after marrying into a family of literary patrons and writers: Milton's *Comus* was produced for a connection, the countess-dowager of Derby; her step-daughters, Elizabeth Egerton and Jane Brackley, are among the earliest women dramatists in England (their "Concealed Fancies" pokes fun at the duchess, then their father's fiancée); and William Cavendish was later to write a treatise on horseman-ship. Margaret Cavendish wrote plays, poems, short stories, essays, life writings, and works that elude traditional classification. We excerpt portions of her autobiography, originally appended to her *Life of William Cavendish*, from *Nature's Pictures* (1656).

FROM A TRUE RELATION OF MY BIRTH, BREEDING, AND LIFE

My father was a gentleman, which title is grounded and given by merit, not by princes; and 'tis the act of Time, not Favor. And though my father was not a peer of the realm, yet there were few peers who had much greater estates or lived more nobly therewith. Yet at that time, great titles were to be sold, and not at so high rates but that his estate might have easily purchased, and was pressed[1] for to take. But my father did not esteem titles unless they were gained by heroic actions, and the kingdom being in a happy peace with all other nations, and in itself being governed by a wise king, King James, there were no employments for heroic spirits.

And towards the latter end of Queen Elizabeth's reign, as soon as he came to man's estate, he unfortunately fortunately killed one Mr. Brooks in a single duel; for my father by the laws of honor could do no less than call him to the field to question him for an injury he did him where their swords were to dispute and one or both of their lives to decide the argument wherein my father had the better.[2] And though my father by honor challenged him, with valor fought him, and in justice killed him, yet he suffered more than any person of quality usually doth in cases of honor, for though the laws be rigorous, yet the present princes most commonly are gracious in those misfortunes, especially to the injured. But my father found it not, for his exile was from the time of his misfortunes to Queen Elizabeth's death. For the Lord Cobham being then a great man with Queen Elizabeth, and this gentleman, Mr. Brooks, a kind of a favorite (and as I take it brother to the then Lord Cobham[3]) which made Queen Elizabeth so severe not to pardon him. But King James of blessed memory graciously gave him his pardon and leave to return home to his native country, wherein he lived happily and died peaceably, leaving a wife and eight children—three sons and five daughters—I being the youngest child he had, and an infant when he died.

As for my breeding, it was according to my birth and the nature of my sex; for my birth was not lost in my breeding, for as my sisters was or had been bred so was I, in plenty or rather with superfluity.[4] Likewise we were bred virtuously, modestly, civilly, honorably, and on honest principles. As for plenty, we had not only for necessity, conveniency, and decency, but for delight and pleasure to a superfluity. 'Tis true we did not riot,[5] but we lived orderly. For riot, even in kings' courts and princes' palaces, brings ruin without content or pleasure when order in less fortunes shall live more plentifully and deliciously than princes that live in a hurly-burly (as I may term it) in which they are seldom well served: for disorder obstructs. Besides, it doth disgust life, distract the appetites, and yield no true

---

1. At hand, prepared.
2. Dueling to settle points of honor was coming under increasing censure.
3. Sir Henry Brooke (1538–1605), diplomat and son of the sixth Lord Cobham.
4. Superabundance.
5. Live in indulgence.

relish to the senses; for pleasure, delight, peace, and felicity live in method and temperance.

As for our garments, my mother did not only delight to see us neat and cleanly, fine and gay, [but] rich and costly, maintaining us to the height of her estate but not beyond it. For we were so far from being in debt, before these wars,[6] as we were rather beforehand with the world, buying all with ready money, not on the score.[7] For although after my father's death the estate was divided between my mother and her sons (paying such a sum of money for portions to her daughters either at the day of their marriage or when they should come to age[8]) yet by reason she and her children agreed with a mutual consent, all their affairs were managed so well as she lived not in a much lower condition than when my father lived. 'Tis true, my mother might have increased her daughters' portions by a thrifty sparing, yet she chose to bestow it on our breeding, honest pleasures, and harmless delights, out of an opinion, that if she bred us with needy necessity it might chance to create in us sharking[9] qualities, mean thoughts, and base actions which she knew my father, as well as herself, did abhor.

Likewise we were bred tenderly, for my mother naturally did strive to please and delight her children, not to cross or torment them, terrifying them with threats, or lashing them with slavish whips. But instead of threats, reason was used to persuade us, and instead of lashes, the deformities of vice was discovered, and the graces and virtues were presented unto us. Also we were bred with respectful attendance, everyone being severally waited upon. And all her servants in general used the same respect to her children (even those that were very young) as they did to herself, for she suffered not her servants either to be rude before us or to domineer over us, which all vulgar servants are apt, and oftimes which some have leave to do. Likewise she never suffered the vulgar serving men to be in the nursery among the nurse maids, lest their rude love-making might do unseemly actions, or speak unhandsome words in the presence of her children, knowing that youth is apt to take infection by ill examples, having not the reason of distinguishing good from bad. Neither were we suffered to have any familiarity with the vulgar servants or conversation: yet caused us to demean ourselves with a humble civility towards them, as they with a dutiful respect to us. Not because they were servants were we so reserved, for many noble persons are forced to serve through necessity, but by reason the vulgar sort of servants are as ill bred as meanly born, giving children ill examples and worse counsel.

As for tutors, although we had for all sorts of virtues, as singing, dancing, playing on music, reading, writing, working, and the like, yet we were not kept strictly thereto. They were rather for formality than benefit, for my mother cared not so much for our dancing and fiddling, singing and prating of several lan-

---

6. The civil wars of the mid-seventeenth century in which many royalists, like William Cavendish, lost fortunes.
7. On credit.
8. The actual estate would normally be inherited by males, with the eldest son the chief heir; daughters would be provided for with "portions."
9. Cheating, sponging.

guages, as that we should be bred virtuously, modestly, civilly, honorably, and on honest principles.

As for my brothers, of which I had three, I know not how they were bred. First, they were bred when I was not capable to observe or before I was born; likewise the breeding of men was after different manner of ways from those of women. But this I know: that they loved virtue, endeavored merit, practiced justice, and spoke truth; they were constantly loyal and truly valiant. Two of my three brothers were excellent soldiers and martial discipliners, being practiced therein. For though they might have lived upon their own estates very honorably, yet they rather chose to serve in the wars under the States of Holland[10] than to live idly at home in peace: my brother, Sir Thomas Lucas, there having a troop of horse,[11] my brother (the youngest) Sir Charles Lucas serving therein. But he served the States not long, for after he had been at the siege and taking of some towns he returned home again. And though he had the less experience, yet he was like to have proved the better soldier, if better could have been, for naturally he had a practic genius to the warlike arts (or arts in war) as natural poets have to poetry. But his life was cut off before he could arrive to the true perfection thereof. Yet he writ "A Treatise of the Arts in War," but by reason it was in characters,[12] and the key thereof lost, we cannot as yet understand anything therein, at least not so as to divulge it. My other brother, the Lord Lucas, who was heir to my father's estate, and as it were the father to take care of us all, is not less valiant than they were, although his skill in the discipline of war was not so much, being not bred therein, yet he had more skill in the use of the sword, and is more learned in other arts and sciences then they were, he being a great scholar, by reason he is given much to studious contemplation.

Their practice was when they met together to exercise themselves with fencing, wrestling, shooting, and such like exercises, for I observed they did seldom hawk or hunt, and very seldom or never dance or play on music, saying it was too effeminate for masculine spirits. Neither had they skill or did use to play, for ought I could hear, at cards or dice or the like games, nor given to any vice, as I did know, unless to love a mistress were a crime—not that I know any they had, but what report did say—and usually reports are false, at least exceed the truth.

As for the pastimes of my sisters when they were in the country, it was to read, work, walk, and discourse with each other. For though two of my three brothers were married—my brother, the Lord Lucas, to a virtuous and beautiful lady, daughter to Sir Christopher Nevil, son to the Lord Abergavenny; and my brother, Sir Thomas Lucas, to a virtuous lady of an ancient family, one Sir John Byron's daughter—likewise, three of my four sisters: one married Sir Peter Killegrew, the other Sir William Walter, the third Sir Edmund Pye, the fourth as yet unmarried—yet most of them lived with my mother, especially when she was

10. A Spanish invasion of the Netherlands in 1567, under the duke of Alva, threatened the Dutch Calvinists. The wars raged intermittently until the Peace of Nijmegen in 1678, with occasional English intervention.
11. Cavalrymen.
12. Shorthand.

at her country house (living most commonly at London half the year, which is the metropolitan city of England). But when they were at London, they were dispersed into several houses of their own, yet for the most part they met every day, feasting each other like Job's children.[13] But this unnatural war came like a whirlwind, which felled down their houses, where some in the wars were crushed to death, as my youngest brother Sir Charles Lucas, and my brother Sir Thomas Lucas. And though my brother Sir Thomas Lucas died not immediately of his wounds, yet a wound he received on his head in Ireland shortened his life.

But to rehearse their recreations. Their customs were in wintertime to go sometimes to plays or to ride in their coaches about the streets to see the concourse and recourse of people, and in the springtime to visit the Spring Garden,[14] Hyde Park, and the like places, and sometimes they would have music and sup in barges upon the water.[15] These harmless recreations they would pass their time away with, for I observed they did seldom make visits, nor never went abroad with strangers in their company, but only themselves in a flock together, agreeing so well that there seemed but one mind amongst them. And not only my brothers and sisters agreed so, but my brothers- and sisters-in-law. And their children, although but young, had the like agreeable natures and affectionable dispositions, for to my best remembrance I do not know that ever they did fall out, or had any angry or unkind disputes. Likewise, I did observe that my sisters were so far from mingling themselves with any other company, that they had no familiar conversation or intimate acquaintance with the families to which each other were linked to by marriage, the family of the one being as great strangers to the rest of my brothers and sisters as the family of the other. . . .

But now I have declared to my readers, my birth, breeding, and actions to this part of my life (I mean the material parts, for should I write every particular, as my childish sports and the like, it would be ridiculous and tedious). But I have been honorably born and nobly matched; I have been bred to elevated thoughts, not to a dejected spirit; my life hath been ruled with honesty, attended by modesty, and directed by truth. But since I have writ in general thus far of my life, I think it fit I should speak something of my humor, particular practice and disposition.

As for my humor, I was from my childhood given to contemplation, being more taken or delighted with thoughts than in conversation with a society, in so much as I would walk two or three hours and never rest, in a musing, considering, contemplating manner, reasoning with myself of every thing my senses did present. But when I was in the company of my natural friends, I was very attentive of what they said or did. But for strangers I regarded not much what they said, but many times I did observe their actions, whereupon my reason as judge, and my thoughts as accusers, or excusers, or approvers and commenders, did plead, or appeal to accuse, or complain thereto. Also I never took delight in clos-

---

13. An unintentionally inappropriate allusion to the children of the suffering Job of the Old Testament (Job 1:4).
14. In Charing Cross; once part of St. James Park, it was in public use by 1634.
15. The Thames River.

ets or cabinets of toys, but in the variety of fine clothes and such toys as only were to adorn my person. Likewise I had a natural stupidity towards the learning of any other language than my native tongue, for I could sooner and with more facility understand the sense than remember the words, and for want of such memory makes me so unlearned in foreign languages as I am.

As for my practice, I was never very active by reason I was given so much to contemplation; besides my brothers and sisters were for the most part serious and staid in their actions, not given to sport nor play, nor dance about, whose company I keeping made me so too. But I observed that although their actions were staid, yet they would be very merry amongst themselves, delighting in each others' company. Also they would in their discourse express the general actions of the world, judging, condemning, approving, commending as they thought good, and with those that were innocently harmless they would make themselves merry therewith.

As for my study of books it was little, yet I chose rather to read than to employ my time in any other work or practice, and when I read what I understood not I would ask my brother, the Lord Lucas (he being learned), the sense or meaning thereof. But my serious study could not be much, by reason I took great delight in attiring, fine dressing, and fashions, especially such fashions as I did invent myself, not taking that pleasure in such fashions as was invented by others. Also I did dislike any should follow my fashions, for I always took delight in a singularity, even in accoutrements of habits, but whatsoever I was addicted to, either in fashion of cloths, contemplation of thoughts, actions of life, they were lawful, honest, honorable, and modest, of which I can avouch to the world with a great confidence, because it is a pure truth.

As for my disposition, it is more inclining to be melancholy than merry, but not crabbed or peevishly melancholy, but soft, melting, solitary, and contemplating melancholy. And I am apt to weep rather than laugh, not that I do often either of them. Also I am tender-natured, for it troubles my conscience to kill a fly, and the groans of a dying beast strike my soul. Also where I place a particular affection, I love extraordinarily and constantly, yet not fondly but soberly and observingly, not to hang about them as a trouble, but to wait upon them as a servant. But this affection will take no root, but where I think or find merit and have leave both from divine and moral laws. Yet I find this passion so troublesome as it is the only torment to my life for fear any evil misfortune, or accident, or sickness, or death should come unto them, insomuch as I am never freely at rest. Likewise I am grateful, for I never received a courtesy but I am impatient and troubled until I can return it. Also I am chaste, both by nature and education, insomuch as I do abhor an unchaste thought. Likewise I am seldom angry, as my servants may witness for me, for I rather choose to suffer some inconveniences than disturb my thoughts, which makes me wink many times at their faults. But when I am angry, I am very angry, but yet it is soon over, and I am easily pacified if it be not such an injury as may create a hate. Neither am I apt to be exceptious or jealous. But if I have the least symptom of this passion I declare it to those it concerns, for I never let it lie smothering in my breast to breed a malignant disease in the mind which might break out into extravagant passions, or railing speeches, or indiscreet actions, but I examine moderately, reason soberly, and plead gently in my own behalf, through a desire to keep those affections I had, or at least thought to have. And truly I am so vain as to be so self-conceited, or so naturally partial, to think my friends have as much reason to love me as another, since none can love more sincerely than I, and it were an injustice to prefer a fainter affection, or to esteem the body more than the mind. Likewise I am neither spiteful, envious, nor malicious; I repine not at the gifts that nature or fortune bestows upon others, yet I am a great emulator; for though I wish none worse than they are, yet it is lawful for me to wish myself the best, and to do my honest endeavor thereunto. For I think it no crime to wish myself the exactest of Nature's works, my thread of life the longest, my chain of destiny the strongest, my mind the peaceablest, my life the pleasantest, my death the easiest, and the greatest saint in heaven; also to do my endeavor, so far as honor and honesty doth allow of to be the highest on Fortune's wheel and to hold the wheel from turning, if I can, and if it be commendable to wish another's good, it were a sin not to wish my own. For as envy is a vice, so emulation is a virtue, but emulation is in the way to ambition, or indeed it is a noble ambition. But I fear my ambition inclines to vain glory, for I am very ambitious; yet 'tis neither for beauty, wit, titles, wealth, or power, but as they are steps to raise me to Fame's tower, which is to live by remembrance in after ages.

Likewise I am what the vulgar calls proud, not out of a self-conceit or to slight or condemn any, but scorning to do a base or mean act and disdaining rude or unworthy persons; insomuch, that if I should find any that were rude or too bold, I should be apt to be so passionate as to affront them, if I can, unless discretion should get betwixt my passion and their boldness, which sometimes perchance it might if discretion should crowd hard for place. For though I am naturally bashful, yet in such a cause my spirits would be all on fire, otherwise I am so well bred, as to be civil to all persons of all degrees or qualities.

Likewise I am so proud, or rather just to my lord, as to abate[16] nothing of the quality of his wife, for if honor be the mark of merit, and his master's royal favor (who will favor none but those that have merit to deserve) it were a baseness for me to neglect the ceremony thereof. Also in some cases I am naturally a coward, and in other cases very valiant: as for example, if any of my nearest[17] friends were in danger I should never consider my life in striving to help them though I were sure to do them no good, and would willingly, nay cheerfully, resign my life for their sakes. Likewise I should not spare my life, if honor bids me die. But in a danger where my friends or my honor is not concerned or engaged but only my life to be unprofitably lost, I am the veriest coward in nature, as upon the sea, or any dangerous places, or of thieves, or fire, or the like. Nay, the shooting of a gun, although but a pot-gun, will make me start and stop my hearing, much less have I courage to discharge one. Or if a sword should be

16. Do away with.
17. Closest.

held against me, although but in jest, I am afraid. Also as I am not covetous, so I am not prodigal but of the two I am inclining to be prodigal, yet I cannot say to a vain prodigality, because I imagine it is to a profitable end. For perceiving the world is given or apt to honor the outside more than the inside, worshipping show more than substance, and I am so vain (if it be a vanity) as to endeavor to be worshipped rather than not to be regarded, yet I shall never be so prodigal as to impoverish my friends or go beyond the limits or facility of our estate. And though I desire to appear at the best advantage whilst I live in the view of the public world, yet I could most willingly exclude myself so as never to see the face of any creature but my lord, as long as I live, enclosing myself like an anchorite[18] wearing a frieze[19] gown tied with a cord about my waist.

But I hope my readers will not think me vain for writing my life, since there have been many that have done the like, as Caesar, Ovid, and many more, both men and women, and I know no reason I may not do it as well as they. But I verily believe some censuring readers will scornfully say, "Why hath this lady writ of her own life since none cares to know whose daughter she was, or whose wife she is, or how she was bred, or what fortunes she had, or how she lived, or what humor or disposition she was of?" I answer that it is true, that 'tis to no purpose to the readers, but it is to the authoress, because I write it for my own sake, not theirs. Neither did I intend this piece for to delight, but to divulge, not to please the fancy, but to tell the truth, lest after ages should mistake in not knowing I was daughter to one Master Lucas of St. Johns, near Colchester, in Essex, second wife to the lord marquis of Newcastle, for my lord having had two wives, I might easily have been mistaken,[20] especially if I should die and my lord marry again.

Richard Brathwait Reflects on the Past

A prolific writer of lyrics, satires, odes, pastorals, romances, psalms, and such tracts as a guide to drinking and *The English Gentlewoman*, Richard Brathwait (1588?–1673) was a gentleman from the English lake district. His parents told him to study law, but he preferred the Muses. When his father died in 1610, Brathwait left London and legal studies for his country estate; there he married in 1617 and had nine children. He continued to write and was still publishing during the Restoration. His *Spiritual Spicery* (1638), a mélange of verse and prose, includes "Holy Memorials, or Heavenly Mementos." These, like the *Confessions* of Augustine that they may be meant to resemble, are as much meditations as memoirs. Given to wordplay, similes, and biblical echoes, Brathwait selects—and doubtless bends—the facts to fit the pattern of the prodigal son, to whom he compares himself. We excerpt some personal memories, especially those of his youth in London as "an author! One of the wits!"

18. Hermit.
19. A coarse woolen cloth.
20. Misidentified.

From Holy Memorials

[Brathwait starts with his conception, when "seeds" of Adam's sin "sprung in me before the light took notice of me," and his birth, when upon leaving his uterine "jail" he "found one worser than that which I left."]

Lachrymae[1] were the only musical airs that ushered me to this vale of woes. My very first voice implied a prophecy, my tears forerunners of my following misery. I came into the world naked, whereas all other creatures come clothed and armed. With what joy was I received, while those that saw me cried, "How like is he to his father!" And they said well, if they pointed at Adam, for his blood made me his son and, like himself, a sinner. . . . Yet for all this did my parents account of me as a rich prize. Dandled must I be till I sleep, wrapped in warm clothes, carefully nursed, tenderly used: and if my too dear parents got but one poor smile from their babe they held their care and cost highly recompensed. . . .

[Brathwait becomes a thoughtless child.]

I found in myself a conceit apt enough for any sports: in these could I lesson[2] others, but in the school of virtue, I was ever slowest in reading or taking out any such lesson to myself. How long seemed that day when learning was enjoined me for a task! How speedy that hour wherein liberty was given me to play! Thus like a bear to the stake was I haled to my book, wherein I found afterwards the happiest state. Wandering, albeit not much harmful, fancies began now to seize on me. I was seldom contented by being seated in that place where I was, nor with that sport I last affected. When I was in my father's house my desire was to be in the field; when I was in the field, I longed to be at home. My childish ambition, indeed, was not high. My delights, as they required no great cost, so were they purchased with less care. Easy and narrow were my desires: they aspired no higher than to points, pins, or cherry-stones. Trifles had so taken up my imagination as it could reach no further. Yet, in these weak vanities, my desire was to be a conqueror. . . .

[Enjoying plenty and dreaming "little of others' scarcity," snitching orchard fruit, seeking popularity with his playmates, Brathwait thought himself "a brave youth" with a toy gun, hobbyhorse, and rattle. Then comes adolescence.]

While roaring[3] was in request, I held it a complete fashion. For civility, I held it for such a rag of unbeseeming gentry as I scorned to take acquaintance of it. I had long before this aspired to a pipe of rich smoke with a tinder-box, and these gave light to my lighter[4] discourses. I held my pockets sufficiently stored if they could but bring me off for my ordinary and after dinner purchase me a stool on the stage.[5] I had cares enough besides hoarding, so as I held it fit to disbur-

---

1. Tears.
2. Teach.
3. Loud and bullying behavior.
4. Frivolous.
5. An "ordinary" was a regular meal, especially at a tavern or eating house. Some theaters sold seats set up on the stage.

den myself of that and resign it over to the worldling. A long winter night seemed but a Midsummer night's dream, being merrily passed in a catch[6] of four parts, a deep health to a light mistress, and a knot of brave blades[7] to make up the consort. . . .

[As a man, Brathwait pulls himself together, listens to his elders, and thinks more of God. Even in old age, though, he can have "green thoughts shrouded under gray locks" and turn "child again" while his eyes darken and teeth blacken. Recalling his past pleasures and labors, he is dismayed.]

My breeding was such as it never acquainted me with any hand-labor; neither was my constitution so strong as to endure it, nor my disposition so low as to brook it. Free-bred were my studies:[8] so as, lapwing-like with shell on head,[9] I began to write before my years could well make me an author. But hence my tears![10] The subjects I made choice of were of love, to close with my fancy, which was very light. I was proud in bearing the title of a "writer," which I must confess, together with the insistancy[11] of such as either truly applauded me or deluded me, made me ambitious after the name of an "author." And what were those light poems I then penned but such as are now pensive odes to my dolorous soul, grieving to peruse what my youth so dearly loved? O how familiar was I with Parnassus, Helicon, Hippocrene, and all the Muses![12] Meantime, I seldom or never thought of that heavenly Olympus which crowns all virtuous labors with true happiness. It was the saying of a holy father, "Those studies which I once loved now condemn me; those which I sometimes praised now disparage me."[13] Far more cause have I to say, "how those labors which I once fancied now afflict me, those which sometimes delighted me now perplex me." I am many times in company where I hear some of my youthful verses repeated; and though I do neither own them nor praise them, yet must I in another place answer for them if He, on Whom I depend, shall not in these tears which I shed drown the memory of them.

For alas! How many chaste ears have I offended, how many light ears have I corrupted with those unhappy works which I have published? What wanton measures have I writ for the nonce to move a light courtesan to hug my conceit, and next her Venus and Adonis, or some other immodest toy, to lodge me in her bosom? Light stuff, to be entertained in so flourishing a state! O how the remembrance of these do grieve me, when that talent which might have been employed to God's glory became a forge of lightness and vanity! O how much better had it

6. A fast secular song for several voices.
7. Young men well-born enough to wear swords.
8. "Free-bred" in the Roman sense of "liberal": meant for freeborn—*liber*—gentlemen and their children, not for slaves.
9. It was said that the newly hatched lapwing "runs about with its head in the shell" (OED).
10. In Terence's *Andria* (I.i.99): a father says "hinc illae lacrimae" (therefore these tears) to explain his son's tears for a pretty girl.
11. Pressure.
12. Parnassus and Helicon were hills sacred to the Muses; the horse Pegasus made a spring, Hippocrene, when he pawed the ground on Helicon.
13. The margin cites Augustine.

been for me to bury it than to use it to His dishonor Who gave me it![14] . . . Neither was I only versed in these, for being put on by my superiors, at whose disposal I was, I addressed my pen to labors historical, moral,[15] and divine. Neither was I in these less blameworthy: for even those, wherein I should only have aimed at God's glory, had ever in them some sprinklings of vainglory: nay, what was more (for enough I cannot speak to my own shame), those cardinal virtues whereof I treated, and which to the imitation of others I commended, found ever the worst example in myself. . . . Was it sufficient for me to commend to others what I meant not to amend in myself? Was this the duty of an Author?
. . .

After such time as my parents had brought me up at school, to get me an inheritance in that wherewith no earthly providence could endow me, I was sent to the university, where (still with a humble acknowledgment of others' favors and seasonable endeavors) I became such a proficient as Time called me and Examination approved me for a graduate.[16] And in these studies I continued, till by universal voice and vote I was put upon a task whose style I have and shall ever retain: the Son of Earth, *Terrae Filius*.[17] From the performance of which exercise, whether it were the extraordinary favor which the University pleased to grace me withal, or that she found some tokens in me of such future proficiency as might answer the hopes of so tender a mother, I know not: but sure I am [that] I received no small encouragement, both in my studies and free tender of ample preferment. And too apt was I to apply this the worse way. For this extraordinary grace begot in me a self-conceit of my own worth, ever thinking that if this had not proceeded from some more deserving parts in me, [then] that rich seminary of all learning would not have shown so graceful a countenance toward me. Notwithstanding, I labored by that grace which was given me to suppress this opinion in me and humbly to acknowledge my wants and weakness in all, my ability in nothing. But applause is a dangerous earring, which I found by giving too easy ear to my own praise, which as it deluded my judgment so it exposed me to censure. True, too true, I found it, that in the sight of our own parts[18] we need no borrowed lights. This it was, and only this, that induced me to put myself forward in public exercises with much confidence, wherein (such happiness it is to be possessed of opinion) I seldom or never came off with disgrace.

Having for sundry years together thus remained in the bounteous bosom of this my nursing mother, all which time in the freedom of those studies I reaped no less private comfort than I received from others' encouragement, I resolved to set my rest upon this: to bestow the most of my time in that place if it stood with my parents' liking. But soon was I crossed by them in these resolves, being enjoined by them to turn the course of my studies from those sweet academic

14. Cf. Jesus' parable of the talents in Matt 25:14–30.
15. Related to ethical and social questions.
16. Brathwait graduated from Oriol College, Oxford, in 1604, remaining there for several more years before moving to Cambridge and then to London.
17. Jocular title at Oxford for someone "privileged to make humorous and satirical strictures in a [public] speech" (OED).
18. To see our own abilities.

exercises wherein I tasted such infinite content and to betake myself to a profession which I must confess suited not well with my disposition. For the fresh fragrant flowers of divine poesy and moral philosophy could not like well to be removed nor transported to those thorny places and plashes[19] of the Law. But no remedy: with an unwilling farewell I took my leave of Philosophy to address my studies to that Knowledge which at first seemed so far different from my element, as if I had been now to be molded to some new dialect; for though I was known to most tongues, I became a mere novice in this. Here I long remained, but lightly profited, being there seated where I studied more for acquaintance than knowledge. Nor was I the only one (though a principal one) who ran deeply in arrears with Time and gulled the eyes of Opinion with a law-gown. For I found many in my case who could not recompense their parents' many years' charge with one book-case.

Yet, amidst these disrelishing studies whereto I was rather enforced than inclined, I bestowed much precious time (better spent than in taverns and brothels) in reviving in me the long-languishing spirit of Poetry, with other moral assays,[20] which so highly delighted me as they kept me from affecting that loose kind of liberty which, through fullness of means and licentiousness of the age, I saw so much followed and eagerly pursued by many. This moved me sometimes to fit my buskined muse[21] for the stage, with other occasional presentations or poems which, being freeborn and not mercenary, received graceful acceptance of all such as understood my rank and quality.[22] For so happily had I crept into Opinion (but weak is that happiness that is grounded on opinion) by closing so well with the temper and humor of the time, as nothing was either presented by me (at the instancy of the noblest and most generous wits and spirits of that time) to the stage or committed by me to the press which passed not with good approvement in the estimate of the world.

Neither did I use these private solaces of my pen otherwise than as a play only to the imagination, rather to allay[23] and season more serious studies than account them any fixed employment. Nor did I only bestow my time on these, for I addressed myself to subjects of stronger digestion, being such as required more maturity of judgment, though less pregnancy of invention—relishing more of the lamp than those lighter measures which I had formerly penned—wherein I grew as strong in the opinion and reputation of others as before. This, I must confess, begot in me a glowing heat and conceit of myself; but this I held an easy error and the more dispensable because arising from the infirmity of nature. Howsoever, I can very well remember (and what other followers can be to such a remembrancer but penitent tears and incessant fears?) that I held it in those days an incomparable grace to be styled one of the "wits." Where, if at any time invited to a public feast or some other meeting of the Muses, we hated nothing

19. Thickets.
20. Attempts.
21. Greek tragic actors wore buskins, thick-soled boots. Brathwait's plays are lost.
22. As a freeborn gentleman he did not write for money.
23. Dilute.

more than losing time, reserving ever some select hours of that solemnity to make proof of our conceits in a present provision of epigrams, anagrams, with other expressive (and many times offensive) fancies.

But wits so ill employed were like weapons put into madmen's hands. They hurt much, benefited little: distasting more than they pleased, for they liked only such men's palates as were malcontents and critically affected.[24] By this time I had got an eye in the world and a finger in the street—"There goes an author! One of the wits!"—which could not choose but make me look big, as if I had been cast in a new mold. O how in privacy, when nothing but the close evening and dark walls accompany me, doth the remembrance of these lightest vanities perplex me! How gladly would I shun the memory of them! How willingly forgo that sweetness which many conceive to be in them! But let me go on, for I am as yet but entering that high beaten path of my younger follies. Having thus for divers years together continued at Inns of Court,[25] where that opinion the world had of my works gained me more friends than the opinion men had of my law got me fees (for such as affected scenes more than suits[26] were my clients), I thought with myself to take a turn or two in Paul's[27] and to peruse a whole gazette in one walk. This I conceived might improve me: first by endearing and ingratiating myself with that society which I must confess were richly endowed with two excellent parts, invention and memory, [and] secondly by screwing some subject from their relations[28] which might set my pen awork upon occasion.

But I found not there what I expected, which made me leave that walk and turn peripatetic, a civil Exchange-man,[29] where in short time I got acquaintance of the best, being such gentle merchants[30] as their wealth could not darken their worth but they would willingly enter [the] lists[31] in a combat of wit. These, I grant, took great felicity in my company; nor did it repent me of bestowing some hours with these, whose discourse of foreign news, strengthened by such able intelligence,[32] did infinitely please. And these, without so much as the least loss to themselves (I may safely vow), would not stick upon occasion to accommodate me, which winged my desires for the Court, the better to accomplish me,[33] where I found graceful acceptance with choicest acquaintance. But Cynthia could not be still in her full orb.[34] I began to withdraw my thoughts from the pursuit of these and recount with myself what I had seen: store of wealth in the one and a

24. Pleased only those with negative attitudes.
25. London's law schools.
26. Enjoyed play-stages more than litigation.
27. St. Paul's cathedral, in the book district, saw much social activity.
28. Talk and reports.
29. "Civil" had a range of meanings, including "urban" and "polite." London's financial center was the Exchange.
30. An ironic oxymoron: "gentle" implies wealth from land, not trade.
31. A tiltyard or tournament.
32. Political and economic information, often secret.
33. Become more socially polished.
34. The moon cannot always be full; conceivably an allusion to Elizabeth's death in 1603 and a shift in courtly culture.

beseeming state in the other. Yet for all this I found myself but a planet[35] in both. Fixed I could not be till some constant calling admitted me.

I resolved then, seeing I found nothing, either in Court or City, but cares: cares in the one of getting to hoard and gather, cares in the other of getting to spend and scatter; in the one more rind than pith, in the other more pith than rind; this partaking more of compliment, that of substance; yet a natural strain of invention in both, but their objects different—the one making a cringe[36] for fashion, the other for gain. While the former makes his vows too familiar with his protestations to be believed, the other sets too deep a gloss of his commodities, with shop-oaths, to be liked. The one, with a low duck of "Your servants' servant," proclaims him the servant of Time[37] and no one's servant. This I wholly disliked, for I found the title of "servant" otherwise applied by that divine vessel of election, that devout sanctuary of sanctuaries, that pure mirror of supreme contemplation. His title was, as it was likewise of others of his fellow-laborers: "Paul a servant of Jesus Christ, Jude a servant of Jesus Christ." With this compliment,[38] these began their Epistles—a saint-like preamble, a heavenly court[ier]ship! Such as all Christians are to imitate.

The other, with his subtle weights and measures (reserving ever my best thoughts for the best), made me suspect him that he sold his commodities by retail and his conscience by wholesale. Upon review of these, I say, I resolved to leave those cinnamon trees of the Court with their sweet rinds and those palms of the City with their broad shades and to turn honest countryman, where my parents' providence had settled a competent estate upon me. Here I looked to find nothing but plain dealing, where I found in very deed nothing less. For upon a more serious perusal of that life, with the benefits that rose from it and conditions of those who were born and bred in it, I found a cunning colt wrapped up in a russet coat,[39] men as apt to catch as if they had been hatched in the Harpies' nest, such as would not stick to hazard their part and portion in the Tabernacle for a simoniacal[40] contract. And still I went on to dive into the quality of those islanders,[41] where I found some pining through want, others repining at their neighbors' wealth, few or none content with their estate, yet none so poor in estate as he would not, though he spared it from his belly, have a fee in store to maintain a [law]suit. Long I had not remained in this fashion till in pleased the Prince to put me in commission for administration of Justice: a virtue, and a choice one too, yet such a one as by the abuse of man, not of time, may be compared to the celedon stone, which retaineth her virtue no longer than it is rubbed with gold. For my carriage therein, I appeal to such as knew me: many imperfections and failings, Heaven knows, accompanied me, which by a humble

35. A wandering body, not a fixed star.
36. An obsequious bow.
37. A time-server, hypocrite.
38. Courteous expression.
39. A coarse woolen, usually reddish coat: simple rustic wear.
40. Corrupt traffic in spiritual things, e.g., the sale of benefices.
41. Isolated, remote persons.

acknowledgment of my own wants, and an earnest desire of supply by God's grace, became so rectified in me as what before seemed crooked was, by that golden rule of His divine will, in me straightened.

Thus have I passed my days, traced many ways, where the longer I lived the more I sinned, which caused me to wash my couch with tears and to remember the follies of my youth, manhood, and age with anguish of heart. O how much it now grieves me to have grieved so much at the sight or thought of gray hairs, and to have grieved so little at the thought or sight of my sins! May it then be my care to call for grace lest I bring my gray hairs with lasting sorrow to the grave. O, may the remainder of my days teach me to number my days, that I may go to Him and live with Him who is the length of days!

2

Elizabeth Cavendish Egerton,
countess of Bridgewater (1626–1663)

Ben Jonson *(1572–1637)*

Elizabeth Cavendish Egerton, Countess of Bridgewater, Mourns Her Children

Daughter of a staunch and wealthy royalist, William Cavendish (later duke of Newcastle) and his first wife, Elizabeth Bassett, Elizabeth Egerton (1626–1663), step-daughter of Margaret Cavendish, grew up in a courtly atmosphere. There is no sign that she was well educated, but she partook of the literary culture in which her family was immersed; a manuscript at Oxford University's Bodleian Library contains poems and "Concealed Fancies," a closet drama she composed with her sister. (Another manuscript, at Yale University, does not include the drama.) After marrying John Egerton, the future second earl of Bridgewater, Elizabeth Egerton lived a retired life at Ashridge, the family estate in Hertfordshire. There she raised a large family until her early death in premature childbed with her tenth child. Egerton's writings after her marriage concern family and religious matters. Like many parents in a time of high childhood mortality, Egerton buried several children. The following selections, mourning two of them, are from a contemporary fair copy of a journal in the British Library (MS Egerton 607).

On My Boy Henry

Here lies a boy, the finest child from me
Which makes my heart and soul sigh for to see.
Nor can I think of any thought but grief,
For joy or pleasure could me not relieve.
It lived days as many as my years,
No more—which caused my grievèd tears.
Twenty and nine was the number,
And death hath parted us asunder.
But thou art happy, sweetest on High,
I mourn not for thy birth, nor cry.

When I lost my Dear Girl Kate

My sorrow is great I confess. I am much grieved for the loss of my dear girl Keatty who was as fine a child as could be. She was but a year and ten months old when, by the fatal disease of the smallpox, it was God's pleasure to take her from me, who spoke anything one bid her, and would call for anything at dinner, and make her mind known at any time, and was kind to all, even to strangers, and had no anger in her.

All thought she loved them. Her brothers and sister loved her with a fond love. She was so good, she never slept nor played at sermon nor prayers. She had received the sacrament of baptism which washed her from her original sin, and she lived holily. She took delight in nothing but me if she had seen me; if absent, ever had me in her words, desiring to come to me. Never was there so fond a child of a mother.

But she now is not in this world which grieves my heart, even my soul. But I must submit and give God my thanks that He once was pleased to bestow so great a blessing as that sweet child upon me.

On the Same Occasion

It was God's pleasure to afflict me, and not her, in calling her from me. For He hath made her happy, giving her the joys of heaven, and to that end I know we bring them: to God, not to our selves. If God gives them grace, which I hope He hath and will, so are they fitter for Him than me. For all our lives is but to live here that we may live with our Savior forever. And He saith "Of such is the

Kingdom of Heaven,"[1] that is of sweet children, so innocent.

Thus do I not doubt her happiness, but yet grieve I for my own loss, and know it was God's punishment for my sins to separate so soon the dear body and soul of my sweet babe. Though her soul is singing hallelujahs, yet is her sweet body here, seized on by worms and turned to dust, till the great day shall come when all appear united, both body and soul, before the Judgment Seat of God. Let me cry unto God, and let none wonder that I should lament for my loss and know 'tis God which hath afflicted me.

And let me ask pardon and beg of the Lord to stay His hand and to preserve my dear husband and those five dear babes I have and my near friends, as my dear sisters and brother, which are dear to me. And let me not think I am abler to bear afflictions than David, who was according to God's own heart, who mourned for his young child and for Absalom—his son who fought against him—crying "Absalom, my son, my son";[2] and Jacob who mourned for Joseph when he thought he had been dead.[3]

Oh, let me beg God's mercy, and pray with David, "Remove Thy stroke away from me: when Thou with rebukes dost correct man for iniquity, Thou makest his beauty to consume away like smoke; surely every man is vanity. Hear my prayer, Oh Lord, give ear unto my cry, hold not Thy peace at my tears, for I am a stranger with Thee, and a sojourner with Thee, as all my fathers were."[4] But, Oh Lord, stay Thy hand of affliction, and pardon my sins, and make me truly to trust in Thee. And let us say, Oh Lord, send "us help from trouble, for vain is the help of man."[5] For 'tis God alone that doth all things; He gives and He takes, and let us say with Job, "Blessed be the name of the Lord."[6] Oh, let us ever look up unto Him, for He is our life and salvation, a very present help in trouble. So let us pray unto Him and beg His blessing to us and our dear ones, and to bless the child I am now withal, infusing His spirit of grace into it, that when our change is come He may call us all to His blessed Kingdom to live with Him forever.

ON THE SAME

In the sight of us, the unwise, the righteous seem to die, and their departure is taken for misery, and their going from hence as utter destruction. But they are in peace. And my dear Jewel, to show she was going to happiness, when her eyes were set, Death having seized upon her, the last word she spoke was to me; when in passion I asked her if I should kiss her, she said, 'Yes," lengthening the word as if she was in high bliss, and lay so sweetly, desiring nothing but her Lord Jesus.

1. Luke 18:16–17.
2. 1 Samuel 12–13; 28:17; 2 Samuel 16–18; 18:33–19:4.
3. Genesis 37:33–35.
4. Psalms 39:10–12.
5. Psalms 108:12.
6. Job 1:21.

Thus her life and death was nothing but sweetness, showing us what we should perform at our last day. And God found her worthy of Himself. So must my sorrow submit.

Ben Jonson's Epitaphs for Two Children

A former bricklayer, Benjamin Jonson (1572–1637) became an immensely learned satirist, playwright, poet, and creator of court masques. He was subject to bursts of passion, as witness his brief imprisonment for manslaughter, but he had many friends and followers (the "Tribe of Ben" as he called them). In 1594 he married Ann Lewis; a son, Ben, was born in 1596 and died of the plague in 1603. In 1598 Jonson temporarily became a Catholic, thereby risking persecution. A daughter, Mary, was born a year or so later but soon died. As David Riggs notes in *Ben Jonson: A Life* (Cambridge: Harvard University Press, 1989), "the odds of an infant's surviving to fifteen were only one out of three" (55). Attitudes toward death varied. Some called intense grief impious (Jonson's epigram "Of Death" says "He that fears death, or mourns it, in the just, / Shows of the Resurrection little trust"); others said God finds tears natural. Presumably the poem on Mary was composed shortly after she died and that on Ben when Jonson was in the country and his family in quarantine in London. Jonson later said that on his son's seventh birthday he had a vision of him grown up but marked for death by a bloody cross on his forehead (Riggs 95). We use the 1616 text and have consulted Jonson's *Complete Poems*, ed. George Parfitt (New Haven: Yale University Press, 1975).

ON MY FIRST DAUGHTER (#22)

Here lies to each her parent's ruth,[1]
Mary, the daughter of their youth:
Yet, all Heaven's gifts, being Heaven's due,
It makes the father less to rue.
At six month's end, she parted hence
With safety of her innocence;
Whose soul Heaven's Queen (whose name she bears),
In comfort of her mother's tears,
Hath placed amongst her virgin train:[2]
Where, while that severed doth remain,[3]
This grave partakes the fleshly birth—
Which cover lightly, gentle earth.

1. Pity, regret, grief.
2. The Virgin Mary has added the baby's soul to her retinue of virgin followers.
3. While soul and body remain severed (until the Resurrection).

ON MY FIRST SON (#45)

Farewell, thou child of my right hand,[4] and joy;
My sin was too much hope of thee, loved boy.
Seven years thou wert lent to me, and I thee pay,
Exacted by thy fate, on the just day.
Oh, could I lose all father, now. For why
Will man lament the state he should envy?
To have so soon 'scaped world's, and flesh's rage,
And, if no other misery, yet age?
Rest in soft peace, and, asked, say here doth lie
Ben Jonson his[5] best piece of poetry.
For whose sake, henceforth, all his vows be such,
As what he loves may never like too much.[6]

4. "Benjamin" means a child of the right hand: favored and blessed.
5. Jonson's; in Renaissance English "his" after a noun indicates a possessive.
6. Be complacently pleased by. Much Christian and classical thought stressed life's fragility and warned against basing happiness on human affection.

3

Mary Sidney Herbert,
countess of Pembroke (1561–1621)

Henry Vaughan *(1622–1695)*

Mary Sidney Herbert, Countess of Pembroke, Mourns her Brother

Daughter of Mary Dudley Sidney and Sir Henry Sidney, Mary Sidney Herbert (1561–1621) received a fine (if not profound) education at the hands of private tutors, served briefly in the court of Elizabeth I, and was married in 1576, at fifteen, to the forty-two-year-old Henry Herbert, earl of Pembroke. While raising four children, she also made her home, Wilton House, a mecca for poetic lights, including her illustrious brother, Sir Philip, with whom she collaborated in translating the Psalter into verse. Philip completed the first 43 psalms before his death in 1586; Mary did the remaining 107. All these, often revised by the countess, circulated widely in manuscript. A number of her other works, including revisions of Sidney's *Arcadia*, saw print, an unusual course for the writings of any woman, particularly for a woman of her rank. A lament for her brother, the "doleful lay" of Clorinda, reproduced here, appeared in Edmund Spenser's *Colin Clouts Come Home Again* (1595) as a conclusion to his "Astrophel," an elegy for the dead Philip Sidney ("Clorinda," in Spenser's myth, is the dead hero's sister). The authorship is debated, but Herbert's modern editor, Margaret Hannay, ascribes it to the countess. Since it is traditional not to modernize Spenser's own English, we retain the original spelling, although not the punctuation. We base our text on the edition by J. C. Smith and E. de Selincourt (Oxford: Oxford University Press, 1912).

THE DOLEFUL LAY[1] OF CLORINDA

Ay me,[2] to whom shall I my case complaine,
That may compassion[3] my impatient griefe?
Or where shall I enfold[4] my inward paine
That my enriuen[5] heart may find reliefe?
Shall I vnto the heauenly powres it show,
Or vnto earthly men that dwell below?

To heauens? Ah, they alas the authors were
And workers of my vnremedied wo;
For they foresee what to vs happens here,
And they foresaw, yet suffred this be so.
  From them comes good, from them comes also il,
  That which they made, who can them warne[6] to spill?[7]

To men? Ah, they, alas, like wretched bee,
And subiect to the heauens' ordinance.[8]
Bound to abide what euer they decree,
Their best redresse is their best sufferance[9].
  How then can they, like wretched, comfort mee,
  The which, no lesse, need comforted to bee?

Then to my selfe will I my sorrow mourne,
Sith none aliue like sorrowful remaines.
And to my selfe my plaints shall back retourne,
To pay their vsury[10] with doubled paines.
  The woods, the hills, the riuers shall resound
  The mournfull accent of my sorrowes ground.[11]

1. A short lyric poem.
2. Alas.
3. Pity.
4. Wrap up.
5. Cleft; torn apart.
6. Forbid.
7. Destroy.
8. Dispensation; decree.
9. Patient endurance.
10. Interest.
11. Basis; also the base line sustaining melodic variations.

Woods, hills and riuers now are desolate,
Sith he is gone the which them all did grace.
And all the fields do waile their widow state,
Sith death their fairest flowre did late deface.
   The fairest flowre in field that euer grew
   Was Astrophel; *that was, we all may rew.*[12]

What cruell hand of cursed foe vnknowne
Hath cropt[13] *the stalke which bore so faire a flowre?*
Vntimely cropt, before it well were growne,
And cleane defacèd[14] *in vntimely howre.*
   Great losse to all that euer him did see,
   Great losse to all, but greatest losse to mee.

Breake now your gyrlonds,[15] *O ye shepheards' lasses,*
Sith the fair flowre which them adornd is gon.
The flowre which them adornd is gone to ashes,
Neuer againe let lasse put gyrlond on.
   In stead of gyrlond, weare sad Cypres[16] *nowe*
   And bitter Elder,[17] *broken from the bowe.*

Ne[18] *euer sing the loue-lays which he made.*
Who euer made such layes of loue as hee?
Ne euer read the riddles which he sayd
Vnto your selues—to make you mery glee.[19]
   Your mery glee is now laid all abed,
   Your mery maker now, alasse, is dead.

Death the deuourer of all world's delight,
Hath robbèd you and reft[20] *fro me my ioy.*
Both you and me and all the world he quight
Hath robd of ioyance[21] *and left sad annoy.*
   Ioy of the world, and shepheards pride was hee,
   Shepheards hope neuer like againe to see.

12. Grieve for.
13. Cut off.
14. Marred.
15. Garlands.
16. A tree associated with mourning.
17. A bush associated with mourning.
18. Nor.
19. Sport.
20. Bereft.
21. Delight.

Oh death that hast vs of such riches reft,
Tell vs, at least, what hast thou with it done?
What is become of him whose flowre here left
Is but the shadow of his likenesse gone?
    Scarce like the shadow of that which he was,
    Nought like, but that he like a shade[22] did pas.

But that immortall spirit which was deckt
With all the dowries of celestiall grace
By soueraine choyce from th'heuenly quires select,
And lineally deriv'd from Angels' race,
    O what is now of it become, aread?[23]
    Ay me, can so diuine a thing be dead?

Ah no: it is not dead, ne can it die,
But liues for aie[24] in blisfull Paradise.
Where like a new-borne babe it soft doth lie,
In bed of lillies wrapt in tender wise,
    And compast[25] all about with roses sweet,
    And daintie violets from head to feet.

There thousand birds, all of celestiall brood,
To him do sweetly caroll day and night.
And with straunge notes, of him well vnderstood,
Lull him a sleep in Angelick delight,
    Whilest in sweet dreame to him presented bee
    Immortall beauties, which no eye may see.

But he them sees and takes exceeding pleasure
Of their diuine aspects, appearing plaine,
And kindling loue in him aboue all measure,
Sweet love still ioyous, neuer feeling paine.
    For what so goodly forme he there doth see,
    He may enioy from iealous rancor[26] free.

22. Specter.
23. Advise.
24. Ever.
25. Encompassed.
26. Animosity.

> *There liueth he in euerlasting blis,*
> *Sweet spirit neuer fearing more to die,*
> *Ne dreading harme from any foes of his,*
> *Ne fearing saluage beasts' more crueltie,*
> > *Whilest we here wretches waile his priuate lack,*
> > *And with vaine vowes do often call him back.*

> *But liue thou there still happie, happie spirit,*
> *And giue us leaue thee here thus to lament:*
> *Not thee that dost thy heauens' ioy inherit,*
> *But our owne selues that here in dole are drent.*[27]
> > *Thus do we weep and waile, and wear*[28] *our eies,*
> > *Mourning in others, our owne miseries.*

Henry Vaughan on His Brother

Henry Vaughan (1622–1695) came from a distinguished Welsh family. His twin, Thomas, also a poet, was an Anglican priest and subtle alchemist who died, it was said, after inhaling mercury fumes. After attending Oxford and studying law, Vaughan became a successful doctor, even if some called him ingenious "but proud and humorous [eccentric]."[1] The amatory and satirical verses he wrote when he was young are excellent, but he is most often remembered for religious lyrics written under the influence of George Herbert. In July 1648, his brother William died; a poem lamenting William's death appeared in *Silex Scintillans* (1650, 1655; the Latin means "sparkling flint": these lyrics are sparks struck from the poet's flinty heart by blows from God and experience). We have used L. C. Martin's edition (Oxford: Clarendon Press, 1957); see also that by Louis Martz (Oxford: Oxford University Press, 1995).

SILENCE, AND STEALTH OF DAYS

> *Silence, and stealth of days! 'Tis now*
> > *Since thou art gone*
> *Twelve hundred hours, and not a brow*
> > *But clouds hang on.*

27. Drowned.
28. Exhaust.

1. Quoted in the *Dictionary of National Biography* from Anthony à Wood's *Athenae Oxoniensis* (1691–1692).

As he that in some cave's thick damp
 Locked from the light,
Fixeth a solitary lamp,
 To brave the night,
And walking from his sun, when past
 That glimm'ring ray
Cuts through the heavy mists in haste
 Back to his day,
So o'er fled minutes I retreat
 Unto that hour
Which showed thee last but did defeat
 Thy light and power.
I search, and rack my soul to see
 Those beams again,
But nothing but the snuff[2] to me
 Appeareth plain;
That dark and dead sleeps in its known
 And common urn.
But those,[3] fled to their Maker's throne,
 There shine, and burn.
O could I track[4] them! but souls must
 Track one the other,
And now the spirit, not the dust,
 Must be thy brother.
Yet I have one pearl[5] by whose light
 All things I see,
And in the heart of earth and night
 Find Heaven, and thee.

2. The dead wick, the burnt residue.
3. The brother's "light and power."
4. Follow; the next line says that only souls, not bodies, can follow souls.
5. Perhaps God's Word, but also the "pearl of great price" symbolizing the Kingdom of Heaven (Matt. 13:45–46).

4

Amelia Bassano Lanyer *(1569–1645)*

Henry Howard,
earl of Surrey (1517–1547)

Amelia Bassano Lanyer Celebrates Cookham

Although from a family of court musicians and possibly of Jewish descent, Amelia Bassano (1569–1645) grew up in contact with noble circles and apparently benefited educationally. A pregnancy resulting from an extended liaison with the elderly Henry Cary, Lord Hunsdon, led to an arranged marriage in 1593 with Alphonso Lanyer, a musician. The marriage was attended by difficulties, at least until Lanyer received a royal patent in 1604. Before 1609 Lanyer came into close contact with Margaret Clifford, countess dowager of Cumberland (1560–1616) and her daughter, Anne Clifford (1590–1676), at Cookham, their country house, an interlude that ended when Anne married Richard Sackville, earl of Dorset. This experience apparently aroused the sense of conscious female community voiced in both Lanyer's *Salve Deus Rex Judaeorum* and the appended early country-house poem, "The Description of Cookham."

The countess as model is the center of both poems: the triangle formed by the countess, Anne Clifford (now known for her diaries), and Lanyer constitutes a nurturing community at Cookham; the countess and still other women (Pilate's wife, the daughters of Jerusalem, the Virgin Mary) take the moral center of the longer poem on the life and death of Christ. In Lanyer's revolutionary rewriting of Christian history, which contains some of the most strikingly feminist poetry by a woman of her time, it is Adam, not Eve, who brings ruin on humanity. Hence Lanyer's clarion call: "Then let us have our liberty again." For our text of "The Description of Cookham" we use the 1611 edition. See also the edition by Susanne Woods (Oxford: Oxford University Press, 1993).

THE DESCRIPTION OF COOKHAM

Farewell, sweet Cookham, where I first obtained
Grace from that grace where perfect grace remained;
And where the muses gave their full consent,
I should have power the virtuous to content;
Where princely palace willed me to indite,[1]
The sacred story of the soul's delight.
Farewell, sweet place, where virtue then did rest,
And all delights did harbor in her breast.
Never shall my sad eyes again behold
Those pleasures which my thoughts did then unfold.
Yet you, great lady, mistress of that place,
From whose desires did spring this work of grace,
Vouchsafe to think upon those pleasures past
As fleeting worldly joys that could not last;
Or, as dim shadows of celestial pleasures
Which are desired above all earthly treasures.
Oh how, methought, against[2] *you thither came,*
Each part did seem some new delight to frame!
The house received all ornaments to grace it,
And would endure no foulness to deface it.
The walks put on their summer liveries,
And all things else did hold like similes:
The trees with leaves, with fruits, with flowers clad,
Embraced each other, seeming to be glad,
Turning themselves to beauteous canopies,
To shade the bright sun from your brighter eyes.
The crystal streams with silver spangles graced,
While by the glorious sun they were embraced;
The little birds in chirping notes did sing,
To entertain both you and that sweet spring.

1. Compose.
2. Anticipating.

And Philomela³ with her sundry lays,
Both you and that delightful place did praise.
Oh, how methought each plant, each flower, each tree
Set forth their beauties then to welcome thee.
The very hills right humbly did descend
When you to tread upon them did intend.
And as you set your feet, they still did rise,
Glad that they could receive so rich a prize.
The gentle winds did take delight to be
Among those woods that were so graced by thee.
And in sad murmur uttered pleasing sound
That pleasure in that place might more abound;
The swelling banks delivered all their pride
When such a phoenix⁴ once they had espied.
Each arbor, bank, each seat, each stately tree,
Thought themselves honored in supporting thee.
The pretty birds would oft come to attend thee,
Yet fly away for fear they should offend thee;
The little creatures in the burrow by
Would come abroad to sport them in your eye;
Yet fearful of the bow in your fair hand,⁵
Would run away when you did make a stand.
Now let me come unto that stately tree,
Wherein such goodly prospects you did see:
That oak that did in height his fellows pass,
As much as lofty trees, low growing grass;
Much like a comely cedar straight and tall,
Whose beauteous stature far exceeded all.
How often did you visit this fair tree,
Which seeming joyful in receiving thee
Would like a palm tree spread his arms abroad,
Desirous that you there should make abode;
Whose fair green leaves, much like a comely veil,
Defended Phoebus⁶ when he would assail;
Whose pleasing boughs did yield a cool, fresh air,

---

3. Daughter of Pandion, king of Athens. Ravished by her brother-in-law, Tereus, who cut out her tongue to prevent her from speaking, she nevertheless made her plight known. Fleeing from Tereus after taking revenge on him, she was turned into a nightingale (some say a swallow) while her sister, Procne, was turned into a swallow (or nightingale).
4. An Egyptian bird fabled to live five hundred years, kill itself on a pile of burning wood, and resurrect itself from the ashes.
5. Perhaps Lanyer identifies Cumberland with Diana.
6. Resisted Apollo, the sun god.

Joying his happiness when you were there.
Where being seated, you might plainly see
Hills, vales, and woods, as if on bended knee
They had appeared your honor to salute
Or to prefer some strange, unlooked-for suit;
All interlaced with brooks and crystal springs,
A prospect fit to please the eyes of kings;
And thirteen shires appeared all in your sight;
Europe could not afford much more delight.
What was there then but gave you all content
While you the time in meditation spent
Of their Creator's power, which there you saw
In all His creatures held a perfect law
And in their beauties did you plain descry
His beauty, wisdom, grace, love, majesty.
In these sweet woods how often did you walk,
With Christ and His apostles there to talk;
Placing His holy writ in some fair tree,
To meditate what you therein did see.
With Moses you did mount His holy hill,[7]
To know His pleasure, and perform His will.
With lovely David you did often sing
His holy hymns to Heaven's eternal king,[8]
And in sweet music did your soul delight
To sound His praises, morning, noon, and night.
With blessèd Joseph you did often feed
Your pinèd brethren,[9] *when they stood in need.*
And that sweet lady[10] *sprung from Clifford's race,*
Of noble Bedford's blood (fair stream of grace)
To honorable Dorset now espoused,
In whose fair breast true virtue then was housed:
Oh what delight did my weak spirits find
In those pure parts of her well-framèd mind.
And yet it grieves me that I cannot be
Near unto her, whose virtues did agree
With those fair ornaments of outward beauty
Which did enforce from all both love and duty.

7. Sinai, from which Moses brought the ten commandments (Exo. 19).
8. The psalms.
9. Joseph, viceroy of Egypt, supplied food to his brothers from famine-stricken Canaan (Gen. 42–47).
10. Anne Clifford, diarist, daughter of the Countess of Cumberland.

Unconstant Fortune, thou art most to blame
Who casts us down into so low a frame
Where our great friends we cannot daily see
So great a difference is there in degree.
Many are placèd in those orbs of state,
Parters in honor, so ordained by Fate;
Nearer in show, yet farther off in love,
In which the lowest always are above.[11]
But whither am I carried in conceit?
My wit too weak to conster[12] *of the great.*
Why not? Although we are but born of earth,
We may behold the heavens, despising death.
And loving heaven that is so far above,
May in the end vouchsafe us entire love.
Therefore sweet Memory do thou retain
Those pleasures past which will not turn again:
Remember beauteous Dorset's[13] *former sports,*
So far from being touched by ill reports,
Wherein myself did always bear a part
While reverend love presented my true heart.
Those recreations let me bear in mind,
Which her sweet youth and noble thoughts did find,
Whereof deprived, I evermore must grieve,
Hating blind Fortune, careless to relieve.
And you, sweet Cookham, whom these ladies leave,
I now must tell the grief you did conceive
At their departure; when they went away
How everything retained a sad dismay.
Nay long before, when once an inkling came,
Methought each thing did unto sorrow frame:
The trees that were so glorious in our view,
Forsook both flowers and fruit; when once they knew
Of your depart, their very leaves did wither,
Changing their colors as they grew together.
But when they saw this had no power to stay you
They often wept; though speechless, could not pray you;
Letting their tears in your fair bosoms fall
As if they said, "Why will you leave us all?"

11. Lower placed persons are superior in loyalty to the more privileged.
12. Interpret; understand.
13. Anne Clifford's.

This being vain, they cast their leaves away,
Hoping that pity would have made you stay.
Their frozen tops, like age's hoary hairs,
Shows their disasters, languishing in fears.
A swarthy, rivelled[14] *rind all overspread*
Their dying bodies, half alive, half dead.
But your occasions called you so away
That nothing there had power to make you stay.
Yet did I see a noble, grateful mind
Requiting each according to their kind,[15]
Forgetting not to turn and take your leave
Of these sad creatures, powerless to receive
Your favor when with grief you did depart,
Placing their former pleasures in your heart,
Giving great charge to noble Memory
There to preserve their love continually.
But specially the love of that fair tree,
That first and last you did vouchsafe to see;
In which it pleased you oft to take the air
With noble Dorset, then a virgin fair;
Where many a learned book was read and scanned.
To this fair tree, taking me by the hand,
You did repeat the pleasures which had past,
Seeming to grieve they could no longer last.
And with a chaste, yet loving kiss took leave,
Of which sweet kiss I did it soon bereave,[16]
Scorning a senseless creature should possess
So rare a favor, so great happiness.
No other kiss it could receive from me
For fear to give back what it took of thee;
So I, ungrateful creature, did deceive it,
Of that which you vouchsafed in love to leave it.
And though it oft had given me much content,
Yet this great wrong I never could repent,
But of the happiest made it most forlorn.
To show that nothing's free from Fortune's scorn,
While all the rest with this most beauteous tree
Made their sad consort Sorrow's harmony,

14. Wrinkled.
15. Species (analogous to social station).
16. Dispossess.

The flowers that on the banks and walks did grow,
Crept in the ground, the grass did weep for woe
Because you went away they know not whither.
And those sweet brooks that ran so fair and clear,
With grief and trouble wrinkled did appear.
Those pretty birds that wonted were to sing,
Now neither sing, nor chirp, nor use their wing,
But with their tender feet on some bare spray
Warble forth sorrow, and their own dismay.
Fair Philomela leaves her mournful ditty,
Drowned in dead sleep, yet can procure no pity.
Each arbor, bank, each seat, each stately tree
Looks bare and desolate now for want of thee,
Turning green tresses into frosty gray,
While in cold grief they wither all away.
The sun grew weak, his beams no comfort gave,
While all green things did make the earth their grave;
Each briar, each bramble, when you went away,
Caught fast your clothes, thinking to make you stay.
Delightful Echo,[17] *wonted to reply*
To our last words, did now for sorrow die.
The house cast off each garment that might grace it,
Putting on dust and cobwebs to deface it.
All desolation then there did appear,
When you were going whom they held so dear.
This last farewell to Cookham here I give,
When I am dead thy name in this may live,
Wherein I have performed her[18] *noble hest,*
Whose virtues lodge in my unworthy breast,
And ever shall, so long as life remains,
Tying my heart to her by those rich chains.

Surrey Meditates on Windsor Castle

As a poet, Henry Howard, earl of Surrey (1517–1547), son of Elizabeth Stafford Howard, helped smooth English meters into new elegance and experimented with English versions of the Petrarchan sonnet, blank verse, and the psalms. Married to Frances Vere and the father of three children, Surrey was so imprudently proud of his

17. A chatty nymph condemned by Hera to use her tongue only to repeat what was said to her.
18. The countess of Cumberland.

lineage—his father was duke of Norfolk—that Henry VIII came to suspect the young aristocrat of wanting his throne and had him beheaded. Surrey and Henry VIII's illegitimate son Henry Fitzroy, duke of Richmond, had been boyhood friends in the royal castle at Windsor, upriver from London. Fitzroy, who married Surrey's sister, Mary, in 1533, died in 1536 at seventeen. In 1537 Surrey was detained in Windsor for having struck Sir Edward Seymour (Seymour had charged Surrey with sympathy for Catholic rebels in northern England). In the following two poems, first published in *Tottel's Miscellany*, Surrey recalls happier days. We follow but modernize texts in the edition by Emrys Jones (Oxford: Clarendon, 1964).

WHEN WINDSOR WALLS

When Windsor walls sustained my wearied arm,
My hand my chin, to ease my restless head,
Each pleasant plot revested[1] green with warm,
The blossomed boughs with lusty Ver yspread,[2]
The flowered meads, the wedded birds so late,[3]
Mine eyes discovered. Then did to mind resort
The jolly woes, the hateless short debate,[4]
The rakehell life that longs[5] to Love's disport.
Wherewith, alas, my heavy charge[6] of care
Heaped in my breast broke forth against my will,
And smoky sighs that overcast the air.
My vapored eyes such dreary tears distill
   The tender spring to quicken where they fall,
   And I half bent to throw me down withal.

SO CRUEL PRISON

So cruel prison how could betide, alas,
As proud Windsor, where I in lust[7] and joy
With a king's son my childish[8] years did pass,
In greater feast than Priam's sons of Troy,

1. Reclad.
2. Spread with vigorous springtime green.
3. Recently mated.
4. Contest.
5. Belongs.
6. Burden.
7. Pleasure.
8. Youthful.

Where each sweet place returns a taste full sour.
The large green courts where we were wont to hove,[9]
With eyes cast up unto the maidens' tower
And easy sighs, such as folk draw in love.

The stately salles;[10] the ladies bright of hue;[11]
The dances short, long tales of great delight,
With words and looks that tigers could but rue,[12]
Where each of us did plead the other's right.

The palm play,[13] where, despoilèd[14] for the game,
With dazèd eyes oft we by gleams of love
Have missed the ball and got sight of our dame
To bait[15] her eyes which kept the leads[16] above.

The graveled ground, with sleeves tied on the helm,[17]
On foaming horse, with swords and friendly hearts,
With cheer[18] as though the one should overwhelm,
Where we have fought and chasèd oft with darts.[19]

With silver drops the meads yet spread for ruth,
In active games of nimbleness and strength
Where we did strain, trailed by swarms of youth,
Our tender limbs that yet shot up in length.

The secret groves, which oft we made resound
Of pleasant plaint and of our ladies' praise,
Recording soft what grace each one had found,
What hope of speed,[20] what dread of long delays.

The wild forest, the clothèd holts[21] with green,
With reins availed and swift ybreathèd horse,[22]
With cry of hounds and merry blasts between,
Where we did chase the fearful hart a force.[23]

9. Linger.
10. Halls.
11. Complexion.
12. Pity.
13. A kind of tennis without racquets.
14. Undressed, stripped down.
15. Attract, lure.
16. Spectators could watch events while seated on the roof near the "leads" (fancy leaden pipes and gutters).
17. In the tiltyard knights sometimes jousted with ladies' detachable sleeves tied on their helmets as favors.
18. Expression.
19. Hunted with arrows.
20. Success.
21. Groves.
22. With loosened reins and a fast, well-exercised horse.
23. By running it down (rather than shooting it).

The void[24] walls eke, that harbored us each night,
Wherewith, alas, revive within my breast
The sweet accord, such sleeps as yet delight,
The pleasant dreams, the quiet bed of rest,
    The secret thoughts imparted with such trust,
The wanton[25] talk, the divers change of play,
The friendship sworn, each promise kept so just,
Wherewith we passed the winter nights away.
    And with this thought the blood forsakes my face,
The tears berain[26] my cheek of deadly hue,
The which, as soon as sobbing sighs, alas,
Upsuppèd[27] have, thus I my plaint renew:
    "O place of bliss, renewer of my woes,
Give me account where is my noble fere,[28]
Whom in thy walls thou didst each night enclose,
To other lief,[29] but unto me most dear."
    Each stone, alas, that doth my sorrow rue,
Returns thereto a hollow sound of plaint.
Thus I alone, where all my freedom grew,
In prison pine with bondage and restraint,
    And with remembrance of the greater grief
    To banish th'less I find my chief relief.

24. Hollow.
25. Unrestrained.
26. Fall on my face like rain.
27. Drunk up, evaporated.
28. Companion.
29. Liked; "other" can be plural.

5

Elizabeth Stafford Howard,
duchess of Norfolk (1497–1558)

Henry Stafford, baron Stafford *(1502–1563)*

Elizabeth Stafford Howard, Duchess of Norfolk,
Quarrels with Some Men in her Life

The marriage in 1512 of Elizabeth Stafford (1497–1558), daughter of Edward Stafford, third duke of Buckingham, to the far older Thomas Howard (1473–1554), third duke of Norfolk, was unusual in leaving evidence of the misery of the parties. The marriage was eagerly sought by Norfolk. An arranged match, it took place despite Elizabeth's earlier attachment to Ralph, fourth earl of Westmoreland (1499–1550), who married her sister Catherine (by whom he had eighteen children). Norfolk must have found his match less valuable after Buckingham's execution for treason[1] rendered his daughter less powerful.

These sober realities did not deter the duchess from protesting when, in 1526, after fourteen years of marriage and five children (including the poet Surrey), Norfolk took a mistress. That this woman, Bess Holland, was lowborn may have intensified the duchess's vituperative efforts to end the relationship. Norfolk's indifference to his wife's anguish and his anger at her public complaints over what was common male behavior led to the involvement of their extended families and even of government officials. Although the duchess was a highly accomplished woman, Norfolk removed her from their home and kept her on a

---

1. Edward Stafford, duke of Buckingham (1478–1521), was executed after an attempt to revive a distant claim to Henry VIII's throne.

tight allowance. Little sympathy was shown her. She was expected to acquiesce in the double standard and, as witness one of the letters reprinted here, to continue to put her husband's influence at her family's disposal. Her situation was further complicated by her refusal to sue for a divorce. Her course of action left a trail of letters now in the British Library and the Public Record Office. We base our texts on reprints in M. A. E. Green Wood, *Letters* (1846) and G. F. Nott, *Works of Henry Howard, Earl of Surrey* (1815).

ELIZABETH DUCHESS OF NORFOLK TO LORD CROMWELL[2]
(DECEMBER 30, 1536)

My very good lord,

In my most loving wise I commend me unto you, and I thank you for all your kindness that you have showed me. You have bound me to love you and all yours that be of your kin during my life.

My lord, since I came home I had a letter from my Aunt Hastings,[3] and she desired me to deny the said two articles.[4] And I do send to Mr. Richard Cromwell[5] a copy of the letter of the answer I made to her to deliver to you, which I pray you take the pain to overread at your convenient leisure. And there you shall perceive that I will never deny the said two articles during my life. And so I pray you show my lord my husband that I will never deny them, for no ill-handling that he can do to me, nor for no prisonment; so I pray you show my lord my husband that he may trust to it. Seeing that I will not do it at the king's commandment, nor at your desire, I will not do it for no friend nor kin I have living.

Nor from this day forward I will never sue to the king, nor to none other, to desire my lord and husband to take me again, for I have made much suit to him and nothing regarded. And I made him no fault but in declaring of his shameful handling of me, as I have written to you, my lord, in other letters before. There shall no imprisonment change my mind, nor a less living.

I pray you, my lord, to be in hand with the king to get me a better living, ere my lord my husband go northwards, for I have but 50 pounds the quarter, and here I lie in a dear country, and I but three hundred marks a year. I have been from my lord my husband, come the Tuesday in the Passion Week, three years. Though I be left poorly, yet I am content withal, for I am out of danger of mine enemies and of the ill life that I had with my lord my husband since he loved Bessy Holland first, which was but washer of my nursery eight years. And

---

2. Thomas Cromwell (1485?–1540), son of a clothmaker, succeeded Wolsey as chief minister of Henry VIII but was himself eventually executed.
3. Anne, daughter of Henry Stafford, second duke of Buckingham, was married to George Hastings, third baron Hastings of Hastings.
4. Presumably from a list of complaints against her husband.
5. We have been unable to identify Richard Cromwell.

she hath been the causer of all my trouble. I pray you, my lord, when you be at leisure, write to me an answer whether I shall have a better living or not, for if my lord my husband go northward I will get me into some other quarter, where I may be better cheap.

I am fully determined never to write nor to send more to my lord my husband as long as I live, how poorly soever I live, for he never sent me answer of the last letter that I did write to him by the king's commandment, nor no answer of the two gentle letters that I did write to him before. And if he should take me again, I know well it is more for the shame of the world than for any love he beareth me. For I know well my life should be as ill as ever it was. I have been well used since I went from him to a quiet life, and if I should come to him, to use me as he did, he would grieve me worse now than it did before because I have lived quiet these three years, without brawling or fighting. I may say I was born in an unhappy hour to be matched with such an ungracious husband, and so ungracious a son and daughter.

My lord, I thank you for all your kindness that you have done for me, which I will never forget. No more to you at this time, but I pray God send you as much honor and as well to do with long life and health, as I would myself, and to overcome your enemies.

> *Written at Redborne,[6] the 30th day of December, by yours*
> *that is most bounden to you during my life, E. Norfolk*
> *My lord, I pray you show my lord my husband this letter.*

ELIZABETH DUCHESS OF NORFOLK TO SECRETARY CROMWELL (JUNE 26, 1537)

My very good lord,

In my most loving wise that my heart can think, I commend me unto you. The cause of my writing unto you is that I may know whether I shall have a better living or not, for an[7] the King's Grace and you would be so good to me to speak to my lord my husband that I might have a better living, by your good means I might live; and my jointure, which is but five hundred marks and three score pounds, changing with Mr. Gorstwek, as he knoweth well I might, at the desire of my lord my husband.[8] An I were once settled in my jointure, I trust my lord, every year once to do you some pleasure, though I be not able to recompense your good lordship the kindness that I have found in you before I was in my present trouble and since, which I will never forget (your kindness dur-

---

6. Locale of a house in Hertfordshire where the duchess was sent.
7. If.
8. A jointure was the amount settled on a wife by her husband.

ing my life), you have so bound me. My trust is in you next God. For if the King's Grace granteth my daughter of Richmond[9] her jointure (which he had never penny for at her marriage) I know well, if the king command my husband, that I shall have my whole jointure. If my daughter's jointure be granted before, he will not let me have the remainder of my jointure by the king's commandment, nor at your good lordship's desire neither, though my lord, my father, paid two thousand marks with me with other great charges, as I have written to you before, which my lord my husband hath forgotten now he hath so much wealth and honors and is so far in doting love with that quean[10] that he neither regardeth God nor his honor.

He knoweth that it is spoken of far and near, to his great dishonor and shame, and he chose me for love. And I am younger than him by twenty years, and he hath put me away four years and a quarter at this midsummer. I have lived always like a good woman, as it is not unknown to him. I was daily waiter in the court sixteen years together, when he hath lived from me more than a year in the king's wars. The King's Grace shall be my record how I used myself without any ill name or fame, and the best in the court that were there that time, both men and women, know how I used myself in my younger days. And here is a poor reward I have in my latter days for my well doing! And it is the least I shall have, without your good help, my lord. He hath taken away all my jewels and my apparel and left me four years and more like a prisoner, as I have written you before. And none comes at me but such as he appointeth.

I have made suit to him three times with three gentle letters. One of them was by the king's commandment, when I was with his majesty at Dunstable, and I have sent you the copies of them all three. I never sent to him since, nor never will during my life. I am full determined, since I was with the King's Grace and you, that I would never make more suit to nobody during my life. I know, my lord, my husband's crafty ways of old: that he hath made me many times promises under a color which he never performed. I will never make more suit unto him, neither for prisonment nor less living during my life.

And besides that, my daughter of Richmond and Bess Holland is come up with her—that harlot which hath put me at this trouble. And it is eleven years since my lord my husband first fell in love with her—and yet she is but a churl's daughter and of no gentle blood, but that my lord my husband hath set him up for her sake because he was so nigh akin to my Lord Hussey[11] that was late made (and died last and was beheaded) and was the head of that drab, Bess Holland's blood. And he keeps her still in his house, and his children maintain the matter; therefore I will never come at him during my life. Another time he

9. Mary Howard married Henry Fitzroy, duke of Richmond (1519–1536), the natural son of Henry VIII.
10. Harlot.
11. Sir John Hussey, Baron Hussey (1466?–1537), eldest son of Sir William Hussey; arrested in 1537 on suspicion of complicity in the Lincolnshire rising, he was reportedly executed the next day.

set his women to bind me till blood come out at my fingers' ends, and pinna-cled me, and set on my breast till I spit blood, and he never punished them. All this was done for Bess Holland's sake, and he sent me word by Master Cornysh[12] that he would serve me so two years before he put me away. I know well if I should come home again my life should be but short.

My lord, whether I have a good living or not, I thank you for it. I have such a trust in you, for I hear say how good you were to my Lady Mary, the king's daughter,[13] in her great trouble, and many now which were too long to rehearse. If you, my lord, do not now give me this command for my living which I have sued for to you so long, I shall think no fault in you. You are called so steadfast to your friends and so true without dissimulation I shall reckon it is the pleasure of God I should have this ill fortune and that no friend should do me good.

I have sued to nobody but to you, my lord, to amend my living, nor never will do. I live in Hertfordshire, and have but 300 marks, 50 pounds a quarter, and keep twenty persons daily besides other great charges which I have rehearsed before. I could live better and cheaper in London than I do here. It may well be called Her forth shire. And here have I lived four years and a quar-ter at this midsummer. My lord, I can say no more to you, but put my trust in you next God. I pray you, my lord, write to me an answer by this bearer where-to I shall trust, and whether I am to have a better living or not. And no more to you, my lord, at this time, but our Lord send you, my lord, long life and as much honor as I would myself. Written at Redborne, the twenty-sixth of June,

By your most bounden during my life, E. Norfolk.

Henry Stafford[14] to Secretary Cromwell (May 13, 1533)

Right worshipful Master Cromwell,

With as hearty recommendations as my heart can think I recommend me unto you and certify you I received this day your loving letters by my lord of Norfolk's servant. And by the content of the same I perceive your advertise-ment touching the taking of my lady of Norfolk into my house whereby you reckon that, by my good counsel, a quietness and tranquility between my lord and her might ensue and continue. Sir, to be assured of that I would not only receive her into my house, but I would fetch her on my feet at London and endure also a greater pain if need were.

---

12. William Cornysh, a leading composer and musician.
13. Mary Tudor (1516–1558), daughter of Henry VIII and Catherine of Aragon who ruled England 1553–1558; Mary suffered deeply after Henry's repudiation of her mother.
14. Henry Stafford (1501–1563), first baron Stafford, was Elizabeth Stafford's only brother.

But the redress of this standeth not in the advertisement of her kin, where-of she hath had sundry times great plenty near in the pitiful exclamation of her poor friends: praying her call to remembrance the great honor that she is come to by that noble man her husband; and in what possibility she was in to do all her friends good if she had followed the king's highness' pleasure—as doth become every true subject to do—which showed her so great favor that had been to move any alien's heart I think living; and the gentle advertisement that his highness hath sent to her divers times, as of some his highness made me privy unto. And also on the other side, to consider what more shame could her enemies wish her than to be at this continual contention with my lord her hus-band which doth not only make him to absent her company and nothing to tender the preferment of any of her friends, but also, beside the common oblo-quy of this world (which every good person would eschew) bring herself in the king's high displeasure, which is to every true heart death, and her poor friends in continual hindrance (whereof our Lord knows they have no need) to the uttermost discomfort of her well-willers and rejoicing of them that bear her no good-will.

Now, since all these considerations, sundry times renewed by the best and wisest of her kin, nor the wisdom nor gentleness of my said lord's grace her husband, cannot induce her to break her sensual and willful mind, only reckon-ing at all times her own wit best, and taking me and all other at all times for flatterers and liars that have advertised her to a better conformity. As this is not to my said lord unknown, I trust that you nor other my good friends will not reckon that in this matter I might do good but rather to put myself in great jeopardy to match myself with her, that by her wild language might undo me and all mine and never deserving the same. But if I had not found you my espe-cial good friend, I would never have opened my mind so far, which is my shame and sorrow, being her brother, to rehearse.

Elizabeth Duchess of Norfolk to the Earl of Westmoreland (April 11, 1541)

My lord of Westmoreland,

In my most loving wise I commend me unto you, and I heartily thank you for the great pain you took for me, which I shall never forget. And I desire you, my lord, to make no more suit to my lord my husband, for there shall no prison-ment make me to lie on myself. I have been so well used to it this seven years, that I care not for it. And I do send you by this bearer two dishes of almond butter, and one to my sister, and another to my niece, Dorothy, and wafer-cakes to you and to my sister and to the gentlewomen, and four dozen cakes to be delivered to Mistress Daniel. And I do send by this bearer to my sister a gold ring, and to my niece, Dorothy, a bow royal of gold. I pray you, if you see mine uncle of Huntingdon, have me heartily recommended unto him and to mine aunt. I pray God that I may break my prisonment that I have had this seven year, that I may come abroad and see my friends. No more to you at this time, but I pray God send you as well to fare as I would myself.

Written at Redborne, the 11th day of April,
by your poor loving sister-in-law during my life, E. Norfolk

Elizabeth Duchess of Norfolk to her Brother, Lord Stafford (after 1547)

Good brother of Stafford,

I commend me unto you, and would be very glad to hear of your health. And I pray you that I may be heartily commended to my good Lady Stafford, and to show her that her daughter Susan and yours is in good health and merry, and desires your blessings. Nevertheless this be, good brother, if you send me any of your daughters, I pray you to send me my niece Dorothy, for I am well acquainted with her conditions already, and so I am not with the others. And she is the youngest, too, and if she be changed, therefore, she is better to break as concerning her youth. And thus I pray God to send you health and as much honor as I would myself. Written at Redborne . . .

By your poor sister loving, E. Norfolk

Brother, I pray you to send me my niece Dorothy, because I know her conditions—she shall not lack as long as I live, an you would be heard by me at [all], or else I think you be own kin to the false drab and cook, [had it not] been I had had her to my comfort.

6

Rachel Wriothesley Vaughan Russell
(1636–1723)

Henry King *(1592–1669)*

Rachel Wriothesley Vaughan Russell Mourns her Husband

Born to loving and privileged parents—Rachel de Rouvigny and Thomas Wriothesley, fourth earl of Southampton—Rachel Wriothesley (1636–1723) lived her early life in undistinguished conformity to the mores of her class, although her early life—like her later years—showed her ability to negotiate personal relationships with great success. Her first marriage, to Francis, Lord Vaughan, was short-lived but placid, and the young widow characteristically maintained excellent relationships with her husband's family. It is her second marriage, to Lord William Russell, a leading Whig, and its aftermath, which has won Lady Russell posterity's attention. The ardor of her attachment did not abate over the fourteen years of their marriage, which ended in 1683 when he was executed for treason after the Rye House Plot. Although Lois Schwoerer stresses Lady Russell's strong personality and the many activities and successes which continued during her long widowhood (*Lady Rachel Russell: One of the Best of Women* [Baltimore: Johns Hopkins University Press, 1988]), here we focus on her relationship to her husband. The letters from which we take our extracts were written to the Reverend John Fitzwilliam (d. 1699), once chaplain to her father and source of sustained advice and comfort in the years following her husband's death. They first reached print as an effort to vindicate Lord Russell's character politically, in part on the basis of his wife's devotion to his memory. We rely here on the edition of 1801, in which the letters are appended to a biography of Lord Russell.

LADY RUSSELL TO DR. FITZWILLIAM (SEPTEMBER 30, 1683)

I need not tell you, good Doctor, how little capable I have been of such an exercise as this. You will soon find how unfit I am still for it, since my yet disordered thoughts can offer me no other than such words as express the deepest sorrows, and confused, as my yet amazed mind is. But such men as you, and particularly one so much my friend, will, I know, bear with my weakness, and compassionate my distress, as you have already done by your good letter and excellent prayer. I endeavor to make the best use I can of both; but I am so evil and unworthy a creature, that though I have desires, yet I have no dispositions, or worthiness, towards receiving comfort. You that knew us both and how we lived must allow I have just cause to bewail my loss. I know it is common with others to lose a friend; but to have lived with such a one, it may be questioned how few can glory in the like happiness, so consequently lament the like loss. Who can but shrink at such a blow, till by the mighty aids of His holy spirit, we will let the gift of God, which He hath put into our hearts, interpose? That reason which sets a measure to our souls in prosperity, will then suggest many things which we have seen and heard, to moderate us in such sad circumstances as mine. But, alas! my understanding is clouded, my faith weak, sense strong, and the devil busy to fill my thoughts with false notions, difficulties, and doubts, as of a future condition [words missing] of prayer: but this I hope to make matter of humiliation, not sin. Lord let me understand the reason of these dark and wounding providences, that I sink not under the discouragements of my own thoughts: I know I have deserved my punishment, and will be silent under it; but yet secretly my heart mourns, too sadly I fear, and cannot be comforted, because I have not the dear companion and sharer of all my joys and sorrows. I want him to talk with, to walk with, to eat and sleep with; all these things are irksome to me now; the day unwelcome, and the night so, too; all company and meals I would avoid if it might be; yet all this is that I enjoy not the world in my own way, and this sure hinders my comfort; when I see my children before me, I remember the pleasure he took in them; this makes my heart shrink. Can I regret his quitting a lesser good for a bigger? O! if I did steadfastly believe, I could not be dejected; for I will not injure myself to say I offer my mind any inferior consolation to supply this loss. No; I most willingly forsake this world—this vexatious, troublesome world, in which I have no other business but to rid my soul from sin; secure by faith and a good conscience my eternal interests; with patience and courage bear my eminent misfortunes, and ever hereafter be above the smiles and frowns of it. And when I have done the remnant of the work appointed me on earth, then joyfully wait for the heavenly perfection in God's good time, when by his infinite mercy I may be accounted worthy to enter into the same place of rest and repose, where he is gone, for whom only I grieve I do [word missing] fear. From that contemplation must come my best support. Good Doctor, you will think, as you have reason, that I set no bounds when I let myself loose to my complaints. But I will release you, first fervently asking the continuance of your prayers for

Your infinitely afflicted,
But very faithful servant,
R. Russell
Woburn Abbey[1]

Lady Russell to Dr. Fitzwilliam (April 20, 1684)

Believe me, good Doctor, I find myself uneasy at reading your short letter of 8th April, (which I have but newly received) before I had answered yours of the 11th March. I have several times taken a pen in my hand to do it and been prevented by dispatching less pleasing dispatches first, and so my time was spent before I came to that I intended before I laid away the pen.

The future part of my life will not, I expect, pass as perhaps I would just choose; sense has been long enough gratified; indeed, so long I know not how to live by faith; yet the pleasant stream that fed it near fourteen years together, being gone, I have no sort of refreshment but when I can repair to that living fountain, from whence all flows; while I look not at the things which are seen, but at those which are not seen, expecting that day which will settle and compose all my tumultuous thoughts in perpetual peace and quiet; but am undone, irrecoverably so, as to my temporal longings and concerns. Time runs on, and usually wears off some of that sharpness of thought inseparable with my circumstances, but I cannot experience such an effect, every week making me more and more sensible of the miserable change in my condition. But the same merciful hand which has held me up from sinking in the extremist calamities, will (I verily believe) do so still, that I faint not to the end in this sharp conflict, nor add sin to my grievous weight of sorrows by too high a discontent, which is all I have now to fear. You do, I doubt not, observe I let my pen run too greedily upon this subject: indeed 'tis very hard upon me to restrain it, especially to such as pity my distress and would assist towards my relief any way in their power. I am glad I have so expressed myself to you as to fix you in resolving to continue the course you have begun with me, which is to set before me plainly my duty in all kinds: 'twas my design to engage you to it; nor shall you be less successful with me in your desires could there happen occasion for it—which is most unlikely, Doctor Fitzwilliam understanding himself and the world so well. On neither of the points, I believe, I shall give you reason to complain, yet please myself in both; so far of one mind we shall be.

1. Seat in Bedfordshire of the earls and dukes of Bedford.

I am entertaining some thoughts of going to that now desolate place, Stratton,[2] for a few days, where I must expect new amazing reflections at first, it being a place where I have lived in sweet and full content; considered the condition of others, and thought none deserved my envy. But I must pass no more such days on earth; however, places are indeed nothing. Where can I dwell that his figure is not present to me! Nor would I have it otherwise; so I resolve that shall be no bar, if it proves requisite for the better acquitting any obligation upon me. That which is the immediate one is settling, and indeed giving up, the trust my dear Lord had from my best sister.[3] Fain[4] would I see that performed as I know he would have done it had he lived. If I find I can do as I desire in it, I will (by God's permission) infallibly go; but indeed not to stay more than two or three weeks, my children remaining here, who shall ever have my diligent attendance, therefore shall hasten back to them.

I do not admit one thought of accepting your kind and religious offer, knowing it is not proper. I take, if I do go, my sister Margaret,[5] and believe Lady Shaftsbury[6] will meet me there. This I choose, as thinking some persons being there to whom I would observe some rules, will engage me to restrain myself, or keep in better bounds my wild and sad thoughts. This is all I can do for myself. But blessed by the good prayers of others for me, they will, I hope, help me forward towards the great end of our creation.

> *I am, most cordially, good Doctor,*
> *Your ever mournful, but*
> *Ever faithful friend, to serve you,*
> *R. Russell*

I hear my Lord Gainsborough and my Lady will be shortly at Chilten.[7] She is one I do truly respect: I can never regret being near her, though my design is to converse with none but lawyers and accountants.

> *Woburn Abbey*

Henry King on his Wife

Henry King (1592–1669), poet, translator, and Bishop of Chichester from 1642, married Anne Berkeley c. 1617. The couple had five children, some of whom died young, and then, on January, 5, 1624, King buried his beloved spouse and "friend." The

---

2. Stratton House and manor in Hampshire, which had descended to Rachel Russell from her father and which she and William Russell used as an idyllic country retreat.
3. Elizabeth Wriothesley Noel, fourteen months older than Rachel Russell, who died in 1680, leaving a trust vested in William Russell for her daughters.
4. Gladly.
5. Apparently her sister-in-law, Margaret Russell.
6. Her cousin, Margaret Spencer, third wife of the Whig leader, Anthony Ashley Cooper, first earl of Shaftsbury, whose Hampshire estate was near her own.
7. Edward Noel, first earl of Gainsborough had married Rachel's sister Elizabeth (d. 1680) in 1661; in 1683 he married Mary Herbert, widow of James Herbert of Buckinghamshire. "Chilten" may be "Chilton," near the Herbert's Buckinghamshire home. We thank Lois Schwoerer and Ann Mitchell (archivist of Woburn Abbey) for this suggestion.

grieving tetrameters he wrote were much admired, being copied into a number of seventeenth-century commonplace books. King was particularly drawn to such verse, writing on the death of Donne and penning a "Deep Groan" on the execution of Charles I in 1649. We follow the edition by Margaret Crum (Oxford: Clarendon, 1965).

An Exequy To his Matchless Never-to-be-Forgotten Friend

Accept, thou shrine of my dead saint,[1]
Instead of dirges this complaint;
And, for sweet flowers to crown thy hearse,
Receive a strew[2] *of weeping verse*
From thy grieved friend, whom thou might'st see
Quite melted into tears for thee.

Dear loss! Since thy untimely fate
My task hath been to meditate
On thee, on thee: thou art the book,
The library whereon I look
Though almost blind. For thee (loved clay!)
I languish out, not live, the day,
Using no other exercise
But what I practice with mine eyes.
By which wet glasses[3] *I find out*
How lazily Time creeps about
To one that mourns. This, only this
My exercise and business is:
So I compute the weary hours
With sighs dissolvèd into showers.

Nor wonder if my time go thus
Backward and most preposterous;[4]
Thou has benighted me. Thy set
This eve of blackness did beget,
Who wast my day (though overcast
Before thou had'st thy noon-tide passed),
And I remember must in tears
Thou scarce had'st seen so many years

1. One of the elect, destined for salvation.
2. A scattering.
3. Optical instruments.
4. In reverse.

As day tells hours.[5] *By thy clear sun*
My love and fortune first did run;
But thou wilt never more appear
Folded within my hemisphere,
Since both thy light and motion
Like a fled star is fall'n and gone;
And 'twixt me and my soul's dear wish
The earth now interposèd is,
Which such a strange eclipse doth make
As ne'er was read in almanac.

   I could allow thee for a time
To darken me and my sad clime,
Were it a month, a year, or ten,
I would thy exile live till then,
And all that space my mirth adjourn
So thou would'st promise to return,
And putting off thy ashy shroud
At length disperse this sorrow's cloud.

   But woe is me! the longest date[6]
Too narrow is to calculate
These empty hopes. Never shall I
Be so much blest as to descry
A glimpse of thee till that day come
Which shall the earth to cinders doom,
And a fierce fever must calcine[7]
The body of this world, like thine
(My little world!). That fit[8] *of fire*
Once off, our bodies shall aspire
To our souls' bliss: then we shall rise
And view ourselves with clearer eyes
In that calm region where no night
Can hide us from each other's sight.

   Meantime, thou hast her, Earth: much good
May my harm do thee. Since it stood
With Heaven's will I might not call
Her longer mine, I give thee all

5. Apparently Anne died when she was about twenty-four.
6. Period of time.
7. Burn to ashes. King anticipates the destruction of the world by fire before he can see his wife in the risen flesh.
8. Feverish spell.

My short-lived right and interest
In her whom living I loved best:
With a most free and bounteous grief
I give thee what I could not keep.
Be kind to her, and prithee look
Thou write into thy Doomsday book[9]
Each parcel of this rarity
Which in thy casket shrined doth lie.
See that thou make thy reck'ning straight
And yield her back again by weight,
For thou must audit on thy trust
Each grain and atom of this dust,
As thou wilt answer Him that lent
(Not gave) thee my dear monument.

So, close the ground and 'bout her shade
Black curtains draw: my bride is laid.[10]

Sleep on, my love, in thy cold bed
Never to be disquieted.
My last "Good night!" Thou wilt not wake
Till I thy fate shall overtake:
Till age, or grief, or sickness must
Marry my body to that dust
It so much loves, and fill the room
My heart keeps empty in thy tomb.
Stay for me there: I will not fail
To meet thee in that hollow vale.
And think not much of my delay:
I am already on the way,
And follow thee with all the speed
Desire can make or sorrows breed.
Each minute is a short degree[11]
And ev'ry hour a step towards thee.
At night when I betake to rest,
Next morn I rise nearer my west
Of life almost by eight hours' sail

9. The "Doomsday book" was a survey of properties and owners. King plays with two senses of "doomsday": the list of land "parcels" and Judgment day, when the earth will yield up the dead. King treats Earth like the servant in Jesus' parable from whom God demands an account of his stewardship.
10. Laid in the grave but recalling the custom of family and friends "laying" a bride in a flower-strewn bed.
11. Stair.

Than when Sleep breathed his drowsy gale.
    Thus from the sun my bottom[12] steers
And my day's compass downward bears.
Nor labor I to stem the tide
Through which to thee I swiftly glide.
    'Tis true, with shame and grief I yield
Thou like the van[13] first took'st the field
And gotten hast the victory
In thus adventuring to die
Before me, whose more years might crave
A just precèdence in the grave.
But hark! My pulse, like a soft drum,
Beats my approach, tells thee I come,
And slow howe'er my marches be,
I shall at last sit down by thee.
    The thought of this bids me go on
And wait my dissolution
With Hope and Comfort. Dear (forgive
The crime), I am content to live
Divided, with but half a heart,
Till we shall meet and never part.

12. A ship's hull, commonly used to mean the ship itself.
13. The vanguard, soldiers moving ahead of the main group. Although younger, Anne has conquered the enemy before Henry could even reach the field.

7

Jane Sharp *(fl.1641–1671)*

John Sadler *(fl. 1636)*

Jane Sharp on Midwifery

Jane Sharp (fl. 1641–1671), author of *The Midwives Book*, the first printed text on midwifery by an Englishwoman, is described on the title page as "practitioner in the art of midwifery above thirty years." The only other historical thread of identification is the dedication to her still unidentified "much esteemed and ever honored friend, the Lady Eleanor Talbot."

Sharp writes that she has chosen plain English terms for a subject traditionally obscured by Latin. While the results, she says in the extracts below, may seem immodest, the text will be intelligible and useful to unlearned readers, who should "use as much modesty in the perusal of it, as I have endeavored to do in the writing of it." Despite her refreshing directness and feminist consciousness, modern readers will notice Sharp's decision to discuss men before women, her Galenic and Aristotelian commonplaces, and her acceptance of such derogatory beliefs as the notion that "fits of the mother" originate in disorders of the female reproductive system. Her work combines shrewd observation with superstition. Also noteworthy are her descriptions of male and female genitalia as well as chapters on nursing and children's diseases. Here Sharp follows (perhaps unknowingly) two earlier works on women's health. The first, a long "prologue to the women readers" in the augmented translation by Dr. Thomas Raynold (1545) of Roesslin's *Birth of Mankind* (1540), asserts the value of making life-saving information available. Admitting that "lewd" persons can misuse the book, Raynold tells readers to "construe everything herein contained according to the best, and to use everything therein entreated of to the purpose wherefore it was written" (sig. C7v). The other is *Child-birth or the Happy Delivery of Women* (1612): like Sharp's later work, it had illustrations. Sharp's work has been edited by Elaine Hobby, who kindly shared information with us. We base our text on *The Midwives Book* (1671).

FROM *THE MIDWIVES BOOK*

To the Midwives of England

Sisters,

I have often sat down sad in the consideration of the many miseries women endure in the hands of unskillful midwives, many professing the art (without any skill in anatomy, which is the principal part effectually necessary for a midwife) merely for lucre's sake. I have been at great cost in translations for all books, either French, Dutch, or Italian of this kind. All which I offer with my own experience. Humbly begging the assistance of almighty God to aid you in this great work, and am

Your affectionate friend,
Jane Sharp.

The Introduction. Of the Necessity and Usefulness of the Art of Midwifery.

The art of midwifery is doubtless one of the most useful and necessary of all arts for the being and well being of mankind, and therefore it is extremely requisite that a midwife be both fearing God, faithful, and exceeding well experienced in that profession. Her fidelity shall find not only a reward here from man, but God hath given a special example of it (Exodus 1) in the midwives of Israel, who were so faithful to their trust that the command of a king could not make them depart from it, viz. "But the midwives feared God, and did not as the King of Egypt commanded them, but saved the men children alive. Therefore God dealt well with the midwives, and because they feared God He made them houses."[1]

As for their knowledge, it must be two-fold: speculative[2] and practical. She that wants the knowledge of speculation is like to one that is blind or wants her sight; she that wants the practice is like one that is lame and wants her legs: the lame may see but they cannot walk; the blind may walk but they cannot see. Such is the condition of those midwives that are not well versed in both these. Some perhaps may think that then it is not proper for women to be of this profession, because they cannot attain so rarely[3] to the knowledge of things as men may, who

1. Exod. 1:21.
2. Theoretical.
3. Finely, splendidly.

are bred up in universities, schools of learning, or serve their apprenticeships for that end and purpose where anatomy lectures being frequently read, the situation[4] of the parts[5] both of men and women and other things of great consequence are often made plain to them.

But that objection is easily answered by the former example of the midwives amongst the Israelites. For though we women cannot deny that men in some things may come to a greater perfection of knowledge than women ordinarily can, by reason of the former helps that women want, yet the holy Scriptures hath recorded midwives to the perpetual honor of the female sex, there being not so much as one word concerning men-midwives mentioned there that we can find, it being the natural propriety of women to be seeing into that art. And though nature be not alone sufficient to the perfection of it, yet farther knowledge may be gained by a long and diligent practice and be communicated to others of our own sex. I cannot deny the honor due to able physicians and surgeons when occasion is. Yet we find that even amongst the Indians and all barbarous people, where there is [sic] no men of learning the women are sufficient to perform this duty. And even in our own nation, that we need go no farther, the poor country people where there are none but women to assist (unless it be those that are exceeding poor and then they have more need of meat than midwives), the women are as fruitful and as safe and well-delivered (if not much more fruitful and better commonly) in childbed than the greatest ladies of the land.

It is not hard words that perform the work, as if none understood the art that cannot understand Greek. Words are but the shell, that we ofttimes break our teeth with them to come at the kernel, I mean our brains to know what is the meaning of them, but to have the same in our mother tongue would save us a great deal of needless labor. It is commendable for men to employ their spare time in some things of deeper speculation than is required of the female sex, but the art of midwifery chiefly concern us which, even the best learned men will grant, yielding something of their own to us, when they are forced to borrow from us the very name they practice by, and to call themselves men-midwives.

But to avoid long preambles in a matter so clear and evident, I shall proceed to set down such rules and method concerning this art as I think needful, and that as plainly and briefly as possibly I can, and with as much modesty in words as the matter will bear. And because it is commonly maintained that the masculine gender is more worthy than the feminine, though perhaps when men have need of us they will yield the priority to us, that I may not forsake the ordinary method I shall begin with men, and treat last of my own sex, so as to be understood by the meanest capacity, desiring the courteous reader to use as much modesty in the perusal of it as I have endeavored to do in the writing of it, considering that such an art as this cannot be set forth but that young men and maids will have much just cause to blush sometimes and be ashamed of their own follies, as I wish they may if they shall chance to read it, that they may not convert that into evil that is really intended for a general good.

4. Position.
5. Privy parts.

Chapter 1. A Brief Description of the Generative Parts in Both Sexes; and First of the Vessels in Men Appropriated to Procreation

There are six parts in men that are fitted for generation: 1. The vessels that prepare the matter to make the seed, called the preparing vessels. 2. There is that part or vessel which works this matter, or transmutes the blood into the real desire for seed. 3. The stones[6] that make the seed fructify.[7] 4. There are the vessels that convey the seed back again from the stones when they have concocted[8] it. 5. There are the seminal or seed-vessels that keep or retain the seed concocted. 6. The yard[9] that from these containing vessels casts the seed prepared into the matrix.[10]

Chapter 7. Of a Man's Yard

The yard is as it were the plow wherewith the ground is tilled and made fit for production of fruit. We see that some fruitful persons have a crop by it almost every year, only plowing up their own ground, and live more plentifully by it than the countryman can with all his toil and cost, and some there are that plow up other men's ground, when they can find such lascivious women that will pay them well for their pains, to their shame be it spoken. But commonly they pay dear for it in the end, if timely they repent not.

The yard is of a ligamental[11] substance, sinewy and hollow as a sponge, having some muscles to help it in its several postures. The yard and the tongue have more great veins and arteries in them than any part of the body for their bigness; by these porosities,[12] by help of imagination, the yard is sometimes raised, and swells with a windy spirit[13] only. For there is a natural inclination and force by which it is raised when men are moved to copulation, as the motion is natural in the heart and arteries. True it is that in these motion is always necessary, but the yard moves only at some times, and riseth sometimes to small purpose.

It stands in the sharebone[14] in the middle as all know, being of a round and long fashion, with a hollow passage within it, through which pass both the urine and seed; the top of it is called the head or nut[15] of the yard, and there it is compact and hard, and not very quick of feeling, lest it should suffer pain in copulation. There is a soft loose skin called the foreskin which covers the head of it and will move forward and backward as it is moved; this foreskin in the lower part, only in the middle, is fastened or tied long ways to the greater part of the head of the yard by a certain skinny part called the string or bridle. It is of temperament hot and moist. And it is joined to the middle of the sharebone and with the

6. Testicles.
7. Become fruitful.
8. Brought to perfection by heat.
9. Penis.
10. Womb.
11. Flexible, fibrous tissue binding body parts together.
12. Porous structures.
13. A sort of animating air; it was believed that the element of air played a role in erections.
14. Pubis.
15. The glans penis.

bladder by the conduit pipe that carrieth the urine, and with the brain by nerves and muscles that come to the skin of it, to the heart and liver by veins and arteries that come from them.

The yard hath three holes or pipes in it: one broad one and that is common to the urine and seed, and two small ones by which the seed comes into the common long conduit pipe. These two arteries or vessels enter into this pipe in the place called the perineum,[16] which in men is the place between the root of the yard and the arse-hole or fundament,[17] but in a woman it is the place between that and the cut[18] of the neck of the womb. From those holes to the bladder that passage is called the neck of the bladder, and from thence to the head of the yard is the common pipe or channel of the yard. The yard hath four muscles: two towards the lower part on both sides, one of them near the channel or pipe of the yard. And these are extended in length, and they dilate the yard and raise it up that the seed may with ease pass through it. Two other muscles there are that come from the root of it near the sharebone that comes slanting toward the top of the yard in the upper part of it. When these are stretched the yard riseth, and when they slacken then it falls again, and if one of these be bent and the other be not, the yard bends to that muscle that is stretched or bent.

If the yard be of a moderate size, not too long nor too short, it is good as the tongue is, but if the yard be too long, the spirits in the seed flee away; if it be too short, it cannot carry the seed home to the place it should do.

The yard also serveth to empty the bladder of the water in it, and that is easily proved by a louse put into the pipe of the yard, which by biting will cause one to make water when the urine is suppressed. The foreskin was made to defend the yard that is tender, and to cause delight in copulation; the Jews were commanded to cut it off.[19] Many diseases are incident to the yard, but a priapism[20] or standing of the yard continually by reason of a windy matter is a disease that properly belongs to this part, and is very dangerous sometimes.

The yard of a man is not bony (as in dogs, and wolves, and foxes) nor gristly, for then it could not stand and fall as need is. It is made of skins, brawns,[21] tendons, veins, arteries, sinews, and great ligaments, yet not so full of veins but it may be emptied and filled again, nor so full of arteries as to beat always. Yet you shall find it beat sometimes. It consists not of nerves for they are not hollow enough for the passages, but it is compounded of a peculiar substance that is not found in any other part of the body. The place of it, as I said, begins at the sharebone, and it is fast knit to the yard between the cods[22] and the fundament, so that there is a seam that comes up along the cods and parts them in the midst between the stones. The yard is not perfectly round, but is somewhat broad on the back or upperside; it differs a little in some from others. The situation of it is so pecu-

16. The area between the anus and the scrotum or vulva.
17. Buttocks, anus.
18. Passage across; opening.
19. Gen. 17.
20. Persistent erection of the penis.
21. Muscles.
22. Testicles.

liar to men that they have herein a preeminence above all other creatures. Some men, but chiefly fools, have yards so long that they are useless for generation. It is generally held that the length or proportion of the yard depends upon cutting the navel string: if you cut it too short and knit it too close in infants it will be too short because of the string that comes from the navel to the bottom of the bladder which draws up the bladder and shortens the yard. And this, beside the general opinion, stands with so much reason that all midwives have cause to be careful to cut the navel string long enough, that when they tie it the yard may have free liberty to move and extend itself—always remembering that moderation is best, that it be not left too long, which may be as bad as too short.

There are six parts to be observed of which the yard consists: 1. two sinewy bodies, 2. a sinewy substance to hold up the two side ligaments and the urinary passage, 3. the urinary passage itself, 4. the nut of the yard, 5. the four muscles, and 6. the vessels.

The two sinewy bodies are really two though they are joined together. They are long and hard; within they are spongy and full of black blood; the spongy substance within seems to be woven network[23] and is made of numberless veins and arteries, and the black blood that is contained in them is full of spirits. Motion and leisure in copulation heats them and makes the yard to stand, and so will imagination; the hollow weaving of them together was to hold the spirits as long as may be that the yard fall not down before it hath performed the work of nature. These side ligaments of the yard (where they are thick and round) spring from the lower part of the sharebone, and not the upper part as Galen[24] supposed. At the beginning they are parted and resemble a pair of horns or the letter y, where the common pipe for urine and seed goes between them. It is thus manifest that the greatest part of the yard is made of two sinewy parts, one of them of each side, and they both end at the top of the head of the yard; they come from two beginnings and lean upon the hip under the sharebone, and so run on to the nut of the yard. Also their substance is double: the outside is sinewy, hard and thick, the inside black, soft, loose, spongy and thin. They are joined by a thin and sinewy skin which is strengthened by some slanting small veins placed there like to a weaver's shuttle; they are parted at their first rising to make way for the water pipe, but they are joined about the middle of the sharebone, and there they lose near a third part of their sinewy substance.

The use of these two sinewy bodies that make the yard is for the vital spirits to run through the thin parts of them and fill the yard with spirits. And they are so thick and compact and strong on the outside that they hinder these spirits from breaking suddenly away, for should they flee out the yard will stand no longer but presently fall down.

In the inside of the substance of the yard (which is wrapped about by the outward sinewy substance) there is seen a thin and tender artery coming from the root of the yard and runs quite through the whole loose substance of it. Besides

23. Arranged in the fashion of a net.
24. Galen (129–c. 200) was a celebrated ancient physician.

these there is a conduit pipe placed at the lower part of the yard that serves both for seed and urine to be put forth by (as common to them both). And it runs through the middle of the foresaid two sinewy bodies and is of the same substance with them, and is loose and thick, soft and tender, and runs equally in all respects from the neck of the bladder to the top of the yard. Only it is something larger where it begins than where it ends at the top of the nut. This pipe, at first, as I said, hath three holes where it riseth from the neck of the bladder; that in the middle is wider than the other two pipes or holes are (which stand on both sides of it and which are derived from the passage that comes from the seed vessels). And they carry the seed into this great pipe. In this great pipe, where it is fastened to the nut of the yard and with the two sinewy bodies, there is a little hollow place wherein (when a man is troubled with the running of the reins[25] by reason of the pox[26]) some corrupt seed or sharp matter lieth which occasions great pains and ulcers. And sometimes the surgeon is forced to cut off the top of the yard, and sometimes from these ulcers there will grow a piece of flesh in the yard's passage for urine which hinders the urine that it cannot come forth till that piece of flesh be taken away by conveying something into that urinary passage that may eat it off. There is one thing more worth taking notice of by surgeons concerning this pipe or urinary passage: that from the place where it begins and goes forward from the neck of the bladder to the spermatic vessels and forestanders[27] that there is a thin and very tender skin which is of a most acute feeling and to stir up delight in the act of venery,[28] and it will make the yard stand upon any delightsome thoughts or desires. If the surgeons be not careful when they thrust the [syringe] in near that place, they will soon break this skin and undo their patient. This common pipe comes from the neck of the bladder; that is, it begins there, but it doth not take its being from it. For boil the bladder of any creature and it will part from it, whereby it is plain that it is only joined to it and so runs on to the nut of the yard.

Chapter 10. Of the Generative or Privy Parts in Women

Man in the act of procreation is the agent and tiller and sower of the ground; women is the patient or ground to be tilled who brings seed also, as well as the man, to sow the ground with. I am now to proceed to speak of this ground or field which is the woman's womb and the parts that serve to this work. We women have no more cause to be angry or be ashamed of what Nature hath given us than men have; we cannot be without ours no more than they can want theirs. The things most considerable to be spoken to are 1) the neck of the womb or privy entrance, 2) the womb itself, 3) the stones, 4) the vessels of seed.

At the bottom of the woman's belly is a little bank called a mountain of pleasure near the wellspring and the place where the hair coming forth shows virgins to be ready for procreation, in some far younger than others; some are more forward at twelve years than some at sixteen years of age, as they are hotter and riper

25. Kidneys.
26. Syphilis.
27. English equivalent of "prostate," once thought to contain semen.
28. The sex act.

in constitution. Under this hill is the springhead, which is a passage having two lips set about it with hair as the upper part is. I shall give you a brief account of the parts of it, both within and without, and of the likeness and proportion between the generative parts in both sexes.

Chapter 11. Of the Womb

The matrix or womb hath two parts: the great hollow part within and the neck that leads to it, and it is a member made by nature for propagation of children. The substance of the concavity[29] of it is sinewy, mingled with flesh, so that it is not very quick of feeling. It is covered with a sinewy coat that it may stretch in time of copulation and may give way when the child is to be born. When it takes in the seed from man, the whole concavity moves towards the center and embraceth it and toucheth it with both its sides. The substance of the neck of it is musculous and gristly with some fat, and it hath one wrinkle upon another, and these cause pleasure in the time of copulation; this part is very quick of feeling. The concavity or hollow of it is called the womb, or house, for the infant to lie in. Between the neck and the womb there is a skinny, fleshy substance within— quick of feeling, hollow in the middle—that will open and shut, called the mouth of the womb. And it is like the head of a tench[30] or of a young kitten, It opens naturally in copulation, in voiding menstrous blood and in child-birth, but at other times, especially when a woman is with child, it shuts so close that the smallest needle cannot get in but by force.

The neck is long, round, hollow. At first it is no wider than a man's yard makes it, but in maids much less. About the middle of it is a pannicle[31] called the virgin pannicle, made like a net with many fine ligaments and veins, but a woman loseth it in the first act, for it is then broken. At the end of the neck there are small skins which are called foreskins; within the neck, a little toward the share-bone, there is a short entrance whose orifice is shut with certain fleshy and skinny additions, whereby (and by the aforesaid foreskin) the air coming between, they make a hissing noise when they make water.

The figure of the concavity of the womb is four [s]quare, with some roundness and hollow below like a bladder. There is towards the neck of the womb on both sides a strong ligament near the haunches,[32] binding the womb to the back; they are like a snail's horns and therefore are called the horns of the womb. About these horns there is one stone on each side, harder and smaller than men's stones and not perfectly round but flat like an almond; seed is bred in them, not thick and hot as in men but cold, watery seed.

These stones have not one purse[33] to hold them both as men's stones have, but each of them hath a covering of its own that springs from the peritoneum,[34] binding them about, the horns, and each of them hath a small muscle to move them by.

29. Hollowness.
30. A freshwater fish.
31. Membrane.
32. The part of the body between the last ribs and the thigh.
33. Receptacle, bag.
34. The membrane lining the cavity of the abdomen.

The foresaid seed-vessels are planted in these stones, and are called preparing vessels, descending from the liver vein, the great artery, and the emulgent[35] veins; then there are other vessels called carriers, that continually dilate themselves and proceed as far as the concavity of the womb (where it is joined to the neck), and they carry the seed to the hollow of the womb. The many orifices of these vessels are called cups; the menstruous blood runs forth by them, and the infant sucks its nutriment from them by the veins and arteries of the navel that are joined to these cups.

A woman hath no forestanders, for a woman's vessels are soft, and do not hurt the stones as they would do in men because they are so hard. The whole matrix considered with the stones and seed vessels is like to a man's yard and privities, but men's parts for generation are complete and appear outwardly by reason of heat, but women's are not so complete, and are made within by reason of their small heat.

The matrix is like the yard turned inside outward. For the neck of the womb is as the yard, and the hollow of it with its receivers and vessels and stones are like the cods. For the cods turned in have a hollowness, and within the womb lie the stones and seed vessels, but men's stones and vessels are larger. The place of the cut of the matrix is between the fundament and the sharebone, and the place between both arteries is called the peritoneum. The neck from the cut by the belly goeth upward as far as the womb, and the place of it is between the right gut and the bladder; all these are placed at length in the cavity of the belly.

The womb is small in maids and less than their bladder; neither is the hollow complete but groweth bigger as the body doth. In maids of ripe years it is not much bigger than you can comprehend[36] in your hand, unless when they come to be with child. Yet it grows by reason of their courses.[37] The sides of it are fleshy, hard, and thick, but when a woman is with child it is stretched out and made thin and seems more sinewy, and then it riseth toward the navel more or less according as the child is in bigness. It hath but one hollow cell, yet this at the bottom is in some manner divided into two, as if there were two wombs fastened to one neck. For the most part, boys are bred in the right side of it, and girls in the left.

It joins to the brain by nerves, to the heart by arteries, to the liver and lights[38] by veins, to the right gut by pannicles, to the bladder by the neck of it— which neck is short, and comes not forth as men's do. It is joined to the haunches by the horns; the concavity of it is loose every way, and therefore it will fall to the sides, and sometimes it will come all forth of the body by the neck of it. Perhaps it is no error to say the wombs are two, because there are two cavities like two hollow hands touching one the other, both covered with one pannicle. And both end in one channel. No man that sees a womb can well discern it unless

35. Milking out the serum through the kidneys.
36. Grasp.
37. Menses.
38. Eyes.

he be well skilled in the aspects concerning limbs and shadows,[39] whereby physicians are much helped in many practices as well as other artificers.[40]

The womb, by reason of that which flows to it, is hot and moist. It is of great use to cleanse the body from superfluous blood, but chiefly to preserve the child. It is subject to all diseases, and the whole womb may be taken forth when it is corrupted, as I have seen, and yet the woman may live in good health when it is all cut away. In the year of our Lord 1520, upon the 5th of October, Domianus,[41] a surgeon, cut out a whole womb from one called Gentil, the wife of Christopher Briant of Milan, in the presence of many learned doctors and other students. And that woman did afterwards follow her ordinary business, and as she and her husband confessed and reported, she kept company with her husband, and cast forth seed in copulation, and had her monthly courses as she was wont to have before.

Chapter 12. Of the Likeness of the Privities of Both Sexes.

But to handle these things more particularly, Galen saith that women have all the parts of generation that men have, but men's are outwardly, women's inwardly.

The womb is like to a man's cod, turned the inside outward, and thrust inward between the bladder and the right gut, for then the stones which were in the cod will stick on the outsides of it, so that what was a cod before will be a matrix. So the neck of the womb, which is the passage for the yard to enter, resembleth a yard turned inwards, for they are both one length. Only they differ like a pipe and the case for it. So then it is plain that when the woman conceives the same members are made in both sexes. But the child proves to be a boy or a girl as the seed is in temper,[42] and the parts are either thrust forth by heat or kept in for want of heat. So a woman is not so perfect as a man because her heat is weaker, but the man can do nothing without the woman to beget children, though some idle coxcombs will needs undertake to show how children may be had without use of the woman.

Dr. Sadler's Advice on the Uterus

According to the title page of *The Sick Woman's Private Looking-Glass*, John Sadler (fl. 1636) was a "doctor in physic in the city of Norwich," a bustling town northeast of London. He is probably not the John Sadler (1615–1674) who was a member of Parliament, Hebrew scholar, and advocate of the right of London Jews to erect a synagogue. *Looking-Glass* was printed by Anne Griffin, one of a number of women in the book trade (although there is little evidence that such women, often widows, were protofeminist). The title page, which quotes a Latin tag from the Roman poet Juvenal on a sound mind in a sound body, claims that Sadler's description of uterine diseases and "affects"—both what affects the womb and its own effects on body and spirit— will help women "inform the physician about the cause of their grief." Sadler's pref-

39. Traces.
40. Craftsmen.
41. Domianus has, so far, resisted identification.
42. Temperature.

ace vows to avoid "hard words and rhetorical phrases," but his margins cite authorities in Latin and Greek and the prefatory matter includes an admiring Latin epistle from a member of London's College of Physicians and a fancy poem in English telling how Apollo and the Muses have crowned Sadler with laurel. In modernizing the 1636 text we transliterate Greek words.

FROM *THE SICK WOMAN'S PRIVATE LOOKING-GLASS*

Chapter 1: Introduction

If any one, but of a mean capacity,[1] were asked what were the wonder of the world, I think that reason would move him to answer, "man," he being a *mikrokosmos*, or little world, to whom all things are subordinate, agreeing in the *genus* with things sensitive, all being animal,[2] but differing in the *species*, for man alone is endued with reason: "Let us make man in our image, after our likeness" [Gen. 1], wherefore of the Greeks he is called *anthropos apo tou anatrepein*, of turning his eyes upward towards Him whose image and superscription he bears. Whence the poet[3] writeth:

> *Nonne vides hominum ut caelos ad sidera vultus*
> *Sustulerit Deus? ac sublimis finxerit ora.*
> *See how the heavens' high Architect*
>   *hath framed man in this wise:*
> *To stand, to go, to look erect,*
>   *with body, face, and eyes.*

And Cicero saith that all creatures were made like moles to root upon the earth, man only excepted: to him was given an upright frame to behold that mansion prepared for him above.[4]

Now, to the end that this so noble and glorious a creature might not quite perish, hath the Almighty given unto woman the field of generation for a receptacle of human seed, whereby that natural and vegetable soul[5] which lies potentially in the seed, may, by the *vis plastica* [shaping force] be produced into act: that man, being mortal and leaving his offspring behind him, may become as it were immortal, and live in his posterity. And because this field of generation—to wit, the womb—is the subject-matter from whence our ensuing discourse is drawn like so many lines from the center, that you may the better judge of that which follows we will in brief lay before you the parts of the womb together with the qualities of the menstrual blood.

1. That is, except for those with poor understanding.
2. People belong to the "genus" of animate beings endowed with senses.
3. The margin cites book 5 of Silius Italicus (26–101), presumably his epic, *Punica*.
4. The margin cites Cicero's *Laws*, book 5.
5. The "vegetable soul" is the principle of growth shared by animals and plants; animals add a "sensitive soul" and we add a "rational" one.

First, touching the womb, of the Grecians it is called *metra* ("the mother") or *delphys*, saith Priscian, because it makes us all brothers.[6] It is placed in the *hyposirium*, or lower part of the belly, in the cavity called "pelvis," having the straight gut on one side, to keep from the hardness of the backbone, and the bladder on the other side, to defend it from blows. The form or figure of it is like a virile member,[7] only this excepted: the manhood is outward and the woman-hood within. It is divided into the neck and the body [the margin reads *auchan tes matras*, meaning "neck of the womb"]. The neck consists of a hard fleshly sub-stance much like a cartilage, at the end whereof there is a membrane transverse-ly placed called *hymen* or *eugion*. Near also unto the neck there is a prominent pannicle[8] which is called of Montanus[9] the "door of the womb" because it pre-serveth the matrix from cold and dust. Of Grecians it is called *seiris*,[10] of the Latins *praeputium muliebre* [female foreskin] because the Jewish women did abuse this part to their own mutual lust, as Saint Paul speaks, for which Juvenal turns satirist against them:

> *Nec distare putant humana carne suillam,*
> *Qua pater abstinnuit mox et praeputia ponnunt.*[11]

The body of the womb is that wherein the child is conceived, and this is not altogether round but dilates itself into two angles, which Herophilus,[12] compar-ing to the horns of a calf, calleth them *kerata*. The outward part of it is nervous[13] and full of sinews, which are the cause of its motion: but inwardly it is fleshy. It is fabulously[14] reported that in the cavity of the womb there are seven divided cells or receptacles for human seed. But those that have seen anatomies[15] do know there are but two, and those not divided by a partition but only by a line or suture running through the midst of it. In the right side of the cavity, by rea-son of the heat of the liver, males are conceived.[16] In the left side, by the cold-ness of the spleen, females are begotten. And this do most of our moderns hold

6. Priscian (6th century) was a North African grammarian who taught at Constantinople. Since "brother" in Greek is *adelph*, he assumes, perhaps wrongly, that it comes from sharing a womb, a *delphys*.
7. Male genitals; like Jane Sharp, Sadler shares the ancient and widespread notion that female genitals are like the male but inside-out and tucked in.
8. Membrane.
9. Dr. Giovanni Battista de Monte (1498–1552) of Padua.
10. The Greek word is nearly illegible in the text from which we have worked, and this is our best guess; *seiris* is from *seira*, the front of the perineum near the vagina.
11. The margin cites Rom. 1:26. The Latin is Juvenal's Satire 14.98–99: "Nor do [Jews] think to distinguish between human flesh and that of a sow—from which their father abstained—and soon remove the foreskin." Perhaps because the pig is female, Sadler reads the verse as obscene, but the subject of Juvenal's sentence ("Quidem") is masculine.
12. A Greek surgeon (335–280 B.C.E.) from Chalcedon (Northwest Turkey).
13. With "nerves" (sinews).
14. As a false tale or rumor.
15. Dissections.
16. It was widely held that males, being more "perfected" than females (hence their complete-ly descended genitalia), have more vital heat; temperature differences in the womb cause sexu-al differentiation.

for an infallible truth. Yet Hippocrates[17] holds it but in the general, for in whom, saith he, the spermatical vessel[18] of the right side comes from the reins and the spermatical vessel of the left side from the hollow vein, in them males are conceived in the left side, and females in the right. Well therefore may I conclude with the saying of Empedocles[19] [that] such sometimes is the power of the seed that a male may be conceived in the left side as well as the right. In the bottom of the cavity there are little holes called the *cotyledons*, which are the ends of certain veins and arteries, serving in breeding women to convey sustenance to the child, which is received by the umbilical vein, and in others to carry the courses into matrix.[20]

Now, touching the menstruals: they are defined to be a monthly flux of excremental and unprofitable blood.[21] In which we are to note that the matter flowing forth is excrementious, which is to be understood of the superplus or redundancy of it, for it is an excrement in quantity, in quality being pure and incorrupt, like unto the blood in the veins. And that the menstrous blood is pure, and simply of itself all one in quality with that in the veins, is proved two ways: first, from the final cause[22] of this blood, which is the propagation and conservation of mankind, that man might be conceived, and being begotten he might be comforted and preserved, both in the womb and out of the womb. And all will grant it for a truth, that the child, while it is in the matrix, is nourished with this blood. And it is as true, that being out of the womb it is still nourished with the same, for the milk is nothing but the menstrual blood made white in the breasts[23]—and I am sure women's milk is not thought to be venomous but of a nutritive quality, answerable to the tender nature of an infant. Secondly, it is proved to be pure from the generation of it, it being the superfluity of the last aliment of the fleshly parts.[24]

It may be objected, if the blood be not of a hurtful quality, how can it cause such venomous effects: as if the same fall upon trees and herbs, it maketh the one barren and mortifies[25] the other. And Averroes[26] writes that if a man accompany with a menstrous woman, if she conceive, she shall bring forth a leper. I answer [that] this malignity is contracted in the womb, for the woman, wanting native heat to digest this superfluity, sends it to the matrix, where seating itself until the mouth of the womb be dilated, it becomes corrupt and venomous, which may

17. The ancient Greek doctor (466–377 B.C.E.).
18. The duct for semen (with sperm, or "seed").
19. A Greek Sicilian poet, philosopher, and scientist (c. 493–c. 433 B.C.E.) who wrote on the four elements and a cosmos based on Love and Strife.
20. That is to carry menstrual blood ("courses") to the womb's lining.
21. To be excreted because not needed. The blood is "unprofitable" since no conception has taken place and the uterine lining must be shed. Sadler will argue that this blood is not impure.
22. In Aristotelian terms, a thing's or phenomenon's ultimate purpose.
23. A common belief derived, as the margin notes, from Aristotle.
24. Menstrual blood, thinks Sadler, is the surplus left by the process of turning food into blood.
25. Makes wither and die.
26. The Arab philosopher and doctor from Spain (1126–1198).

easily be, considering the heat and moistness of the place. This blood, therefore, being out of his vessels, offends in quality. In this sense let us understand Pliny, Fernelius, Florus, and the rest of that torrent.[27]

But if frigidity[28] be the cause why women cannot digest all their last nourishment, and consequently that they have these purgations, it remains to give a reason why they are of so cold a constitution more than men, which is this: The natural end[29] of man's and woman's being is to propagate; and this injunction was imposed upon them by God at their first creation, and again after the deluge (Gen. 1:28, 9:1). Now, in the act of conception there must be an agent and a patient,[30] for if they be both every way of one constitution they cannot propagate. Man therefore is hot and dry, women cold and moist. He is the agent, she the patient, or weaker vessel, that she should be subject unto the office of the man. It is necessary likewise that woman should be of a cold constitution, because in her is required a redundancy of matter for the infant depending on her, for otherwise, if there were not a superplus of nourishment for the child, more than is convenient for the mother, then would the infant detract and weaken the principal parts of the mother, and like unto the viper, the generation of the infant would be the destruction of the parent.[31] These monthly purgations continue from the fifteenth year to the forty-sixth or fiftieth. Yet often there happens a suppression, which is either natural or morbisical.[32] They are naturally suppressed in breeding women and such as give suck. The morbisical suppression falls now into our method to be spoken of. [The next chapter tells why some women fail to menstruate. Amazons, e.g., are so active that they bleed very little, and cold, tumors, or ulcers may have the same effect. We append Sadler's concluding prayer.]

The Author's Prayer for his Patient

What cure I undertake within this roof,	*Luke 7:6*
Lord say the word, "Be whole," and 'tis enough.	
Thy word alone, did make the lame to walk,	*Acts 3:7*
The deaf to hear, yea and the dumb to talk.	*Mark 7:3*
The servant's palsy by Thy word was cured,	*Matt 8:13*

27. The *Natural History* of Pliny the Elder (23/4–79) was a major source of (mis)information on natural history. Sadler has earlier cited Fernelius as the author of *De Hominis Procreatione* (*On Human Procreation*). We have not located a medical authority named Florus.
28. The coldness that stops women from fully "digesting" the blood made by the conversion of food (excess blood, Sadler has just speculated, can collect near the cervix and, rotting, give the fetus leprosy). With her lower temperature, a woman has excess blood that goes to the womb and is then, in the absence of pregnancy, expelled.
29. Purpose according to Nature; having souls, we also have a spiritual "end."
30. That is, one who acts and one who receives.
31. Vipers were thought to exit their mother by chewing their way through her side. If women were as "hot" as men, says Sadler, they would fully "digest" their blood and there would be no excess to nourish the fetus; the fetus would perforce live off its mother's blood and she would die.
32. Pathological.

The lepers cleansèd, and of health assured.　　　　*Matt 8:3*
By it the born blind man was made to see;　　　　*John 11:44*
By it the dead to life, ev'n raisèd be.
By it were these cures wrought; O Lord, grant, then,
Unto my prayer that Thou wilt say, "Amen."
For neither herb nor plaster[33] will do well　　　*Wisd 16:12*
Unless therewith Thy benedict[34] doth dwell.

33. Medicated bandage.
34. Blessing.

8

Rachel Speght [Procter] *(c. 1597–after 1621)*

Richard Hyrde *(d. 1528)*

Rachel Speght [Procter] on Learning

Rachel Speght (c. 1597–after 1621), the daughter of James Speght, rector of two London churches, was the author of *A Muzzle for Melastomus* (1617), the earliest of three responses in a female voice to Joseph Swetnam's *Arraignment of Lewd, Idle, Froward, and Unconstant Women* (1615). Speght's strong but fairly good-mannered response shows her grounding in the Bible and secular learning and her self-respect as a woman. Hers is the first unquestionably female answer in English to male attacks in the pamphlet wars (though Christine de Pisan's *City of Ladies* had been translated in 1521). Speght shows her sense of this fledgling tradition in her later *Dream* when she refers to the pseudonymous Ester Sowernam and Constantia Munda, who had also responded to Swetnam. *Mortalities Memorandum*, to which Speght's *Dream* was appended, appeared several months before her marriage in 1621 to William Procter (the births of children are recorded in 1627 and 1630; Procter died in 1653) and was occasioned by the death of Speght's mother. *Dream*, which merges dream vision with the autobiographical form so congenial to early modern women, relates Speght's quest for knowledge, bolstered by such personified allies as Industry, Truth, and Desire against the efforts of Dissuasion. Speght's struggle is ended by Death (i.e., news of her mother's demise) and followed by tributes to her mother's piety and influence. It is ironic—but typical of our loss of information about women of the period—that nothing else is known of this parent. Indeed Speght's own voice is heard no more after this publication, in which her interrupted dream-vision is followed by the title poem, a meditation on death marked by Speght's feminism (for want of a better term) and faith: "Death was at first inflicted as a curse, / But woman's seed hath broke the serpent's head." We use the 1621 edition; see also the edition by Barbara Lewalski (Oxford: Oxford University Press, 1996).

THE DREAM

When splendent Sol[1] which riseth in the East
Returning thence took harbor in the West,
When Phoebus[2] laid her head in Titan's lap
And creatures sensitive[3] made haste to rest,
When sky which erst[4] looked like to azure blue
Left color bright and put on sable hue,

Then did Morpheus[5] close my drowsy eyes
And stood as porter at my senses' door,
Diurnal[6] cares excluding from my mind
Including rest (the salve for labors sore).
Night's greatest part in quiet sleep I spent,
But nothing in this world is permanent.

For ere Aurora[7] spread her glittering beams
Or did with robes of light herself invest,
My mental quiet sleep did interdict[8]
By entertaining a nocturnal guest:
A dream, which did my mind and sense possess
With more than I by pen can well express.

At the appointment of supernal[9] power
By instrumental means methought I came
Into a place most pleasant to the eye
Which for the beauty some did "cosmos"[10] name,

1. The resplendent sun.
2. The Titaness Phoebe, lunar consort of Coeus.
3. Capable of sensation.
4. Earlier.
5. Son of Sleep, god of dreams.
6. Daily.
7. Goddess of dawn.
8. Forbid.
9. Heavenly.
10. In Greek, "Cosmos" (the world) also means "ornament."

Where stranger-like on everything I gazed,
But wanting wisdom was as one amazed.

Upon a sudden, as I gazing stood,
Thought came to me and asked me of my state,
Inquiring what I was, and what I would,
And why I seemed as one disconsolate.
To whose demand I thus again replied,
"I as a stranger in this place abide."

"The haven of my voyage is remote,
I have not yet attained my journey's end;
Yet know I not nor can I give a guess
How short a time I in this place shall spend.
For that high power which sent me to this place
Doth only know the period of my race.

"The reason of my sadness at this time
Is 'cause I feel myself not very well.
Unto you I shall much obligèd be
If for my grief a remedy you'll tell."
Quoth she, "If you your malady will show,
My best advice I'll willingly bestow."

"My grief," quoth I, "Is callèd Ignorance
Which makes me differ little from a brute;
For animals are led by nature's lore,
Their seeming science is but custom's fruit.
When they are hurt they have a sense of pain
But want the sense to cure themselves again.

"And ever since this grief did me oppress
Instinct of nature is my chiefest guide;
I feel disease, yet know not what I ail;
I find a sore but can no salve provide.
I hungry am yet cannot seek for food,
Because I know not what is bad or good.

"And sometimes when I seek the golden mean[11]
My weakness makes me fail of mine intent,

11. Moderation, the median.

That suddenly I fall into extremes
Nor can I see a mischief to prevent,
But feel the pain when I the peril find
Because my malady doth make me blind.

"What is without the compass of my brain
My sickness makes me say it cannot be;
What I conceive not cannot come to pass
Because for it I can no reason see.
I measure all men's feet by mine own shoe
And count all well which I appoint or do.

"The pestilent effects of my disease
Exceed report, their number is so great.
The evils which through it I do incur
Are more than I am able to repeat.
Wherefore, good Thought, I sue to thee again
To tell me how my cure I may obtain."

Quoth she, "I wish I could prescribe your help.
Your state I pity much and do bewail.
But for my part, though I am much employed,
Yet in my judgment I do often fail.
And therefore I'll commend unto your trial
Experience, of whom take no denial.

"For she can best direct you what is meet
To work your cure and satisfy your mind."
I thanked her for her love and took my leave,
Demanding where I might Experience find.
She told me if I did abroad enquire,
'Twas likely Age could answer my desire.

I sought, I found, she asked me what I would.
Quoth I, "Your best direction I implore,
For I am troubled with an irksome grief."
Which when I named, quoth she, "Declare no more,
For I can tell as much as you can say,
And for your cure I'll help you what I may.

"The only medicine for your malady
By which, and nothing else, your help is wrought

Is Knowledge, of the which there is two sorts:
The one is good, the other bad and naught.
The former sort by labor is attained,
The latter may without much toil be gained.

"But 'tis the good which must effect your cure."
I prayed her then that she would further show
Where I might have it. "That I will," quoth she,
"In Erudition's garden it doth grow;
And in compassion of your woeful case,
Industry shall conduct you to the place."

Dissuasion hearing her assign my help
(And seeing that consent I did detect)[12]
Did many remoras[13] *to me propose*
As dullness and my memory's defect,
The difficulty of attaining lore,
My time, and sex, with many others more.

Which when I heard my mind was much perplexed,
And as a horse new come into the field
Who with a harquebus[14] *at first doth start,*
So did this shot make me recoil and yield.
But of my fear when some did notice take
In my behalf they this reply did make:

First quoth Desire, "Dissuasion hold thy peace,
These oppositions come not from above."
Quoth Truth, "They cannot spring from reason's root
And therefore now thou shalt no victor prove."
"No," quoth Industry, "Be assured this,
Her friends shall make thee of thy purpose miss.

"For with my sickle I will cut away
All obstacles that in her way can grow.
And by the issue of her own attempt,
I'll make thee 'labor omnia vincet'[15] *know."*

---

12. Display.
13. Impediments (the remora is a fish once rumored to attach itself to a ship, slowing it down).
14. An early, portable type of artillery.
15. Labor will conquer all; a play on Ovid's famous "Love conquers all."

Quoth Truth, "And sith[16] her sex thou do'st object
Thy folly I by reason will detect.

"Both man and woman of three parts consist,
Which Paul[17] doth body, soul, and spirit call.
And from the soul three faculties arise:
The mind, the will, the power. Then wherefore shall
A woman have her intellect in vain
Or not endeavor knowledge to attain?

"The talent God doth give must be employed;
His own with vantage he must have again.
All parts and faculties were made for use;
The God of knowledge nothing gave in vain.
'Twas Mary's choice our Savior did approve,
Because that she the better part did love.[18]

"Cleobulina[19] and Demophila[20]
With Telefilla,[21] as historians tell
(Whose fame doth live, though they have long been dead),
Did all of them in poetry excel.
A Roman matron that Cornelia hight,[22]
An eloquent and learned style did write.

"Hypatia[23] in astronomy had skill;
Aspasia[24] was in rhetoric so expert
As that Duke Pericles of her did learn;
Areta[25] did devote herself to art:
And by consent (which shows she was no fool)
She did succeed her father in his school.

---

16. Since.
17. 1 Thess. 5:23.
18. Luke 10:42.
19. Or Eumetus (6th c. B.C.E.), daughter of one of the seven sages.
20. Demophyle (c. 600 B.C.E.), a lyric poet.
21. A lyric poet, fl. 6th century B.C.E..
22. Named Cornelia. Daughter of Scipio Africanus and mother of the Gracchi, she was a skilled orator.
23. Hypatia (370–415), daughter of Theon of Alexandria, was a noted mathematician.
24. Aspasia (470–410 B.C.E.) was at the center of cultered Athenian society; a courtesan, she was the mistress of Pericles, ruler of Athens from 440 to 430 B.C.E.
25. Arete (fl. 370–340 B.C.E.) was daughter of the philosopher Aristippus and succeeded him as head of the Cyrenian school.

"And many others here I could produce
Who were in science counted excellent.
But these examples which I have rehearsed,
To show thy error are sufficient."
Thus having said, she turned her speech to me
That in my purpose I might constant be.

"My friend," quoth she, "Regard not vulgar talk;
For dunghill cocks at precious stones will spurn,
And swine-like natures prize not crystal streams;
Contemnèd[26] *mire and mud will serve their turn.*
Good purpose seldom oppositions want
But constant minds Dissuasion cannot daunt.

"Shall every blast disturb the sailor's peace?
Or boughs and bushes travelers affright?
True valor doth not start at every noise
Small combats must instruct for greater fight.
Disdain to be with every dart dismayed
'Tis childish to be suddenly afraid.

"If thou didst know the pleasure of the place,
Where knowledge grows and where thou mayst it gain,
Or rather knew the virtue of the plant,
Thou wouldst not grudge at any cost or pain
Thou canst bestow to purchase for thy cure
This plant, by which of help thou shalt be sure.

"Let not Dissuasion alter thy intent;
'Tis sin to nip good notions in the head.
Take courage and be constant in thy course,
Though irksome be the path which thou must tread.
Sick folks drink bitter medicines to be well,
And to enjoy the nut men crack the shell."

When Truth had ended what she meant to say,
Desire did move me to obey her will;
Whereto consenting I did soon proceed
Her counsel and my purpose to fulfill.
And by the help of Industry, my friend,
I quickly did attain my journey's end.

26. Despised.

Where being come, Instruction's pleasant air[27]
Refreshed my senses which were almost dead.
And fragrant flowers of sage and fruitful plants
Did send sweet savors up into my head.
And taste of science appetite did move
To augment theory of things above.

There did the harmony of those sweet birds
(Which higher soar with Contemplation's wings
Then barely with a superficial view,
Denote the value of created things)
Yield such delight as made me to implore
That I might reap this pleasure more and more.

And as I walked, wandering with Desire,
To gather that for which I thither came
(Which by the help of Industry I found),
I met my old acquaintance, Truth by name,
Whom I requested briefly to declare
The virtue of that plant I found so rare.

Quoth she, "By it God's image man doth bear;
Without it he is but a human shape,
Worse than the devil, for he knoweth much.
Without it who can any ill escape?
By virtue of it evils are withstood;
The mind without it is not counted good.

"Who wanteth Knowledge is a scripture fool;
Against the ignorant the prophets pray.
And Hosea threatens judgment unto those,
Whom want of Knowledge made to run astray.
Without it thou no practique[28] good canst show
More than by hap,[29] as blind men hit a crow.

"True knowledge is the window of the soul
Through which her objects she doth speculate.[30]
It is the mother of faith, hope, and love;

27. Manner, mien.
28. Practical.
29. Chance.
30. Examine.

Without it who can virtue estimate?[31]
By it in grace thou shalt desire to grow;
'Tis life eternal God and Christ to know.

"Great Alexander made so great account
Of knowledge, that he oftentimes would say
That he to Aristotle was more bound
For knowledge (upon which Death could not prey)
Than to his father Philip[32] *for his life,*
Which was uncertain, irksome, full of strife."

This true report put edge unto Desire,
Who did incite me to increase my store
And told me 'twas a lawful avarice
To covet knowledge daily more and more.
This counsel I did willingly obey,
Till some occurrence callèd me away

And made me rest content with that I had,
Which was but little, as effect doth show,
And quenchèd hope for gaining any more
For I my time must other ways bestow.
I therefore to that place returned again
From whence I came, and where I must remain.

But by the way I saw a full-fed beast,
Which roarèd like some monster, or a devil,
And on Eve's sex he foamèd filthy froth
As if that he had had the falling evil.[33]
To whom I went to free them from mishaps
And with a muzzle[34] *sought to bind his chaps.*

But, as it seems, my mood out run my might
Which, when a self-conceited creature saw,
She past her censure on my weak exploit
And gave the beast a harder bone to gnaw:

---

31. Esteem, appraise.
32. Alexander the Great (356–323 B.C.E.), son of Philip II of Macedonia, was tutored by Aristotle.
33. Epilepsy.
34. Allusion to her *Muzzle for Melastomus* (1617).

Haman she hangs, 'tis past, he cannot shun it,
For Ester in the pretertense hath done it.[35]

And yet her enterprise had some defect;
The monster surely was not hangèd quite.
For as the child of Prudence did conceive,
His throat not stopped he still had power to bite.
She therefore gave to Cerberus a sop[36]
Which is of force his beastly breath to stop

But yet if he do swallow down that bit,
She other ways hath bound him to the peace.
And like an artist takes away the cause
That the effect by consequence may cease,
This frantic dog, whose rage did women wrong,
Hath Constance wormed to make him hold his tongue.

Thus leaving them I passèd on my way.
But ere that I had little further gone,
I saw a fierce, insatiable foe
Depopulating countries, sparing none.
Without respect of age, sex, or degree,
It did devour and could not daunted be.

Some feared this foe, some loved it as a friend.
For though none could the force of it withstand,
Yet some by it were sent to Tophet's[37] flames,
But others led to heavenly Canaan land.[38]
On some it seizèd with a gentle power,
And others furiously it did devour.

The name of this impartial foe was Death
Whose rigor, whilst I furiously did view,
Upon a sudden, ere I was aware,
With piercing dart my mother dear it slew,

35. The past; an allusion to Ester Sowernam's *Ester hath Hanged Haman* (1617).
36. "Constantia Munda," author of *The Worming of a Mad Dog* (1617), styled herself the daughter of Prudentia Munda. In Virgil's *Aeneid*, Aeneas gives Cerberus, watchdog of Hades, a pacifying sop of honey- and drug-soaked bread.
37. Hell.
38. Promised land (Gen. 12:6–7).

Which when I saw it made me so to weep
That tears and sobs did rouse me from my sleep.

But when I waked I found my dream was true,
For Death had ta'en[39] *my mother's breath away,*
Though of her life it could not her bereave
Sith she in glory lives with Christ for aye,
Which makes me glad and thankful for her bliss
Though still bewail her absence, whom I miss.

A sudden sorrow pierceth to the quick;
Speedy encounters fortitude doth try;
Unarmèd men receive the deepest wound;
Expected perils time doth lenify[40]
Her sudden loss hath cut my feeble heart
So deep that daily I endure the smart.

The root is killed. How can the boughs but fade?
But sith that Death this cruel deed hath done,
I'll blaze[41] *the nature of this mortal foe*
And show how it to tyrannize begun.
The sequel then with judgment view aright;
The profit may and will the pains requite.
Esto Memor Mortis.[42]

Richard Hyrde Discusses Women's Learning

Although Richard Hyrde (d. 1528) was a diplomat and moved in the international humanist circle of Thomas More, possibly acting as tutor or physician to More's household, little is known about him. He probably studied at Oxford, where he supplicated for a degree in 1519. Sometime between 1524—when Juan Luis Vives's *Instruction of a Christian Woman* appeared in Latin—and his death in 1528, Hyrde translated this influential conduct book into English. His introduction says he did so because More, his "singular good master," lacked the time. Hyrde's death from exposure while on a mission connected to the king's divorce from Catherine of Aragon was noted in a letter by Stephen Gardiner calling him "a young man learned in physic,

39. Taken.
40. Assuage, mitigate.
41. Proclaim.
42. Be mindful of death.

Greek and Latin."[1] In the mid 1520s (the date is uncertain; the *Revised Short Title Catalogue* [*STC*] has "1526?") Hyrde saw to the printing of *A Devout Treatise upon the Pater Noster*, a translation by More's daughter, Margaret Roper, of Erasmus's *Precatio Dominica* (1523). He addresses his preface to Frances Staverton, Margaret's cousin, offering what Foster Watson calls "the first reasoned claim of the Renascance period written in English for the higher education of women (14)." We base our text on the first edition; see also the diplomatic edition by Richard DeMolen (New York: Twayne, 1971).

FROM *A DEVOUT TREATISE*

Richard Hyrde, unto the most studious and virtuous young maid, Frances S[taverton], sendeth greeting and well-to-fare:

I have heard many men put great doubt whether it should be expedient and requisite or not [for] a woman to have learning in books of Latin and Greek. And some utterly affirm that it is not only neither necessary nor profitable, but also very noisome and jeopardous,[2] alleging for their opinion that the frail kind[3] of women, being inclined of their own courage[4] unto vice and mutable at every novelty, if they should have skill in many things that be written in the Latin and Greek tongue, compiled and made with great craft and eloquence (where the matter is happily sometime more sweet unto the ear than wholesome for the mind), it would of likelihood both inflame their stomachs[5] a great deal the more to that vice that men say they be too much given unto of their own nature already, and instruct them also with more subtlety and conveyance[6] to set forward and accomplish their froward[7] intent and purpose. But these men that so say do, in my judgment, either regard but little what they speak in this matter, or else, as they be for the more part unlearned, they envy it, and take it sore to heart that others should have that precious jewel which they neither have themselves nor can find in their hearts to take the pain to get. For first, where they reckon such instability and mutable nature in women, they say therein their pleasure of a contentious mind for the maintenance of their matter. For if they would look thereon with one even eye, and consider the matter equally, they should find and well perceive that women be not only of no less constancy and discretion than men, but also more steadfast and sure to trust unto than they.

---

1. Quoted by Foster Watson, *Vives and the Renascence Education of Women* (London: Edward Arnold, 1912), p. 160.
2. Injurious and hazardous.
3. Nature.
4. Disposition.
5. Their wills and appetites.
6. Contrivance.
7. Perverse, evilly disposed.

For whether, I pray you, was more light and more to be discommended: Helen (that with much labor and suit and many crafty means was at the last overcome and enticed to go away with the king's son of Troy) or Paris (which with one sight of her was so doted in her love that neither the great cheer and kindness showed unto him of her husband King Menelaus, nor shame of the abominable deed, nor fear of the peril that was like to come thereupon, nor the dread of God, might let[8] him to convey her away, contrary to all gentleness, contrary to all right, all laws and conscience)? Nor the woman casteth her mind neither to one nor other of her own proper will, which thing is a sure token of an upright and a steadfast mind, but by the suit and means of the man, when he with one look of her is ravished of all his wits.

Now if here, peradventure,[9] a man would say, "Yes, they be moved as well as men, but they dissemble, forbear, and will not utter their stomachs, neither it is so convenient the woman to speak as the man,"[10] that shall not help his excuse, but rather hinder it. For they be the more worthy to be allowed that will not be so far overseen in that affection which is so naturally given to all things living, but they can remember their duty and honesty, where the man is many times so far beside his reason that he seeth neither where nor when, neither to whom, nor how to behave himself, neither can regard what is comely and what is not. For verily it is as inconvenient for the man to demand that thing that is unlawful, if he could perceive, as for the woman. And if both their vices were all open and showed, the man should have much more that he ought to be ashamed of, saving that he is also in that point worse than the woman, inasmuch as she is ashamed of her fault, be it never so small, and he is so far from that virtue, that when he hath done naught,[11] he rejoiceth of it and avaunceth himself[12] as though it were well done. And yet he is so unreasonable in judging the woman that as Isocrates[13] sayth, wherein he hath no consideration how oft or how sore he offend his wife he will not suffer once to be offended himself by her never so little, where he would that she should take his deeds all well in worth. Wherefore, indeed, women be in gay case[14] and happy, if their honesty and praise must hang at the girdles of such people.

Now as for learning, if it were cause of any evil as they say it is, it were worse in the man than in the woman, because (as I have said here before) he can both worse stay[15] and refrain himself than she. And moreover than that, he cometh ofter and in more occasions than the woman, inasmuch as he liveth more forth abroad among company daily, where he shall be moved to utter such craft as he hath gotten by his learning. And women abide most at home, occupied ever with some good or necessary business. And the Latin and the

---

8. Check, hinder.
9. Perchance.
10. Cf. 1 Cor. 14:34–35.
11. Acted naughtily.
12. Boasts.
13. An Athenian orator (436–338 B.C.E.).
14. Fine case, used ironically.
15. Steady, restrain.

Greek tongue, I see not but there is as little hurt in them as in books of English and French which men both read themself for the proper pastimes that be written in them and for the witty and crafty conveyance of the makings. And also can bear well enough that women read them if they will never so much, which commodities be far better handled in the Latin and Greek than any other language. And in them be many holy doctor's writings, so devout and effectuous that whosoever readeth them must needs be either much better or less evil, which every good body, both man and woman, will read and follow, rather than other.

But as for that that I hear many men lay for the greatest jeopardy in this matter; in good faith, to be plain, methink it is so foolish that scantly it is worthy either to be rehearsed or answered unto. That is, where they say if their wives [knew] Latin or Greek then might they talk more boldly with priests and friars, as who sayth there were no better means (if they were ill disposed) to execute their purposes than by speaking Latin or Greek, other else that priests and friars were commonly so well learned, that they can make their bargain in Latin and Greek so readily, which thing is also far contrary, that I suppose nowadays a man could not devise a better way to keep his wife safe from them than if he teach her the Latin and Greek tongue and such good sciences as are written in them, the which now most part of priests, and specially such as be naught, abhor and fly from, yea, as fast in a manner, as they fly from beggars that ask them alms in the street.

And where they find fault with learning because they say it engendreth wit and craft, there they reprehend it for that that it is most worthy to be commended for, and the which is one singular cause wherefore learning ought to be desired. For he that had lever[16] have his wife a fool than a wise woman, I hold him worse than twice frantic. Also, reading and studying of books so occupieth the mind, that it can have no leisure to muse or delight in other fantasies, when in all handiworks that men say be more meet for a woman, the body may be busy in one place, and the mind walking in another. And while they sit sewing and spinning with their fingers, may cast and compass many peevish fantasies in their minds, which must needs be occupied, either with good or bad, so long as they be waking. And those that be evil disposed, will find the means to be naught though they [know] never a letter on the book. And she that will be good, learning shall cause her to be much the better. For it showeth the image and ways of good living, even right as a mirror showeth the similitude and proportion of the body.

And doubtless the daily experience proveth that such as are naught are those that never knew what learning meant. For I never heard tell nor read of any woman well learned that ever was (as plenteous as evil tongues be) spotted or infamed as vicious. But on the other side, many by their learning taken such increase of goodness that many may bear them witness of their virtue, of which sort I could rehearse a great number, both of old time and late, saving that I

16. Would rather.

will be content as for now with one example of our own country and time, that is this gentlewoman which translated this little book hereafter following, whose virtuous conversation, living, and sad[17] demeanor may be proof evident enough what good learning doth where it is surely rooted, of whom other women may take example of prudent, humble, and wifely behavior, charitable and very Christian virtue, with which she hath with God's help endeavored herself no less to garnish her soul than it hath liked His goodness with lovely beauty and comeliness to garnish and set out her body. And undoubted is it, that to th'increase of her virtue, she hath taken and taketh no little occasion of her learning. Besides her other manifold and great commodities taken of the same, among which commodities this is not the least: that with her virtuous, worshipful, wise, and well-learned husband she hath by the occasion of her learning and his delight therein, such especial comfort, pleasure, and pastime as were not well possible for one unlearned couple either to take together or to conceive in their minds what pleasure is therein.

Therefore, good Frances, seeing that such fruit, profit, and pleasure cometh of learning, take no heed unto the lewd words of those that dispraise it, as verily no man doth save such as neither have learning, nor wotteth[18] what it meaneth, which is, indeed, the most part of men. And as the most part and the best part be not alway of one mind, so if this matter should be tried not by wit and reason but by heads or hands, the greater part is like as it often doth to vanquish and overcome the better. For the best part (as I reckon) whom I account the wisest of every age—as among the Gentiles the old philosophers, and among the Christian men, the ancient doctors of Christ's church—all affirm learning to be very good and profitable, not only for men but also for women (the which Plato the wise philosopher calleth a bridle for young people against vice).

Wherefore, good Frances, take you the best part and leave the most; follow the wise men and regard not the foolish sort, but apply all your might, will, and diligence to obtain that especial treasure which is delectable in youth, comfortable in age, and profitable at all seasons. Of whom, without doubt, cometh much goodness and virtue. Which virtue whoso lacketh, he is without that thing that only maketh a man, yea, and without the which a man is worse than an unreasonable beast, nor once worthy to have the name of a man. It maketh fair and amiable that that is of nature deformed, as Diogenes[19] the philosopher, when he saw a young man foul and evil-favored of person, but very virtuous of living, "Thy virtue," said he, "maketh thee beautiful." And that that is goodly of itelf already, it maketh more excellent and bright. Which as Plato the wise philosopher sayth, "If it could be seen with our bodily eyes, it would make men wondrously enamored and taken in the love of it."

Wherefore, unto those especial gifts of grace that God hath lent you and endowed you withal, endeavor yourself that this precious diamond and ornament

17. Grave, serious.
18. Knows.
19. A cynic philosopher (412?–323? B.C.E.).

be not lacking, which had shall flourish and lighten all your other gifts of grace and make them more gay, and lacked shall darken and blemish them sore. And surely the beauty of it, though ye had none other, shall get you both greater love, more faithful and longer to continue of all good folks, than shall the beauty of the body, be it never so excellent, whose love decayeth together with it that was the cause of it, and most commonly before, as by daily experience we may see them that go together for the love of the bodily beauty, within a small while when their appetite is satisfied, repent themself.

But the love that cometh by means of virtue and goodness shall ever be fresh and increase, right as doth the virtue itself. And it shall you come by none otherwise so readily, as if you continue the study of learning, which you be entered well in already. And for your time and age, I would say, had greatly profited, saving that child's age is so frail accounted that it needeth rather admonition and continual calling upon, than the deserved praise. Howbeit, I have no doubt in you, whom I see naturally born unto virtue, and having so good bringing up of a babe, not only among your honorable uncle's children, of whose conversation and company they that were right evil might take occasion of goodness and amendment, but also with your own mother,[20] of whose precepts and teaching, and also very virtuous living, if you take heed (as I put no fear you will and also do), you can not fail to come to such grace and goodness as I have ever had opinion in you that ye should. Wherefore I have ever in my mind favored you, and furthered to my power your profit and increase thereunto, and shall as long as I see you delight in learning and virtue, no kind of pain or labor refused on my part that may do you good.

And as a token of my good mind,[21] and an instrument toward your success and furtherance, I send you this book, little in quantity but big in value, turned out of Latin into English by your own forenamed kinswoman, whose goodness and virtue, two things there be that let[22] me much to speak of. The one, because it were a thing superfluous to spend many words unto you about that matter which yourself know well enough by long experience and daily use. The other cause is for I would eschew the slander of flattery, howbeit I count it no flattery to speak good of them that deserve it, but yet I know that she is as loath to have praise given her as she is worthy to have it, and had leaver her praise to rest in men's hearts than in their tongues, or rather in God's estimation and pleasure than any man's words or thought. And as touching the book itself, I refer and leave it to the judgments of those that shall read it and unto such as are learned. The only[23] name of the maker putteth out of question the goodness and perfection of the work, which as to mine own opinion and fantasy can not be amended in any point. And as for the translation thereof, I dare be bold to say it, that who so list and well can confer and examine the translation with the original, he shall not fail to find that she hath showed herself not only erudite and elegant in either

20. More's sister Joan, who was married to Richard Staverton.
21. Opinion, intention.
22. Hinder.
23. Mere.

tongue, but hath also used such wisdom, such discreet and substantial judgment in expressing lively the Latin, as a man may peradventure miss in many things translated and turned by them that bare the name of right wise and very well learned men.

And the labor that I have had with it about the printing I yield wholly, and freely give unto you, in whose good manners and virtue, as in a child, I have so great affection, and unto your good mother, unto whom I am so much beholden, of whose company I take so great joy and pleasure, in whose godly communication I find such spiritual fruit and sweetness that as oft as I talk with her, so oft methink I feel myself the better. Therefore, now, good Frances, follow still[24] on her steps, look ever upon her life to inform your own thereafter, like as ye would look in a glass to tire[25] your body by. Yea, and that more diligently, in so much as the beauty of the body, though it be never so well attended, will soon fade and fall away; good living and virtue, once gotten, tarrieth still, whose fruit ye shall feel not only in this world, which is transitory and of short continuance, but also in another. And also it should be great shame, dishonesty, and rebuke unto you—borne of such a mother, and also nourished up with her own teat—for to degenerate and go out of kind. Behold her in this age of hers, in this almost continual disease and sickness, how busy she is to learn, and in the small time that she hath had, how much she hath yet profited in the Latin tongue, how great comfort she taketh of that learning that she hath gotten, and consider thereby what pleasure and profit you may have hereafter (if God lend you life, as I pray He do) of the learning that you may have ere you come to her age, if you spend your time well.

Which doing, you shall be able to do yourself good, and be great joy and comfort to all your friends and all that ever would you well. Among whom, I would you should reckon me for one not among the least, if not among the chief.

And so, fare you well, mine own good, gentle, and fair Frances.
At Chelsea, the year of our Lord God,
a thousand five hundred twenty-four,
the first day of October.

24. Always.
25. Dress, adorn.

9

Elizabeth Talbot Grey,
countess of Kent (1581–1651)

Hugh Platt *(1552–c. 1611)*

Elizabeth Talbot Grey, Countess of Kent, Compiles Recipes

The compilation of cooking recipes and medical "receipts" (remedies) commonly ascribed to Elizabeth Talbot Grey, countess of Kent (1581–1651), first appeared in print after her death. While her authorship has been questioned, we note that the countess, a granddaughter of Bess of Hardwick, came from a family boasting a number of women authors, including two women excerpted in this volume, Elizabeth Egerton and Margaret Cavendish. Reprinted sixteen times by 1683, *A True Gentlewoman's Delight Wherein Is Contained All Manner of Cookery* and *A Choice Manual of Rare and Select Secrets in Physic and Surgery* were printed together, with separate title pages, from the first edition (1653). Noblewomen had traditionally assumed responsibility for providing health care to their many dependents and for managing household affairs on often huge estates. The diary (1599–1605) of Lady Margaret Dakins Hoby (1571–1633) is filled with accounts of the well-intended but sometimes horrifying medical attention she bestowed on those in her neighborhood. Such women often kept manuscript collections of recipes and remedies; a portion of the copious papers of Lady Grace Mildmay (1552–1620) was published in 1993 under the title *With Faith and Physic*. Below are some excerpts from the 1653 edition of Grey's collection.

From *A True Gentlewoman's Delight*

How to Make a Fresh Cheese

Take a pint of fresh cream, set it on the fire, then take the white of six eggs, beat them very well, and wring in the juice of a good lemon to the whites. When the cream seethes up[1] put in the whites and stir it about till it be turned, and then take it off, and put it into the cheesecloth, and let the whey[2] be drawn from it. Then take the curd[3] and pound it in a stone mortar with a little rosewater[4] and sugar and put it into an earthen colander, and so let it stand till you send it to the table. Then put it into a dish, put a little sweet cream to it, and so serve it in.

How to Make a Sack Posset[5]

Take two quarts of pure good cream, a quarter of a pound of the best almonds, stamp them in the cream, and boil amber[6] and musk[7] therein. Then take a pint of sack in a basin and set it on a chafing dish till it be blood warm. Then take the yolks of twelve eggs with four whites and beat them very well together, and so put the eggs into the sack and make it good and hot. Let the cream cool a little before you put it into the sack, then stir all together over the coals till it be as thick as you would have it. If you take some amber and musk and grind it small with sugar, and strew it on the top of the posset, it will give it a most delicate and pleasant taste.

To Make a Chicken Pie

Make your paste with good store of butter and yolks of eggs and sugar. Then take six small chickens, taking out the breast bone and stuffing them round. Take two nutmegs and a good quantity of cinnamon and put it in little pieces. Take two yolks of eggs and beat them with six spoonfuls of verjuice.[8] Then take your juice and verjuice and a little salt, stir them well together, take a good deal of butter and wet it in the verjuice, and put it in the bellies of the chickens. So lay them in the pie with butter under them. Then take half a pound of currants washed and dried. So lay them on the top of the chickens, with a piece of marrow, barberries,[9] grapes, and good store of butter and sugar as will season it. A little before you draw out your pie, put in verjuice and sugar boiled together.

1. Boils.
2. Watery part of the milk.
3. The fatty substance formed in the milk.
4. Water distilled from roses.
5. A drink made of strong white wine and hot milk.
6. Obscure; a plant or ambergris—the whale musk also used in perfume.
7. Any of a number of musky plants.
8. The acid juice of green or unripe grapes.
9. The fruit of the barberry bush.

To Bake Beef Like Red Deer

Take a pound of beef and slice it thin, and half a pint of good wine vinegar, some three cloves, and mace above an ounce, three nutmegs. Pound them altogether. Pepper and salt, according to your discretion, and a little sugar. Mix these together, take a pound and a half of suet, shred and beat it small in a mortar. Then lay a row of suet, a row of beef. Strew your spices between every lane, then your vinegar. So do till you have laid in all. Then make it up, but first beat it close with a rolling pin. Then press it a day before you put it in your paste.

To Keep Quinces[10] All the Year

First you must core them, and take out the kernels clean, and keep the cores and kernels. Then set over some water to boil them. Then put them in when you set over the water. Then let them boil till they be a little soft, and then take them up and set them down till they be cold. Then take the kernels and stamp them and put them into the same water they were boiled in, and let them boil till they be thick; see you have as much liquor as will cover the quinces, and if you have not enough, take of the smallest quinces and stamp them to make more liquor. And when it is boiled good and thick, you must strain it through a coarse cloth. And when the quinces be cold, then put them into a pot and the liquor also, and be sure the liquor cover them. You must lay some weight upon them to keep them under. So cover them close, let them stand fourteen days, and they will work of their own accord. And they will have a thick rind upon them. And when they wax hoary[11] or thick, then take it from the liquor, for it will have a skin on it within a month or six weeks.

To Pickle Cucumbers

Take the cucumbers and wash them clean and dry them clean in a cloth. Then take some water, vinegar, salt, fennel tops and some dill tops, and a little mace. Make it fast enough and sharp enough to the taste, then boil it a while, and then take it off and let it stand and cool. Then put in the cucumbers and a board on the top to keep them down and tie them close, and within a week they will be fit to eat.

To Do Clove Gillyflowers Up for Salletting[12] All the Year

Take as many clove gillyflowers as you please, and slip off the leaves. Then strew some sugar in the bottom of the gallipot[13] that you do them in, and then a lane of gillyflowers, and then a lane of sugar, and so do till all the gillyflowers be done. Then pour some claret wine into them (as much as will cover them). Then cut a piece of thin board and lay it on them to keep them down. Then tie them close,

10. A pear-shaped fruit.
11. Grey or white.
12. That is, to preserve clove-scented flowers for use in salad.
13. Small, glazed earthen pot.

and sit them in the sun, and let them stand a month or thereabouts, but keep them from any rain or wet.

How to Preserve Grapes to Look Clear[14] and Green

Take a pound of grapes with no stalks on them when they do begin to be ripe. Then weigh as much double refined sugar beaten small. Then take the grapes that were weighed, stone them at the place where the stalks are, pull off the skins, and strain some sugar in the bottom of the thing you do them in. And so lay them in the sugar you did weigh till you have stoned and peeled them, and so strew the sugar upon them. Then set them on the fire and let them boil as fast as can be till the syrup be pretty thick. Then take them off and put them up till they be cold.

Recipes and Advice from Sir Hugh Platt

Sir Hugh Platt (1552–c. 1611) was the third son of a rich London brewer; twice married, he had at least five children. After graduating from Cambridge, studying law, and having a fling at literature, he discovered a talent for "projects": ingenious notions, sometimes presented with a show of revealing secrets, that might ameliorate life and serve the state. Among his ideas were methods to upgrade coal, waterproof clothes, rustproof armor, and make bullets go faster. Platt won a knighthood, yet some scorned such ingenuity as mere fantasy or tied it to greed and monopolies. We excerpt recipes from a work for well-off women involved in countryhouse life but also a scheme to keep beef edible at sea, for Platt remembers England's larger "project": to explore and colonize abroad. We follow the 1609 edition used by G. E. and Kathleen Rosemary Fussell (London: Crosby Lockwood, 1948); their introductions describe Platt's career and the sort of household for which he wrote.

FROM *DELIGHTS FOR LADIES TO ADORN THEIR PERSONS, TABLES, CLOSETS, AND DISTILLERIES*

Part 3 (Cookery and Houswifery):
5. To Boil a Capon in White Broth.

Boil your capon by itself in fair water, then take a ladleful or two of mutton broth and a little white wine, a little whole mace, a bundle of sweet herbs, a little marrow. Thicken it with almonds, season it with sugar and a little verjuice.[1] Boil a

---

14. Lustrous.

1. A sour sauce made from unripe crab apples or other fruit.

few currants by themselves, and a date quartered, lest you discolor your broth, and put on the breast of your capon, chicken, or rabbit. If you have no almonds, thicken it with cream or with yolks of eggs. Garnish your dishes on the side with a lemon sliced and sugar.

20. A Conceit[2] of the Author's: How Beef May be Carried at the Sea Without that Strong and Violent Impression of Salt Which Is Usually Purchased[3] by Long and Extreme Powdering.[4]

Here, with the good leave and favor of those courteous gentlewomen for whom I did principally, if not only, intend this little treatise, I will make bold to launch a little from the shore and try what may be done in the vast and wide ocean, and in long and dangerous voyages, for the better preservation of such usual victuals as for want of this skill do oftentimes merely perish, or else by the extreme piercing of the salt do lose even their nutritive strength and virtue. And if any future experience do happen to control[5] my present conceit, let this excuse a scholar: "quod in magnis est voluisse satis."[6] But now to our purpose. Let all the blood be first well gotten out of the beef by leaving the same some nine or ten days in our usual brine; then barrel up all the pieces in vessels full of holes, fastening them with ropes at the stern of the ship; and so dragging them through the salt seawater (which by his infinite change and succession of water will suffer no putrefaction, as I suppose), you may happily find your beef both sweet and savory enough when you come to spend the same. And if this happen to fall out true upon some trial thereof had, then either at my next impression,[7] or when I shall be urged thereunto upon any necessity of service, I hope to discover the means also whereby every ship may carry sufficient store of victual for herself in more close and convenient carriages than those loose vessels are able to perform. But if I may be allowed to carry either roasted or sodden[8] flesh to the sea, then I dare adventure my poor credit therein to preserve, for five whole months together, either beef, mutton, capons, rabbits, etc. both in a cheap manner and also as fresh as we do now usually eat them at our tables. And this I hold to be a most singular and necessary secret for all our English navy, which at all times upon reasonable terms I will be ready to disclose for the good of my country.

22. How to Make a Larger and Daintier Cheese of the Same Proportion of Milk than Is Commonly Used or Known by Any of our Best Dairy Women at This Day.

Having brought your milk into curds by ordinary rennet,[9] either break them with your hands according to the usual manner of other cheeses and after with a fleet-

2. A fancy, an inventive notion.
3. Obtained.
4. Preserving with salt and spice.
5. Overcome, disprove.
6. "In great matters it is enough to have wished [to do them]."
7. Edition.
8. Boiled.
9. A substance (from a plant or a calf's stomach) that curdles milk.

ing[10] dish, taking away as much of the whey as you can, or else put in the curds, without breaking, into your moat.[11] Let them so repose one hour, or two or three, and then to a cheese of two gallons of milk add a weight of ten or twelve pounds, which weight must rest upon a cover that [fits] with the moat or case, wherein it must truly descend by degrees as you increase your weight, or as the curds do sink and settle. Let your curds remain so all that day and night following until the next morning, and then turn your cheese or curds and place your weight again thereon, adding from time to time some more small weight as you shall see cause. Note that you must lay a cloth both under and over your curds at the least, if you will not wrap them all over as they do in other cheeses, changing your cloth at every turning. Also, if you will work in any ordinary moat, you must place a round and broad hoop upon the moat, being just of the self-same bigness or circumference, or else you shall make a very thin cheese.

Turn these cheeses every morning and evening, or as often as you shall see cause, till the whey be all run out, and then proceed as in ordinary cheeses. Note that these moats would be full of holes, both in the sides and bottom, that the whey may have the speedier passage. You may also make them in square boxes full of holes, or else you may devise moats or cases either round or square of fine wicker, which having wicker covers, may by some sleight[12] be so stayed,[13] as that you shall need only morning and evening to turn the wrong side upward, both the bottoms being made loose and so close and fitting as they may sink truly within the moat or mold, by reason of the weight that lieth thereon. Note that in other cheeses the cover of the moat shutteth over the moat, but in these the covers descend and fall within the moats. Also, your ordinary cheeses are more spongious and full of eyes than these by reason of the violent pressing of them, whereas these cheeses, settling gently and by degrees, do cut as close and firm as marmalade. Also, in those cheeses which are pressed out after the usual manner, the whey that cometh from them, if it stand a while, will carry a cream upon it, whereby the cheese must of necessity be much less, and as I guess by a fourth part, whereas the whey that cometh from these new kind of cheeses is like fair water in color and carrieth no strength with it. Note also that if you put in your curds unbroken, not taking away the whey that issueth in the breaking of them, that so the cheeses will yet be so much the greater; but that is the more troublesome way, because the curds being tender will hardly endure the turning unless you be very careful. I suppose that the Angelotes in France may be made in this manner in small baskets, and so likewise of the Parmesan; and if your whole cheese consist of unflatten[14] milk, they will be full of butter and eat most daintily, being taken in their time before they be too dry, for which purpose you may keep them when they begin to grow dry upon green rushes or nettles.

10. Skimming.
11. Cheese-vat.
12. Trick, mechanism.
13. Supported, steadied.
14. Citing Platt, the *Oxford English Dictionary* speculates that this means unskimmed.

I have robbed my wife's dairy of this secret, who hath hitherto refused all recompenses that have been offered her by gentlewomen for the same: and had I loved a cheese myself so well as I like the receipt, I think I should not so easily have imparted the same at this time. And yet I must needs confess that for the better gracing of the title wherewith I have fronted this pamphlet, I have been willing to publish this with some other secrets of worth, for the which I have many times refused good store both of crowns and angels:[15] and therefore let no gentlewoman think this book too dear at what price so ever it shall be valued upon the sale thereof; neither can I esteem the work to be of less then twenty years' gathering.

Part 4 (Cosmetics, Ointments, "Beauties"):

17. [For a Red or Pimply Face]

Take of those little whelks[16] or shells which some do call "giny money," wash five or six of them and beat them to fine powder and infuse the juice of lemons upon them, and it will presently boil: but if it offer to boil out of your glass then stop the mouth thereof with your finger, or blow into it. This will in a short time be like an ointment, with which you must anoint the heat or pimples of the face oftentimes in a day until you find help. As the ointment drieth, put more juice of lemons to it. This of an outlandish[17] gentlewoman and it is an assured remedy if the heat be not very extreme. Some have found by experience that bathing of the face with hot vinegar every night when they go to bed doth mightily repel the humor.[18]

27. A Delicate Stove to Sweat in.

I know that many Gentlewomen as well for the clearing of their skins as cleansing of their bodies, do now and then delight to sweat. For the which purpose I have set down in this manner following, as the best that ever I observed. Put into a brass pot of some good content such proportion of sweet herbs, and of such kind as shall be most appropriate for your infirmity, with some reasonable quantity of water; close the same with an apt cover, and well luted[19] with some paste made of flour and whites of eggs. At some part of the cover you must let in a leaden pipe, the entrance whereof must also be well luted; this pipe must be conveyed through the side of the chimney, where the pot standeth in a thick hollow stake, of a bathing tub crossed with hoops according to the usual manner in the top, which you may cover with a sheet at your pleasure. Now the steam of the pot passing through the pipe under the false bottom of the bathing tub, which must be bored full of big holes, will breath so sweet and warm a vapor upon your body,

---

15. Crowns and angels were valuable coins.
16. A common edible sea-mollusc; since "whelk" also meant boil or pimple, there may be a trace of sympathetic magic in this recipe.
17. Foreign.
18. The hot "humor" or bodily fluid that reddens the complexion.
19. Sealed or made snug with "lute" (sticky clay).

as that (receiving air by holding your head without[20] the tub as you sit therein) you shall sweat most temperately and continue the same a long time without fainting. And this is performed with a small charcoal fire maintained under the pot for this purpose. Note that the room would be closed wherein you place your bathing tub, lest any sudden cold should happen to offend you while your body is made open and porous to the air.

20. Outside.

RELIGION

10

Sarah Chevers *(fl. 1663)* and
Katherine Evans *(d. 1692)*

William Weston *(1550–1615)*

Sarah Chevers and Katherine Evans on Their Imprisonment

Sarah Chevers (or Cheevers) (fl. 1663) of Slaughterford, Wiltshire, and Katherine
Evans (d. 1692) of Somerset, wife of John Evans, a Quaker minister and landowner
there, left their families in 1658 on a missionary trip to Alexandria. En route, they
were imprisoned by the Inquisition in Malta for three years. Both women remained
steadfast despite harsh treatment and the danger to their lives. They were visited in
Malta by another Quaker, Daniel Baker, who interceded for them with the authorities (unsuccessfully) and encouraged them to hold fast to their faith. After their
release, achieved through such strategies as a hunger strike and threatening prophecies on their own part, as well as diplomatic negotiations, they traveled to Tangiers,
where they were well received. Evans was imprisoned twice more—in London's
Newgate in 1682 and in the city of Bristol. *A Short Relation* is the story of their experiences, interspersed with prayers, meditations, hymns, letters, visions, and prophecies; the introduction by Daniel Baker justifies the women's mission: "the living God
Eternal hath chosen the weak things to confound and bring to naught the things that
are mighty, subtle, and potent." The book was expanded by Evans in 1663 as *A True
Account* and revised again that year as *A Brief Discovery* in order to include Chevers's
account of her visions. Our selections from *A Short Relation* are from the 1662 edition.

FROM *A Short Relation of . . . the Inquisition in Malta*

A TRUE DECLARATION CONCERNING THE
LORD'S LOVE TO US IN ALL OUR VOYAGE

We were at sea between London and Plymouth many weeks, and one day we had some trials. And between Plymouth and Leghorn we were 31 days, and we had many trials and storms within and without, but the Lord did deliver us out of all. And when we came to Leghorn with the rest of our friends, we went into the town (after we had produced[1]) and stayed there many days, where we had service every day. For all sorts of people came unto us, but no man did offer to hurt us; yet we gave them books. And having got passage in a Dutch ship we sailed towards Cyprus, intending to go to Alexandria, but the Lord had appointed something for us to do by the way, as he did make it manifest to us (as I did speak). For the master of the ship had no business at the city of Malta (in the island of Malta where Paul suffered shipwreck). And being in the harbor on the first day of the week, we, being moved of the Lord, went into the town. And the English consul met us on the shore and asked us concerning our coming. And we told him truth and gave him some books and a paper, and he told us there was an Inquisition, and he kindly entreated us to go to his house and said all that he had was at our service while we were there. And in the fear and dread of the Lord we went, and there came many to see us. And we called them to repentance, and many of them were tender, but the whole city is given to idolatry. And we went a shipboard that night.

And the next day, we, being moved to go into the city again, dared not to fly the cross but in obedience went, desiring the will of God to be done. And when we came to the governor, he told us that he had a sister in the nunnery did desire to see us if we were free. And in the fear of God we went, and talked with them and gave them a book. And one of their priests was with us (at the nunnery) and had us into their place of worship, and some would have us bow to the high altar, which we did deny. And having a great burden, we went to the consul again and were waiting upon the Lord what to do that we might know.

And the inquisitors sent for us. And when we came before them they asked our names, and the names of our husbands, and the names of our fathers and mothers, and how many children we had. And they asked us wherefore we came into that country. And we told them we were the servants of the living God and were moved to come and call them to repentance and many other questions. And they went away but commanded that we should be stayed there.

And the next day they came again and called for us, and we came. But they would examine us apart, and called Sarah, and they asked whether she was a true Catholic. She said that she was a true Christian that worshippeth God in spirit and in truth, and they proffered her the crucifix and would have had her swear

1. In context, this is obscure; brought forth witness?

that she would speak the truth. And she said she should speak the truth, but she would not swear. For Christ commanded her not to swear, saying, "Swear not at all."[2] And the English consul persuaded her with much entreating to swear, saying none should do her any harm. But she denied, and they took some books from her and would have had her swear by them, but she would not. And they asked wherefore she brought the books. And she said because we could not speak their language, and they might know wherefore we came. And they asked of her what George Fox[3] was, and she said he was a minister. And they asked wherefore she came thither. She said to do the will of God, as she was moved of the Lord. And they asked how the Lord did appear unto her. And she said, "By His spirit." And they asked where she was when the Lord appeared unto her. And she said, "Upon the way." And they asked whether she did see His presence and hear His voice. And she said she did hear His voice and saw His presence. And they asked what He said to her. And she said the Lord told her she must go over the seas to do His will, and then they asked how she knew it was the Lord. And she said He bid her go and His living presence should go with her, and He was faithful that had promised, for she did feel His living presence. And so they went away.

Two days after they came again, and called for me, and offered me the crucifix, and told me the magistrate commanded me to swear that I would speak the truth. And I told them that I should speak the truth, for I was a witness for God, but I should not swear, for a greater than the magistrate saith, "Swear not at all, but let your yea be yea and your nay be nay, for whatsoever is more cometh of evil." "But," said they, "You must obey the justice, and he commands you to swear." I said I should obey justice, but if I should swear I should do an unjust thing. For (the just) Christ said, "Swear not at all." And they asked me whether I did own that Christ which died at Jerusalem. I answered we owned the same Christ and no other: He is the same yesterday, today, and forever.

And they asked me what I would do at Jerusalem. I said I did not know that I should go there, but I should go to Alexandria. And they said, "What to do?" And I said, "To do the will of God. And if the Lord did open my mouth I should call them to repentance, and declare to them the day of the Lord, and direct their minds from darkness to light." Then they asked me whether I did tremble when I did preach. And I told them I did tremble when the power of the Lord was upon me. And they asked whether I did see the Lord with my eyes. I said God was a spirit, and He was spiritually discerned. . . .

And there came a man with a black rod, and the chancellor, and the consul and had us before their Lord Inquisitor, and he asked us whether we had changed our minds yet. We said, "Nay, we should not change from the truth." He asked what new light we talked of. We said, "No new light, but the same the prophets and apostles bare testimony to." Then he said, "How came this light to be lost ever since the primitive times?" We said it was not lost; men had it still in them, but they did not know it by reason that the night of apostacy[4] had and hath over-

2. Matt. 5:33–37.
3. Son of a Puritan weaver, Fox (1624–1691) founded the Society of Friends (Quakers).
4. Abandonment of faith.

spread the nations. Then he said if we would change our minds and do as they would have us to do we should say so, or else they would use us as they pleased. We said, "The will of the Lord be done." And he arose up and went his way with the consul and left us there. And the man with the black rod and the keeper took us, and put us into an inner room in the Inquisition, which had but two little holes in it for light or air. But the glory of the Lord did shine round us. . . .

They said it was impossible we could live long in that hot room. So the next week day they sat in council. But, oh, how the swelling sea did rage, and the proud waves did foam even unto the clouds of heaven! And proclamation was made at the prison gate. We did not know the words, but the fire of the Lord flamed against it. . . .

The room was so hot and so close that we were fain to rise often out of our bed and lie down at a chink of their door for air to fetch breath. And with the fire within, and the heat without, our skin was like sheep's leather, and the hair did fall off our heads, and we did fail often. Our afflictions and burdens were so great that when it was night we wished for day. We sought death but could not find it; we desired to die, but death fled from us. We did eat our bread weeping and mingled our drink with our tears.

We did write to the Inquisitor and laid before him our innocence and our faithfulness in giving our testimony for the Lord amongst them. And I told him if it were our blood they did thirst after they might take it any other way as well as to smother us up in that hot room. So he sent the friar, and he took away our inkhorns. (They had our Bibles before.) We asked why they took away our goods. They said it was all theirs and our lives too, if they would. We asked how we had forfeited our lives unto them; they said for bringing books and papers. We said if there were anything in them that was not true they might write against it. They said they did scorn to write to fools and asses that did not know true Latin. . . .

They did not part us till ten weeks after. But, oh, the dark clouds and the sharp showers the Lord did carry us through! Death itself had been better than to have parted in that place. They said we corrupted each other and that they thought when we were parted we would have bowed to them. But they found we were more stronger afterwards than we were before. The Lord our God did fit us for every condition. . . .

Many did think we should not have been heard nor seen after we were in the Inquisition, but the Lord did work wonderfully for us and His truth. For they new built the Inquisition, and there were many laborers for a year and a half, and the great men came to see the building. And we were carried forth with great power to declare in the name of the Lord Jesus, not fearing the face of man. The Lord was our strength. But behold they threatened us with irons and halters for preaching the light so boldly, and they said none ought to preach but prelates to a bishop (as they use to say in England). Now their Lord Inquisitor (so called) and the magistrates were kept moderate towards us and gave order we should have ink and paper to write to England. But we were hindered still. And we do believe they would have set us at liberty had it not been for the friars: it was they that wrought against us still to the Pope and to the Inquisitor, and we told them so.

They sought three quarters of a year to part us before they could bring it to pass. And when they did part us, they prepared a bed for Sarah, and their own Catholics lay upon the boards that had not beds of their own. When we were parted the Lord would not suffer me to keep any money; I knew not the mind of God in it. Their friars came and said we should never see one another's faces again, but the Inquisitor should send me my food. But the Lord would not suffer him to send it: Sarah did send me such as she could get near three weeks. Then the friar came and asked me what I did want. I said, "One to wash my linen and something hot to eat." I was weak. He sent to Sarah to know if she would do it for me. She said she would. And by that means we did hear of each other every day. . . .

But there was a poor Englishman heard that Sarah was in a room with a window next the street. It was high; he got up and spake a few words to her, and they came violently and hauled him down and cast him into prison upon life and death. And the friars came to know of us whether he had brought any letters. We said no. I did not see him. They said they did think he would be hanged for it. He was one that they had taken from the Turks and made a Catholic of him.

Sarah wrote a few lines to me of it and said she did think the English friars were the chief actors of it—we had a private way to send to each other. I wrote to her again, and after my salvation I said whereas she said the friars were the chief actors, she might be sure of that, for they did hasten to fill up their measures. But I believe the Lord will preserve the poor man for his love; I am made to seek the Lord for him with tears. And I desired she would send him something once a day if the keeper would carry it. And I told her of the glorious manifestations of God to my soul (for her comfort) so that I was ravished with love, and my beloved was the chiefest of ten thousands; and how I did not fear the face of any man though I did feel their arrows, for my physician is nigh me; and how I was waiting upon the Lord and saw our safe return into England, and I was talking with G. F. to my great refreshment. The name of G. F. did prick them to the heart. I said it was much they did not tempt us with money. I bid her take heed: the light would discover it and many more things, let it come under what cover it would.

And this paper came to the friar's hands, by what means we could never tell. But as the light did show us, the Lord would have it so. It smote the friar that he was tormented many days, and he translated it into Italian and laid it before their Lord Inquisitor, and got the Inquisitor's lieutenant, and came to me with both the papers in his hand and asked me if I could read it. I said, "Yea, I writ it." "Oh! Did you indeed!" said he. "And what is it you say of me here?" "That which is truth," said I. Then he said, "Where is the paper Sarah sent? Bring it, or else I will search the trunk and everywhere else." I bid him search where he would. He said I must tell what man it was that brought me the ink or else I would be tied with chains presently. I told him I had done nothing but what was just and right in the sight of God, and what I did suffer would be for truth's sake, and I did not care; I would not meddle nor make with the poor workmen. He said, "For God's sake tell me what Sarah did write." I told him a few words and said it was truth.

Said he, "You say it is much we do not tempt you with money." And in few hours they came and tempted us with money often.

So the lieutenant took my ink and threw it away, and they were smitten as if they would have fallen to the ground and went their way. I saw them no more in three weeks, but the poor man was set free the next morning. . . .

Our money served us a year and seven weeks, and when it was almost gone the friars brought the Inquisitor's chamberlain to buy our hats. We said we came not there to sell our clothes nor anything we had. Then the friar did commend us for that and told us we might have kept our money to serve us otherwise. We said no, we could not keep any money and be chargeable to any; we could trust God. He said he did see we could, but they should have maintained us while they kept us prisoners.

And then the Lord did take away our stomachs; we did eat but little for three or four weeks. And then the Lord called us to fasting for eleven days together, but it was so little that the friars came and said that it was impossible that creatures could live with so little meat as they did see we did for so long time together, and asked what we would do, and said their Lord Inquisitor said we might have anything we would. We said we must wait to know the mind of God, what he would have us to do; we did not fast in our own wills, but in obedience to the Lord. They were much troubled and sent us meat and said the English consul sent it. We could not take anything till the Lord's time was come.

We were weak, so that Sarah did dress her head as she would lie in her grave (poor lamb). I lay looking for the Lord to put an end to the sad trial which way it seemed good in his sight. Then I heard a voice saying, "Ye shall not die." I believed the Lord, and His glory did appear much in our fast. He was very gracious to us and did refresh us with His living presence continually, and we did behold His beauty to our great joy and comfort. And He was large to us in His promises, so that we were kept quiet and still (the sting of death being taken away): our souls, hearts, and minds were at peace with the Lord, so that they could not tell whether we were dead or alive but as they did call to us once a day, till the time the Lord had appointed we should eat. . . .

There were of divers nations brought into the Inquisition prisoners, and the friars and the rest that were great would gain their way to make Christians of them. And we were made to stand up against them and their ways and deny them in the name of the Lord, and declare the truth to the simple-hearted continually, if we did suffer death for it. We could not endure to hear the name of the Lord blasphemed, nor His pure way of truth perverted, nor the ignorant deceived. They did write all they understood of what we spake and sent it to the court chamber before the Inquisitor and magistrates, but the Lord did blast it with the mildews of His wrathful indignation and burnt it up with the brightness of His son, and we rejoiced in our God.

But still our burdens continued very heavy, and our righteous souls were vexed with the filthy conversation of the wicked. And the pure seed of God was pressed from day to day, that our spirits did mourn. And our hearts were grieved because of the hardness of their hearts, and their rebellion against their Maker who was so gracious to them—to suffer them so long in all their abominations, and waited to be gracious to them, and knock at the door of their hearts calling for justice, mercy, and humility. But behold oppression, cruelty, and self-exaltation, notwithstanding the Lord did strive so much with them and sent so many undeniable truths and infallible testimonies of the coming of His son to judgment and so clear a manifestation of the way to eternal salvation, given forth of His own mouth by His eternal spirit, and having us for an example who were kept by His power and holiness. They had not a jot nor tittle against us but for righteousness' sake, though they had winnowed and fanned[5] us so long. Glory, honor, and praises be given to our God forever.

Oh, they would not let us know of any English ship that came into the harbor, as near as they could, but the Lord would make it manifest to us. We had a great working and striving in our bodies, but we knew not what it meant. The arrows of the wicked did fly, so that my soul was plunged and overwhelmed from head to feet. And the terrors of the unrighteous had taken hold of us, and the flames of hell compassed us about. Then the Lord appeared unto me in a dream and said there were two English friends in the city which did plead for our liberty in our behalf, and He had taken all fear away from them and made them bold. And in a little while after, the magistrates sent for us forth, and asked us whether we were sick or whether we did want anything and were very tender to us, and said we should write to England, and bid the scribe give us ink and paper. He said he would, but he was so wicked he did not. They did not tell us of any English that were there. But there was one Francis Steward of London (a captain of a ship) and a friar of Ireland which came to the city together (for what we know). And they did take great pains for us and went to their ruler and the Inquisitor and to several magistrates and friars, and the new English consul with them, and wrought much amongst them that all were willing to let us go save the Inquisitor, they said. And he said he could not free us without an order from the Pope. But we had many heavy enemies besides, which would not be seen, but they obtained the favor to come and speak with us, which was a great thing in such a place.

They sent for us to the court chamber, and the English consul asked us if we were willing to go back to England. We said if it were the will of God we might. The captain spake to us with tears in his eyes, and told us what they had done for us, but could not prevail. "It is this Inquisitor," said he, "The rest were made free; you have preached among these people," he said. We told him we were called upon the testimony of our conscience, and the truth that we have witnessed forth among them we should stand to maintain with our blood. He said if they could get us off he would freely give us our passage and provide for us, and the vessel was his own. We told him his love was as well accepted of the Lord as if he did carry us. He offered us money; he saw the Lord would not suffer us to take any. He took our names. We told them they took us out of our way, and put us into the Inquisition, and bid us change our minds, and we could not: the Lord had changed us into that which changed not if they would burn us to ashes or chop

5. A technique for cleaning grain by tossing it until the chaff blows away.

us as herbs to the pot. The friar said we did not work—which was false; we had work of our own and did work as we were able. We told him our work and maintenance was in England. And they said it was true. He said we would not accept of the Inquisitor's diet.

We did not know who did prepare for us; we did receive our meat as we had freedom in the Lord. Then he said we had suffered long enough and too long, but we should have our freedom in few days, and that they would send to the Pope for an order. And there were many English ships that way, but the captain saw it was a very hard thing, so that it grieved him to the heart. He prayed God to comfort us, and he went away, and we do beseech God to bless and preserve him unto everlasting life, and never to let him nor his go without a blessing from Him for his love: he did venture himself exceedingly in that place.

But after he was gone they arose up against us with one accord. The Inquisitor came up into a tower and looked down upon us as if he would have eaten us, and they did try us for our lives again, and did shut up our doors many weeks; we could not tell for what. At length the Inquisitor came into the tower again, and Sarah was moved to call to him to have the door opened for us to go down into the court to wash our clothes. Then he gave command for the door to be opened once a week, and in a little while 'twas open every day. But great was our affliction indeed. And she told him if we were the Pope's prisoners we would appeal to the Pope, and he should send us to him. But them in the prison with us, especially the friar, were mortal enemies to us, but yet they would have fed us with the choicest of their meat, and would gladly give us whole bottles of wine if we would receive it, and were greatly troubled because we did refuse to eat and drink with them, and did persecute us exceedingly. But the Lord did visit them with his dreadful judgments: the friar was tormented night and day; his body did perish; the doctors and surgeons did follow him a long time.

And there were two or three English ships there, came into harbor. And Sarah saw the coming of them in a vision of the night. And there was a great pleading for us, that we saw. But she heard a voice saying we could not go now. So we were made willing to wait the Lord's time.

Then they sent for us forth when the ships were gone and asked us if we would be Catholics. And we said we were true Christians and had received the spirit of Christ, and he that had not the spirit of Christ was none of His. The English consul told us of the ships, and said they would not let us go unless we would be Catholics, and that we must suffer more imprisonment yet, and said he did what he could for us. One of the magistrates showed us the cross. We told them and said we did take up the cross of Christ daily, which is the great power of God to crucify sin and iniquity. So we told them that one of their fathers did promise us our liberty. We did think that friar was too tender-hearted to stay among them; he did take a great deal of pains for us (the captain said). We told him he would never have cause to repent it: the blessing of God would be upon him for anything he should do for us, for we were the servants of the living God. And he promised us our freedoms in a little time.

CONCERNING THE CROSS OF CHRIST . . .

Christ's cross I do embrace
Which gives me an entrance into grace.
Sin and death it doth deface,
And makes me run a glorious race.
A crown of life and grace I do obtain
And sin and death is daily slain,
And Christ Himself alone to reign
Through the cross I do obtain.

The cross of Christ is more to me
Than all the treasures I can see.
It brings me to my resting place
For to behold God's lovely face.
The cross of Christ is power indeed
Against the serpent and his seed,
And salvation it doth bring
To all that do believe therein.

The cross of Christ is my delight;
It doth uphold me day and night.
It keeps me from the power of sin
Through Christ, who is my heavenly king.
Without the cross I cannot be
From sin and death at all set free.
The cross alone doth crucify
Transgression, sin, iniquity.
It doth break down the middle wall,
And slays the enmity withal,
And makes of twain one perfect man,
And so renews Christ for me again.

The Cross of Christ it doth destroy
That nature that doth disobey—
In those that do themselves deny,
And take it up most willingly,
And daily bear it after Him,
Who is our Lord, and Prince, and King,
And not at all to let it down
Till they come to enjoy the crown.

The cross of Christ is power and life:
It doth destroy all mortal strife.

> *It keepeth from the power of sin*
> *All those that love to walk therein.*
> *All that do own Christ Jesus' cross*
> *Through self-denial they must pass*
> *For to be purgèd from their sin*
> *And no longer live therein.*
>   *The cross of Christ doth operate*
> *Through every vein and vital part.*
> *The heart and reins[6] to cleanse from sin*
> *Of them that's exercised therein.*
> *They that live in sin and wickedness*
> *Are enemies to Christ Jesus' cross,*
> *For all sin and uncleanness*
> *Doth pierce the life of Christ Jesus.*

Father William Weston in the Jesuit Underground

In 1584, the Jesuit William Weston (1550–1615), born in Kent, educated at Oxford and Lincoln's Inn, and ordained in Spain, returned to England to aid the Catholic resistance. Eventually captured, he spent many years incarcerated in Wisbech Castle in Ely and then in solitary confinement in the Tower of London. Released by James I in 1603, he returned to Spain, teaching Greek and Hebrew at the English College in Seville until becoming rector at Valladolid, where he died in 1615. In 1611 Weston wrote his autobiography, recounting his adventures in England: keeping a step ahead of would-be captors (often with the aid of Catholic women), disentangling himself from conspiracies, and until his capture bringing sacraments and comfort to many who rejected the Reformation but not their country. Our selections are from the translation by Philip Caraman (New York: Farrar Strauss, 1955), lightly modified.

FROM WESTON'S AUTOBIOGRAPHY

To the Tower

So the morning dawned when once again we were made a spectacle to men and to the world. A countless crowd of people gathered to watch us, both within and beyond the castle enclosure. And while they stood by, the horses were saddled and nine, perhaps ten, guards assembled who were to escort us the whole length of the journey and take us to court. It was also their business to prevent us conferring privately with one another or having any word at all save in the presence of a witness. Then, after much fussing and bustling, we mounted our horses in

---

6. Kidneys; seat of the feelings.

full view of the spectators and set out with a large guard of soldiers. Scarcely had we gone a mile and a half when a fast rider was posted after us. In as short a time as possible he had caught up with us, and at once stripped us of the packbags in which we carried our cassocks,[1] shirts and those few other things we needed, as men do who are bidden off to prison. They suspected we had secretly taken away certain things and by coming on us unexpectedly had hoped to discover our deceit.

We then continued on our way. The man, however, returned with the packs as fast as he had first come. Only our breviaries[2] had been stolen. Apart from them there was nothing that took their fancy or was worth snatching.

A little further along, two of those men they call pursuivants[3] met us on the high road. They had been sent on the authority of the [Queen's] Council for the very task that had just been completed: to arrange for our transference to London and to carry out a close search of all our cells and common rooms, examining the walls and ceilings for our secret hiding places. As they had been forestalled in their work, they spared themselves the rest of the journey and attached themselves to our party. Hereafter I was handed over to these two guards, who clung to my side incessantly and did not leave my room even at night.

It was winter, and very wet and cold. The roads were muddy, and when we came to an inn we warmed ourselves and dried our clothes. My companions, also, had their own rooms with their own guards assigned to each. I took great pains to show consideration to my keepers. I told them to light a blazing fire and to lie down while supper was got ready, or ordered a glass of wine or other refreshment for them and said that I would pay. The whole day we had gone without a meal and had toiled, practically fasting, on a tedious journey. So while they were busy looking after the horses, I took their cloaks and laid them out before the fire, and with these and other attentions I gained the good-will of them both.

"Beware of my companion," one of them said. "He is a great rascal. Don't confide in him the slightest thing that could be used against you." And the other man told me the same about his mate, each giving reasons why I should do well to suspect the other of special knavery. But actually there was no need for this. Their loathsome occupation as pursuivants of Catholics told me enough about them, and I knew how little trust I could place in either. Without scruple or risk of rash judgment one might well have presumed they were more than ordinarily wicked men.

These men told me the reason why I had been summoned: namely, that I was deeply attached to the Spanish party,[4] and had defended their claim to the English succession, both privately and in company, even in open debate; and they added that the priests in Wisbech were split into factions in support of conflicting princes. Some were for the Spanish side, others the Scottish. Hence the dis-

1. Priestly garments, and hence evidence of their identity.
2. Catholic prayer books.
3. Agents sent to arrest Catholics whose activities offended the authorities.
4. A segment of the Catholic community that looked for Spanish help in overthrowing Elizabeth.

cord among them. Now these accusations were very serious. (No greater calumny against me could have been fabricated.) And it was easy, therefore, to understand the alarm of the Queen's Council and their sending for me. Furthermore they named the chief people who had accused me, and mentioned many other things that certainly could never have reached the ears of the heretics[5] unless certain persons had manifestly betrayed me.

So a great part of the journey I spent talking to them on these subjects. And because I was well in their favor, they allowed me to have private conversations with other persons, and once actually kept watch at the door while I heard a man's confession—saying, as they did it, "We don't want to pay large fines in money for letting one of those rogues find you in secret conference." They said this, I am certain, to make much of the small kindness they had done. Nevertheless, I knew that on this present journey they were behaving abominably to the men who, against their wishes, had joined the escort. They had hoped for greater profit, and would have got it, if the transportation had been in their undivided charge.

In three days we reached London. From our inn we were taken to the Queen's court. Spattered all over with mud and grime from the road, we must have presented a sorry sight to the courtiers. For two whole hours, at very least, we were kept waiting on their decision. Then, after a long deliberation, without even seeing us, they sent us back to the inn. But I must mention an incident that occurred there. One of my companions, getting cold with the long waiting and becoming rather restive, interrupted the protracted sitting by taking an occasional brief walk up and down. I tried to do the same. But some seedy-looking courtier or other, who had been sitting with his arms crossed, charged at me heartily and squarely, with the whole weight of his body, as I was walking between two guards. I saw him coming, stepped aside, and made way for him. A large number of people were watching. On my return, he came at me again. Again I side-stepped. Then, yielding place to him, I sat down. Possibly he thought that here were priests—and Jesuits at that (they were despised more than the dregs of the rabble and loathed by men of every class)—giving themselves airs at court. No doubt he thought that this was no place for such men to presume to walk up and down, or even raise their eyes and look another man in the face.

So we were dismissed and returned to the inn with our full accompaniment of guards. Back at the inn, we had supper. It was time now we retired to rest. We were weary from the day's business. But two messengers from court came to hustle us off to prison immediately. One of them entered my room. He had a large number of attendants with him. "In the Queen's name," he said, bringing down his arm on me, "I arrest you." "There's no need for that," I said. "I have been the Queen's prisoner many years already." "I am obliged to put you through a thorough examination," he said, "to see whether you are carrying any arms or letters on your person, or in your baggage." This he did. He delved into every pocket and corner of my clothes and baggage. Then he fastened my arm with a rope.

5. Weston's term for Protestants.

"Get along with you," he ordered, "you're to go to the Tower of London." The priest Giles Archer received the same treatment. But my other two companions were taken off separately to different prisons.

So the two of us were led away. I went first. He followed with his own escort. We were dragged through a long city street until at last we reached the Tower and were brought before the Lieutenant. He asked us many questions, principally concerning Father [John] Gerard,[6] who a few months earlier had made good his escape. He said he would give a vast sum to recapture him. Then two warders were summoned and assigned us each to our cells; but before being led off we embraced and took leave of each other as for the last time. How he fared, I do not know. But it was my lot to fall into the hands of another brutal plunderer. As soon as the door was shut on me the fellow appeared. "You are Edmunds,"[7] he said, "and you are a Jesuit. I belong to the Queen's service and it's my job to deal with you and the likes of you in the way you deserve. First, hand over your crucifix. You always go about with crucifixes, rosaries and medals." Then he put both hands on my chest and with one tug ripped my gown from the neck to my ankles. "Where's that crucifix?" he said, and searched the rest of my person and clothing all over. "If I don't find your crucifix," he continued, "I will unstitch every garment you have on." At last he hit upon it. Delighted with the prize, he gave me no more trouble.

I wondered now what new accusation they would find to bring against me and what witnesses they would produce to support it. But they gave me a very long respite, and during several weeks of concern and anxiety as to my ultimate fate nothing further was said or done. Eventually they did summon me and brought me before the commissioners. First they asked me the usual preliminary questions. What was my name? my country? birthplace? place of education, and ordination to the diaconate and priesthood? Then they sought to put me under oath to give direct and truthful answers to the rest of their questions. I told them they could ask whatever they wished. In what was lawful for me to mention, I would satisfy them without being bound by an oath. If they asked anything unlawful, no oath would make me answer. "It's not our present business," they said, "to deal with religious questions: for instance, the fact that you are a Jesuit and a priest and have entered the realm against the established laws and will of the Sovereign. Nor do we intend to inquire about the Masses you have said since your entry; the houses where you have stayed; the people you have drawn from the Queen's allegiance and reconciled to the Pope. We release you from anxiety on all these counts. You have nothing to fear there. You are charged with graver things, matters of life and death for you." Then, in sequence, they brought out the four principal heads of accusation against me. I had in my possession seditious books treating perniciously of the state of the realm, principally one, ascribed to Father [Robert] Parsons,[8] which discussed the rights of various claims

6. Jesuit writer (1564–1637) whose autobiography recounts his escape from the Tower in 1597.
7. Weston's alias at the time.
8. Influential English Jesuit, author, and missionary to England (1546–1610).

to the succession. Then, that the priests at Wisbech had fostered panics and factions among themselves, and had held public discussions on these claims and made them subjects of daily conversation; and while some favored one successor, and others another, I was the chief protagonist of the Spanish faction. Moreover, I had known of the approach of the vast Armada of the Spaniards against England[9] and had not given information about it; and, in addition, through couriers and correspondence, I had previous knowledge of two of their warlike expeditions, the first against England, the second against Ireland, and I had held my tongue. . . .

Finally, after they had failed to get the information they wanted, they covered me pretty well with insults and jibes and sent me back to prison. Even considering the range and number of their questions, they had shown themselves fair adepts at abuse; but still, with that strange inner hatred they nursed, they gave signs of regretting that they had not said everything they might have done. I do not refer to all. Some, indeed, if not from moderation then out of respect for their own persons and position, wished to appear more balanced than the rest. But even one of these men threatened to squeeze blood from my nails and finger tips—a sufficiently ill-concealed threat of the horrors of the rack and torture to fill me with fear.

Shut again in my cell, I lay there hourly and daily expecting sentence of death. The time and place were well suited to prayer, and, had not my eyes failed me, to reading and study also. But the sight of one eye was completely gone, and a film forming over the other made it more than half blind, so that I very nearly suffered complete loss of sight. Moreover, because of a chronic headache, sleep had become all but impossible. I had, in fact, practically none, and for the space of eight, nine, ten or more days I scarcely had two or three hours' sleep, and that only with the aid of sleeping draughts. So all the time I suffered severely from a most grievous inflammation of the eyes and head. Indeed these troubles caused me much greater suffering and depression than the tedium of prison life, my close confinement, or the excessive solitude due to my total segregation from the world outside.

Once, right under my eyes, a Catholic was carried out for burial in most mean style. Unless I am mistaken, he had endured eleven whole years in this vile prison for the sake of his religion, yet his spirit remained undaunted. Humberstone was his name. My warder told me that an unsparingly cruel man had been deputed to look after him. Apart from his habitual brutalities, he would inflict savage blows and lashes on Humberstone until, in the end, under these and all the other countless sufferings of his imprisonment—the squalor, the confinement, the solitude, the underfeeding, the scourges and cudgeling—he lost the balance of his mind. Drained utterly of bodily strength he became helpless for nearly three years before his death and was confined to bed: without help—and it was very rarely given him—he could not even turn over and lie on his other side. The same warder told me this also about Humberstone: his father, a heretic

9. The 1588 expeditionary force sent by Philip II against Elizabeth.

who had obtained the favor of the Queen, had been granted permission to remove his son from prison and bring him home. He begged his son to come. He implored him insistently again and again, but he could not get him to yield to his entreaties. In the midst of all his tribulations the son preferred to remain gloriously in prison for his faith, with a most assured hope of salvation, rather than pass his days with a heretic, even his own father. Indeed, he knew for certain that with him he could never escape the deceits, blandishments, persuasions and other wiles of heretical company.

Not unlike this was the case of another gentleman, a pattern of singular probity. He was my prison neighbor, though we were separated by massive walls and heavily barred and bolted doors. Formerly he had held high rank in the Catholic army fighting the heretics in Flanders. But after striving bravely in the line for several years, some matter of business brought him back to England. Here he fell into the hands of the heretics. On interrogation he replied that he was a Catholic—forthrightly, as became a soldier. He was clapped into the Tower, and there I found him on my arrival, bravely completing his fifth year of imprisonment, worn down by many infirmities and wants. His mother was anxious to take him out, and a short time before I left the fortress she went to great expense and effort and employed intercessors with the Queen to this end. At length she obtained permission. But he would not avail himself of it for fear of admitting that he had ever offended the Queen and broken the law by going out of the kingdom without a license—an admission that was made a condition of his release. It was for reasons of religion and conscience that he had gone abroad. He saw no crime in it and refused to regret his action and proclaim himself sorry. So he stood firmly by his resolution, and though his mother, sisters and friends came every day beseeching him and striving to move him with tears, he remained steadfast in his conviction.

Escapes

[Weston recounts "a story that has its amusing side" as told to him by the warder. It concerns a Catholic, "but his Catholicism was not the reason for his imprisonment" in the Tower.]

He had been detained a long, almost interminable, time, and though his case had been heard and examined it appeared that justice had fallen asleep. There was no sentence. He seemed, so to speak, to lie buried in the darkness of the tomb, having passed out of the recollection of his fellow men. Then he started to consider by what means he could make his escape. So, being a skilled artisan, he made a file from a scrap of wrought iron. With this he began slowly to saw through the iron bars and eventually by working at them every day he made a way out for himself. He then scaled the wall, swam across the moat, and got away. The next day, on entering the cell, the warder saw it was empty, its inmate flown. The news was cried by heralds throughout the whole city and a hunt was started for his recapture. Meanwhile, by walking hard, he put six miles between himself and the city; but on the road he stopped at a glover's shop to buy a pair of gloves, and here a traveler who had left London that same morning, looking the man up and down, noticed that his clothes were soaked.

"The heralds were crying for a man all over the city," he said, "a prisoner who escaped from the Tower. He could have got out only by scaling the walls and swimming the moat. Look at this fellow. All his clothes are wet! See! He may be the very man!" They had him arrested and brought back. When the matter was gone into, be was identified and once again locked in, heavily loaded with irons, and fastened by a long chain to a wooden pillar in the middle of his cell.

With patience laboriously come by, he put a good face on the discomforts he suffered. But afterwards, when it was thought that he had been sufficiently punished for his escape, his fetters were undone and once again he was given the freedom of his cell. The incident was forgotten and he was treated the same as before. Nevertheless, this did not satisfy him and he now began to think out some fresh plan. By the same means as last time—the secret of his file had not been detected—he found a way of escape. But as the wall he had to descend was higher this time, he procured a rope (where he got it I do not know) and slid down it. But it was too short and left him dangling a good distance above the water. So, releasing his hold, he dropped into the moat. There was a heavy splash, and in the silence of the night the guards pacing the other side heard the noise. At once they guessed that a prisoner had escaped from the Tower and began running about in every direction. But the man watched for his moment carefully, emerged from the water, and took to flight. Feeling his pursuers upon him, he began to shout, "There, there he goes!" The runner hardest on his heels dashed forward, hoping to win commendation for recapturing the fugitive. He came level with him, then brought his hand down on his shoulder to hold him back a second until he could overtake him. But he felt the wet clothes. "You're the fellow," he cried. "Stop!"

So he was rearrested. They took him back again and this time locked him up and guarded him with still greater care. But after the lapse of some time a new plan occurred to him. He was most ingenious at devising fresh stratagems. First of all he made a habit of never greeting the warder when he came into his cell and never speaking to him when he left. He did not even look at him. Pretending to be busily occupied, he sat facing the window with his back turned to him. Meanwhile he had manufactured a number of things which he fancied would be a help in his new escape.

The day came which he had fixed for his flight. Previously he had completed a dummy of himself in a long gown of the kind he usually wore. Then covering its head with a hat or cap, he placed it in position facing the window, hoping that when the warder entered and saw the model he would notice nothing unusual but simply take it for the same person he always found sitting silently in that place with his back turned on him. Meanwhile he had transformed himself into the perfect blacksmith, made up and dressed in every detail, tools in his hand and slung from his belt. At the usual time the warder entered the cell. He briskly put down the things he was carrying in the place he always did. But the prisoner, who had been hiding behind the door, quickly gave him the slip and hurried downstairs, leaving the warder completely unaware of the trick that had been played upon him. A woman, however, happened to be passing and noticed the man. It was at a time of the day and in a place where no one was allowed to be about without a warder. "Good fellow," she said, "who are you? where do you come from?" He answered that he had just done a blacksmith's job upstairs. "But you can't go visiting prisoners' cells," she said, "unless a warder is with you. Stop! Let's check and see who you are."

While this conversation was going on, the warder returned on his round. "Do you know this fellow?" asked the woman. "Just a minute ago he came down from where you were." The warder looked him up and down, and only after some while did he succeed in recognizing him, so completely transformed were his appearance and his clothes. "Will you never stop trying your tricks?" he said. "Now, get back with me." Again he locked him up in his cell. But one or two years later, after his own warder had given security that he would behave as a loyal subject—for he was under suspicion of some treason or machination against the Queen—he was released on no initiative of his own.

11

Anne Vaughan Lock [Dering, Prowse]

(c. 1534–after 1590)

Henry Lock *(1553?–1608?)*

Anne Vaughan Lock [Dering, Prowse] Meditates on Sin

Anne Lock (c. 1534–after 1590) was the older daughter of Stephen Vaughan, a businessman and diplomat in the time of Henry VIII with strong Protestant leanings. Her first husband, Henry Lock, to whom she was married sometime before 1557, was also a staunch Protestant. As a result of a close friendship with the Scottish preacher John Knox, Anne Lock journeyed to Geneva with two young children in 1557—leaving her husband behind—and remained there about two years; she then returned to London. Letters to her by Knox, often considered to be a dour man, show his warmer side; even though Lock's letters to him are lost, Knox's letters also shed light on her interiority. The sonnet sequence appended to her translation of *Sermons of John Calvin upon the Song that Ezechias Made* (1560) plus the creation by her son, Henry, of more than two hundred religious sonnets, caused William Stull to dub her "literally the mother of English religious sonneteering."[1]

After her husband's death in 1571, Anne Lock remarried twice. Her second husband, Edward Dering, was a rising young Puritan preacher, ten years her junior, who died in 1576 at the age of thirty-six. Her third husband, John Prowse, was an important merchant and political figure in Exeter, where she lived after their marriage (c. 1583). Anne Lock's unwavering faith shows in her translation of Jean Taffin's *Of the Marks of the Children of God* (1590); in her introduction she

---

1. " 'Why Are Not Sonnets Made of Thee?': A New Context," *Modern Philology* 80 (1982): 132.

forecasts troubles for the faithful, commenting that she has "according to my duty, brought my poor basket of stones to the strengthening of the walls of that Jerusalem whereof (by grace) we are all both citizens and members." Our text is based on the 1560 *Sermons*. We have also consulted the edition by Susan M. Felch (Medieval and Renaissance Texts and Studies 185, for the Renaissance English Text Society, 1999); we thank Professor Felch for helping us with cruces in the text.

A MEDITATION OF A PENITENT SINNER
WRITTEN IN MANNER OF A PARAPHRASE[2]
UPON THE 51ST PSALM OF DAVID[3]

THE PREFACE, EXPRESSING THE PASSIONED[4] MIND
OF THE PENITENT SINNER

The heinous guilt of my forsaken ghost [5]
So threats,[6] alas, unto my feebled sprite [7]
Deservèd death, and (that me grieveth most)
Still stand so fixed before my dazzled sight
The loathsome filth of my distainèd[8] life,
The mighty wrath of mine offended Lord—
My Lord whose wrath is sharper than the knife—
And deeper wounds than double-edged sword
That, as the dimmèd and fordullèd[9] eyn
Full fraught with tears and more and more oppressed
With growing streams of the distillèd brine
Sent from the furnace of a grief-full breast
Can not enjoy the comfort of the light
Nor find the way wherein to walk aright

So I, blind wretch—whom God's enflamèd ire
With piercing stroke hath thrown unto the ground
Amid my sins—still groveling in the mire
Find not the way that other oft have found
Whom cheerful glimpse of God's abounding grace

---

2. Amplification of a passage.
3. (Miserere Mei, Deus). Felch traces the prose text of psalm 51 in Lock's margins to the Gallician version of the Latin psalms (i.e., that frequently used in France).
4. Grieved.
5. Spirit.
6. Threatens.
7. Spirit.
8. Dimmed; Felch prefers "defiled."
9. Made dull.

Hath oft relieved and oft with shining light
Hath brought to joy out of the ugly place
Where I in dark of everlasting night
Bewail my woeful and unhappy case
And fret my dying soul with gnawing pain.
Yet blind, alas, I grope about for grace
While blind for grace I grope about in vain.
My fainting breath I gather up and strain
"Mercy, mercy," to cry and cry again.

But mercy while I found with shrieking cry
For grant of grace and pardon while I pray
Even then Despair before my ruthful eye
Spreads forth my sin and shame, and seems to say,
"In vain thou brayest[10] forth thy bootless[11] noise
To Him for mercy, O refusèd wight,[12]
That hears not the forsaken sinner's voice.
Thy reprobate[13] and foreordainèd sprite,
Foredamnèd vessel of His heavy wrath
(As self-witness of thy unknowing heart
And secret guilt of thine own conscience saith),
Of His sweet promises can claim no part.
But thee, caitiff,[14] deservèd curse doeth draw
To Hell, by justice, for offended law."

This horror when my trembling soul doth hear,
When marks and tokens of the reprobate,
My growing sins, of grace my senseless cheer
Enforce the proof of everlasting hate
That I conceive the heaven's king to bear
Against my sinful and forsaken ghost,
As in the throat of Hell, I quake for fear,
And then in present peril to be lost
(Although by[15] conscience wanteth to reply,
But with remorse enforcing mine offense
Doth argue vain my not-availing cry)
With woeful sighs and bitter penitence

10. Cry out; utter harshly.
11. Unavailing, useless.
12. Creature.
13. Wicked; rejected and condemned by God.
14. Wretch.
15. Conceivably a typo for "my."

To Him from whom the endless mercy flows
A cry for mercy to relieve my woes.

And then not daring with presuming eye
Once to behold the angry heavens' face
From troubled sprite I send confusèd cry
To crave the crumbs of all-sufficing grace.
With faltering knee I falling to the ground,
Bending my yielding hands to heaven's throne,
Pour forth my piteous plaint with woeful sound,
With smoking sighs and oft repeated groan
Before the Lord, the Lord, whom sinner I
I cursèd wretch, I have offended so
That dreading in his wreakfull[16] *wrath to die*
And damnèd, down to depth of Hell to go,
Thus tossed with pangs and passions of despair
Thus crave I mercy with repentant cheer.

A Meditation of a Penitent Sinner upon the 51st Psalm

Have mercy   *Have mercy, God, for Thy great mercy's sake.*
upon me (O God)   *O God, my God, unto my shame I say*
after Thy great mercy *Being fled from Thee, so as I dread to take*
        Thy name in wretched mouth, and fear to pray
        Or ask the mercy that I have abused.
        But, God of mercy, let me come to Thee,
        Not for justice, that justly am accused,
        Which self[17] *word justice so amazeth me,*
        That scarce I dare thy mercy sound[18] *again.*
        But mercy, Lord, yet suffer me to crave.
        Mercy is thine; let me not cry in vain
        Thy great mercy for my great fault to have.
        Have mercy, God, pity my penitence
        With greater mercy than my great offense.

And according   *My many sins in number are increased.*
unto the   *With weight whereof, in sea of deep despair,*

16. Vengeful, wreaking destruction.
17. Same.
18. Mention, utter.

multitude
of Thy mercies
do away
mine
offenses.

My sinking soul is now so sore oppressed
That now in peril and in present fear
I cry: "Sustain me, Lord, and Lord, I pray,
With endless number of Thy mercies take
The endless number of my sins away.
So, by Thy mercy, for Thy mercy's sake,
Rue on me, Lord, relieve me with Thy grace
My sin is cause that I so need to have
Thy mercy's aid in my so woeful case.
My sin is cause that scarce I dare to crave
Thy mercy manifold, which only may
Relieve my soul and take my sins away."

Wash me
yet more
from my
wickedness,
and cleanse
me from
my sin

So foul in sin and loathsome in Thy sight,
So foul with sin I see myself to be,
That till from sin I may be washèd white,
So foul I dare not, Lord, approach to Thee.
Oft hath Thy mercy washèd me before
Thou madest me clean. But I am foul again.
Yet wash me Lord again, and wash me more.
Wash me, O Lord, and do away the stain
Of ugly sins that in my soul appear.
Let flow Thy plenteous streams of cleansing grace.
Wash me again, yea, wash me everywhere,
Both lep'rous body and defilèd face.
Yea, wash me all, for I am all unclean,
And from my sin, Lord, cleanse me once again.

For I knowledge
my
wickedness,
and my
sin is ever
before
me.

Have mercy, Lord, have mercy, for I know
How much I need Thy mercy in this case.
The horror of my guilt doth daily grow,
And growing wears my feeble hope of grace.
I feel and suffer in my thrallèd breast
Secret remorse and gnawing of my heart.
I feel my sin, my sin that hath oppressed
My soul with sorrow and surmounting smart.
Draw me to mercy, for so oft as I
Presume to mercy to direct my sight
My chaos and my heap of sin doth lie
Between me and Thy mercy's shining light.
Whatever way I gaze about for grace,
My filth and fault are ever in my face.

Against Thee only
have I sinned
and done
evil in Thy
sight.

Grant Thou me mercy, Lord. Thee, Thee alone
I have offended. And offending Thee,
For mercy, lo, how I do lie and groan.
Thou with all-piercing eye beheldest me
Without regard that sinnèd in thy sight.
Behold, again, how now my spirit it rues
And wails the time when I with foul delight
Thy sweet, forbearing mercy did abuse.
My cruel conscience with sharpened knife
Doth splat[19] *my rippèd*[20] *heart and lays abroad*
The loathsome secrets of my filthy life
And spreads them forth before the face of God
Whom shame from deed shameless could not restrain
Shame for my deed is added to my pain.

That Thou
mayest be
found just
in the sayings, and
mayest overcome
when
Thou art judged.

But mercy, Lord; O Lord, some pity take.
Withdraw my soul from the deservèd Hell,
O Lord of glory, for Thy glory's sake:
That I may savèd of Thy mercy tell
And show how Thou, which mercy hath behight[21]
To sighing sinners that have broke Thy laws,
Performest mercy; so as in the sight
Of them that judge the justice of Thy cause
Thou only just be deemèd, and no more
The world's injustice wholly to confound;
That damming me to depth of during[22] *woe,*
Just in Thy judgment shouldest Thou be found,
And from deservèd flames relieving me,
Just in Thy mercy may'st Thou also be.

For lo, I
was shapen
in wickedness
and in
sin my
mother conceived
me.

For lo, in sin, Lord, I begotten was;
With seed and shape my sin I took also.
Sin is my nature and my kind, alas;
In sin my mother me conceivèd. Lo,
I am but sin, and sinful ought to die,
Die in His wrath that hath forbidden sin.
Such bloom and fruit, lo sin doth multiply.

19. Split open.
20. Searched, examined; Felch suggests "split."
21. Promised.
22. Enduring.

Such was my root, such is my juice[23] within.
I plead not this as to excuse my blame,
On kind or parents mine own guilt to lay,
But, by disclosing of my sin, my shame,
And need of help the plainer to display
Thy mighty mercy: if with plenteous grace
My plenteous sins it please Thee to deface.

But lo, Thou hast loved truth, the hidden and secret things of Thy wisdom Thou hast opened unto me.

Thou lovest simple sooth, not hidden face
With truthless visor of deceiving show.
Lo simply, Lord, I do confess my case,
And simply crave Thy mercy in my woe.
This secret wisdom hast Thou granted me,
To see my sins and whence my sins do grow:
This hidden knowledge have I learned of Thee
To feel my sins and how my sins do flow
With such excess that with unfeignèd heart,
Dreading to drown, my Lord, lo how I flee,
Simply with tears bewailing my desert,
Believèd simply by Thy hand to be.
Thou lovest truth, Thou taughtest me the same.
Help, Lord of truth, for glory of Thy name.

Sprinkle me, Lord, and I shall be clean. Wash me and I shall be whiter than snow.

With sweet hyssop[24] besprinkle Thou my sprite
Not such hyssop, nor so besprinkle me,
As law unperfect, shade of perfect light,
Did use as an appointed sign to be
Foreshowing figure of Thy grace behight.
With death and bloodshed of Thine only son
Th[y] sweet hyssop, cleanse me, defilèd wight,
Sprinkle my soul. And when Thou so hast done,
Bedewed with drops of mercy and of grace,
I shall be clean as cleansèd of my sin.
Oh wash me, Lord, for I am foul, alas,
That only canst, Lord, wash me well within.
Wash me, O Lord. When I am washèd so,
I shall be whiter than the whitest snow.

Thou shalt make me

Long have I heard, and yet I hear the sounds
Of dreadful threats and thunders of the law

23. Sap (reinforcing the tree metaphor).
24. An aromatic herb noted for purifying in the Bible.

hear joy
and gladness.
All
the bones
which Thou
hast broken
shall rejoice.

Which echo of my guilty mind resounds,
And with redoubled horror doth so draw
My listening soul from Mercy's gentle voice
That louder, Lord, I am constrained to call:
"Lord, pierce mine ears and make me to rejoice
When I shall hear and when Thy mercy shall
Sound in my heart the gospel of Thy grace.
Then shalt Thou give my hearing joy again,
The joy that only may relieve my case.
And then my bruisèd bones, that Thou with pain
Hast made too weak my feebled corpse to bear
Shall leap for joy, to show mine inward cheer."

Turn a-
way Thy
face from
my sins,
and do away
all my misdeeds.

Look on me, Lord: though trembling I beknowe,[25]
That sight of sin so sore offendeth Thee,
That seeing sin, how it doth overflow
My whelmèd[26] soul, Thou canst not look on me
But with disdain, with horror, and despite.
Look on me Lord, but look not on my sin.
Not that I hope to hide it from Thy sight,
Which seest me all without and eke within,
But to remove it from Thy wrathful eye
And from the justice of Thine angry face
That Thou impute[27] it not. Look not how I
Am foul by sin, but make me by Thy grace
Pure in Thy mercy's sight, and, Lord, I pray,
That hatest sin, wipe all my sins away.

Create a
clean heart
within me,
O God, and
renew a
steadfast spirit
within
my bowels.

Sin and despair have so possessed my heart,
And hold my captive soul in such restraint
As of Thy mercies I can feel no part
But still in languor[28] do I lie and faint.
Create a new, pure heart within my breast,
Mine old can hold no liquor of Thy grace.
My feeble faith with heavy load oppressed
Stagg'ring doth scarcely creep a reeling[29] pace
And fallen it is too faint to rise again.
Renew, O Lord, in me a constant sprite,

25. Recognize, confess.
26. Engulfed.
27. Charge against.
28. Distress.
29. Winding.

That stayed with mercy may my soul sustain,
A sprite so settled and so firmly pight[30]
Within my bowels that it never move,
But still behold th'assurance of Thy love.

Cast me
not away
from Thy
face, and
take not
Thy holy
spirit from
me.

Lo, prostrate, Lord, before Thy face I lie,
With sighs deep drawn, deep sorrow to express
O, Lord of mercy, mercy do I cry;
Drive me not from Thy face in my distress:
Thy face of mercy and of sweet relief,
The face that feeds angels with only sight,
The face of comfort in extremest grief.
Take not away the succor of Thy sprite:
Thy Holy Sprite, which is mine only stay,
The stay that when despair assaileth me,
In faintest hope yet moveth me to pray,
To pray for mercy, and to pray to Thee.
Lord, cast me not from presence of Thy face,
Nor take from me the spirit of Thy grace.

Restore to
me the comfort
of Thy
saving help
and stablish
me
with Thy
free spirit.

But render me my wonted joys again,
Which sin hath reft,[31] and planted in their place
Doubt of Thy mercy, ground of all my pain.
The taste that Thy love whilome[32] did embrace
My cheerful soul, the signs that did assure
My feeling ghost of favor in Thy sight
Are fled from me, and wretched I endure
Senseless of grace, the absence of Thy sprite.
Restore my joys and make me feel again
The sweet return of grace that I have lost:
That I may hope I pray not all in vain.
With Thy free sprite confirm my feeble ghost
To hold my faith from ruin and decay
With fast affiance[33] and assured stay.

I shall teach
Thy ways
unto the

Lord, of Thy mercy, if Thou me withdraw
From gasping throat of deep, devouring Hell,
Lo, I shall preach the justice of Thy law,

30. Fixed.
31. Robbed.
32. Formerly.
33. Trust.

wicked, and
sinners shall
be turned
unto Thee.

By mercy saved, Thy mercy shall I tell.
The wicked I will teach Thine only way,
Thy ways to take, and man's device[34] to flee,
And such as lewd delight hath led astray,
To rue their error and return to Thee.
So shall the proof[35] of mine example teach
The bitter fruit of lust and foul delight.
So shall my pardon by Thy mercy teach
The way to find sweet mercy in Thy sight.
Have mercy, Lord, in me example make
Of law and mercy, for Thy mercy's sake.

Deliver me
from blood,
O God, God
of my health,
and my tongue
shall joyfully
talk of
Thy justice.

O God, God of my health, my saving God,
Have mercy, Lord, and show Thy might
Assoil[36] me, God, from guilt of guiltless blood
And eke from sin that I ingrowing[37] have
By flesh and blood and by corrupted kind.
Upon my blood and soul extend not, Lord,
Vengeance for blood, but mercy let me find,
And strike me not with Thy revenging sword.
So, Lord, my joying tongue shall talk Thy praise.
Thy name my mouth shall utter in delight,
My voice shall sound Thy justice and Thy ways,
Thy ways to justify thy sinful wight.
God of my health, from blood I savèd so
Shall spread Thy praise for all the world to know.

Lord, open
Thou my lips,
and my mouth
shall
show Thy
praise.

Lo, straining cramp of cold despair again
In feeble breast doth pinch my pining heart.
So as in greatest need to cry and plain[38]
My speech doth fail to utter Thee my smart.
Refresh my yielding heart with warming grace,
And loose my speech, and make me call to Thee.
Lord, open Thou my lips to show my case;
My Lord, for mercy, lo, to Thee I flee.
I cannot pray without Thy moving aid,
Ne can I rise, ne can I stand alone.
Lord, make me pray, and grant when I have prayed.

34. Scheme.
35. Experience.
36. Absolve.
37. Innate; growing within.
38. Lament.

Lord, loose my lips I may express my moan,
And finding grace with open mouth I may
Thy mercies' praise and holy name display.

If Thou
hadst desired
sacrifice, I would
have given;
Thou delightest
not in
burnt offerings.

Thy mercies' praise, instead of sacrifice,
With thankful mind so shall I yield to Thee.
For if it were delightful in Thine eyes,
Or thereby might thy wrath appeasèd be,
Of cattle slain and burnt with sacred flame
Up to the heaven the hazy smoke to send,
Of beasts, to purge my guilt and blame,
On altars broiled the savor should ascend,
To pease[39] Thy wrath. But Thy sweet son alone
With one sufficing sacrifice for all
Appeaseth Thee, and maketh Thee at one
With sinful man, and hath repaired our fall.
That sacred host is ever in Thine eyes.
The praise of that I yield for sacrifice.

The sacrifice
to God
is a troubled
spirit; a broken
and an
humbled
heart, O God,
Thou wilt
not despise.

I yield myself, I offer up my ghost,
My slain delights, my dying heart to Thee.
To God a troubled sprite is pleasing host.
My troubled sprite doth dread like him to be
In whom tasteless languor with lingering pains
Hath feebled so the starvèd appetite,
That food too late is offered all in vain,
To hold in fainting corpse the fleeing sprite.
My pining soul for famine of Thy grace
So fears, alas, the faintness of my faith.
I offer up my troubled sprite. Alas,
My troubled sprite refuse not in Thy wrath.
Such offering likes Thee, ne wilt thou despise
The broken, humbled heart in angry wise.

Show favor
O Lord
in Thy good
will unto
Sion, that

Show mercy, Lord, not unto me alone,
But stretch Thy favor and Thy pleasèd will,
To spread Thy bounty and Thy grace upon
Sion, for Sion is Thy holy hill.
That Thy Jerusalem with mighty wall

39. Appease.

the walls	*May be enclosèd under Thy defense,*
of Jerusalem may	*And buildèd so that it may never fall*
be builded.	*By mining*[40] *fraud or mighty violence.*
	Defend Thy church, Lord, and advance it
	So in despite of tyranny to stand,
	That trembling at Thy power the world may know
	It is upholden by Thy mighty hand,
	That Sion and Jerusalem may be
	A safe abode for them that honor Thee.

Then shalt	*Then on Thy hill and in Thy wallèd town*
Thou accept	*Thou shalt receive the pleasing sacrifice.*
the sacrifice	*The bruit*[41] *shall of Thy praisèd name resound*
of righteousness,	*In thankful mouths, and then with gentle eyes*
burnt	*Thou shalt behold upon Thine altar lie*
offerings and	*Many a yielded host of humbled heart.*
oblations.	*And round about then shall Thy people cry,*
Then shall	*We praise Thee, God our God: Thou only art*
they offer	*The God of might, of mercy, and of grace."*
young bullocks upon	*That I, then, Lord, may also honor Thee,*
Thine altar.	*Relieve my sorrow and my sins deface;*
	Be, Lord of mercy, merciful to me;
	Restore my feeling of Thy grace again;
	Assure my soul, I crave it not in vain.

Sonnets by Henry Lock

Sharing his mother Anne's interest in devout poetry, Henry Lock, often spelled Lok (1553?–1608?), wrote *Sundry Christian Passions* (1593), a pair of sonnet sequences dedicated to Elizabeth I. In 1597 he reprinted it, adding another set of sonnets, together with a verse paraphrase of Ecclesiastes. A would-be courtier, Lock got work as a spy and in the early 1590s carried messages between James VI and Elizabeth. Despite his good connections, though, he spent time in jail for debts and died poor. His sonnets are often voiced in the person of scriptural figures such as Jonah, David, or Judith, adopting and allegorizing for Protestant poetry the participatory role-playing taught, in a very different way, by Catholic manuals on meditation. We add two sonnets from a concluding set of poems addressed to important people. Lock's work was edited by A. B. Grosart in 1871.

40. Undermining, subversive.
41. Noise.

SONNET 2 (JONAH AND THE WHALE)

From out the darkness of this sea of fear,
Where I in whale remain devoured of sin,
With true remorse of former life I rear
My heart to heaven, in hope some help to win:
I do confess my fault, who did begin
To fly from Thee, O Lord, and leave undone
Thy service, which of right should first have been
Performed, by which so many should be won
To praise Thy name. But fear, alas, begun
To represent to me my journey long,
The dangers of the world my life should run,
Which made me to my soul to offer wrong.
But since by show of death Thou call'dst me back,
Thy gracious help at need let me not lack.

SONNET 3 (NOAH'S ARK)

Within this ark wherein my soul doth dwell,
My body floating on world's troubled wave,
Which winds of fierce affections cause to swell,
And hardly can my power from sinking save,
I cry to Thee, O Lord, and comfort crave.
Close up this fountain of still-flowing sin;
Let me by faith again once footing have
On fruitful earth, and holy life begin;
Lighten the burden so unclean within
Of brutish vices raging in my mind;
Let clean affects[1] the greater party win,
And so increase that plenty I may find
Of sacrifices, pleasing in Thy sight,
Of faith and love, which are Thy soul's delight.

1. Desires.

Sonnet 11 (David and Goliath)

Since with Goliath I am now to fight
And lack the flight of holy David's sling,
Arm Thou me, Lord, with heav'nly armor bright,
Which power of flesh and world to foil[2] may bring:
Thy righteous breast-plate gird on me with truth,[3]
Prepare my feet with Gospel of Thy peace,
The shield of faith (which fiery darts bear forth[4]
Of wicked Satan, whose assaults not cease),
The helmet of salvation, and the sword
Of spirit, which is founded on Thy law.
All these my prayers are: that Thou afford
To make me steadfast, spite of lion's claw,
Who roaring daily seeks as wishèd prey
My silly[5] soul from Thee to take away.[6]

Sonnet 17 (The Foolish Virgins)

Five foolish virgins[7] in my senses dwell
And seek to make me slumber over-long.
They dream that all my deeds do fall out well,
Whereas indeed I headlong run to wrong;
To vanities their humors[8] do belong,
And sin, who doth their fancy chiefly feed;
They chainèd are to links of lust so strong
That their best soil brings forth but bitter weed;
They lack the oil which should be used, indeed,
To lead them to the everlasting light:

2. Defeat.
3. David himself insists on fighting armed only with staff and sling (1 Sam. 17:38–40); Lock's armor is from Eph. 6:11–17.
4. Repel.
5. Weak, harmless.
6. Cf. 1 Sam. 17:34 (David recalls his fight with a lion) and 1 Pet. 5:8 (comparing Satan to a roaring lion seeking prey).
7. Jesus compares God's Kingdom to five wise virgins who keep their lamps filled while awaiting the bridegroom; five foolish ones, having no lamp-oil ready when he comes at midnight, miss the wedding (Matt. 25:1–13).
8. Tendencies generated by "humors"—the body's mix of cold, hot, moist, dry elements.

It grows not, Lord, in fruit of human seed.
Man sleeps all day and gropes his way at night:
Unless Thou lend Thy hand and fill our lamps,
Our light goes forth with smoth'ring sinful damps.

SONNET 18 (THE SAMARITAN WOMAN AT THE WELL)

Out of the fountain of eternal life
I, poor Samaritan,[9] here ready stand
(To sinful lust an old betrothèd wife)
With pitcher ready in my trembling hand
To draw a draught of liquor most divine
To quench the thirst of my inflamèd heart
With heav'nly dew, ere that my soul do pine,[10]
And qualify the rigor of my smart.
A Prophet true Thou art, I understand,
Or rather Father of all truth Thou art.
A stranger I am from fair Judea land,
With these Thy blessings crave for to impart.
Then guide my hand and teach my soul to taste
True faith—the fountain where all bliss is placed.

SONNET 21 (THE MERCHANT AND THE PEARL)

A merchant I, full long abroad have strayed
By sea and land true happiness to gain;[11]
The riches of the earth my eyes have weighed
And seen their profit to be light and vain.
Such trifling trash my soul doth now disdain,
And jewels of more value I espy:
Among the rest one doth all other stain,[12]
Which with my wealth I wish that I might buy;
But this rare pearl is of a price so high

---

9. When in Samaria, Jesus asked a woman at a well for some water; their conversation persuaded her that he was a prophet and the Christ (John 4:5–42).
10. Starve.
11. A parable in Matt. 13:45–46 tells of a merchant who sells everything in order to buy a "pearl of great price" (Heaven).
12. Make dingy by comparison.

As all the earth cannot esteem[13] the same,
Much less to purchase it can I come nigh;
Yet doth the love thereof my heart inflame.
Be Thou the pledge, sweet Savior, then for me,
That heavenly bliss shall so my riches be.

SONNET 22 (THE WIDOW'S MITE)

Among the press of many that draw near
Unto the feast of grace in Temple Thine,
I silly widow also do appear
With humble heart, O Lord, who here incline,
And unto Thee a mite for offering mine
Present as precious to my poor estate;[14]
For herds or flocks, for store of corn and wine,
Without obedience, Lord, Thou aye didst hate.
But broken hearts and souls which lie prostrate
Before Thy throne of grace, and mercy crave,
Do mercy find, though it be ne'er so late;[15]
Thy promise hereof us assurance gave,
In trust whereof, obeying Thy behest,
My prayers to Thy praise, O Lord, are pressed.

SONNET 26 (CAIN AND ABEL)

Of parents first two brothers born that were
The body and the soul did represent:
The elder Cain, who Enoch's walls did rear,[16]
The younger Abel dwelt in silly tent:
First man with plow the virgin soil he rent,[17]
The other served and shore[18] the silly sheep.
To worldly lusts of flesh the one was bent;

13. Estimate, recognize.
14. In Mark 12:41–44 Jesus praises a poor widow whose gift of two "mites" (small coins) to the temple takes more real sacrifice than do the large sums donated by the rich.
15. An echo of Ps. 51.
16. Gen. 4:17 (the name, which was also the name of Cain's son, means "wandering." Cain murdered his brother Abel.
17. Abel was the first farmer; Cain was a herder.
18. Sheared.

Thy heavenly laws the other sought to keep.
A deadly discord 'twixt them so did creep,
The elder did the guiltless younger slay.
That ancient hatred grounded is so deep
It strives in me, alas, unto this day.
Accept my sacrifice, Lord; me defend:
My powers unto Thy holy pleasure bend.

SONNET 51 (SUSANNA AND THE ELDERS)[19]

Whilst in the garden of this earthly soil
My self to solace and to bath I bend,
And fain would quench sin's heat, which seems to boil
Amidst my secret thoughts which shadow lend.
My Sense and Reason, which should me defend
As judges chosen to the commonweal,
Allured by Lust my ruin do pretend[20]
By force of Sin, which shameless they reveal.
They secretly on my affections steal
When Modesty (my maids) I sent away,
To whom for help I thought I might appeal.
But Grace yet strengthens me to say them nay,
Yet they accuse me, Lord, and die I shall
If Christ (my Daniel) me not judge of all.

SONNET 70 (WITH MOSES IN THE DESERT)

Whilst in this worldly wilderness about,
For want of faith I back am forced to go
(Afraid of sins, which Giant-like are stout,[21]
And foul affections, which like cruel foe
Of Esau's race[22] *their might and power bestow*

---

19. Protestants assign the famous story of Susanna to the Apocrypha, although the Geneva Bible says that "some join [it] to the end of Daniel, and make it the 13. chap."
20. Aim at. Lock refers to the lusting elders who hypocritically accuse Susanna.
21. Strong.
22. Esau, Jacob's older brother, sold his birthright for a bowl of stew (Gen. 25); his people held a land that God tells Moses the Israelites may not have (Deut. 2). In the Promised Land, the Israelites encounter giants, sometimes read as tyrants and "mighty men."

To stop my passage to the Promised Land),
I gin to faint, and to repine also,
Against the power of Thy most mighty hand,
For which the Serpent Satan now doth stand
In readiness my silly soul to sting
And close me up in Death's eternal band,
Unless to me Thy mercy succor bring:
That brazen Serpent—Christ nailed on the tree—
Whose sight by faith alone is cure to me.[23]

SONNET 79 (WITH ISRAELITE SLAVES)

In bondage long to Satan have I been
A maker of the brick of Babel tower,
By birth a thrall to gross and filthy sin,
Whom lust's taskmasters do attend each hour.
Affection to the flesh doth clean deflower
The memory and love of promised lands:
The fiend (even Pharaoh) seeketh to devour
My soul and chain me to his dreadful bands.
But Lord receive me safe into Thy hands:
Protect me from the rigor of his might,
Quench thou the force of lust's inflamèd brands,
In my defense give me true faith to fight.
Send Moses, Lord, with power of heav'nly sword,
And Aaron[24] to direct me by thy Word.

SONNET 83 (JUDITH AND HOLOFERNES)

This slender city, Lord, of strength behold,
Wherein I dwell: Bethulia,[25] my bower
Of flesh whereto sin lays a batt'ry bold
And seeks with sword and dearth my soul devour.

23. When the Israelites were dying from snakebites in the desert, Moses made a brazen serpent and put it on a pole so that the sight of it would cure those bitten by lesser serpents (Num. 21; see 2 Kings 18 for its necessary destruction by Hezekiah). In John 3:14, Jesus associates himself with Moses's serpent; the cross was often called a "tree."
24. The great Israelite priest, brother of Moses.
25. When the city of Bethulia was besieged by Holofernes, a young Israelite widow, Judith, visited his tent with seemingly seductive friendliness; while he slept, she beheaded him. Although calling the story noncanonical, Protestants read and admired it.

Suppress Thou hellish Holofernes's power,
Who prides himself in prey of children Thine.[26]
I have no trust in mountains, walls, nor tower;
For want of faith (true fountain) we shall pine.
Raise up this female courage heart of mine;
Strengthen my hand to reave[27] this monster's head;
Let me not taste deceitful folly's wine,
Nor be polluted with world's sinful bed,
But constantly by faith fight in defense
Of feeble flesh, and drive Thy enemies thence.

SONNET 87 (THE PARABLE OF THE TALENTS)[28]

The talent which Thou pleased'st, Lord, to give
To me Thy servant, that I should bestow,
Whilst in Thy service on the earth I live,
My diligent increase thereof to show,
I have abusèd Lord, too long, I know,
And fear Thy coming to be nigh at hand;
I see for breach of duty what I owe,
And of Thy judgments do in terror stand.
Thy grace hath left me in a foreign land,
Where inexpert of virtue I do stray;
I shall be thrown to Satan's thrallful band,
Void of Thy heavenly joy and bliss for aye,
Unless Thou help: for Thou dost use to give
Grace unto grace, and faith from faithless drive.

SONNET 93 (PHARAOH'S DREAM)

The dream which Thou to Pharaoh didst reveal
Thou in myself hast made me see indeed
The state, alas, of man's weak commonweal,
Whereas[29] affections of all sorts do feed.

26. In preying on God's children.
27. Cut off.
28. On the servants given talents (coins) to invest, see Matt. 25:14–30.
29. Where. Pharaoh dreams of seven fat and seven lean cattle, which Joseph correctly reads as seven years of plenty and then seven of dearth (Gen. 41).

The fruitful soil of grace some whiles did breed
Full fair effects in truth of heav'nly kind,
But many barren thoughts, alas, succeed
And threaten famine to a virtuous mind.
Store of such years as yet I fare behind,
Which, Lord, will starve the comforts of my faith,
Unless Thy mercy and Thy wisdom find
A storehouse to lay up what Scripture saith:
In hope of which Thy goodness, lo, I live,
Which of Thy grace, Lord, do Thou to me give.

PART 2. SONNET 41

O Perfect Sun, whereof this shadow[30] is
A slender light, though it some beauty show,
On whom Thy influence dost bestow,
Whose constant course still shines in endless bliss:
To scan Thy glory wit of man doth miss.
How far Thy mercy's beams abroad extend
Tongue cannot speak nor wit can comprehend,
And human frailty is bewrayed[31] in this;
The fire, air, water, earth they wholly bend,
The host of heaven and creatures below,
To pay their duty unto Thee they owe,
Which didst their being and their virtue send.
And I intend with them, in what I may,
To witness forth Thy laud and praise for aye.

TO THE RIGHT HONORABLE, THE COUNTESS OF PEMBROKE

Of all the nymphs of fruitful Britain's race,
Of all the troops in our Diana's[32] train,
You seem not least, the Muses' trophies' grace,
In whom true honor spotless doth remain.
Your name, your match, your virtues, honor gain;

---

30. That is, the visible material sun in the sky.
31. Shown, revealed.
32. Queen Elizabeth. The Countess is Mary Sidney.

But not the least, that pregnancy of sprite
Whereby you equal honor do attain
To that extinguished lamp of heav'nly light
Who now no doubt doth shine near angels bright:[33]
While you, fair star, make clear our darkened sky,
He heavens.[34] Earth's comfort you are and delight,
Whose (more than their mortal) gifts you do apply
To serve their Giver, and your guider's grace,
Whose share in this my work hath greater place.

To the Honorable Lady, The Lady Rich[35]

The perfect beauty which doth most reclaim
The purest thoughts from base and vain desire
Not seen nor levied is by common aim
Of eyes, whom coullers[36] use to set on fire;
The rare-seen beauty men on earth admire
Doth rather dazzle than content the sight,
For grace and wisdom soonest do retire
A wand'ring heart to feed on true delight;
Seldom all gifts do in one subject light,
But all are crowned with double honor then,
And shine the more, adorned with virtue bright,
But (with religion graced) adored of men.
These gifts of nature, since they meet with grace,
In you have power more than fair Venus' face.

33. Mary Sidney's brother, Philip, dead from his battle wounds in 1586.
34. While you brighten earth's sky he brightens the heavens.
35. Penelope Rich, sister of the Earl of Essex and the "Stella" of Philip Sidney's *Astrophil and Stella*.
36. Probably colliers; if so, Lock means that Lady Rich's eyes can ignite coals.

12

Elizabeth Melville Colville of Culross
(fl. 1603–1630)

Thomas Sackville *(1536–1608)*

Elizabeth Melville Colville of Culross Visits the Afterworld

Elizabeth Colville, (fl. 1603–1630), daughter of Sir James Melville of Halhill, Scotland, and wife of Lord John Colville, was a staunch Presbyterian, famed in her own time for her devout comportment at public prayers as well as for the composition reprinted below. Another poem by her, addressed to a fellow Presbyterian who had been imprisoned in 1605, was reprinted in David Laing's *Early Metrical Tales* (1826). *Ane Godlie Dreame, Compylit in Scottish Meter* (1603) was first printed by Robert Charteris in Scots under the initials M. M., probably for "Mistress Melville." The poem, in ottava rima, is a dream-vision, a genre congenial to a number of early seventeenth-century women. Despite the chronological gap we juxtapose it to passages from Thomas Sackville's long "Induction" to *The Mirror for Magistrates*, a more secular but analogous visit to a personification-filled world. In Colville's vivid Calvinist vision of Hell, reprinted at least seven times before 1700, a pilgrim narrates a guided tour of the afterworld. Colville at first calls the guide an angel but later reveals His true identity: "I am thy God for whom thou sighs so sore." We follow the Anglicized version of 1604: *A Godly Dream, Compiled by Eliz. Melville, Lady Culros Younger, at the Request of a Friend*, with a few readings from the 1620 edition. All editions before 1640 append "A Very Comfortable Song."

FROM *A GODLY DREAM*

Upon a day as I did mourn full sore
For sundry things wherewith my soul was grieved
My grief increasèd and grew more and more,
I comfort fled and could not be relieved.
With heaviness my heart was so mischieved[1]
I loathed my life, I could not eat nor drink
I might not speak, nor look to none that lived
But mused alone and divers things did think.

This wretched world did so molest[2] *my mind*
I thought upon this false and iron age
And how our hearts were so to vice inclined
That Satan seemed most fearfully to rage.
Nothing in earth my sorrow could assuage,
I felt my sin most strongly to increase:
I grieved the spirit that wont to be my pledge
My soul was plunged into most deep distress.

All merriness did aggravate my pain,
And earthly joys did still increase my woe.
In company I no wise could remain,
But fled resort[3] *and so alone did go.*
My silly[4] *soul was tossèd to and fro*
With sundry thoughts which troubled me full sore;
I pressed to pray, but sighs o'erset[5] *me so*
I could do naught but groan and say no more.

The twinkling[6] *tears abundantly ran down,*
My heart was eased when I had mourned my fill:
Then I began my lamentation,
And said, "O Lord, how long is it Thy will
That Thy poor saints shall be afflicted still?

1. Hurt, overwhelmed; the accent falls on the second syllable.
2. Annoy.
3. Company.
4. Simple.
5. Overwhelmed.
6. Glimmering.

Alas, how long shall subtle Satan rage?
Make haste, O Lord, Thy promise to fulfill
Make haste to end our painful pilgrimage.

"Thy silly saints are tossèd to and fro.
Awake, O Lord, why sleepest Thou so long?
We have no strength against our cruel foe,
In sighs and sobs now changèd is our song,
The world prevails, our enemies are strong,
The wicked rage, but we are poor and weak:
O show Thyself, with speed revenge our wrong,
Make short these days even for Thy chosens' sake.

"Lord Jesus come and save Thy own elect
For Satan seeks our simple souls to slay.
The wicked world doth strongly us infect,
Most monstrous sins increases day by day.
Our love grows cold, our zeal is worn away,
Our faith is failed and we are like to fall:
The lion roars to catch us for his prey,
Make haste, O Lord, before we perish all.

"These are the days that Thou so long foretold
Should come before this wretched world should end
Now vice abounds, and charity grows cold,
And even Thine own most strongly do offend.
The devil prevails; his forces he doth bend
If it could be to wreck Thy children dear.
But we are Thine, therefore some succor send,
Receive our souls, we weary wandering here.

"What can we do? We cloggèd[7] are with sin,
In filthy vice our senseless souls are drowned.
Though we resolve, we never can begin
To mend our lives, but sin doth still abound.
When wilt Thou come? When shall Thy trumpet sound?
When shall we see that great and glorious day?
O save us Lord, out of this pit profound,
And reave[8] us from this loathsome lump of clay." . . .

7. Encumbered; a "clog" was a weight attached to a prisoner.
8. Take, snatch.

[The narrator falls asleep, praying, "Lord Jesus, come," when an "angel bright" appears, saying, "Lift up thy heart, declare thy grief to me, / Perchance thy pain brings pleasure in the end."]

I sighed again and said, "Alas for woe,
My grief is great, I can it not declare.
Into this earth I wander to and fro,
A pilgrim poor, consumed with sighing sore.
My sins, alas, increases more and more,
I loath my life, I weary wand'ring here.
I long for heaven, my heritage is there,
I long to live with my Redeemer dear."

"Is this the cause?" said He, "Rise up anon
And follow me, and I shall be thy guide.
And from thy sighs leave off thy heavy moan,
Refrain from tears and cast thy care aside.
Trust in My strength, and in My word confide,[9]
And thou shalt have thy heavy heart's desire.
Rise up with speed, I may not long abide.
Great diligence this matter doth require."

My soul rejoiced to hear His words so sweet;
I lookèd up and saw His face most fair,
His countenance revived my weary spirit;
Incontinent[10] *I cast aside my care.*
With humble heart I prayed Him to declare
What was His name; He answered me again
"I am thy God for whom thou sigh'st so sore
I now am come, thy tears are not in vain.

"I am the way, I am the truth and life,
I am thy spouse that brings thee store of grace:
I am thy Lord that soon shall end thy strife,
I am thy love whom thou would'st fain embrace.
I am thy joy, I am thy rest and peace,
Rise up anon and follow after Me:
I shall thee lead unto thy dwelling place,
The land of rest thou longest so sore to see."

9. Have faith.
10. Immediately.

With joyful heart I thankèd Him again,
"Ready am I," said I, "and well content
To follow Thee, for here I live in pain.
O wretch unworth, my days are vainly spent.
Not one is just, but all are fiercely bent
To run to vice; I have no force to stand.
My sins increase, which makes me sore lament,
Make haste, O Lord, I long to see that land."

"Thy haste is great," He answered me again,
"Thou think'st thee there, thou art transported so.
That pleasant place must purchased be with pain,
The way is strait, and thou hast far to go.
Art thou content to wander to and fro,
Through great deserts, through water and through fire:
Through thorns and briars and many dangers mo?
What say'st thou now? Thy feeble flesh will tire."

"Alas," said I, "although my flesh be weak
My spirit is strong, and willing for to fly.
O leave me not but for Thy mercy's sake
Perform Thy word, or else for dole I die.
I fear no pain since I should walk with Thee,
The way is long, yet bring me through at last."
"Thou answerest Me, I am content," said He,
To be thy guide, but see thou grip Me fast."

Then up I rose and made no more delay,
My feeble arms about His neck I cast,
He went before and still did guide the way,
Though I was weak, my spirit did follow fast.
Through moss and mire, through ditches deep we passed,
Through pricking thorns, through water and through fire,
Through dreadful dens which made my heart aghast,
He bare me up when I began to tire.

Sometime we climbed on craggy mountains high,
And sometime stayed on ugly brayes[11] of sand:
They were so stay[12] that wonder was to see,

11. Dikes, shoals.
12. Steep, hard to negotiate.

But when I feared He held me by the hand.
Through thick and thin, through sea and eke[13] through land,
Through great deserts we wandered on our way.
When I was weak and had no strength to stand,
Yet with a look He did refresh me ay.

Through waters great we were compelled to wade,
Which was so deep that I was like to drown;
Sometimes I sank, but yet my gracious guide
Did draw me up half dead and in a swoon
In woods most wild, and far from any town,
We thrusted through, the briars together stack[14]
I was so weak, their strength did beat me down,
That I was forced for fear to flee aback.

"Courage," said He, "thou art midway and more;
Thou may not tire, nor turn aback again.
Hold fast thy grip, on Me cast all thy care,
Assay thy strength, thou shalt not fight in vain.
I told thee first that thou should'st suffer pain,
The nearer heaven the harder is the way:
Lift up thy heart and let thy hope remain,
Since I am guide thou shalt not go astray."

Forward we passed on narrow brigs of tree[15]
Over waters great that hideously did roar;
There lay below that fearful was to see
Most ugly beasts that gapèd to devour.
My head grew light and troubled wondrous sore,
My heart did fear, my feet began to slide.
But when I cried, He heard me evermore
And held me up. O blessed be my guide!

Weary I was, and thought to sit at rest,
But He said, "No, thou may not sit nor stand.
Hold on thy course, and thou shalt find it best
If thou desirest to see that pleasant land."
Though I was weak, I rose at His command

13. Also.
14. Stuck together.
15. Bridges of wood.

And held Him fast. At length He let me see
That pleasant place that seemed to be at hand.
"Take courage now, for thou art near," said He.

I lookèd up unto that castle fair,
Glist'ring like gold and shining silver bright,
The stately towers did mount above the air,
They blinded me, they cast so great a light.
My heart was glad to see that joyful sight.
My voyage then I thought was not in vain.
I Him besought to guide me there aright,
With many vows never to tire again.

[The dreamer hurries ahead to the castle but fails to reach it; Jesus directs her to look down and see "another kind of way."]

I lookèd down and saw a pit most black,
Most full of smoke and flaming fire most fell.
That ugly sight made me to flee aback.
I feared to hear so many shout and yell.
I Him besought that He the truth would tell.
"Is this," said I, "the Papists' purging place[16]
Where they affirm that seely[17] *souls do dwell*
To purge their sin before they rest in peace?"

"The brain of man most warely[18] *did invent*
That purging place," He answered me again.
"For greediness together they consent
To say that souls in torments must remain,
While gold and goods relieve them of their pain.
O spiteful spirits that did the same begin;
O blinded beasts your thoughts are all in vain;
My blood alone doth cleanse the soul from sin.

"This pit is Hell where through thou now must go,
There is the way that leads thee to thy land.
Now play the man, thou need'st not tremble so,
For I shall help and hold thee by the hand."
"Alas," said I, "I have no force to stand,

16. Purgatory, where Catholics say sinful souls are made fit for Heaven.
17. Not guilty enough for Hell.
18. Prudently (ironic).

For fear I faint to see that ugly sight.
How can I come amongst that baleful band
Oh help me now, I have no force nor might.

"Oft have I heard that he that enters here,
In this great gulf shall never come again."
"Courage," said He. "Have I not bought thee dear?
My precious blood it was not shed in vain.
I saw this place, My soul did taste this pain,
Ere ever I went into My Father's glore.[19]
Through must thou go, but thou shalt not remain,
Thou need'st not fear for I shall go before."

"I am content to do Thy whole command,"
Said I again, and did Him fast embrace.
Then lovingly He held me by the hand,
And in we went into that fearful place.
"Hold fast thy grip," said He, "in any case,
Let me not slip[20] *whatever thou shalt see;*
Dread not the death but stoutly forward press,
For death nor Hell shall never vanquish thee."

His words so sweet did cheer my heavy heart,
Incontinent I cast my care aside.
"Courage," said He. "Play not a coward's part,
Though thou be weak, yet in My strength confide."
I thought me blest to have so good a guide;
Though I was weak I knew that He was strong:
Under His wings I thought me for to hide,
If any there should press to do me wrong.

Into that pit when I did enter in,
I saw a sight which made my heart aghast:
Poor damnèd souls tormented sore for sin,
In flaming fire were frying wonder fast,
And ugly spirits. And as I thought them past
My heart grew faint, and I began to tire.
Ere I was ware[21] *one grippèd me at last,*
And held me high above a flaming fire.

19. Glory.
20. Get away, let go.
21. On guard.

The fire was great, the heat did pierce me sore,
My faith grew weak, my grip was wondrous small.
I trembled fast, my fear grew more and more,
My hands did shake that I Him held withal.
At length they loosed, then I began to fall
And cried aloud, and caught Him fast again,
"Lord Jesus come and rid me out of thrall."
"Courage," said He. "Now thou art past the pain."

With this great fear I started and awoke,
Crying aloud, "Lord Jesus come again."
But after this no kind of rest I took;
I pressed to sleep, but it was all in vain.
I would have dreamed of pleasure after pain,
Because I know I shall it find at last.
God grant my guide may still with me remain:
It is to come what I believed was past.

This is a dream, and yet I thought it best
To write the same and keep it still in mind
Because I knew there was no earthly rest
Prepared for us that hath our hearts inclined
To seek the Lord. We must be purged and fined.[22]
Our dross is great, the fire must try us sore,
But yet our God is merciful and kind,
He shall remain and help us evermore.

The way to Heaven I see is wondrous hard.
My dream declares that we have far to go.
We must be stout, for cowards are debarred,
Our flesh of force must suffer pain and woe,
These dreary ways and many dangers mo
Awaits for us, we can not live in rest;
But let us learn since we are warnèd so
To cleave to Christ, for He can help us best.

O seely souls with pains so sore oppressed,
That love the Lord and long for heaven so high:
Change not your minds, for ye have chosen the best
Prepare yourselves, for troubled must ye be.

22. Refined.

Faint not for fear in your adversity.
It is the way that leads you unto life,
Suffer a while and ye shall shortly see
The land of rest when ended is your strife.

In wilderness ye must be tried awhile,
Yet forward press and never flee aback:
Like pilgrims poor and strangers in exile
Through fair and foul your journey ye must take.
The devil, the world, and all that they can make,
Will send their force to stop you in the way.
Your flesh will faint and sometime will grow slack,
Yet come to Christ and He shall help you ay.

The thorny cares of this deceitful life
Will rend your heart and make your soul to bleed.
Your flesh and spirit will be at deadly strife,
Your cruel foe will hold you still in dread
And throw you down. Yet rise again with speed;
And though ye fall, yet lie not loitering still,
But call on Christ to help you in your need,
Who will not fail His promise to fulfill.

In floods of woe when we are like to drown
Yet climb to Christ and grasp Him wonder fast,
And though ye sink and in the deep fall down
Yet cry aloud and He will hear at last.
Dread not the death, nor be not sore aghast
Though all the earth against you should conspire.
Christ is your guide, and when your pain is past
Ye shall have joy above your heart's desire.

Though in this earth ye shall exalted be,
Fear shall be left to humble you withal.
For if ye climb on tops of mountains high,
The higher up the nearer is your fall.
Your honey sweet shall mixèd be with gall,
Your short delight shall end with pain and grief.
Yet trust in God, for His assistance call,
And He shall help and send you soon relief.

Though waters great do compass you about,
Though tyrants threat, though lions rage and roar,
Defy them all and fear not to win out,
Your guide is near to help you evermore.
Though pricks of iron do prick you wondrous sore,
As noisome lusts that seek your soul to slay
Yet cry on Christ and He shall go before,
The nearer heaven, the harder is the way.

[The narrator continues her exhortation to persevere, call on God, be humble even if "ye seem to fly / With golden wings above the firmament," keep hoping, and trust Christ.]

The joy of heaven is worth one moment's pain;
Take courage then, lift up your hearts on high.
To judge the earth when Christ shall come again
Above the clouds ye shall exalted be.
A crown of joy and true felicity
Awaits for you when finished is your fight;
Suffer awhile and ye shall shortly see
A glore most great and infinite of weight.

Prepare yourselves, be valiant men of war,
And thrust with force out through the narrow way.
Hold on your course and shrink not back for fear.
Christ is your guide, ye shall not go astray.
The time is near; be sober, watch, and pray.
He sees your tears, and He hath laid in store
A rich reward which in that joyful day
Ye shall receive and reign forever more.

Now to the King that create all of naught,
The Lord of Lords that rules both land and sea,
That saved our souls, and with His blood us bought,
And vanquished death triumphing on the tree,[23]
Unto the great and glorious Trinity
That saves the poor and doth His own defend,
Be laud and glore, honor and majesty,
Power and praise, Amen, world without end.

23. The cross.

Thomas Sackville Visits Hades

The Elizabethan statesman and diplomat, Sir Thomas Sackville (1536–1608), first earl of Dorset and baron Buckhurst, coauthored the political drama *Gorboduc* and contributed to the hugely popular *Mirror for Magistrates* compiled by William Baldwin. This set of verse complaints, supposedly said by the ghosts of dead celebrities destroyed by fortune, fate, folly, or divine justice, appeared in 1559 and was enlarged as new editions followed. We excerpt Sackville's "Induction" to the complaint spoken by Henry, duke of Buckingham, friend and victim of Richard III. The narrator tells how one evening, in the sterility of late autumn under the melancholy planet Saturn, he meets Sorrow. Sorrow takes him on a tour of the underworld (which Baldwin's prose comment prudently identifies as a literary fiction, not Purgatory) to meet historical figures and allegorical personifications. We modernize the text in Lily B. Campbell's edition of the *Mirror* (Cambridge: Cambridge University Press, 1938).

FROM SACKVILLE'S *INDUCTION*

A hideous hole all vast, withouten shape,
Of endless depth, o'erwhelmed with ragged stone,
With ugly mouth and grisly jaws doth gape,
And to our sight confounds itself in one.
Here entered we, and yeding[1] *forth anon*
A horrible loathly lake we might discern
As black as pitch, that clepèd is Averne.[2]

A deadly gulf where naught but rubbish grows,
With foul black swelth[3] *in thickened lumps that lies,*
Which up the air such stinking vapors throws
That over there may fly no fowl but dies,
Choked with the pestilent savors that arise.
Hither we come, whence forth we still did pace,
In dreadful fear amid the dreadful place.

And first within the porch and jaws of Hell
Sat deep Remorse of Conscience, all besprent[4]
With tears: and to herself oft would she tell
Her wretchedness, and cursing never stent[5]

---

1. Going.
2. Is named Avernus (a river in Hades).
3. Usually a whirlpool, but used here to mean "foul troubled water" (*Oxford English Dictionary*).
4. Besprinkled.
5. Ceased.

> *To sob and sigh: but ever this lament*
> *With thoughtful care, as she that all in vain*
> *Would wear and waste continually in pain.*

[Sackville and Sorrow meet Dread, Revenge, Misery, Greedy Care, Heavy Sleep (who makes equal beggar and king), and now Old Age.]

> *Crookbacked he was, tooth-shaken and blear-eyed,*
> *Went on three feet, and sometimes crept on four;*[6]
> *With old lame bones that rattled by his side,*
> *His scalp all pilled*[7] *and he with eld forlore:*[8]
> *His withered fist still knocking at Death's door,*
> *Fumbling and driveling as he draws his breath;*
> *For brief: the shape and messenger of Death.*

[Next come Malady, Famine, Death, and War with a huge shield on which is painted "Deadly Debate, all full of snaky hair"; ancient warriors such as Alexander, Hannibal, Pompey, Caesar, and Xerxes; and ruined cities.]

> *But Troy alas methought above them all;*
> *It made mine eyes in very tears consume,*
> *When I beheld the woeful weird*[9] *befall*
> *That by the wrathful will of gods was come:*
> *And Jove's unmovèd sentence and foredoom*
> *Of Priam*[10] *king and on his town so bent.*
> *I could not lin,*[11] *but there I must lament.*

> *And that the more, since Destiny was so stern*
> *As force perforce there might no force avail*
> *But she*[12] *must fall: and by her fall we learn*
> *That cities, towers, wealth, world, and all shall quail.*[13]
> *No manhood, might, nor nothing might prevail,*
> *All were*[14] *there pressed full many a prince and peer*
> *And many a knight that sold his death full dear.*

---

6. Used a cane or crawled—Sackville's ironic version of the Sphinx's famous riddle: what goes on four legs in the morning, two at noon, and three in the evening? (The answer: a human being.) Old age is second babyhood.
7. Bald.
8. Utterly lost in old age.
9. Fate (unless Sackville's "werd" means a divine "word"). The Renaissance èlite was fascinated by Troy, partly because many European royal houses, including the Tudors, claimed Trojan descent.
10. The king of Troy.
11. Cease.
12. Troy.
13. Yield, be destroyed.
14. Even if.

Not worthy Hector,[15] *worthiest of them all,*
Her hope, her joy: his force is now for naught.
Oh Troy, Troy, there is no boot but bale.[16]
The hugie horse within thy walls is brought:[17]
Thy turrets fall, thy knights that whilome[18] *fought*
In arms amid the field are slain in bed,
Thy gods defiled, and all thy honor dead. . . .

Cassandra yet there saw I how they haled[19]
From Pallas' house[20] *with spercled*[21] *tress undone,*
Her wrists fast bound, and with Greeks' rout empaled:[22]
And Priam eke in vain how he did run
To arms, whom Pyrrhus[23] *with despite hath done*
To cruel death, and bathed him in the bane[24]
Of his sons' blood before the altar slain.
But how can I describe the doleful sight

That in the shield so lifelike fair did shine?
Since in this world I think was never wight[25]
Could have set forth the half, not half so fine.
I can no more but tell how there is seen
Fair Ilium[26] *fall in burning red gledes*[27] *down*
And from the soil great Troy, Neptunus' town.[28]

[Sackville and Sorrow come to the stinking river Acheron and meet Charon, Hades' ferryman who transports the shades of the departed to Hades, and Cerberus, Hades' three-headed watchdog. Charon welcomes them aboard and the two cross further into Hell.]

Thence come we to the horror and the Hell:
The large great kingdoms, and the dreadful reign

15. The great Trojan champion, killed by the Greek Achilles.
16. There is no remedy except grief.
17. The "Trojan horse" was filled with armed Greek soldiers who, once the huge hollow horse was inside Troy, emerged and captured the city.
18. Once, formerly.
19. Dragged.
20. The temple of Pallas Athena.
21. Disheveled (and possibly bespattered, presumably with blood).
22. Walled in by a crowd of Greeks.
23. A Greek soldier.
24. Bath (from French "bain") and/or poisonous ruin or curse.
25. Person.
26. Troy.
27. Hot coals.
28. Troy was dedicated to Neptune (Poseidon), god of the sea.

Of Pluto[29] *in his throne where he did dwell,*
The wide waste places, and the hugie plain,
The wailings, shrieks, and sundry sorts of pain,
The sighs, the sobs, the deep and deadly groan,
Earth, air, and all resounding plaint and moan.

    Here puled[30] *the babes, and here the maids unwed*
With folded hands their sorry chance bewailed;
Here wept the guiltless slain and lovers dead
That slew themselves when nothing else availed;
A thousand sorts of sorrows here that wailed
With sighs and tears, sobs, shrieks, and all yfere,[31]
That, oh alas, it was a Hell to hear. . . .

    "Lo here," quoth Sorrow, "princes of renown
That whilome sat on top of Fortune's wheel
Now laid full low like wretches whirlèd[32] *down,*
Even with one frown that stayed but with a smile.[33]
And now behold the thing that thou erewhile
Saw only in thought, and what thou now shalt hear
Recount the same to Caesar, king, and peer."

[The duke of Buckingham, now enters to make his "complaint."]

---

29. God of the underworld. He kidnapped Ceres' daughter Proserpina, who must stay with him in Hades half of each year.
30. Whimpered, cried.
31. Together.
32. Sackville's "whurled" combines "whirled" (by a rotating wheel) and "hurled," thown.
33. Presumably the frown and smile are Fortune's.

13

A Medley of Christian Religious Poetry

The religious underpinnings of early modern English life occasioned the bulk of the period's writing. Despite the efforts of successive English monarchs to enforce the religious settlement initiated by Henry VIII, the break with Rome left some subjects part of an embattled Catholic minority and others divided in belief among proliferating Protestant sects. These divisions eventually led to a self-imposed exile by many recusants (as Catholics came to be called) and to an acrimony among the sects that fed the growth of British colonies and erupted in civil war in the mid-seventeenth century. Women were active players in the Protestant camp and an important glue in the recusant community. We print here poems by two Protestant women: Anne Collins, who remained in Britain, and Anne Bradstreet, who emigrated, and two recusants: Gertrude Aston Thimelby, who spent her married life in England and then professed abroad, and Gertrude More, who in 1623 cofounded and entered a Benedictine convent at Cambrai, now part of northern France but then Flemish. To these we add poems by two Protestant men, Henry Coleman and John Collop, and the recusant Henry Constable.

Anne Collins on Strife

Occasional self-references in *Divine Songs and Meditations Composed by An[ne] Collins* (1653), a slender volume of deeply religious verses that survives in only one exemplar, provide our few bits of information about Anne Collins (fl. 1653): she suffered chronic illness, was childless, had experienced despair, and was past her youth when the volume appeared. She was undoubtedly opposed to strife. Critics have placed her quite variously in the religious grid of mid-seventeenth-century England—as Puritan, as anti-Sectarian, as anti-Calvinist, even (less convincingly) as Catholic. It is certain from the verses themselves that Collins took no delight in secular composition but found spiritual refreshment in religious writing. Although she counsels withdrawal from the turmoil of her age, her poetry treats current matters; even poems on political broils, though, turn on their religious aspect. We use the 1653 edition and have consulted that by Sidney Gottlieb (Tempe: Medieval and Renaissance Texts and Studies 161, for the Renaissance English Text Society, 1996).

ANOTHER SONG

Time past we understood by story
The strength of sin a land to waste,
Now God to manifest his glory
The truth hereof did let us taste.[1]
For many years this land appears
Of useful things the nursery,
Refreshed and fenced with unity.

But that which crowned each other blessing
Was evidence of truth divine:
The word of grace such light expressing,
Which in some prudent hearts did shine,
Whose flame inclines those noble minds
To stop the course of profanation
And so make way for reformation.

But he that watcheth to devour[2]
This their intent did soon descry,
For which he straight improves his power
This worthy work to nullify.
With sophistry and tyranny
His agents he forthwith did fill
Who gladly execute his will.

And first they prove by elocution
And hellish logic to traduce
Those that would put in execution
Restraint of every known abuse.

1. An allusion to the recent civil wars.
2. Satan.

They separate and 'sturb the state
And would all order overthrow;
The better sort were chargèd so.

Such false reports did fill all places
Corrupting some of high degree,
To whom the highest title graces
From hearing slanders was not free;
Which scruple bred and put the head
With primest members so at bait[3]
Which did the body dislocate.

A lying spirit misinformed
The common people, who suppose
If things went on to be reformed
They should their ancient customs lose,
And be beside to courses tied
Which they nor yet their fathers knew,
And so be wrapped in fangles[4] new.

Great multitudes therefore were joined
To Satan's pliant instruments.
With Malice Ignorance combined
And both at Truth their fury vents.
First Piety as enemy
They persecute, oppose, revile
Then friend as well as foe they spoil.[5]

The beauty of the land's abolished,
With faberics[6] by art contrived.
The many of them quite demolished,
And many of their homes deprived.
Some mourn for friends' untimely ends,
And some for necessaries faint[7]
With which they parted by constraint.

3. In conflict with.
4. Novelties.
5. Despoil. Pronounced "spile" in Collins's day.
6. Edifices.
7. Languish.

But from those storms hath God preserved
A people to record His praise.
Who, since they were therefore reserved,
Must to the height their spirits raise
To magnify His lenity [8]
Who safely brought them through the fire
To let them see their hearts' desire

Which many faithful ones deceased
With tears desirèd to behold:
Which is the light of truth professed
Without obscuring shadows old
(When spirits free not tied shall be
To frozen forms long since composed
When lesser knowledge was disclosed).

Who are preserved from foes outrageous,
Noting the Lord's unfound-out ways,
Should strive to leave to after ages
Some memorandums of His praise,
That others may admiring say:
Unsearchable His judgments are,
As do His works always declare.

Anne Dudley Bradstreet on Vanity

Born to moderately prosperous and highly literate Puritan parents—her father, himself a poet, was steward for the earl of Lincoln—young Anne Bradstreet (1613–1672) had access to the libraries of her father and the earl and was well educated. From her teen years, like her father and her sister, Mercy, she composed verses. In 1630, after her marriage to Simon Bradstreet, steward of the countess of Warwick, she emigrated to New England with her husband and parents. There she was at the center of colonial society: her father served as governor of Massachusetts and, after her death, so did her husband. Despite increasing illness, Bradstreet raised eight children while, with the approval of her family, continuing to compose poetry. In 1650 an uncorrected manuscript of her poems was brought to London by her brother-in-law, John Woodbridge, and published as *The Tenth Muse, Lately Sprung up in America*; it established Bradstreet as the first American poet. A corrected and augmented posthumous edition, *Several Poems Compiled with Great Variety of Wit*, appeared in 1678. The

8. Mildness.

poems include commentaries on history and politics, lyrics expressing love for her family, and deservedly well-known religious poems. For our text we rely on *Early New England Meditative Poetry: Anne Bradstreet and Edward Taylor*, ed. Charles E. Hambrick-Stowe (Mahwah: Paulist Press, 1989).

The Vanity of All Worldly Things[9]

As he said vanity, so vain say I;
Oh! vanity, O vain all under sky.
Where is the man can say, "Lo I have found
On brittle earth a consolation sound?"
What, is't in honor to be set on high?
No, they like beasts and sons of man shall die.
And whilst they live, how oft doth turn their fate?
He's now a captive that was king of late!
What, is't in wealth great treasures to obtain?
No, that's but labor, anxious care, and pain.
He heaps up riches, and he heaps up sorrow;
It's his today, but who's his heir tomorrow?
What then? Content in pleasures canst thou find?
More vain than all, that's but to grasp the wind.
The sensual senses for a time they please,
Meanwhile the conscience' rage who shall appease?
What, is't in beauty? No, that's but a snare;
They're foul enough today that once were fair.
What, is't in flowering youth, or manly age?
The first is prone to vice, the last to rage.
Where is it then? In wisdom, learning, arts?
Sure, if on earth, it must be in those parts.
Yet these the wisest man of men did find
But vanity, vexation of mind;
And he that knows the most doth still bemoan
He knows not all that here is to be known.
What is it then? To do as Stoics[10] tell:
Nor laugh, nor weep, let things go ill or well?
Such Stoics are but stocks,[11] such teaching vain:

9. Cf. Eccles. 1:1: "Vanity of vanities, all is vanity."
10. An ancient school of philosophy emphasizing duty and wisdom's mastery of desire and pain. The "wisest man" several lines earlier is Solomon.
11. Senseless persons; literally, tree trunks and stumps.

While man is man he shall have ease or pain.
If not in honor, beauty, age, nor treasure,
Nor yet in learning, wisdom, youth, nor pleasure,
Where shall I climb, sound, seek, search, or find
That Summum Bonum[12] *which may stay my mind?*
There is a path no vulture's eye hath seen,
Where lion fierce, nor lion's whelps have been,
Which leads unto that living crystal fount:
Who drinks thereof the world doth naught account.
The depth and sea have said 'tis not in me,
With pearl and gold it shall not valued be.
For sapphire, onyx, topaz who would change?
It's hid from eyes of men; they count it strange.
Death and destruction the same hath heard,
But where and what it is from heaven's declared.
It brings to honor which shall ne'er decay;
It stores with wealth which time can't wear away.
It yieldeth pleasures far beyond conceit,
And truly beautifies without deceit.
Nor strength, nor wisdom, nor fresh youth shall fade,
Nor death shall see, but are immortal made.
This pearl of price, this tree of life, this spring:
Who is possessed of—shall reign a king,
Nor change of state, nor cares shall ever see,
But wear his crown unto eternity.
This satiates the soul, this stays the mind.
And all the rest, but vanity we find.

Dame Gertrude More on Sanctity

The great-great granddaughter of Sir Thomas More was born Helen More (1601?–1633) at Leyton, near London, but left England in 1623 to found, with eight other women, the Benedictine convent at Cambrai in what is now northern France. Eventually she found a sympathetic confessor in Dom Augustine Baker, who published her anthologies posthumously: *The Holy Practices* (1657) includes works by Baker and others; *The Spiritual Exercises* (1658), on which we base our text, includes More's description of life in a convent. On More see also Dorothy Latz, *Glow-Worm Light* (Salzburg: Universität Salzburg, 1989) and *Neglected English Literature: Recusant Writings of the Sixteenth and Seventeenth Centuries* (Salzburg: Universität Salzburg, 1997).

12. Chief good.

"O GLORIOUS SAINT WHOSE HEART DID BURN"[13]

O glorious saint whose heart did burn
And flame with love divine,
Remember me, most sinful wretch,
Who hunger-starved doth pine
For want of that which thou enjoyst
In such abundant measure,
It is my God that I do mean,
My joy and all my treasure.
Thy words, O Saint, are truly sweet
Because thou dost address
Them unto Him Who's only meet
Our miseries to redress.

TO OUR BLESSED LADY THE ADVOCATE OF SINNERS[14]

All hail, O Virgin, crowned with stars,
*   and moon under thy feet,*
Obtain us pardon of our sins
*   of Christ our Saviour sweet.*
For though thou art mother of my God,
*   yet thy humility*
Disdaineth not this simple wretch
*   that flies for help to thee.*
Thou knowest thou art more dear to me
*   than any can express*
And that I do congratulate
*   with joy thy happiness;*
Who art the Queen of heaven and earth
*   thy helping hand me lend,*
That I may love and praise my God,
*   and have a happy end.*
And though my sins me terrify
*   yet hoping still in thee*

13. St. Augustine, fifth-century bishop, theologian, and author of *Confessions*. More's untitled poem, addressed to "my beloved S. Augustine," is from "The Second Confession" of *Spiritual Exercises*.
14. From *Spiritual Exercises*.

I find my soul refreshèd much
  when I unto thee fly.
For thou most willingly to God
  petitions dost present
And dost obtain much grace for us
  in this our banishment.
The honor and the glorious praise
  by all be given to thee
Which Jesus, thy beloved Son,
  ordained eternally.
For thee whom He exalts in heaven
  above the angels all
And whom we find a patroness
  when unto thee we call.
      Amen.
O Mater Dei
Memento Mei[15]

ON SIR THOMAS MORE[16]

Renownèd More, whose bloody fate
England ne'er yet could expiate,
Such was thy constant faith, so much
Thy hope, thy charity was such,
As made thee twice a martyr prove:
Of faith in death, in life of love!
View here thy grandchild's broken heart,
Wounded with a seraphic dart,
Who while she lived mortals among
Thus to her Spouse divine she sung:
"Mirror of beauty in Whose face
The essence lives of every grace,
True luster dwells in thy sole sphere.
Those glimmerings that sometimes appear
In this dark vale, this gloomy night,
Are shadows tipped with glow-worm light.
Show me thy radiant parts above

15. O, Mother of God, remember me.
16. This untitled poem from *Spiritual Exercises* carries these words in the margin. Latz, who reprints the poem in *Glow Worm Light*, titles it "Magnes Amoris Amor" ("love the magnet of love"), after the caption beneath a portrait of Gertrude More on the facing page.

> *Where angels unconsumèd move,*
> *Where amorous fire maintains their lives,*
> *As man by breathing air survives.*
> *But if perchance the mortal eye*
> *That views thy dazzling looks must die,*
> *With blind faith here I'll kiss them and desire*
> *To feel the heat before I see the fire."*

Gertrude Aston Thimelby on Varieties of Love

Gertrude Aston (c. 1617–1668) spent time in Spain during the two embassies of her father, Sir Walter Aston. One short poem, "On Saint Catherine's Day," survives from her youth. Also extant are some witty, metaphysical poems written during the ten years of her marriage to Henry Thimelby (which took place c. 1645) celebrating family occasions and marital love. Henry Thimelby and their only child died in 1655, and in 1658 Gertrude Thimelby professed her Catholicism, joining her sister-in-law, Winefrid Thimelby, in St. Monica's Convent at Louvain, in Belgium. The correspondence and poetry of the Aston-Thimelby-Fowler family circle were anthologized by Arthur Clifford as *Tixall Poetry* (1813) and *Tixall Letters* (1815), named for the Aston family seat. We base our selections on his entries in *Tixall Poetry*.

ON SAINT CATHERINE'S DAY[17]

> *You glorious saint, though born of royal blood,*
> *All greatness scorned but that of being good.*
> *Though learned in many knowledges, were still,*
> *Best knowing and most practicing God's will.*
> *And though more fair than is the rosy morn,*
> *The charms of virtue did you most adorn.*
> *Pray I not great, not wise, not fair may seem*
> *In the world's false, but in heaven's just, esteem.*

NO LOVE LIKE THAT OF THE SOUL

> *Some forward[18] heretics in Love there be,*
> *Willful abusers of his deity;*

---

17. Either November 25, feast day of Catherine of Alexandria (fourth century), or September 15, feast day of Catherine of Genoa (1447–1510).
18. Perverse, refractory.

Whose weak opinions, and whose feverish flame,
Pretend his right but do abuse his name.
Such are the idle likers of a face,
Who leave the soul for the fantastic case,
Which, though today like some bright shrine of art
Th'amazèd gazers bend to, Death's cold dart
May ere tomorrow so deform: dismayed
The adorer stands, of what he loved afraid.
Ah, then who would this busy nothing prize:
No sooner liked but vanished from our eyes!
Yet this unlucky passion is renewed
As oft as some fair and new prospect's viewed.
How falsely these usurp a lover's name,
Who merit, rather, what the abused dame
Gave the unconstant Pamphilus: new smart
For every change of his removing heart.[19]
And is not theirs like his vain exercise
Who lost his misspent time in killing flies?
Since the pursuit of beauty nothing gains,
When the reward is never worth the pains.
'Tis only they with justice may pretend
A lasting joy, whose love can know no end.
These are the wise admirers of the soul,
And these Fame only Lovers does enroll;
Nor heat nor cold they feel, no change of state,
Who all their thoughts to this do consecrate.
For as that is forever, so their flame:
The object one, the passion is the same.
Then choose, frail mortals, which you'd rather be:
Joyed for a while, or pleased eternally.

Henry Colman on the Divine Marriage

Little is known about Henry Colman (fl. 1640) except that he probably attended Cambridge, had Yorkshire connections, and remained loyal to king and church. His poetry, which shows the impact of the Anglican liturgy and the manner of George Herbert and other "metaphysical" poets, exists in two manuscripts dated 1640, one now in Oxford's Bodleian Library and the other, somewhat longer, at the Beineke Library at Yale University. We base our selections on transcriptions in Colman's *Divine Meditations (1640)*, ed. Karen E. Steanson (New Haven: Yale University Press, 1978)

19. Cf. the torture of Pamphilus in Sidney's *Arcadia*, Book 2.

ON MARRIAGE [20]

Marriage is that sacred tie
That joins two loving hearts in one,
Nor can love be parted ever,
Though bodies far asunder lie,
Firm affections' strength alone
Is such as death could conquer never,
For death can only part the clay,
So takes but the worst half away.

But divine love's mansion is
Seated in the starry heav'n
And admits of no mutation;
Its pure eyrie [21] *soars to bliss,*
And by God alone was giv'n
To inhabit that blessed station.
Who saith he loves and changes seat,
His flame's but an adulterate heat.

Such hearts then as are joined by love
Are first in heaven marrièd;
In vain do mortals then deny
To such the marriage bed to prove
Or hope they can be varièd
From th'old and new affection try:
For whom God once hath joined in heart
Let sinful mortals fear to part.

Marriage hath ever been esteemed
An honored tie, and chiefly such
Whose chaster virgin beds ne'er knew
But one live love, and dead him deemed
Worthy alone t'be loved so much
That they would ne'er admit a new;

---

20. For Christians, Christ is the bridegroom of the Church as the body of all believers, a marriage allegorized for them by the Song of Songs and Jesus' parable of the wise and foolish virgins (Matt. 25). Christ can also "marry" an individual soul.
21. Nesting place of eagles and hawks.

And happy is that marriage bed
Where both are truly marrièd.

Happy, indeed, but far more blessed
Is that rich soul whose love is placed
Upon the God of Love, and He
Is pleased to marry to His rest
Where in heaven it shall be graced
With honor to eternity:
This indeed's the happiest bride
That ever sat her Spouse beside.

And thus th'Almighty's pleased to wed:
Whenas the soul unto Him sues
With fervent love He ne'er denies,
But straight she shall be marrièd;
God will not coy it, nor refuse
The loving soul that to Him flies.
O sacred rite, O honored life:
Since God is pleased to take a wife.

And art Thou pleased to fall in love
With that sick soul that seeks to Thee
In fervent love and earnestness?
Grant then mine may truly move,
And to th'Lamb may married be
In perpetual happiness:
He who's thus sped and wed shall ne'er
Need a separation fear.

John Collop on the Spirit's Struggles

Doctor John Collop (1625–after 1676) was a royalist and moderate Anglican from
Bedfordshire who studied at Cambridge and admired the great scientist William
Harvey. Many poems in his *Poesis Rediviva or Poesy Revived* (1656) and *Itur Satyricum*
(1660) are satirical (such as some witty if disturbing verses in praise of an ugly mistress); others, from which we select three, are devout in a style that, like Colman's,
recalls Herbert. We base our texts on *The Poems of John Collop*, ed. Conrad Hilberry
(Madison: University of Wisconsin Press, 1962).

Vox Penitentiae [22]

I, I, ah, I thee, Lord, betrayed!
While sin strange insurrections made;
I, I, like him with lips durst kiss,
Who sought out's [23] Hell at gates of bliss.
My sins, ah, scourges, buffets are;
My sins, ah, thorns, Thy temples tear.
My sin presents the spear, nails, gall,
Renews Thy sweat, death, burial.
Yet while I, Lord, with Mary come
Early with spices to Thy tomb,
With balm of penance waiting there
To offer odors up in prayer,
After repentant show'rs of dew,
Angels my sun's arise shall show.
Hark, hark: Who's both the light and way
Calls thee, my soul: make haste, obey.
Ah, loads of sin and flesh! can I,
A camel, pass a needle's eye? [24]
Say, oh say not that Heaven gate
Too narrow is, or way too strait! [25]
Faith and good works can dispossess
Thee both thy loads of sin and flesh;
And so conveyed on wings of prayer
Thou mayst like incense enter there.
So shalt thou find a way not strait: [26]
He kneels who enters at Heaven gate.

22. That is, "The Voice of Penitence."
23. "Out his." Collop means the kiss Judas gave Jesus as he betrayed him. The next lines recall Jesus' passion and resurrection.
24. Cf. Matt. 19: "it is easier for a camel to go through a needle's eye than for a rich man to enter Heaven."
25. Matt. 7:14: "strait is the gate, and narrow is the way, which leadeth unto life, and few there be that find it."
26. A pun on "strait" (narrow) and "straight" (unbent).

ON POVERTY

What art thou, Poverty, thou so much art fled,
Christ spoused [27] thee living, us bequeathed thee dead:
Ambition never tenters thee on racks; [28]
No vulture gnaws thy heart, plot thy brain cracks;
No emulous [29] rival hast, no hollow friend;
Dost in the place thou'rt born securely end:
By healthful hunger sauced, meats happy be;
No table made a snare by gluttony;
By neighb'ring floods sav'st charges of excise;
Drink which the wise makes fools, can make thee wise!
No dropsies fear'st, no gout, nor no catarrh;
Palate with body ne'er commences war;
Thy body and thy conscience both are clear;
Hast nothing here to hope, or ought to fear;
No man to cut this shrub down his ax whets,
Nor a self-wounding conscience by regrets.
While others, sport of winds, hoist into th'deep,
Along the shore he doth securely keep.
The ostrich's body hindereth her wings,
While such a lark mounts up with ease and sings.
Who desires little, he thinks little much;
Such as desires are, ev'n our riches such.
What dead thou canst enjoy, alive despise.
Who sets his heart on others' goods, not wise.
For this, ah this, princes changed crowns for cells;
He's crowned with joy with whom contentment dwells.

SPIRIT, FLESH

Soul: Arise, make haste.
Flesh: Whither? Ah, whither flies my soul so fast?
Soul: Heav'n calls, obey.
Flesh: 'Tis night; Ah stay! 'Tis night! Thou'lt lose thy way;

---

27. Married.
28. Uses tenterhooks to torture you on the rack.
29. Enviously competitive.

Soul: The day springs rose.
Flesh: Ah, but thy sin black clouds doth interpose!
Soul: Those penance clears;
The sun succeeds a sacred dew of tears:
See a full shower!
Heav'n suffers violence by a holy power.
Flesh: Ah, Heav'n is high!
Soul: Prayer lends a Jacob's ladder to the sky.[30]
Angels descend,
Flesh: Wrestle, ah, wrestle! Blessing crowns the end.

Henry Constable Turns to a Catholic Piety

Born in Yorkshire, Henry Constable (1562–1613) studied at Cambridge and the Inns of Court, served as a diplomat in the 1580s, and wrote love sonnets in the elegant French style. With friends at court, including Sir Francis Walsingham, he had a successful career, but around 1590 he became a Catholic and left England. On a visit home he found himself briefly in the Tower and spent some years in poverty before returning abroad in 1610. His sonnet sequence, *Diana*, appeared in 1592, but his devout verses were unprinted in his lifetime. The intensity of their elaborate conceits anticipates the poetry of another Catholic convert, Richard Crashaw. We adapt the transcriptions from Harleian MS 7553 in *The Poems of Henry Constable*, ed. Joan Grundy (Liverpool: Liverpool University Press, 1960).

TO THE BLESSED SACRAMENT[31]

When Thee, O holy sacrificèd Lamb,
In severed signs I white and liquid see:[32]
As on Thy body slain I think on Thee,
Which pale by shedding of Thy blood became.
And when again I do behold the same
Veilèd in white to be received of me:[33]
Thou seemest in thy sindon[34] *wrapped to be,*
Like to a corpse whose monument I am.

---

30. Jacob wrestled with an angel and dreamed of a ladder to Heaven on which angels passed up and down (Gen. 28).
31. The bread and wine of Communion, which Catholics believe are transformed during the Mass into Christ's body and blood in a re-enactment of Jesus' sacrifice.
32. "Severed" because two "signs": white bread and red wine.
33. As bread consumed by the communicant.
34. Burial shroud.

Buried in me, unto my soul appear,
  Prisoned in earth and banished from Thy sight,
  Like our forefathers who in Limbo were.[35]
Clear Thou my thoughts, as Thou did'st give the light:
  And as Thou others freed from purging fire,
  Quench in my heart the flames of bad desire.

To Saint Margaret[36]

Fair Amazon of Heaven, who took'st in hand
  St. Michael and St. George to imitate,[37]
  And for a tyrant's love transformed to hate
  Wast for thy lily faith retained in band.[38]
Alone on foot, and with thy naked hand,
  Thou did'st like Michael and his host, and that
  For which on horse armed George we celebrate,
  Whilst thou like them a dragon did'st withstand.
Behold my soul shut in my body's jail,
  The which the drake[39] of Hell gapes to devour:
  Teach me, O virgin, how thou did'st prevail.
Virginity, thou say'st, was all thy aid:
  Give me then purity instead of power,
  And let my soul, made chaste, pass for a maid.

35. As the dead Christ descended to Hell and rescued the good Israelites (the "harrowing of Hell"), so he can enter Constable's body and illuminate that inner prison. Souls in Limbo suffer only from lacking the sight of God.
36. When Margaret was jailed by the Roman governor of Antioch for rejecting his advances, the devil came to her disguised as a dragon. Unfooled, she fought and defeated him.
37. The archangel Michael and England's patron saint, George, both defeated evil dragons.
38. Imprisoned.
39. Dragon.

14

Jane Ward Lead *(1624–1704)*

John Milton *(1608–1674)*

Jane Ward Lead Celebrates Holy Wisdom

Following an early experience of revelation, Jane Ward of Norfolk (1624–1704) lived a relatively conventional married life for more than twenty-five years. As a widow, however, she experienced a vision of a female figure, Sophia, and began a life of "spiritual virginity." A follower of Jacob Boehme, the German mystic and writer, she entered the household of John Pordage, leader of a nonconformist congregation, in 1674. After the death of Pordage, she published more than twenty tracts. With Dr. Francis Lee, a follower who was to become her son-in-law, she established the Philadelphian Society, a group based on Boehme's principles. Many of Lead's mystical visions center on a female figure. Such a figure, Sophia (Holy Wisdom), appears in "Solomon's Porch, or the Beautiful Gate to Wisdom's Temple," the long prefatory poem to her *Fountain of Gardens* (1697–1701). Our extract is based on the 1697 edition.

FROM "SOLOMON'S PORCH"

> *Arise, ye lovers true;*
> *Arise, arise, ye wondrous few;*
> *Apparitors[1] divine, ordained, fore-sent*

---

1. Public servants.

Heaven's beauteous virgin queen[2]
    To attend and usher in.
The mother to adore, the bride to compliment,
    Blest virgin, mother, bride in one:
Thrice sacred band of love, and mystic union!
    Arise, arise, ye wondrous few,
        Arise, ye lovers true.

Long in inglorious ease obscured ye lie,
Despised, neglected, yet neglecting too,
Nor caring what the impious, trifling world
        Could either say or do.
O'erlooked by man, yet loved and favored high
In heaven's regard and God's auspicious eye—
Whom neither high preferment's charm can move,
Ambition fire, or beauty prompt to love—
        And yet to love most true.
Out of the everlasting virgin's womb,
Sons of the morn already born anew,
        Born into time,
And winged at will to ascend the ethereal clime.[3]
Angelic men, embodied seraphim,[4]
All captives to the blest Sophia's charms;
        Through wisdom's mazes bright,
        Wand'ring in tracks of light,
By her still guided and exempt from harms.
        Still kept
From mazy error's tangling step
        From paths untrue
By her fair, silver-twined, mercurial clue:[5]
Dear captives to the bright Sophia's charms.
        And yet more loudly to proclaim
        Transcendent love's and beauty's fame,
Long wrapped in the divine Urania's[6] arms:
Wrapped in the dear, divine Urania's arms,
Plund'ring her sweets, and rifling all her charms.

2. Almost certainly Sophia, not the Virgin Mary.
3. Region.
4. Six-winged angels that hover over God's throne (Isa. 6:2).
5. Possibly Mercury's caduceus or winged staff.
6. Muse of astronomy, who became the often invoked muse of "divine poetry," especially that based on the Bible. At times she merges with the Holy Spirit: cf. Milton's invocation in *Paradise Lost*.

Ye wondrous few, arise.
God's herald true, throw off your mortal guise.
Now lift your sweet, loud, speaking, trumpets high.
Now let your jocund levets[7] fill the sky.
Tell, tell the drowsy world their God is nigh.

Now let eternal song unbounded flow
With torrent deep, serene, majestic, slow
          Disdaining art's control.
     Like heaven's full-spangled canopy,
          Most nice and yet most free
Ranged by Dame Nature's artful liberty.
     Let every point[8] a star, each line
          In constellation shine;
               Each living word a soul:
          In thousand differing ways,
          Varying to God new praise.
Now, now let your inspired seraphic strains
          In mighty numbers roll.

Proclaim, proclaim the gracious jubilee,[9]
     And set the sin-bound captives free.
Proclaim, proclaim the gracious jubilee.

O may through me the mighty trumpet sound,
And spread its fame the woods, and plains,
          The isles, and seas around.
     Let sportful echoes play
     And dancing all the way
Swell and intune the trembling sounds anew.
     All well-tuned voices raise
     To great Elchajah's praise,
Peace to all worlds, dear love to man, to God His honor due.

O may through me the mighty trumpet sound,
And spread His fame the woods, the hills, and plains,
          The isles, and seas around.

7. Mirthful trumpet calls.
8. Spot in space.
9. Year of celebration. Biblically, a year when the holy land rested and slaves were emancipated (Lev. 25:8–17).

And ye fair virgin-daughters *of the morn,*
Sion's *first blossoms, from new* Salem[10] *born,*
  High paradisial *nymphs appear,*
The virgin queen's *attendant graces dear:*
   Haste, haste away
And join your powers unanimous to proclaim
  The wondrous year.
The great, the good, the now-revolving day,
Full period-circle bright, of endless fame.
  Ye paradisial nymphs appear,
The *virgin queen's* attendant graces dear,
Sion's first blossoms, from new *Salem* born:
Rise ye fair *virgin daughters* of the morn.

  Arise and shine,
Illustrious troop of heroines *divine,*
Celestial Amazons, *untaught to yield,*
With heaven-aspiring ardors, sprightly vigor filled.
In this, the virgin's *day, most forward bent*
Zealous their very heroes to prevent[11]
In terrible, majestic, gay parade,
Hell's fierce embattled legions first t'invade.
  With orient beams of light,
  Scattering the misty gloom of night,
And chasing every black infernal shade.
  Arise and shine,
  Illustrious heroines,
Cherubic phalanx[12] *bright of Amazons divine,*
Arise, arise and shine.

Yet though deep-skilled in spirits' war-like arts,
Nature has framed, love armed ye too, too free
Far deeper wounds to give and nobler darts
To fix in pure and captivated hearts,
In whose high-tinctured forms harmonious move
The fiery, quick serpentine[13] *energy*
Charmed by the mildness of the peaceful dove,

---

10. Zion is one of Jerusalem's hills (2 Sam. 5:7); Salem is Jerusalem.
11. Precede.
12. A battleline of Cherubs.
13. Tortuous, winding.

Inviting still to love.
Contraries here agree
In strictest unity,
Each other to improve,
The fierce and powerful sting and lofty spire
Co-mingling to exalt *the amorous fire,*
You, at whose presence mortal beauty must
Abscond[14] *and in confusion kiss the dust.*
Beauties too flaming bright
To be endured by human sight,
Which but unveiled would quench the inferior, outward light,

The glances of whose eyes are lucid beams
In-drawn from the all-radiant one,
Divine, super-celestial *sun,*
Where his full streams,
Pointed in central union,
Himself *produce in lustrous image fair*
Of His beloved eternal son.
Hence darting every way
In each reflecting, subdivided ray.
The little loves entranced
With innocent and wanton dance,
Thousand enshrined, celestial Cupids *play,*

From whose coraline lip
Angels their spicy draughts of nectar *sip,*
Quick darting the divine love-flaming kiss
In free, enormous *bliss.*
In whose fair cheeks the tinctures[15] *pure combine,*
The matchless diamonds sparkle paler *bright,*
And in their orbs of light
Enchase[16] *the glittering rubies' sanguine*[17] *flame*
In radiant blush of modesty divine,
Exempt from mortal shame.
Here, re-aspiring from their humble vale
To meet the inclining, vigorous-scented male

14. Hide away.
15. Hues, colors.
16. Serve as a setting for.
17. Blood red.

In their dewy, fruitful bed,
Their Sharon rose[18] *the virgin lilies wed,*
    Whom, as with strict embrace enrapped,
    They lock within their flowery lap,
A stock of graces numberless proceed
    A spring of lesser beauties breed.

The clear, translucent forms all shade disdain
    Disclosing freely to be seen
    The wonder-world within:
Each argent[19] *nerve and every* azure *vein*
The beauteous love-eye *burning in the heart*
From whence love's centers endless multiply
As thick-set spangles of the sky
Raising a sting of joy in every part.
    In every point a Venus *bright,*
    Each star a world of new delight,
Opening an unexhausted spring of bliss.
    Each nymph herself a paradise,
So fine, so pliant the external mold
    That even therein the brighter soul
        With all its graces' train
    Imprints itself distinct and plain,
        And as in fabled streams
        Where silver currents roll
    On orient pearl and sands of gold
Displays her rich, inestimable gems
        Which free exposed to view
    In their untarnished, native hue,
    Reflex through bodies crystalline
    In their transparent mirror *shine,*
But deeper yet and more amazing fair
      Outshines, outflames through her
Express, the only *son's refulgent character.*
Now, now, ye paradisial nymphs appear;
The *virgin queen's* attendant graces dear.
    Arise, arise, and shine
    Illustrious brigade
    Of heroines divine;

18. Cf. The Song of Sol. 2:1; lines from this appear on Lead's title page.
19. Silver.

In terrible-majestic-gay parade.
    With orient beams of light
    Scatter the misty gloom of night,
And *banish* every black infernal shade.
    Arise and shine
    Illustrious Heroines,
Cherubic *phalanx* bright *of Amazons* divine,
    Arise, arise, and shine.

    Haste, haste away,
And let your well-trimmed flowing tresses fair,
Waving in wanton ringlets, gild the air
Out-beaming sun, bright with pellucid ray.
    And as they loosely move
    Fanned by fresh odorous gales of love,
With heaven's warm, gentle-breathing zephyrs [20] *play.*
    Haste to proclaim
The great, the good, the *now-revolving day:*
Amen, hosanna, hallelujah.

Haste to proclaim
The *period-circle* full of endless fame:
The great, the good, the *now-revolving* day.
For this we shout aloud, we sing, we pray:
Amen, amen, hosanna, hallelujah.
    Heroes fall back again.
    Lead up the virgin train.
And hand in hand, as love-paired twins, advance
    In sacred, well-paced mystic dance,
    Tracing on holy ground,
    Circling Jehovah's *altar round,*
Where ay [21] *love-incense burns, goodness and grace abound.*
    Whence living coals out-fly,
    Generate and multiply,
Seraphic ardors every way to impart
To each bright-flaming and love-melting heart.

The quick celestial fires
    Straight their sweet-warbling tongues inspire

---

20. Mild breezes; Zephyr is the west wind.
21. Ever.

While every voice and every trumpet sings:
Glory to the returning King of Kings.
Love's golden era now, now, now begins
Now, now in every breath, in every sound
    The universe around.
     Love's everlasting gospel *rings:*
Glory to the returning King of Kings.
Love's glorious era now, now, now begins.

Fresh springing still th'inspired harmonious vein
Tunes up to higher key and loftier strain,
    In more enchanting lays,
    Varying new hymns of praise,
Jointly th'ascending voice and soul to raise.
    Even till they both aspire,
    And join with the seraphic choir,
    And under God's bright eye
    In influence serene they lie
Dissolved in rapturous hallelujahs.

As that sweet little chorister[22] *that flies*
    And singing mounts the skies
    Till all his breath and song be spent,
Then down he falls in sweeter languishment,[23]
So do angelic souls in sounds aspire.
    They mount and sing
    Upon the dove's bright wing
That gently fans and feeds th'ethereal fire
All emulous[24] *to win the steep ascent.*
    The mighty mountains seven,
Those lily-decked and rosy-flow'ring hills
    Formed by th'all-bounteous hand of heaven,
Its darling sons with mere[25] *delight to fill*
    Till in melodious ravishment,
Their powers, their voice, their very soul be spent.
    The light
    Becomes too blazing bright.

22. A skylark, said to fly straight up at dawn.
23. Faintness.
24. Competing.
25. Pure.

        The bliss
      Unsufferable[26] *is.*
Then down with speed they take their humble flight,
In adoration deep, yet but retire
T'embrace more near and be exalted higher.
Now, love's last, sweetest, mystic death *to try,*
Rapt in sublime, ecstatic joys expire
      Entranced and silent *lie.*
Thus in soft languent[27] *slumbers sweet, true sleep,*
    That rests in God's abyssal deep,[28]
The rest in visionary dreams they see.
    They taste, they feel,
What is unknown, immense, unspeakable.

Proclaim, proclaim, the mighty *jubilee*
  That sets each world of captives free.
Proclaim, proclaim aloud the mighty *jubilee.*

O may through me the mighty trumpet sound,
      And spread its fame the woods, and hills, and plains,
    The isles, and seas around.
    Let sportful echoes play,
    And dancing all the way,
Swell and intune the trembling sounds anew.
    All well-tuned voices raise
    To great *ELCHAJAH's* praise:
Peace to all worlds, dear love to man, to God His honor due.
O may through me the mighty trumpet sound,
And spread His fame the woods, and isles, and seas,
    And heaven, and earth around.

  Too long, too long, the wretched world
Lies waste; in wild confusion hurled,
Unhinged in every part; each property
Struggling, disranged in fiercest enmity.
    The whole creation groans
    And laboring with perpetual toil
    In man's rebellion vile,

26. Insupportable.
27. Faint.
28. Ocean.

Her own hard fate bemoans.
But now shall Nature's jar
Cease her intestine[29] war.
Now shall the long six working days of strife
Attain their line[30] and to their crown arrive.
At last set free
In peaceful rest of Sabbath true
Heaven and earth created new;
To celebrate a universal jubilee.

Concord divine now meets in every part,
And love subdues and reigns in every heart.
O'er all,
In sum or individual,
Triumphant harmony, triumphant love,
In sweetest unity,
Combined, together move.
Even from the zenith high
Of the clear, boundless, empyrean[31] sky—
The throne of God—
Down to earth's inmost, central, deep abode,
All is consent and perfect amity,
All in proportion due,
In weight and number true,
Even from the zenith high,
Th'all radiant throne of God,
Down to earth's inmost, central, deep, abode
Nothing but love, but love and harmony,
Where every voice and every trumpet sings:
Glory to the eternal King of Kings.
Love's golden era now, now, now begins.
Now, now in every breath, in every sound
The universe around
Her everlasting gospel rings:
Glory to the returning King of Kings.
Love's glorious, golden era now, now, now begins.

29. Internal.
30. An allusion to the six ages, paralleling the six "days" of creation, before the millennium.
Perhaps "line" is a finish line.
31. Highest heaven.

Now harmless through the sky
Let the sweet, whisking,[32] treble lightnings fly.
Full base from shore to shore
Shall in deep thunders roar
Not death, not horror now, but melody.
Now, mighty bard,[33] sing out thy sonnet free,
Nor doubt it true shall be.
Come thou and join
Thy loud prophetic voice with mine.
Ring out ye crystal spheres,
Now bless our human ears,
For ye have *power to touch our senses so.*
Now shall *your silver chime*
Move in melodious time
And the deep *base of Heaven's great* orb *shall blow.*
From the bright zenith high
Of the clear, boundless, empyrean sky
From the all-radiant throne of God
Down to earth's inmost, central, deep abode—
Nothing but pure consent and unity.
All in proportion due,
In weight and number true,[34]
All universal love and harmony.

This globe terrene,[35] no longer turned askance,
Hitched in her poles shall now direct advance,
And through the liquid ether dance,
And on her axle spin,
In an harmonious round,
Breathing substantial, dense, embodied sound.
Then shall surcease the ungrateful din
Of jarring spheres and clashing orbs around,
While this wonder-machine,
Engine of harmony divine,
Shall through the echoing welkin[36] play.
And everywhere

32. Rapidly moving.
33. Milton (see our next selection for the passage Lead adapts).
34. Wisdom 11:17, from the Apochrypha, says that God created the universe according to number, weight, and measure.
35. Earthly.
36. Sky.

Its melting air
In clear, triumphant sounds convey
Into each obvious, rolling sphere
   Mingling her ringing atmosphere,
   Which as it springs
Still more transparent, bright, and sounding clear,
  At first divides in lesser rings,
Compacted close, in voice acute and shrill,
  More to the surface near.
  Then wider waves indented, till
The circles swell, the sounds begin to fill.
   Still widening more and more
   Till with deep gamut[37]
In full-mouthed peals orb within orb resound.

   Here in epitome
Shall the vast, heavenly spheres collected be
And down through them transmit their harmony.
Each sphere, each star, shall now dispense
   With passage free in direct line
   And full aspect benign
Its various powers and proper influence.
   Which in her hallow womb
   This globe shall deep entomb
Where from her central, working urn
They shall arise, and into body turn
And shoot from center to circumference.
Her caverns dark must now enlightened be,
   Unfettered, free,
As one transparent, vast, self-moving wheel
Of liquid crystal, open to reveal
  Her rich innumerable stores,
Her various wonders great, and her own acting powers.
These upward move and on the surface play,
Adorned all beauteous, bright, amazing, gay.
   And there,
Themselves in radiant flowers, fruits, metals, gems display
All living, breathing, sounding free
Into the all-uniting element,
   The one capacious air,

37. Musical scale, octave.

Blowing from every pipe a different harmony
Still from the lower circlets upward sent.
Thus every grateful note to heaven repays
The melody it lent. . . .

John Milton on the Birth of Christ

As a birthday present for Christ, Milton (1608–1674) wrote his friend Charles Diodati in 1629, he had sung of the "peace-bearing king," "ethereal quires," "banished pagan gods." The poem marshals a range of pagan and Christian discourses: an ode, a hymn, some pastoral (with a nod at Virgil's "Messianic" fourth eclogue), all in a Homeric or Orphic style now inflected by a fashion for exalted poetry based on the Bible. This fashion, intensified by the popularity of Guillaume Du Bartas's *Sepmaines* as translated by Joshua Sylvester, was to find its greatest fulfillment in Milton's own *Paradise Lost*. In Milton's Christmas poem the cosmic sweep mixed with affective tenderness suggests baroque art, but the opening stanzas' rhyme royal with a concluding hexameter also recalls Spenser. Unlike Spenser, though, Milton treats Graeco-Roman myth ambivalently: he adopts the legend that when Jesus was born, the old gods (really devils, said one tradition) fled their temples and their oracles fell silent. Even while celebrating a new age, Milton thus shows a "fascination with departure."[1] Our text adapts that in *Paradise Regained and the Minor Poems and Samson Agonistes*, ed. Merritt Y. Hughes (New York: Odyssey Press, 1937); we have also consulted *The Complete English Poetry of John Milton*, ed. John Shawcross (New York: New York University Press, 1963).

ON THE MORNING OF CHRIST'S NATIVITY

I

This is the month, and this is the happy morn
Wherein the Son of Heav'n's eternal King,
Of wedded maid and virgin mother born,
Our great redemption from above did bring;
For so the holy sages[2] once did sing,
  That he our deadly forfeit should release,[3]
And with his Father work us a perpetual peace.

II

That glorious form, that light unsufferable,
And that far-beaming blaze of majesty

---

1. James A. Freeman, "Milton and Heroic Literature," in Dennis Danielson, ed., *The Cambridge Companion to Milton* (Cambridge: Cambridge University Press, 1989), p. 56.
2. Hebrew prophets such as Isaiah.
3. Pay for our sins.

Wherewith he wont at Heav'n's high council table,
To sit the midst of trinal unity,[4]
He laid aside; and, here with us to be,
 Forsook the courts of everlasting day
And chose with us a darksome house of mortal clay.
III
Say, heav'nly muse, shall not thy sacred vein
Afford a present to the infant God?
Hast thou no verse, no hymn, or solemn strain,
To welcome Him to this His new abode,
Now while the heav'n, by the sun's team untrod,
 Hath took no print of the approaching light,
And all the spangled host keep watch in squadrons bright?
IV
See how from far upon the eastern road
The star-led wizards[5] *haste with odors sweet;*
O run, prevent[6] *them with thy humble ode,*
And lay it lowly at his blessèd feet;
Have thou the honor first thy Lord to greet,
 And join thy voice unto the angel quire
From out his secret altar touched with hallowed fire.

THE HYMN

1
It was the winter wild,
While the Heav'n-born child,
   All meanly wrapped in the rude manger lies;
Nature, in awe to him,
Had doffed her gaudy trim,
   With her great Master so to sympathize;
It was no season then for her
To wanton with the sun, her lusty paramour.[7]

2
Only with speeches fair
She woos the gentle air

4. God as Father, Son, and Holy Spirit.
5. The Magi who, led by a star, gave Jesus gold, frankincense, and myrrh (Matt. 2:1). Persia was associated with mystic wisdom.
6. Arrive first. Traditionally, the Magi came on January 6 (Epiphany).
7. Lover.

To hide her guilty front with innocent snow,
And on her naked shame,
Pollute[8] with sinful blame,
    The saintly veil of maiden white to throw,
Confounded that her Maker's eyes
Should look so near upon her foul deformities.

3

But He, her fears to cease,
Sent down the meek-eyed Peace;
    She, crowned with olive green, came softly sliding
Down through the turning sphere,
His ready harbinger,
    With turtle[9] wing the amorous clouds dividing,
And waving wide her myrtle wand,
She strikes a universal peace through sea and land.

4

No war, or battle's sound
Was heard the world around;
    The idle spear and shield were high up hung;
The hookèd chariot[10] stood
Unstained with hostile blood;
    The trumpet spake not to the armèd throng,
And kings sat still with awful eye,
As if they surely knew their sov'reign Lord was by.

5

But peaceful was the night
Wherein the Prince of light
    His reign of peace upon the earth began;
The winds, with wonder whist,[11]
Smoothly the waters kissed,
    Whisp'ring new joys to the mild ocean,
Who now hath quite forgot to rave,
While birds of calm[12] sit brooding on the charmèd wave.

6

The stars with deep amaze
Stand fixed in steadfast gaze,

---

8. Polluted: humanity's fall infected Nature too.
9. The turtledove, like the olive a symbol of peace. Associated with Venus, the dove also represents the Holy Spirit.
10. A chariot armed with projecting hooks on the wheels. Tradition held that Jesus was born during an interval of peace.
11. Hushed.
12. Halcyons, said to nest on the waves during a time of calm at the solstice.

> Bending one way their precious influence,
> And will not take their flight,
> For all the morning light,
>   Or Lucifer[13] that often warned them thence;
> But in their glimmering orbs did glow,
> Until their Lord himself bespake, and bid them go.

7

> And though the shady gloom
> Had given day her room,
> The sun himself withheld his wonted speed,
> And hid his head for shame,
> As his inferior flame,
>   The new enlightened world no more should need;
> He saw a greater Sun appear
> Than his bright throne or burning axletree could bear.

8

> The shepherds on the lawn,[14]
> Or ere[15] the point of dawn,
>   Sat simply chatting in a rustic row;
> Full little thought they than,[16]
> That the mighty Pan[17]
>   Was kindly come to live with them below;
> Perhaps their loves, or else their sheep,
> Was all that did their silly[18] thoughts so busy keep.

9

> When such music sweet
> Their hearts and ears did greet,
>   As never was by mortal finger strook,[19]
> Divinely-warbled voice
> Answering the stringèd noise,
>   As all their souls in blissful rapture took;
> The air, such pleasure loath to lose,
> With thousand echoes still prolongs each heav'nly close.[20]

10

> Nature that heard such sound

---

13. "Light-bearer": the morning star or, possibly, the sun.
14. Tending their sheep in the pasture (Luke 2:8ff.).
15. Or ere: before.
16. Then.
17. God of shepherds, hence God.
18. Lowly, simple.
19. Struck.
20. Musical phrase, cadence.

Beneath the hollow round
　　Of Cynthia's seat,[21] the airy region thrilling,
Now was almost won
To think her part was done,
　　And that her reign had here its last fulfilling;
She knew such harmony alone
Could hold all Heav'n and Earth in happier union.

11

At last surrounds their sight
A globe of circular light,
　　That with long beams the shame-faced night arrayed,
The helmèd Cherubim
And sworded Seraphim
　　Are seen in glittering ranks with wings displayed,
Harping in loud and solemn quire,
With unexpressive[22] notes to Heav'n's new-born Heir.

12

Such music (as 'tis said)
Before was never made
　　But when of old the sons of morning sung,[23]
While the Creator great
His constellations set,
　　And the well-balanced world on hinges hung,
And cast the dark foundations deep,
And bid the welt'ring waves their oozy channel keep.

13

Ring out ye crystal spheres,
Once bless our human ears
　　(If ye have power to touch our senses so),
And let your silver chime
Move in melodious time;
　　And let the bass of Heav'n's deep organ blow;
And with your ninefold harmony
Make up full consort to th'angelic symphony.[24]

14

For if such holy song
Enwrap our fancy long,

---

21. The moon and its sphere.
22. Inexpressible (by mortals).
23. Job 38:6–7: "the stars of the morning praised me together."
24. One tradition held that the nine angelic orders guided the heavens' concentric crystal spheres while making music inaudible to mortals.

Time will run back, and fetch the age of gold,[25]
And speckled vanity
Will sicken soon and die,
     And leprous sin will melt from earthly mold,
And Hell itself will pass away,
And leave her dolorous mansions to the peering day.
15
Yea, Truth and Justice then
Will down return to men,
     Th'enameled arras[26] *of the rainbow wearing,*
And Mercy set between,
Throned in celestial sheen,
     With radiant feet the tissued clouds down steering,
And Heav'n as at some festival,
Will open wide the gates of her high palace hall.
16
But wisest Fate says no,
This must not yet be so:
     The Babe lies yet in smiling infancy,
That on the bitter cross
Must redeem our loss,
     So both himself and us to glorify;
Yet first to those ychained in sleep,
The wakeful trump of doom[27] *must thunder through the deep,*
17
With such a horrid clang
As on Mount Sinai rang
     While the red fire and smold'ring clouds out break;[28]
The aged Earth aghast
With terror of that blast,
     Shall from the surface to the center shake,
When at the world's last session,
The dreadful Judge in middle air shall spread his throne.
18
And then at last our bliss
Full and perfect is,
     But now begins; for from this happy day

25. That pure time before the ages of silver, bronze, and now iron.
26. Often a tapestry; here a robe of colored drapery.
27. Gabriel's trumpet call when the dead will waken to be judged.
28. Exod. 19:16ff., when God gives Moses the Ten Commandments.

Th'old dragon[29] *under ground,*
In straiter limits bound,
　　Not half so far casts his usurpèd sway,
　　And wrath to see his kingdom fail,
Swinges the scaly horror of his folded tail.
19
The oracles are dumb,
No voice or hideous hum
　　Runs through the archèd roof in words deceiving.
Apollo from his shrine
Can no more divine,
　　With hollow shriek the steep of Delphos[30] *leaving.*
No nightly trance, or breathèd spell,
Inspires the pale-eyed priest from the prophetic cell.
20
The lonely mountains o'er,
And the resounding shore,
　　A voice of weeping heard, and loud lament;
From haunted spring and dale
Edged with poplar pale,
　　The parting genius[31] *is with sighing sent;*
With flow'r-inwoven tresses torn
The nymphs in twilight shade of tangled thickets mourn.
21
In consecrated earth,
And on the holy hearth,
　　The Lars and Lemurs[32] *moan with midnight plaint;*
In urns and altars round,
A drear and dying sound
　　Affrights the Flamens[33] *at their service quaint;*
And the chill marble seems to sweat,
While each peculiar[34] *power forgoes his wonted seat.*
22
Peor and Baalim[35]

---

29. Satan; cf. Rev. 20:2–3.
30. The Greek mount and town where Apollo would speak, often cryptically, through his priestess.
31. The spirit of some particular locality.
32. In ancient Rome *lares* were household gods, *lemures* spirits of the dead.
33. Roman priests serving some particular god.
34. Particular, the one who owns the "seat" or place.
35. Phoenician deities: Peor was a sun god; Baalim were nature gods, sometimes aspects of the god Baal.

Forsake their temples dim,
   With that twice-battered god of Palestine,[36]
And moonèd Ashtaroth,[37]
Heav'n's queen and mother both,
   Now sits not girt with tapers' holy shine,
The Lybic Hammon[38] shrinks his horn,
In vain the Tyrian maids their wounded Thammuz mourn.[39]

23

And sullen Moloch,[40] fled,
Hath left in shadows dread
   His burning idol all of blackest hue;
In vain with cymbals' ring
They call the grisly king,
   In dismal dance about the furnace blue;
The brutish gods of Nile as fast,
Isis and Orus, and the dog Anubis haste.[41]

24

Nor is Osiris seen
In Memphian[42] grove or green,
   Trampling the unshow'red grass with lowings loud;
Nor can he be at rest
Within his sacred chest
   Naught but profoundest Hell can be his shroud;
In vain with timbreled anthems dark
The sable-stoled sorcerers bear his worshiped ark.

25

He feels from Juda's land
The dreaded Infant's hand,
   The rays of Bethlehem blind his dusky eyn;[43]
Nor all the gods beside
Longer dare abide,
   Nor Typhon huge ending in snaky twine;[44]

---

36. Dagon, a Philistine god whose idol was twice cast down (1 Sam. 5).
37. Astarte, a Phoenician fertility goddess bearing a lunar crescent.
38. The ram-god Ammon had his chief shrine in Lybia.
39. Phoenician maids wept annually for Astarte's beloved Thammuz (whom the Greeks called Adonis), object of a fertility cult.
40. A near-eastern god to whom children were sacrificed.
41. The Egyptian goddess Isis, wife of the creator god Osiris and mother of Horus, hawk-headed sun god, had cow horns; Anubis had a jackal head.
42. In Memphis, the Egyptian city.
43. Eyes.
44. Osiris' enemy, often equated with a snake-legged giant rebel against Jove.

Our Babe, to show his Godhead true,
Can in his swaddling bands control the damnèd crew.[45]
26
So when the sun in bed
Curtained with cloudy red,
 Pillows his chin upon an orient wave,
The flocking shadows pale
Troop to th'infernal jail;
 Each fettered ghost slips to his several grave,
 And the yellow-skirted fays
Fly after the night-steeds, leaving their moon-loved maze.
27
But see! The Virgin blest
Hath laid her Babe to rest:
 Time is our tedious song should here have ending;
Heav'n's youngest teemèd [46] *star*
Hath fixed her polished car, [47]
 Her sleeping Lord with handmaid lamp attending,
And all about the courtly stable
Bright-harnessed [48] *angels sit in order serviceable.*

45. Like Hercules, who strangled two serpents in his cradle.
46. Born.
47. Has stationed her shining chariot.
48. In shining armor.

15

The Jewish Question in Early Modern England

Although the Jews had been officially expelled from England in 1290 following an accusation of a ritual murder,[1] the persecution of Jews in the Iberian peninsula in the late fifteenth century scattered Spanish and Portuguese refugees across Europe. Approximately two dozen Jews settled in Elizabethan London. Ostensibly converted, these "New Christians" were often, as many suspected, Marranos ("Secret Jews") who at risk to themselves continued secretly to practice remnants of their old faith. Among the Jews in early modern England's tiny colony were a mother and daughter who left some written records. Sara Ames Lopez (1550–after 1594) was the daughter of Constance Ruys and Dunstan Añes, a Portuguese Marrano merchant. Born in London, she married another Marrano, Dr. Roderigo Lopez, an immigrant Portuguese physician who rose to become Queen Elizabeth's trusted doctor before being executed in 1594 on what many now think a trumped-up charge—originating with spies of the rambunctious Essex—of plotting to poison the queen.

A normal concomitant of execution for treason was seizure of the felon's goods by the crown. After Lopez's execution, his widow petitioned the queen to return his goods to her and her now orphaned children. In a very unusual response, Elizabeth agreed, returning to Sara Lopez all Dr. Lopez's goods except a ring given him by King Philip of Spain, the ring Lopez had once offered to the

---

1. A libel accusing Jews of murdering a Christian child to reenact the crucifixion and then using the blood of the innocent to prepare matzot for Passover. The earliest accusation in England was in Norwich in 1144. The most notorious was in 1255 and involved eight-year old Hugh of Lincoln, later canonized.

queen as a gift. Elizabeth wore the ring at her waist for the rest of her life, a gesture that supports the scholarly consensus that she believed Lopez innocent. Sara Lopez's petition and an inventory of her goods (Cecil Papers 28/8–11) are now in the library at Hatfield House. We have transcribed and modernized them for what we believe to be their first appearance in print, doing so with the kind permission of the Marquess of Salisbury. We thank Peter Blayney for reviewing our transcription.

Next is a plea dating from 1624 by another Marrano widow, Anne Lopez alias Pinto de Britto, presumably that Anne, daughter of Dr. Lopez, who was born in London in 1579. In 1594 her father was executed and Anne's grandfather Anes also died. By 1613 three of her siblings had moved to Constantinople, practicing Judaism openly. Anne, however, remained in London, one of the few Marranos to do so under James I. There she married Francisco Pinto de Britto of Lisbon, a suspected "Secret Jew" who died in 1618 (suspiciously, his body was buried abroad). In 1624, two years before her own death, Anne petitioned the Court of Chancery for relief against two merchants who had entered an action against her as executrix of her late husband's estate. A transcription by Edgar Samuel of her plea and the abstract of the counter pleas were published in the appendix to an article by Samuel in *Transactions of the Jewish Historical Society of England* (1958). Given the emphasis on female silence, we note a comment in the counter plea that although Anne "pretendeth poverty and disability of language, these defendants do well know her readiness of tongue and her great riches in estate." We give a modernized version of the text, with Edgar Samuel's kind permission.

These petitions document the lives of women from a group that has until recently attracted minimal recognition and its women virtually none. While undoubtedly drafted by lawyers acting for these two women, the petitions give voice to the vitality of women from a despised (when not invisible) segment of early modern English society. They take on added significance when read in tandem with arguments about the profitability of the Jews in the other documents that we reproduce here. An interesting argument gave unexpected urgency to the "Jewish question" during the unsettled years at mid-seventeenth century that saw an increased millenarianism and a desire to put all things in place for the Second Coming: the argument that Jews should be readmitted to England since their total dispersal was a precondition to their ultimate ingathering and hence to the Millennium. Given the frenzy of petitioning in these years, it is not surprising that the readmission of the Jews to England was the subject of a number of petitions and tracts, including those dating between 1649 and 1656 from which we take our excerpts.

One of the earliest of such petitions is by an unknown woman and her son. We have no information about Joanna and Ebenezer Cartwright, self-described as "freeborn of England." Another was penned by Manasseh Ben Israel, alias Manoel Dias Soeiro (1604–1657), the Lisbon-born junior Haham[2] of the

---

2. Literally, a wise person; in Sephardic tradition a religious leader.

Portuguese Synagogue in Amsterdam. Contacted in 1651 by English ambassadors visiting that city to build up English trade, he was invited in 1655 to come to London to petition Oliver Cromwell[3] publicly for the readmission of his fellow Jews to England. Although the measure was unpopular and the petition unsuccessful, a ruling that it was not illegal for Jews to live in England led the sympathetic Cromwell to allow some Portuguese Jewish merchants to open a synagogue, lease a cemetery, and practice Judaism openly. Immigration, however, was strictly limited. Menasseh Ben Israel was pensioned by Cromwell but died in Amsterdam, in 1657, a deeply disappointed man.

The argument for resettlement was mounted by diverse persons, including Quakers such as Margaret Fell Foxe (1614–1702), who addressed "the seed of Abraham" repeatedly in her tracts (e.g., *A Loving Salutation* [1656]; *A Call Unto the Seed of Israel* [1668?]). In one tract (*For Manasseth Ben Israel* [1656]), she addresses the Portuguese Haham. A Hebrew translation of her tracts on resettlement was apparently undertaken by Spinoza, excommunicated by the Amsterdam community around this time; this may be his first publication.

The "Jewish Question" also found its way into the poetry of George Herbert (1593–1633). Born to an aristocratic family, Herbert gave up the prospect of a glamorous life at court or in the upper reaches of the church so as to be a parish priest in the rural town of Bemerton. He was a major poet of the sort now called metaphysical—given to witty conceits and wordplay that in his case press intriguingly against his usual simplicity of rhythm and diction. In *The Temple*, published posthumously in 1633, one poem hopes that Christian prayers will persuade God to convert the Jews. Herbert means to be generous, even if many would now think his hope condescending. See the Everyman edition by C. A. Patrides (London: Dent, 1974).

THE PETITION OF SARA LOPEZ

To the Queen's Most Excellent Majesty:

Humbly lamenting, beseecheth your Majesty, for God's sake, to have pitiful consideration of her afflicted and miserable estate, Sara Lopez, the condemned and poor widow of Doctor Lopez:

That where your suppliant (utterly confounded and dismayed with the heavy ruin of her late husband) lieth at this present in woeful agony and extremity of sickness, utterly despairing the recovery of her former health and strength and rather expecting the speedy shortening of her perplexed life through the inward conceit of her present desolation (being the sorrowful mother of five comfortless and distressed children born within your Majesty's realm, three of them being maiden children, and only relying upon your suppliant's hands).

---

3. Cromwell (1599–1658) was Lord Protector of the commonwealth established after the execution of Charles I.

And forasmuch as your poor suppliant and all her poor children are innocent of her said husband's crime and have in no sort (as they hope) offended your highness or the state of this realm, she most humbly beseecheth your highness, for God's sake, that her said husband's offense and the rigor of the punishment thereof may cease and be determined [4] with the infamous loss of his life.

And that your poor suppliant and her children may have the lease of your suppliant's house for their habitation, with her household stuff and such goods and other things as have been taken from her during her husband's first imprisonment, being their whole stay and substance for their relief and succor.

Whereof, pleaseth it your highness to be advertised that one John Gatherne[5] detaineth[6] from your oratrice[7] 50 or 60 pounds due by the licenses of sumac[8] and aniseeds[9] before her husband's imprisonment which he will not restore without my Lord Treasurer's[10] warrant, who referreth your oratrice to sue[11] for your highness' warrant[12] in that behalf, which said license of sumac and aniseed is also taken away from your suppliant.

As also one Mr. Conway[13] hath made stay[14] of certain plate to the value of 100 pounds of her late husband's, remaining in the court, pretending a debt of 30 pounds to be owing him by her husband, whereof your oratrice can make good proof that the same is long since paid and discharged.

And whereas it pleased your highness of your princely bounty to vouchsafe the gift of a parsonage[15] to the value of 30 pounds per annum upon Anthony Lopez, one of your suppliant's miserable children, for his maintenance at school and learning, the same is likewise taken from him.

In tender consideration of the premises it may please your most excellent Majesty to stand so gracious sovereign to your miserable suppliant as to redress and cause restitution of the premises to be made unto her according to your highness' special bounty for her and her poor children's succor, who are at this present utterly destitute and forsaken of all friends and comfort and, without such your highness' great mercy and compassion towards them, ready to perish and to be driven to extreme begging and penury.[16]

Whereof, it may please your highness, for God's sake, of your princely clemency towards the poor widow and fatherless, to have tender consideration. And your poor suppliant and her poor children (as duty bindeth) shall daily pray for your highness' long life with increase of continual felicity in this life and in the world to come. Amen.

4. Terminated.
5. Identified below as a custom house official.
6. Retains.
7. Female petitioner.
8. A plant used in tanning.
9. Seeds of an aromatic (licorice-like) plant.
10. William Cecil, first Lord Burghley.
11. Take legal action.
12. Authorizing document.
13. Identified later as a gentleman usher.
14. Stoppage.
15. Benefice or living of a parson, based on land and rents.
16. Destitution.

A TRUE INVENTORY OF ALL SUCH PLATE, JEWELS, LICENSES, DEBTS, AND
HOUSEHOLD STUFF AS WAS OF LATE DUE AND BELONGING TO
DOCTOR LOPEZ AND IS NOW IN THE POSSESSION OF THOSE
WHOSE NAMES ARE UNDERWRITTEN:

Plate at the court:

A deep basin and ewer of silver
One great wine pot of silver
Two wine bowls of silver
One gilt wine bowl with a cover
One gilt salt
Six gilt spoons
One gilt pot for beer

(This quantity of plate was valued at 80 pounds. These parcels are now in the hands of Mr. Conway, gentleman usher. Other parcels of plate were likewise at his house of the like esteem,[17] which his widow was constrained to sell for the relief of herself and her poor children.)

One jewel with a fair diamond and a ruby in it, now in the hands of Mr. Wade, clerk of the council.

Licenses and debts

An especial license granted by letters patent to Doctor Lopez for aniseeds and sumac, bearing date the 25th of June in the 26th year of her majesty's reign.

John Gatherne of the Customs House, being constituted[18] by Doctor Lopez to receive such money as should arise out of the profits of this license as is above written, hath received 30 pounds to the doctor's use, all which he detaineth in his own hands.

Almost at the expiration of the said license, was a new license granted to Doctor Lopez, bearing date the 4th of January in the 35th year of her highness' reign. Which license is already obtained by Mister Mompesson[19] and Mr. Alexander.[20]

The House

A lease thereof was taken of Doctor Bayly and Edmund Barber anno domini 1586 for the term of 40 years, paying yearly to New College in Oxford the yearly rent of 10 marks.

A garden joining to the said house, taken of Edmund Barber in the same year, for the term of 21 years, paying yearly to William Flecton, merchant 4 marks.

17. Value.
18. Appointed.
19. Blayney suggests a Richard Mompesson who was "actively seeking grants of spurious kinds in the 1580s and 1590s."
20. Blayney suggests a Robert Alexander, granted a license in April 1593/4.

The two sheriffs, Mr. Haughton[21] and Mr. Banning,[22] seized the goods for which William Anes (Doctor Lopez, his widow's brother) is bound . . . to answer them at such times as they shall be by them demanded. Lest this bond should be returned into the exchequer they crave a discharge.

Sir Richard Martin[23] likewise seized the goods for a debt of 126 pounds which the king, Don Antony,[24] owed him, and for the payment whereof Doctor Lopez stood bound. Sir Richard was then compounded withal, and had 40 pounds paid in hand, and William Anes aforesaid stands bound in a bond . . . for the performance of the rest.

There is a license granted to certain merchants for their traffic to Guinea, provided for them by the king Don Antony. They, in consideration hereof, contracted themselves in a bond of 500 pounds to allow the king out of all the goods they should bring forth of those parts, five pounds in the hundred.

The king, in respect of a debt of 600 pounds due by him to Doctor Lopez, besides other debts, whereof Sir Richard Martin is one, made over the contract to Doctor Lopez, authorizing him to receive and pay all men.

The poor widow's request is it may please her majesty to grant her the benefit of this license whereof there are three years yet to come, as well to satisfy herself as others of the king's creditors.

This license is in the hands of Mr. Wade, aforesaid.

Household stuff in the parlor

One court cupboard[25]
One table
One desk
Four joint stools[26]
Four little leather stools
Three chairs of leather
One pair of andirons

In the hall

Two tables
One bedstead
Three chairs of leather
One pair of andirons

21. Blayney identifies Peter Haughton as sheriff of London in 1594.
22. Blayney also identifies Paul Banning as sheriff of London in 1594.
23. Presumably the Sir Richard Martin (1532–1617) who was warden of the mint from 1559/60 until at least 1594/95; master of the mint from 1580/81 until his death; and at various times alderman, sheriff, and lord mayor of London. Sir Richard has been identified as the husband of Dorcas Martin, translator of a catechism for the use of mother and child that was included in Thomas Bentley's *Monument of Matrons* (1582).
24. Don Antony, pretender to the Portuguese throne, was an important actor in the fall of Roderigo Lopez.
25. A cabinet for displaying plate.
26. Stools made of parts joined together.

In the chambers

Three bedsteads with furniture[27]

Other necessaries there were, which the widow was constrained to sell for the relief of herself and her poor children.

The Plea of Anne Lopez alias Pinto de Britto

To the right honorable and right reverend father in God, John, Lord Bishop of Lincoln, Lord Keeper of the great seal of England.[28]

Humbly complaining, showeth unto your good Lordship your daily oratrice Anne Lopez alias Pinto, administratrix[29] of the goods and chattels[30] of Francis Lopez alias Pinto de Britto, her late husband deceased:

That John Francisco Soprani and Philip Bernardi, merchant strangers,[31] unjustly pretending[32] that the said intestate,[33] together with Anthony da Costa Olivario of London, merchants, did by charter party indentures[34] bearing the date about the sixteenth day of March in the twelfth year of his Majesty's reign of England [c. 1615] became bound in . . . unto the said John Francisco Soprani and the said Philip Bernardi, being proprietors of a ship called the *Susan Bonadventure* of London then riding at anchor in the River of Thames, a port of London, and to William Oakes, master of the said ship in a voyage then, shortly after the making of the said charter party, to be made from London to Dunkirk in Flanders and from thence to Lisbon in Portugal, from thence again unto London, and to pay for the same according to a certain date in the said charter party mentioned.

And further pretending that the said intestate and the said Anthony da Costa de Olivario did not lade[35] the said ship, being at Lisbon aforesaid, within thirty days next after her arrival at Lisbon aforesaid, such quantities of sugars and other merchandises as by the pretended charter party they ought to have done within the time aforesaid, and thereby did forfeit unto them the said bond of three hundred pounds.

And the said John Francisco Soprani and Philip Bernardi do now unjustly pretend that thereby they have lately caused your oratrix to be arrested per writ[36] awarded out of his Majesty's court of king's bench, and by their bill or declara-

27. Coverlets and linen.
28. John Williams, Archbishop of Lincoln (1621–1641)
29. Female administrator.
30. Personal property.
31. Foreigners.
32. Claiming.
33. Person who dies without a will.
34. A deed for hire of a ship and the safe delivery of the cargo.
35. Load with cargo.
36. Legal document or instrument.

tion thereupon filed against your oratrix, as administratrix of the said Francis Lopez alias Pinto de Britto, deceased, have demanded the said penal sum of three hundred pounds supposed to be forfeited as aforesaid, alleging only for breach on behalf of the said Francis Pinto de Britto and Anthony da Costa, that they nor their factors[37] within the said thirty days, which was the time limited for their reloading at Lisbon aforesaid, had caused the said ship to be reladen with such quantities of sugar and sugar chests and other goods as in and by the said pretended charter party was appointed, upon which pretended breach they do not only demand the said three hundred pounds, but further damages by them supposed to be sustained by reason of the default aforesaid, as by their bill or declaration in that behalf now at large it doth and may appear.

Whereas in truth there was no such charter party made or sealed by the said intestate to the knowledge of your oratrix, or if any such charter party indentures were ever by him made or sealed, yet there was no default of performance thereof on the part of the said intestate, either in lading or getting aboard of the merchandise as is pretended or in paying for the same or for the hire of the said ship. But the said John Francisco Soprani and Philip Bernardi and William Oakes and any of them were by the said intestate in his lifetime and long since fully paid, contented, and satisfied all that was due unto them from the said intestate in that behalf or in any otherwise concerning the promised and so much would most plainly appear by divers books and notes of account now remaining in the hands of the said John Francisco Soprani and Philip Bernardi, or one of them, or in the hands of some other by their privity[38] covertly there delivered for their use, if the same might be produced. And the said Philip Bernardi hath of late time confessed that there be in truth nothing due unto him from the oratrix upon the said charter party, but said that he would, notwithstanding, cause the same to be put in suit at common law against your oratrix—being a widow and a stranger and not well able to defend or solicit the same—of purpose only to trouble her and thereby to draw her to compound[39] with him, the said Philip Bernardi, concerning another suit which your said oratrix, upon bond of three hundred pounds, made to the said intestate.

In consideration whereof, and forasmuch as it is now almost ten years complete since the said charter party was made, and forasmuch as there were after that time divers other dealings and reckonings between the said John Francisco Soprani and the said Philip Bernardi and the said intestate while he lived, whereupon the said charter party (if any such there were) all demands concerning the same were fully discharged and cleared, and the said John Francisco Soprani and the said Philip Bernardi were thereof fully satisfied by and from the said intestate.

And since that they, the said John Francisco Soprani and Philip Bernardi, both of them upon account and reckoning and otherwise, became indebted to the

37. Agents, representatives.
38. Secret design.
39. Agree, bargain.

said intestate and so much doth and will most evidently appear by divers books and other notes and writings of account remaining in the hands of them the said Soprani and Bernardi.

And the said Soprani doth but rake up[40] the said charter party, if any such there be, as an old specialty,[41] thereby of purpose only to gain a composition[42] for later just and due debt.

And forasmuch as upon receipt of all the said moneys and satisfaction given for the hire of the said ship to the said Soprani and Bernardi, they never pretended themselves then to be damnified[43] by any such supposed breach of the said covenants on the part of the said Pinto and Anthony da Costa nor demanded of them any satisfaction.

Therefore then, was by them then released and forasmuch as the said supposed breach of the said covenants is only pretended to be made by the said Pinto and Anthony da Costa for that which in the time of thirty days they nor their factors did reload or cause to be reladen at Lisbon aforesaid with such quantity of sugar and other goods as was by them pretended to be undertaken by the said charter party, which if it were true—as your oratrix is persuaded is very false— yet might not the said Bernardi and Soprani be much damnified by the stay of their said ship some few days after the said thirty days at Lisbon aforesaid, nor indeed in any way damnified at all if at the end of the said thirty days the wind and weather did not serve for them for their sail towards England.

And forasmuch as they wonto[44] now put the said charter party in suit, nor so much as demand any thing thereupon as or against the said intestate while he lived or against the said Anthony da Costa (who is yet alive and now resideth beyond the seas) while the said Anthony da Costa was resident here in England, where he remained during 6 years after the making of the said pretended charter party and after the return of the said ship from the said voyage and after payment and full satisfaction given to them, the said Soprani and Bernardi, for the wages and hire of the said ship.

But now after the death of the said Pinto and departure of the said Anthony da Costa do put the same in suit as aforesaid against your oratrix being no party thereunto, nor privy to the matter whereupon the same was made, nor to the means whereby the same was discharged, otherwise than administratrix of the goods and chattels of the said intestate, and have laid their said action at law in the City of London, suing to bring the same to a speedy trial before that your oratrix, being a poor widow and a stranger and not able to speak English can prepare herself and be in readiness for the defense thereof.

May it therefore please your Lordship, the premises considered, to grant unto your oratrix his Majesty's most gracious writ of subpoena to be awarded out of their honorable court and to be directed to the said John Francisco Soprani

40. Search up and bring forward.
41. Special contract or bond.
42. Settling, compounding.
43. Injured.
44. Want to.

and Philip Bernardi thereby commanding them and either of them at a certain time and under certain pains, therein to be limited by your lordship personally, to be and appear before your lordship in the court of chancery then and there to answer the [?complaynte] to abide the order and judgment of your lordship and that honorable court concerning the same.

And further to grant his Majesty's most gracious writ of . . . for payment of their proceedings in the said suit at the common law upon the said charter party.

And your oratrix shall as, in duty notwithstanding she is bound, and pray for your lordship health and happiness with much increase of honor.

THE PETITION OF THE JEWS FOR THE REPEALING OF THE ACT OF PARLIAMENT FOR THEIR BANISHMENT OUT OF ENGLAND (PRESENTED TO HIS EXCELLENCY AND THE GENERAL COUNCIL OF OFFICERS ON FRIDAY, JANUARY 5, 1648, WITH THEIR FAVORABLE ACCEPTANCE THEREOF)

The humble petition of Johanna Cartwright,[45] widow, and Ebenezer Cartwright her son, freeborn of England, and now inhabitants of the City of Amsterdam.

To the Right Honorable, Thomas Lord Fairfax (His Excellency), England's General, and the Honorable Council of War Convened for God's Glory, Israel's Freedom, Peace, and Safety.

Humbly Showeth:

That your petitioners being conversant in that city, with and amongst some of Israel's race (called Jews), and growing sensible of their heavy outcries and clamors against the intolerable cruelty of this our English nation exercised against them by that and (other) inhumane exceeding great massacre of them in the reign of Richard the Second, king of this land, and their banishment ever since, with the penalty of death to be inflicted upon any of their return into this land. That by discourse with them, and serious perusal of the prophets, both they and we find that the time of her call draweth nigh, whereby they together with us shall come to know the Emanuel,[46] the Lord of life, light, and glory, even as we are now known of Him. And that this nation of England, with the inhabitants of the Netherlands, shall be the first and readiest to transport Israel's sons and daughters in their ships to the land promised to their forefathers Abraham, Isaac, and Jacob, for an everlasting inheritance.

For the glorious manifestation whereof, and pious means thereunto, your petitioners humbly pray that the inhumane cruel statute of banishment made

45. The original document reads "Cartentight" at this point only.
46. Christ; the Hebrew means literally "God is with us."

against them may be repealed, and they (under the Christian banner of charity and brotherly love) may again be received and permitted to trade and dwell amongst you in this land, as now they do in the Netherlands.

By which act of mercy, your petitioners are assured of the wrath of God will be much appeased towards you, for their innocent blood shed, and they daily enlightened in the saving knowledge of Him for Whom they look daily and expect as their King of eternal glory, and both their and our Lord God of salvation (Christ Jesus). For the glorious accomplishing whereof, your petitioners do and shall ever address themselves to the true peace, and pray, etc.

This petition was presented to the General Council of the Officers of the Army, under the command of his excellency, Thomas Lord Fairfax, at White Hall, on January 5. And favorably received with a promise to take it into speedy consideration, when the present more public affairs are dispatched.

From *The Humble Addresses of Menasseh Ben Israel, a Divine, and Doctor of Physic, in Behalf of the Jewish Nation*

To His Highness the Lord Protector of the Commonwealth of England, Scotland, and Ireland:

Give me leave, at such a juncture of time, to your Highness, in a style and manner fitting to us Jews and our condition. It is a thing most certain that the great God of Israel, Creator of Heaven and Earth, doth give and take away dominions and empires, according to His own pleasure, exalting some and overthrowing others. Who, seeing He hath the hearts of kings in His hand, He easily moves them whithersoever Himself pleaseth, to put in execution His divine commands.

This, my lord, appears most evidently out of those words of Daniel, where he, rendering thanks unto God for revealing unto him that prodigious dream of Nebuchadnezzar, doth say: "Thou that removest kings, and sets up kings."[47] And elsewhere, "To the end the living might know that the Highest hath dominion in man's kingdom and giveth the same to whom He please."[48] Of the very same mind are talmudists likewise, affirming that a good government or governor is a heavenly gift, and that there is no governor but is first called by God to that dignity. And this they prove from that passage of Exodus: "Behold I have called Bazalel by name," etc., all things being governed by divine providence, God dispensing rewards unto virtues and punishments unto vices, according to His own good will.[49]

47. Dan. 2:21.
48. Dan. 4:17.
49. Exod. 31:2.

This the examples of great monarchs make good, especially of such who have afflicted the people of Israel. For none hath ever afflicted them who hath not been by some ominous exit most heavily punished of God Almighty, as is manifest from the histories of those kings: Pharaoh, Nebuchadnezzar, Antiochus Epiphanes, Pompey,[50] and others. And, on the contrary, none ever was a benefactor to that people, and cherished them in their countries, who thereupon hath not presently begun very much to flourish. Insomuch that the oracle to Abraham ("I will bless them that bless thee and curse them that curse thee"[51]) seemeth yet daily to have its accomplishment. Hence, I, one of the least among the Hebrews (since by experience I have found that through God's great bounty toward us many considerable and eminent persons both for piety and power, are moved with sincere and inward pity and compassion towards us and do comfort us concerning the approaching deliverance of Israel) could not but for myself, and in the behalf of my countrymen, make this my humble address to your Highness and beseech you—for God's sake—that ye would, according to that piety and power wherein you are eminent beyond others, vouchsafe to grant that the great and glorious name of the Lord our God may be extolled and solemnly worshipped and praised by us through all the bounds of this commonwealth, and grant us place in your country that we may have our synagogues and free exercise of our religion.

I, nothing doubting, but that your clemency will easily grant this most equitable petition of ours. Pagans have of old, out of reverence to the God of Israel, and the esteem they had to His people, granted most willingly free liberty, even to apostated[52] Jews, as Onias the High Priest, to build another temple in their country, like unto that in Jerusalem.[53] How much more then may we, that are not apostate or renegade Jews, hope it from your Highness and your Christian council, since you have so great knowledge of and adore the same one only God of Israel, together with us. Besides, it increases our confidence of your bounty towards us, in that so soon as ever the rumor of that most wished for liberty that ye were thinking to grant us, was made known among our countrymen, I, in the name of my nation (the Jews that live in Holland) did congratulate and entertain the ambassadors of England, who were received in our synagogue with as great pomp and applause, hymns and cheerfulness of mind, as ever any sovereign prince was.

·

50. Pharaoh: Egyptian king who refused to free Jacob's descendants and was drowned in the Red Sea (Exod. 1–15:21, esp. 14:26–15:21); Nebuchadnezzar: King of Babylon, who dispersed the kingdom of Judah (Jer. 21:2) but lost his kingdom (Dan. 4); Antiochus IV Epiphanes: king of the Syrian Greeks (175–164 B.C.E.) who despoiled the Temple and sparked the Maccabean revolt (1 Maccabees); Pompey the Great (106–48 B.C.E.) settled Judea in 63 B.C.E. Defeated in battle at Pharsalus, he was murdered after fleeing to Egypt in 48 B.C.E.
51. Gen. 12:3.
52. Fallen from faith, i.e., in building a substitute Temple in an unconsecrated place.
53. According to Josephus, Onias was the son of one of the chief priests in Jerusalem; he settled in Alexandria and built a sanctuary near Memphis (in Egypt). See Josephus, *The Jewish War*, trans. G. A. Williamson; rev. E. Mary Smallwood (New York: Dorset Press, 1981).

For our people did in their own minds presage that the kingly government being now changed into that of a commonwealth, the ancient hatred towards them would also be changed into good will; that those rigorous laws (if any there be yet extant, made under the kings) against so innocent a people, would happily be repealed. So that we hope now for better from your gentleness, and goodness, since from the beginning of your government of this commonwealth, Your Highness hath professed much respect and favor towards us. Wherefore I humbly entreat your Highness that you would with a gracious eye have regard unto us and our petition, and grant unto us, as you have done unto others, free exercise of our religion, that we may have our synagogues and keep our own public worship as our brethren do in Italy, Germany, Poland, and many other places. And we shall pray for the happiness and peace of this your much renowned and puissant commonwealth.

A Declaration to the Commonwealth of England, by Rabbi Menasseh Ben Israel, Showing the Motives of His Coming into England

Having some years since often perceived that in this nation God hath a people that is very tender-hearted and well-wishing to our sore afflicted nation, yea, I myself having some experience thereof in divers eminent persons excelling both in piety and learning, I thought with myself I should do no small service to my own nation, as also to the people and inhabitants of this commonwealth, if by humble addresses to the late honorable Parliament I might obtain a safe conduct once to transport myself thither. Which I having done, and according to my desire received a most kind and satisfactory answer, I now am come. And to the end all men may know the true motives and intent of this my coming, I shall briefly comprehend and deliver them in these particulars:

First and foremost, my intention is to try if by God's good hand over me I may obtain here for my nation the liberty of a free and public synagogue, wherein we may daily call upon the Lord our God that once He may be pleased to remember His mercies and promises done to our forefathers, forgiving our trespasses, and restoring us once again into our fathers' inheritance; and besides to sue also for a blessing upon this nation and people of England for receiving us into their bosoms and comforting Zion in her distress.

My second motive is because the opinion of many Christians and mine do concur herein, that we both believe that the restoring time of our nation into their native country is very near at hand. I, believing more particularly that this restoration cannot be before these words of Daniel (chapter 12, verse 7) be first accomplished, when he saith: "And when the dispersion of the holy people shall be completed in all places, then shall all these things be completed," signifying therewith that before all be fulfilled the people of God must be first dispersed into all places and countries of the world. Now we know how our nation at the present is spread all about, and hath its seat and dwelling in the most flourishing parts of all the kingdoms and countries of the world, as well in America as in the other three parts thereof, except only in this considerable and mighty island. And therefore this remains only in my judgment before the Messiah come and restore our nation: that first we must have our seat here likewise.

My third motive is rounded on the profit that I conceive this commonwealth is to reap, if it shall vouchsafe to receive us. For thence, I hope, there will follow a great blessing from God upon them and a very abundant trading into and from all parts of the world, not only without prejudice to the English nation, but for their profit, both in importation and exportation of goods. Yet, if any shall doubt hereof, I trust their charity towards the people of God will satisfy them, especially when they shall read the ensuing treatise.

The fourth motive of my coming hither is my sincere affection to this commonwealth, by reason of so many worthy, learned, and pious men in this nation, whose loving kindness and piety I have experience of. Hoping to find the like affection in all the people generally, the more because I always have, both by writing and deeds, professed much inclination to this commonwealth, and that I persuade myself they will be mindful of that command of the Lord our God who so highly recommends unto all men the love of strangers,[54] much more to those that profess their good affection to them. For this I desire all may be confident of: that I am not come to make any disturbance, or to move any disputes about matters of religion, but only to live with my nation in the fear of the Lord, under the shadow of your protection, whiles we expect with you the hope of Israel to be revealed.

How Profitable the Nation of the Jews Are

Three things, if it please Your Highness, there are that make a strange nation well-beloved amongst the natives of a land where they dwell. And on the contrary, three things that make them hateful, viz., profit they may receive from them; fidelity they hold towards their princes; and the nobleness and purity of their blood. Now when I shall have made good that all these three things are found in the Jewish nation, I shall certainly persuade your highness that with a favorable eye (monarchy being changed into a republic), you shall be pleased to receive again the nation of the Jews who in time past lived in that island, but (by I know not what false informations) were cruelly handled and banished.

Profit is a most powerful motive, and which all the world prefers before all other things, and therefore we shall handle that point first.

It is a thing confirmed that merchandising is, as it were, the proper profession of the nation of the Jews. I attribute this in the first place to the particular providence and mercy of God towards His people. For having banished them from their own country, yet not from His protection, He hath given them, as it were, a natural instinct by which they might not only gain what was necessary for their need, but that they should also thrive in riches and possessions, whereby they should not only become gracious to their princes and lords, but that they should be invited by others to come and dwell in their lands.

54. Deut. 10:19.

Moreover, it cannot be denied but that necessity stirs up a man's ability and industry, and that it gives him great incitement by all means to try the favor of Fortune. Besides, seeing it is no wisdom for them to endeavor the gaining of land and other immovable goods, and so to imprison their possessions here where their persons are subject to so many causalities, banishments, and peregrinations, they are forced to use merchandising until that time when they shall return to their own country, that then, as God hath promised by the Prophet Zechariah, "There shall be found no more any merchant amongst them in the House of the Lord."[55]

From that very thing we have said, there riseth an infallible profit, commodity, and gain to all those princes in whose lands they dwell above all other strange nations whatsoever, as experience by divers reasons doth confirm. . . .

From hence (if it please Your Highness) it results that the Jewish nation, though scattered through the whole world, are not therefore a despisable people, but as a plant worthy to be planted in the whole world, received into populous cities, who ought to plant them in those places which are most secure from danger—being trees of most savory fruit and profit—to be always most favored with laws and privileges or prerogatives, secured and defended by arms. . . .

In all these places the Jews live (in a manner) all of them merchants, and that without any prejudice at all to the natives. For the natives, and those especially that are most rich, they build themselves houses and palaces, buy lands and firm goods, aim at titles and dignities, and so seek their rest and contentment that way. But as for the Jews, they aspire at nothing but to prefer themselves in their way of merchandise. And so, employing their capitals, they send forth the benefit of their labor amongst many and sundry of the natives, which they, by the traffic of their negotiation, do enrich. From whence it's easy to judge of the profit that princes and commonwealths do reap by giving liberty of religion to the Jews and gathering them by some special privileges into their countries, as trees that bring forth such excellent fruits.

So that if one prince, ill-advised, driveth them out of his land, yet another invites them to his and shows them favor. Wherein we may see the prophecy of Jacob fulfilled in the letter: "The staff (to support him) shall not depart from Jacob, until Messias shall come."[56] And this shall suffice concerning the profit of the Jewish nation.

How Faithful the Nation of the Jews Are

The fidelity of vassals and subjects is a thing that princes much most esteem of, for thereon—both in peace and war—depends the preservation of their estates. And as for this point, in my opinion they owe much to the nation of the Jews, by reason of the faithfulness and loyalty they show to all potentates that receive and protect them in their countries. For setting aside the histories of the Ptolemies, kings of Egypt, who did not trust the guard of their persons, nor the

55. Possibly an allusion to Zech. 14:21: "In that day there shall be no more the Canaanite in the house of the Lord of hosts."
56. Gen. 49:10.

keeping of their forts, nor the most important affairs of their kingdom to any other nation with greater satisfaction than to the Jews; the wounds of Antipater showed to Julius Caesar in token of his loyalty, and the brazen tablets of our ancestors amongst the Romans are evident witnesses enough of their fidelity showed unto them. . . . [57]

The same affection is confirmed by the inviolable custom of all the Jews wheresoever they live. For on every Sabbath or festival day, they everywhere are used to pray for the safety of all kings, princes, and commonwealths under whose jurisdiction they live, of what profession soever, unto which duty they are bound by the prophets and the talmudists, from the Law, as by Jeremiah (chapter 29, verse 7): "Seek the peace of the city unto which I have made you to wander: and pray for her unto the Lord, for in her peace you shall enjoy peace." He speaks of Babylon, where the Jews at that time were captives. From the Talmud (Ord. 4, Tract. 4, Aboda Zara, Perek 1): "Pray for the peace of the kingdom, for unless there were fear of the kingdom, men should swallow one the other alive, etc."[58]

From the continual and never broken custom of the Jews wheresoever they are, on the Sabbath day, or other solemn feasts, at which time all the Jews from all places come together to the synagogue, after the benediction of the holy law. Before the minister of the synagogue blesseth the people of the Jews, with a loud voice he blesseth the prince of the country under whom they live, that all the Jews may hear it and say "Amen." . . .

Now I will not conceal to say, but that always there have been found some calumniators that, endeavoring to make the nation infamous, laid upon them three most false reports, as if they were dangerous to the goods, the lives, and withal to the very souls of the natives. They urge against them their usuries, the slaying of infants to celebrate their Passover, and the inducing Christians to become Jews. . . .

1. As for usury, such dealing is not the essential property of the Jews, for though in Germany there be some indeed that practice usury, yet the most part of them that live in Turkey, Italy, Holland, and Hamburg, being come out of Spain, they hold it infamous to use it. . . . In our law it is a greater sin to rob or defraud a stranger than if I did it to one of my own profession, because a Jew is bound to show his charity to all men. For he hath a precept not to abhor an Idumean, nor an Egyptian, and that he shall love and protect a stranger that comes to live in his land. If notwithstanding there be some that do contrary to this, they do it not as Jews simply, but as wicked Jews, as amongst all nations there are found generally some usurers.

2. As for killing of the young children of Christians, it is an infallible truth what is reported of the Negroes of Guinea and Brazil: that if they see any miserable man that hath escaped from the danger of the sea or hath fallen or suffered

57. The Ptolemies were a dynasty of Greek kings of Egypt, founded by Ptolemy I (367?–283 B.C.E.); Josephus (1:2) relates that Antipater, father of Herod the Great, proved his loyalty to Caesar by showing him the many scars that spoke for him. Josephus also refers to "bronze tablets engraved with the Jews' privileges" in Antioch, in the time of Titus Caesar after his conquest of Jerusalem (8:122).
58. A reference to the Talmudic explication of the cited passage in Jeremiah.

any kind of ill-fortune or shipwreck, they persecute and vex him so much the more saying, "God curse thee." And we that live not amongst the blackamoors[59] and wild men, but amongst the white and civilized people of the world, yet we find this an ordinary course: that men are very prone to hate and despise him that hath ill fortune, and on the other side, to make much of those whom fortune doth favor. Hereof the Christians themselves have good experience, for during the times of their suppression and persecution under the Roman empire, they were falsely slandered of divers emperors and tyrannical princes. Nero accused them that they had set Rome on fire; others that they were witches and conjurers, and others again that they slew their children to celebrate their ceremonies, as we find in divers authors.[60] Even so likewise it is with the Jewish nation that now is dispersed and afflicted, though they have moneys. There is no slander nor calumny that is not cast upon them; even the very same ancient scandal that was cast of old upon the innocent Christians is now laid upon the Jews. Whereas the whole world may easily perceive it is but a mere slander, seeing it is known that at this day, out of Jerusalem, no sacrifice nor blood is in any use by them; even that blood which is found in an egg is forbidden them. How much more man's blood? . . .

3. As for the third point, I say, that although Ferdinand and Isabel, giving color to so indiscreet a determination, said that they induced the nobles to become Jews, yet truly this cannot be said but by some false informations . . . seeing the Jews do not entice any man to profess their law. But if any man of his own free will come to them, they by their rites and ceremonies are obliged to make proof of them whether they come for any temporal interest, and to persuade them to look well to themselves what they do; that the law unto which they are to submit themselves is of many precepts and doth oblige the transgressor to many sore punishments. And so we follow the example of Naomi, cited in the sacred scripture, who did not persuade Ruth to go along with her, but said first to her: "Orpha thy sister returned to her nation and her gods, go thou and follow her."[61] But Ruth continuing constant, then at length she received her.

Besides this, the Jews indeed have reason to take care for their own preservation, and therefore will not go about by such ways to make themselves odious to princes and commonwealths, under whose dominions they live.

Now because I believe that with a good conscience I have discharged our nation of the Jews of those three slanders or calumnies, as elsewhere I have more at large written about it, I conceive I may from those two qualities of profitableness and fidelity conclude that such a nation ought to be well entertained and also beloved and protected generally of all. . . .

---

59. Dark-skinned African.
60. Nero (37–68) falsely blamed Christians for the burning of Rome in 64. Pagan Romans often thought that Communion involved human blood; turned against Jews, a related misunderstanding is termed a blood libel. It is ironic that the early modern witchcraze was intertwined with Christian demonology, given the earlier accusations that Christians used witchcraft.
61. Ruth 1:15.

Now, having proved the two former points, I could add a third, viz, of the nobility of the Jews, but because that point is enough known amongst all Christians, . . . therefore I will here forbear and rest on that saying of King Solomon, the wisest on earth, "Let another man's mouth praise thee, and not thine own."[62]

FROM MARGARET FELL FOXE, *FOR MANASSETH BEN ISRAEL: THE CALL OF THE JEWS OUT OF BABYLON,*
WHICH IS GOOD TIDINGS TO THE MEEK,
LIBERTY TO THE CAPTIVES,
AND FOR THE OPENING OF THE PRISON DOORS.

To the Jewish Nation, Greeks and Hebrews:

Who are scattered up and down the face of the earth through their rebellion against the Lord, and for the breaking of His commandments and statutes which He commanded them by His servant, Moses, which the Lord sent to bring their forefathers out of Egypt. . . . Now, O Israel, is that fulfilled upon you which Moses the servant of the Lord foretold of you. . . .

Therefore hear the word of the Lord, thou who art called Mannasseth Ben Israel (who art come into this English nation with all the rest of thy Brethren) which is a Land of gathering, where the Lord God is fulfilling His promise, who hath said, "For a small moment have I forsaken thee, but with great mercy will I gather thee" (Isaiah 54:7–8). And this is fulfilled in our day. . . .

Here the Lord God testifies against you, and the abomination of your worship, and here you are found worshipping the imagination of your own hearts, and the host of heaven which the Lord God declares against, this is fulfilled upon you this day. . . . If thou wilt hearken to the voice of the Lord thy God, to keep His commandments and His statutes which are written in this book of the law, and if thou turn unto the lord thy God with all thy heart, and with all thy soul, for this commandment which I command thee this day is not hidden from thee, neither is it far off . . . but the word is very nigh unto thee, in thy mouth, and in thy heart, that thou mayst do it (Deuteronomy 30:10–14). Therefore return to the law and to the testimony. If they speak not according to this word it is because is no light in them. . . . So to the sure law and testimony turn your minds, that it may be unto you a lamp unto your feet, and a light unto your paths. . . . Therefore now that ye may escape the overflowing scourge and be hid in the day of the Lord's fierce wrath, turn to the Lord God who calls you, who waits to be gracious to you and give over making a covenant with Hell and Death. . . .

62. Prov. 27:2.

Therefore to this Law turn your minds to the pure light in your consciences, that you may come to witness the word of the Lord fulfilled. . . . Now here you may see where the Lord will be worshipped, not in outward Temples, or outward synagogues made with hands, but the time is come that the Lord will be worshipped in spirit, in the inward man. . . . Therefore to that which circumciseth the heart, turn your minds to within; for that is not circumcision which is outward, but that is circumcision which is of the heart. . . . And for your Sabbaths which ye look upon to be outward, this likewise you must come to know to be within. . . . Therefore turn to the Lord God who is the rest of His people, and turn your minds to the measure of God in you, by which the Lord God leads and teacheth and guides His people, and there you will come to know and find the true Sabbath and rest to your souls. . . .

Give over your outward washings, your outward observances and ceremonies, and carnal ordinances; they are beggarly and filthy; the Lord abhors them: your temple and your synagogues, that is outward; your circumcision, that is outward; your Sabbath, that is outward; your burnt offerings and sacrifices which is outward, your calling of assemblies and solemn feasts. For all those things, saith the Lord, doth my soul hate. . . .[63]

I charge thee, Manasseth Ben Israel, as thou wilt answer it before the living God, that thou let this be read and published among thy brethren, and to go abroad among them where they are scattered.

Given forth from the redeemed seed from Babylon and Egypt, by the mighty power and outstretched arm of the Lord, to which power all nations shall bow and tremble, who for an ensign is set for the gathering of the nations together, who desires the good of all souls, and waits for the redemption and the bringing back out of captivity of the whole seed. Which the promise and covenant of the Lord is too. That they to us may arise out of Babylon, Sodom, and Egypt, and with us serve the Lord in the land of the living. And this shall answered be with that of God in all consciences.

The figures, and the types, and the shadows are ceased; the Lord God is departed out of them. And the substance of them is come, the holy seed is risen the substance thereof. The Lord hath sent the strength of His rod out of Sion, who is the covenant of light, to open the blind eyes and bring out the prisoners out of prison, and them that sit in darkness out of the prison house, that they may sing a new song unto the Lord and His praise from the end of the earth. And the day of the Lord's power is come, in which He makes His people willing, and as many as receives Him, to them He gives power.

63. Cf. Isa. 1:11–14 and such passages in Ps. as 40:6; 51:16.

GEORGE HERBERT, "THE JEWS"

Poor nation, whose sweet sap, and juice
Our scions[64] *have purloined and left you dry;*
Whose streams we got by the Apostles' sluice
And use in baptism while ye pine and die:
Who by not keeping once became a debtor:[65]
And now by keeping lose the letter:[66]
O that my prayers! mine, alas!
Oh that some angel might a trumpet sound;
At which the Church, falling upon her face,
Should cry so loud until the trump[67] *were drowned,*
And by that cry of her dear Lord obtain
That your sweet sap might come again!

64. The slips used in grafting a new plant on to an old one. Herbert means that Christians, grafted onto Judaism, have taken ("purloined" can mean "stolen") the moisture of that older stock.
65. Fallen into spiritual debt by failing to "keep" Jesus as Messiah.
66. By clinging to the letter of the law, they lose the truth of the spirit.
67. Trumpet call.

POLITICAL LIFE

AND

SOCIAL STRUCTURES

16

Mary Tudor Brandon, *dowager of France (1496–1533)*

Thomas Howard, *duke of Norfolk (1473–1554)*

Mary Tudor Brandon Pleads to Wed Her Choice

The younger of Henry VIII's two surviving sisters, beautiful Mary Tudor (1496–1533) became in October 1514—at the age of eighteen—wife of the feeble, recently widowed, fifty-two-year-old Louis XII of France. Mary was crowned queen of France on November 5, 1514, but Louis died on January 1, 1515. The marriage had been arranged by Henry VIII as a retaliation against Charles V, who had broken an arrangement to marry Mary. Mary had agreed to marry Louis only after she had been promised that she could choose a new husband after Louis's expected death. She chose Charles Brandon, duke of Suffolk (d. 1545). Although Brandon was a royal favorite, Henry was reluctant to keep his word, and Mary may have won out only by inducing Brandon, who had been sent to Paris to congratulate François I on his accession, to marry her before she left France. The couple had to pay heavy fines in recompense for the expenses Henry had incurred in connection with her first marriage. By the time of her death, however, she and Brandon were reasonably reconciled with the English court. The letters that follow, which testify to the use of high-born women as political pawns, rely on transcriptions in Mary Anne Everett Green's *Letters of Royal and Illustrious Ladies of Great Britain* (1846). They record Mary's anguish in 1515 when, after the death of Louis XII, she found herself a beautiful, relatively unprotected young widow in a foreign court, pursued—possibly with less than reputable intentions—even by François I. The words in brackets follow Green's efforts at restoration of texts damaged in the 1731 fire at the Cotton Library, Ashburnham House, Westminster.

MARY, QUEEN-DOWAGER OF FRANCE, TO HER BROTHER, HENRY VIII

Mine own good and most kind brother,

I recommend me unto your grace and thank you for the good and kind letters that you have sent me, the which has been the greatest comfort might be unto me in this world. Desiring your grace so for to continue, for there is nothing so great a store[1] [to] me as for to see you, the which I would very fain[2] have the time for to come—as I trust it shall be—or else I would be very sorry. For I think every day a thousand till I may see you.

Sire, whereas your grace sends me word that I will not give no credence [to the]m for no suit,[3] nor for no other words that shall be given me; sire, I promise your grace that I never made them no promise, nor no other fo[r the]m, nor never will [until] that I know your [grace's mind] for nobody alive. For [your grace] is all the comfort t[hat I have] in this world, [and I trus]t your grace w[ill not] fail. For I have noth[ing in this] world that I care for but to have the good and [kind] mind that your grace had ever toward me, [which] I beseech your grace to continue. For therein is my trust that I have in this world.

Sire, as for the letter that your grace did send me by [Master] Clinton[4] (whereas you send m[e word] that I should provide myself [and make] me ready for to come to your grace): sire, an[5] it were tomorrow I would be ready. And as for my lord of Suffolk, and Sir Richard [Wingfield],[6] and Doctor West[7] there be two or [three th]at came from the k[ing m]y son[8] for to have [brought the]m to him by the w[ay as they] came hitherward, [and so hindere]d them coming [hithe]rward that th___ as I trust shall c[onclude in] a day or two. And then [let me] know your mind, for an when I do I will do thereafter.

Sire, I beseech your grace for to be good lord to Mr. John, your surgeon, for my sake, and that you will not be miscontented with him for his long tarrying here with me. For I bore him an [ha]nd[9] that your grace were contented that he should be here with me awhile. And so I pray your grace to give him leave for to tarry here awhile with me for because I am very ill-diseased with the toothache and the mother[10] withal, that some times I wot not what for to

1. Treasure.
2. Gladly.
3. Courtship.
4. Possibly Thomas, eighth Lord Clinton.
5. If.
6. Sir Richard Wingfield (1469?–1525) was a soldier and diplomat.
7. Doctor Nicolas West (1461–1533), Bishop of Ely and diplomat.
8. François I (1494–1547), son-in-law and successor to Louis XII.
9. Persuaded.
10. Hysteria.

be. But [an I] might see your grace I were he[aled]. No more to you at this [time], but I pray God [to send] your grace good [life and long].

By your loving [sister], Mary

MARY, QUEEN-DOWAGER OF FRANCE, TO HER BROTHER, HENRY VIII

To the King my brother this be delivered in haste:

[In my] most kind and [loving wise] I recommend me unto your grace. I would be very glad to hear that your grace were in good health and p[eace], the which should be a great comfort to me and that it will please your grace to send more oft time to me than you do. For as now I am all out of comfort, saving that all my trust is in your grace, and so shall be during my life.

Sire, I pray your grace that it will please your grace to be so good lord and brother to me that you will send hither as soon as you may possibly hither to me. Sire, I beseech your grace that you will keep all the promises that you promised me when I took my leave of you by the w[ater s]ide. Sire, your grace knoweth well that I did marry for your pl[easure a]t this time, and now I trust that you will suffer me to [marry as] me l[iketh fo]r to do. For, sire, I k[now that yo]u shall have ___ s that they ___. For I assure your grace that [my mi]nd is not there where they would have me, and I trust [your grace] will not do so to me that has always been so glad to fulfill your mind as I have been. Wherefore I beseech your grace for to be good lord and brother to me. For sire, an if your grace will have gran[ted] me married in any place, [sav]ing whereas my mind is, I will be there, whereas your grace nor no other shall have any joy of me. For I promise your grace you shall hear that I will be in some religious house, the which I think your grace would be very sorry of and all your realm. Also, sire, I know well that the king, that is [my so]n, will send to your grace by his uncle the duke of ___ for to ma[rry me here, but I tru]st you[r grace ___ I sha]ll never be merry at my heart, (for an ever that I d[o marr]y while I live).

I trow your grace knoweth as well as I do and did before I came hither. And so I trust your grace will be contented, unless I would never marry while I live but be there where never [no] man nor woman shall have joy of me. Wherefore I beseech your grace to be good lord to him and to me both, for I know well that he hath m[et ma]ny hindrances to your grace of him and me both. Wherefore, an your grace be good lord to us both, I will not care for all the world else but beseech your grace to be good lord and brother to me, as you have been here aforetime. F[or in you] is all the trust that I have in this world after God. No m[ore from m]e at this [time]. God send your grace [long life an]d your heart's de[sires]

By your humble and loving sister,
Mary Queen of France

MARY, QUEEN-DOWAGER OF FRANCE, TO HER BROTHER HENRY VIII

Pleaseth it your grace, the French [king], on Tuesday night last [past], came to visit me and [had] with me many diverse [discoursin]g. Among the which he demanded me whether I had [ever] made any promise of marriage in any place, assuring me upon his honor and upon the word of a prince, that in case I would be plain [with] him in that affair, that he would do for me therein to the best of his power, whether it were in his realm or out of the same. Whereunto I answered, that I would disclose unto him the [secre]t of my heart in hu[mili]ty, as unto the prince of the world after your grace in whom I had m[ost trust]. And so declar[ed unto him] the good mind [which] for divers consi[derations I] bear to my lord of Suffolk, asking him not only [to grant] me his favor and consent thereunto, but [also] that he would of his [own] hand write unto your grace and to pray you to bear your like favor unto me and to be content with the same. The which he granted me to do and so hath done, according as shall appear unto your grace by his said [letters].

And sire, I most humbly beseech you to take this answer which I have [made u]nto the French king in good part, the which [I did] only to be discharg[ed of t]he extreme pain and annoyance I was i[n, by reason] of such suit as t[he French kin]g made unt[o me not accordi]ng with mine honor, [the whi]ch he hath clearly left [off]. Also, sire, I feared greatly [lest, in] case that I had kept the matter from his knowledge that he might have not well entreated my said lord of Suffolk, and the rather [for] to have returned to his [former] malfantasy and suits.

Wherefore sire, [sinc]e it hath pleased the said king to desire and pray you of your favor and consent, I most humbly and heartily beseech you that it may like your grace to bear your favor and consent to the same, and to advertise the said king by your writing of your own hand of your pleasure. [And] in that he hath ac[ted after] mine opinion [in his] letter of request, [it] shall be to your great honor ___ nem to content w[ith all] your council and [with] all the other no[bles of the] realm and agr[ee thereto] for your grace a[nd for all] the world. And therefore I eftsoons requi[re you], for all the love that it liked your grace to bear me, that you do not refuse but grant me your favor and consent in form before rehearsed. The which, if you shall deny me, I am well assured to [lead] as desolate a life as ever had creature, the which I know well shall be mine end.

Always praying your grace to have compassion of me, my most loving and sovereign lord and [brother, where]unto I have [entreated] you, beseeching [God al]ways to [preserve your] most royal [estate. Written] at Paris the 15th day of February.

[I mo]st humbly beseech your grace to consider (in case that you make difficulty to condescend to the promises [as I] wish): the French king will take new courage to renew his suits to me (assuring you that I had rather to be out of the world than it should so happen). And how he shall entreat my lord of Suffolk—

God knoweth, with many other inconveniences which might ensue of the same, the which I pray our Lord that I may ne[ver ha]ve life to see.

By your loving sister and true servant,
Mary Queen of France

The Duke of Norfolk Interviews Marguerite de Navarre

In 1533 Henry VIII sent Thomas Howard, third duke of Norfolk (1473–1554), to France to encourage French support for Henry's foreign and domestic policies. Although not a very good diplomat, the duke knew enough to cultivate the French king's famous and talented sister, Marguerite, queen of Navarre. Marguerite, together with the king's mistress, the duchesse d'Estampes, and the powerful Cardinal, Jean du Bellay, led a faction friendly to England. Opposing them was a pro-Imperial group that preferred Henry's occasional enemy and occasional ally, Emperor Charles V, whose sister had married the French king and whose aunt, Catherine of Aragon, was Henry's divorced wife. Norfolk's account of his talk with the astute Marguerite (already a poet and future author of *The Heptameron*) is summarized with much quotation in *Letters and Papers, Foreign and Domestic, of the Reign of Henry VIII*, vol. 6, ed. James Gairdner (London, 1882; Vaduz: Kraus Reprint, 1965), #692, June 23, 1533. The dispatch is damaged and has gaps, here indicated by ellipses. Norfolk was to preside over the trial that condemned his niece, Anne Boleyn, to death and he saw his son, the poet Surrey, beheaded for treason, a fate he narrowly escaped himself. The *Dictionary of National Biography* calls him "hot-tempered, self-seeking, and brutal," but he seems to have hit it off with Marguerite, or to have thought he did.

THE DUKE OF NORFOLK TO HENRY VIII, JUNE 23, 1533.

Since coming here [Paris] I have been twice with the queen of Navarre, and both times for at least five hours. She is one of the most wisest frank women, and best setter forth of her purpose, that I have spoken with, and as affectionate to your Highness as if she were your own sister, and likewise to the queen.[1] She told me she had divers matters of importance to open to me, if I would promise to disclose them only to you and the queen. This I promised to observe. She said, "I advise you at your coming to the court to have good regard how the king my brother's council do proceed, . . . that whatsoever the Great Master[2] shall say . . . " [what follows is badly damaged but the gist is that the Great Master, Montmorency, is pro-Imperial, a friend of the French queen Eleanor, and not to be trusted], showing me fur[ther] . . . he did not only show

1. Anne Boleyn. Marguerite in fact responded ambivalently to Henry's divorce.
2. Duc de Montmorency, leader of the pro-Charles V faction at court.

the same by his favorable acts in all the Emperor's affairs, but that also I should well perceive that no man in France was so ready to serve and please the queen[3] here as he. To prove his affection she told me that the gentleman lately returned from Scotland told her that the marriage between the Scotch king and the daughter of the duke of Vendôme was fully agreed upon by the Great Master's means, if one of them shall like the other. There was no nobleman in France so Imperial as the said Duke, which he openly showed when his master was prisoner, by not doing his best for him nor his realm.[4] She assured me I should find the Grand Master more friendly in words than deeds, if the cause touched anything against the Emperor.

She told me also that about three months ago the Great Master told the Dauphin[5] that he did not well to set his love upon a damsel who neither was wise, fair, nor yet had "bonne grace."[6] The Dauphin replied that he used his love as became him to do, and he would not make him his judge where he would bear favor or displeasure, saying [to Montmorency], "Look upon your own deeds, and see they be honest, and care not for mine." A few days after the Great Master found fault with a garment the Dauphin wore, saying it [became] not him to wear such one; whereunto he answered [with many] . . . sore words; so that the Great Master was not a little [a]bashed therewith. Among which one was, "I see your doings well enough. When ye are present with the king my father, he is never content with me; and when ye are absent I can wish him to be no better to me than he is. Your crafty dealings shall not abuse me, nor I shall never forget it. But everything hath his time, which I can well abide for his pleasure that I am bound unto, and not for yours." The Great Master has sought many ways to win him, but without effect, and has lately got the damsel whom the Dauphin loves a place near the queen so that he may haunt the queen's company and be induced to marry her daughter by the king of Portugal, her late husband. In the queen's chamber there are two bands, of those who take the king's or the queen's part, and they keep different sides of the chamber. The Dauphin and his mistress were upon the queen's side, with which the king was much displeased and rebuked the Dauphin very sore for being so much in the queen's company, considering that he knew she did not behave as she ought to his father; saying in anger, "I shall keep thee well enough out of her comp[any], and so determined to go to Toulouse, the most . . . and worst country of the [whole] realm." [The Dauphin has been ill], so that . . . last they were marvelously afraid of his life . . . since he is something amended; but with tears running down her face, she said, that unless God gave him grace to order his person otherwise than he had done hitherto, she feared

3. Eleanor, wife of François I.
4. Some years earlier François had been defeated by Charles V at the battle of Pavia and held prisoner in Spain. Marguerite had visited him in Madrid and was largely responsible for negotiating his release; the resulting treaty led to François's marriage to Charles's sister.
5. Heir to the French throne.
6. A good air, fine manners.

his friends should not long have joy of him. She assured me that if God did his pleasure of him, with wise handling you would have the Dauphin as sure to you as ever you had his father; ever casting out words against the Great Master, which should be too tedious for you. She told me also that no man can be worse content with his wife than her brother is, so that these seven months he neither lay with her, nor yet meddled with her. I asked her the cause why; and she said, "Parce qu'il ne le trouve plaisant à son appétit;[7] nor when he doth lie with her, he cannot sleep; and when he lieth from her, no man sleepeth better." I said, "Madame, what should be the cause?" She said, "She is very hot in bed, and desireth to be too much embraced"; and therewith she fell upon a great laughter, saying, "I would [not] for all the good in Paris that the king of Navarre were [no be]tter pleased to be in my bed than my brother is to be [in hers]." And therewith she showed me that a little before the . . . began a new . . . . and the Admiral which she . . . thereof; now, methinks, she doth repent, and [w]ell I perceive by her words that she, the Legate, the cardinal of Lorraine, and the Admiral draw one way, and Dauphin doth all lean to them, whereof she doth not a little rejoice. She wished me also to tell you that Béda[8] is banished from this town, and she has procured that his writings will be searched by Le Bar, provost of Paris, and others, among which will be found shameful railings against the kings of England and of France, saying that they do not live like good Christian princes. I hope to have copies of them.

She wished to know whether the marriage of the duke of Vendôme's daughter to the king of Scots would be more to your purpose than the King of Navarre's sister. The duke is and ever will be fast Imperial, as the greatest part of his living is in the Emperor's dominions. The Emperor is continually trying to marry his niece, whom the duke of Milan should have had, to the Scottish king, and has broken that marriage only to do you displeasure, which duke of Milan's marriage, Sir John Wallop doth write to me, is broken. She would . . . your Highness's pleasure if ye would be content she . . . Isabel of Navarre which . . . may be with your pleasure. I showed her if . . . concluded, it were too late to speak thereof . . . for both the duke of Vendôme's daughters . . . sore made awry, and that known she doubted not the young King would refuse them. By this means, she said, you would disappoint the Emperor's malicious purpose towards you; and if hereafter Madame Isabel had any credit with him, she would cause him to be a fast enemy to the Emperor, who keeps her brother's realm of Navarre from him wrongfully. After his only daughter, she is the next heir.

I think the marriage with Madame Isabel much better than the other, because if any business should chance between the King, your nephew, and yourself, the aid of the duke of Vendôme would be much more advantageous to Scotland than that of the other, whose lands are near Spain and who is not of

7. "Because he doesn't find her appealing to his taste."
8. Noël Béda, a conservative theologian, had tried to have Marguerite's *Miroir de l'âme pécheresse* (later translated by Elizabeth I) censored.

the blood royal. And [no par]t of his lands within a hundred miles of the sea, ... [I] perceive [by her w]ords the chief cause why she would have this [marria]ge take effect is that she trusteth surely that a perpetual peace shall be taken between your Highness and your nephew, and then by your help she trusts to recover her husband's realm.[9] She does not think the young king will be able to do her good but[10] through your help and sufferance. She trusts more in the Dauphin's help than her brother's while the Great Master is in authority, which will not continue long if she can impeach it, and few of the nobles will be sorry.

Le Bar told her that the Emperor's ambassador, when he spoke of your great cause,[11] was wont to set his words with such a violence as an hackbut[12] had shot, but now, hearing how you had proceeded in England, he is as mild as a lamb, and says to the King, "Sir, since it is done of such sort in England, now help your Grace that yonder noble woman[13] may be nobly entertained and handled." This is the effect of her sayings to me, about which I wish to know your pleasure, and request that it may be kept secret. My opinion is that she is your good and sure friend.

9. Spain, under Charles V, had taken part of Navarre.
10. Except.
11. Henry's divorce; Henry had insisted that his marriage to Catherine had been invalid from the start, so Norfolk avoids the word "divorce."
12. A portable firearm.
13. Anne Boleyn, now queen of England.

17

Margaret Douglas [Stuart],
countess of Lennox (1515–1578)

Thomas Howard *(d. 1537)*

Margaret Douglas [Stuart] and Thomas Howard Write of Their Love

Varied manuscript communications witnessing to the ill-fated courtship of two young nobles, Margaret Douglas (1515–1578), niece of Henry VIII, and Thomas Howard (d. October 31, 1537), the half-brother of the Duke of Norfolk, have been printed since the sixteenth century. Poems exchanged by the lovers and pre-served in the Devonshire Manuscript (BL Additional MS 17492) were written during their imprisonment in separate cells when their secret, politically unset-tling engagement became known in May 1536, about a month after Anne Boleyn's execution. Following Howard's death in the Tower, Douglas capitulat-ed to her political superiors.

Embedded in the context of the lovers' imprisonment, these poems also comment on power relations. They have, moreover, a hitherto unnoted signifi-cance as currency of Eros, being the earliest known exchange of actual love poems in English between a nobleman and noblewoman. We have used the texts in "Unpublished Poems in the Devonshire Manuscript," Kenneth Muir, ed. (*Proceedings of the Leeds Philosophical Society: Literature and History Section* 6, 1947). The letter from Douglas to Thomas Cromwell is reproduced by both Henry Ellis and Mary Green from a holograph (Cotton MS. Vespasian, F. XIII. ART. 188, fol. 173); Green speculates that Douglas might have been attempting to win favor for Howard. The plaintive poem, "Now That Ye Be Assembled Here," appears in a later portion of the Devonshire Manuscript than the others. In Douglas's hand, it seems to address her father after Howard's death, when she thought she too was going to die. Her distress, though, takes on some irony when one recalls that she was to be the mother of Henry Stuart, Lord Darnley, ill-fated consort of Mary Stuart. Douglas's hatred for her daughter-in-law (whose attachment to the earl of Bothwell may have led to Darnley's murder) is particularly fascinating on the part of one who had herself experienced a heart-wrenching love affair. We have deliberately left the authorship of the individual poems ambiguous.

NOW MAY I MOURN AS ONE OF LATE

Now may I mourn as one of late
Driven by force from my delight
And cannot see my lonely mate
To whom forever my heart is plight.[1]

Alas, that ever prison strong
Should such two lovers separate!
Yet though our body suffereth wrong
Our hearts shall be of one estate.

I will not swerve I you ensure
For gold nor yet for worldly fear;
But like as iron I will endure
Such faithful love to you I bear.

Thus fare ye well to me most dear,
Of all the world both most and least;
I pray you be of right good cheer,
And think on me that loves you best.

And I will promise you again
To think of you I will not let:[2]
For nothing could release my pain
But to think on you, my lover sweet.

1. Pledged.
2. Stop.

With Sorrowful Sighs and Wounds Smart

With sorrowful sighs and woundès smart
    My heart is piercèd suddenly;
To mourn of right it is my part,
    To weep, to wail full grievously.

The bitter tears doth me constrain,
    Although that I would it eschew[3]
To write of them that doth disdain
    Faithful lovers that be so true.

The one of us from the other they do absent,
    Which unto us is a deadly wound,
Seeing we love in this intent
    In God's laws for to be bound.

With sighs deep my heart is pressed,
    During[4] of great pains among
To see her daily whom I love best
    In great and untolerable sorrows strong.

There doth not live no loving heart
    But will lament our grievous woe,
And pray to God to ease our smart
    And shortly together that we may go.

What Thing Should Cause Me To Be Sad?

What thing should cause me to be sad?
    As long (as) ye rejoice with heart
My part it is for to be glad:
    Since you have taken me to your part
    Ye do release my pain and smart
Which would me very sore ensue[5]
But that for you my trust so true.

3. Avoid.
4. Enduring.
5. Follow upon.

If I should write and make report
What faithfulness in you I find
The term of life it were too short
With pen in letters it to bind:
Wherefore whereas ye be so kind,
As for my part it is but due
Like case to you to be as true.

My love truly shall not decay
For threatening nor for punishment;
For let them think and let them say
Toward you alone I am full bent:[6]
Therefore I will be diligent
Our faithful love for to renew,
And still to keep me trusty and true.

Thus fare ye well my worldly treasure,
Desiring God that of His grace
To send us time His will and pleasure
And shortly to get us out of this place:
Then shall I be in as good case
As a hawk that gets out of his mew,[7]
And straight doth seek his trust so true.

ALAS THAT MEN BE SO UNGENT

Alas that men be so ungent[8]
To order me so cruelly!
Of right they should themself repent
If they regard their honesty.

They know my heart is set so sure
That all their words cannot prevail,
Though that they think me to allure
With doubtful tongue and flattering tale.

Alas, me think they do me wrong
That they would have me to resign

6. Inclined.
7. A coop or cage for hawks.
8. Graceless.

My title which is good and strong,
  That I am yours and you are mine.

I think they would that I should swear
  Your company for to forsake
But once there is no worldly fear
  Shall cause me such an oath to make.

For I do trust ere it be long
  That God of his benignity,[9]
Will send us right where we have wrong,
  For serving him thus faithfully.

Now fare ye well my own sweet wife,
  Trusting that shortly I shall hear
From you the stay of all my life,
  Whose health alone is all my cheer.

WHO HATH MORE CAUSE FOR TO COMPLAIN

Who hath more cause for to complain
Or to lament his sorrow and pain
Then I which loves and loved again
  Yet cannot obtain?

I cannot obtain what is my own,
Which causeth me still to make great moan
To see thus right with wrong overthrown,
  As not unknown.

It is not unknown how wrongfully
They will me her for to deny,
Whom I will love most heartily
  Until I die.

Until I die I will not let
To seek her out in cold and heat,
Which hath my heart as firmly set
As tongue or pen can it repeat.

9. Kindness.

I May Well Say with Joyful Heart

I may well say with joyful heart
As never woman might say before
That I have taken to my part
The faithfulest lover that ever was born.

Great pains he suffereth for my sake
Continually both night and day,
For all the pains that he doth take
From me his love will not decay.

With threatening great he hath been paid
Of pain and eke[10] *of punishment,*
Yet all fear aside he hath laid:
To love me best was his intent.

Who shall let[11] *me then of right*
Unto myself him to retain
And love him best both day and night
In recompense of his great pain?

If I had more, more he should have,
And that I know he knows full well;
To love him best unto my grave,
Of that he may both buy and sell.

And thus fare well, my heart's desire,
The only stay[12] *of me and mine;*
Unto god daily I make my prayer
To bring us shortly both in one line.

10. Also.
11. Hinder, prevent.
12. Support.

To Your Gentle Letters An Answer To Recite

To your gentle letters, an answer to recite,
    Both I and my pen thereto will apply.
And though that I cannot your goodness acquite[13]
    In rhyme and meter elegantly
    Yet do I mean as faithfully
As ever did lover for his part.
I take God to record which knoweth my heart.

And whereas ye will continue mine
    To report for me ye may be bold,
That if I had lives as Argus had eyne,[14]
    Yet sooner all them lose I would
    Than to be tempt for fear or for gold
You to refuse or to forsake
Which is my faithful and loving make.[15]

Which faithfulness ye did ever pretend[16]
    And gentleness as now I see
Of me which was your poor old friend,
    Your loving husband now to be;
    Since ye descend from your degree[17]
Take ye this unto your part,
My faithful, true, and loving heart.

For term of life this gift ye have.
    Thus now adieu my own sweet wife,
From T. H. which naught doth crave
    But you, the stay of all my life;
    And they that would other bait or strife
To be tied within our loving bands,
I would they were on Goodwin Sands.[18]

13. Acquit, recompense.
14. A monster with one hundred eyes (eyne) that Juno sent to guard one of Jove's beloveds.
15. Mate.
16. Profess.
17. Position, rank.
18. A well-known drowned island; the wish here is that enemies be drowned or wrecked.

NOW MY PEN, ALAS, WITH WHICH I WRITE

And now my pen, alas, with which I write,
Quaketh for dread of that I must endite.[19]

O very lord, O love, O god, alas!
*   That knowest best mine heart and all my thought,*
What shall my sorrowful life done in this case
*   If I forgo that I so dear have bought*
*   Since ye and me have fully brought*
Into your grace and both our hearts sealed,
How may ye suffer, alas, it be repealed?

What I may do I shall while I may dure
*   On live, in torment and in cruel pain,*
This infortune,[20] *or this disadventure.*
*   Alone as I was born I will complain,*
*   Ne never will I see it shine or rain*
But end I will as Edyppe[21] *in darkness*
My sorrowful life and so die in distress.

O weary ghost that errest[22] *to and fro*
*   Why would thou not fly out of the woefullest*
Body that ever might on ground go?
*   O soul, lurking in this woeful nest*
*   Fly forth my heart and that breast*
And follow alway thy lady dear!
Thy right place is now no longer here.

O ye lovers that high upon the wheel
*   Be set of fortune in good adventure,*[23]
God grant that ye finden aye[24] *love of steel.*
*   And long may your life in joy endure;*
*   But when ye comen by my sepulture*
Remember that your fellow resteth there,
For I loved eke, though I unworthy were.

19. Compose.
20. Ill fortune.
21. Oedipus blinded himself after learning about his patricide and incest.
22. Wanders.
23. Having the good luck to sit atop Fortune's traditional wheel.
24. Ever.

LADY MARGARET DOUGLAS TO LORD CROMWELL (1536)

My lord,

What cause have I to give you thanks and how much bound am I unto you that by your means hath gotten me, as I trust, the king's grace's favor again! And besides that, that it pleaseth you to write and to give me knowledge wherein I might have his grace's displeasure against which I pray our Lord sooner to send me death than that. And I assure you, my lord, I will never do that thing willingly that should offend his grace.

And, my lord, whereas it is informed you that I do charge the house with a greater number than is convenient, I assure you I have but two more than I had in the court, which, indeed, were my lord Thomas' servants. And the cause that I took them for was for the poverty that I saw them in, and for no cause else.

But seeing, my lord, that it is your pleasure that I shall keep none that did belong unto my Lord Thomas, I will put them from me. And I beseech you not to think that any fancy doth remain in me touching him, but that all my study and care is how to please the king's grace and to continue in his favor. And, my lord, where it is your pleasure that I shall keep but a few here with me, I trust you will think that I can have no fewer than I have, for I have but a gentleman and a groom that keeps my apparel, and another that keeps my chamber, and a chaplain that was with me always in the court.

Now, my lord, I beseech you that I may know your pleasure, if you would that I should keep any fewer. Howbeit, my lord, my servants have put the house to small charge, for they have nothing but the reversion of my board, nor I do call for nothing but that that is given me. Howbeit, I am very well entreated. And, my lord, as for resort,[25] I promise you I have none except it be gentlewomen that comes to see me, nor never had since I came hither. For if any resort of men had come, it should neither have become me to have seen them nor yet to have kept them company, being a maid as I am.

Now, my lord, I beseech you to be so good as to get my poor servants their wages. And thus I pray our Lord to preserve you, both soul and body.

By her that has her trust in you,
Margaret Douglas

25. Company, visitors.

NOW THAT YE BE ASSEMBLED HERE

Now that ye be assembled here,
All ye my friends at my request,
'Specially you, my father dear,
That of my blood are the nearest,
This unto you is my request:
That ye will patiently hear
By this my last words expressed
My testament entire.

And think not to interrupt me
For such wise provided have I
That though ye willed it will not be.
This tower ye see is strong and high
And the doors fast barred have I
That no wight[26] *my purpose let should.*
For to be queen of all Italy
Not one day longer live I would.

Therefore, sweet father, I you pray
Bear this my death with patience,
And torment not your hairs gray
But freely pardon mine offense
Since it proceedeth of lover's fervence[27]
And of my heart's constancy.
Let me not from the sweet presence
Of him that I have caused to die.

26. Person.
27. Fervor.

18

Divers Well-Affected Women (1649)

John Taylor (1578–1653)

Divers Well-Affected Women (1649)

Traditionally, women have been expected to maintain public silence and act under what St. Paul calls the "headship" of men in this life (1 Tim. 2:12–14). But the participation of women in public affairs has often been welcomed at times of crisis. During the political and religious tumult of the mid-seventeenth century, when such "Levelers" as John Lilburne (1614?–1657), William Walwyn (fl. 1649), and the even more radical Gerrard Winstanley (1609–1676) were agitating for profound social and political change, women also acted in many forthright ways. Among royalists, many defended homes under siege (Lady Brilliana Harley, notably, died soon after such an episode); many were sent to negotiate concerning the family estates. Humbler women, too, often took a direct part in public affairs, as witness the flurry of mass petitions from which we take our excerpts. These petitions, which occasionally allude to an "ancient" English right of any person to petition, ground that right in Paul's insistence (Gal. 3:28) that in Christ there is neither male nor female. Other traces of what we would today term feminist sentiment are sometimes discernible. For our two sample texts, we rely on the original petitions, arranged chronologically.

THE HUMBLE PETITION OF DIVERS WELL-AFFECTED[1] WOMEN OF THE CITIES OF LONDON AND WESTMINSTER, THE BOROUGH OF SOUTHWARK, HAMLETS AND PARTS ADJACENT, AFFECTERS[2] AND APPROVERS OF THE LATE LARGE PETITION OF THE ELEVENTH OF SEPTEMBER, 1648

To The Supreme Authority of England, The Commons Assembled in Parliament:

Showeth that since we are assured of our creation in the image of God and of an interest in Christ equal unto men, as also of a proportionable share in the freedoms of this commonwealth, we cannot but wonder and grieve that we should appear so despicable in your eyes as to be thought unworthy to petition or represent our grievances to this honorable House.

Have we not an equal interest with the men of this nation in those liberties and securities contained in the Petition of Right[3] and other the good laws of the land? Are any of our lives, limbs, liberties, or goods to be taken from us more than from men but by due process of law and conviction of twelve sworn men of the neighborhood?

And can you imagine us to be so sottish or stupid as not to perceive (or not to be sensible) when daily those strong defenses of our peace and welfare are broken down and trod underfoot by force and arbitrary power?

Would you have us keep at home in our houses, when men of such faithfulness and integrity as the four prisoners our friends in the Tower are fetched out of their beds and forced from their houses by soldiers to the affrighting and undoing of themselves, their wives, children, and families? Are not our husbands, ourselves, our children, and families by the same rule as liable to the like unjust cruelties as they?

Shall such men as Captain Bray[4] be made close prisoners? And such as Mr. Sawyer[5] snatched up and carried away, beaten, and buffeted at the pleasure of some officers of the army? And such as Mr. Blanck[6] kept close prisoner and after most barbarous usage be forced to run the gauntlet and be most slave-like and cruelly whipped? And must we keep at home in our houses as if we, our lives, and liberties, and all were not concerned?

---

1. Well-intentioned.
2. Likers.
3. The Petition of Right (1628) affirmed the first statutory restraints on the crown since the start of the Tudor dynasty in 1485.
4. Laud's chaplain (d. 1644).
5. Presumably William Sawyer, one of five troopers cashiered from the army on March 6, 1649, for passing around petitions and Leveler tracts.
6. Presumably William Blanck or Blancks Jr. of Coleman Street, a barber employed to spy on Lilburne, Walwyn, and other Levelers; he was arrested with other Leveler leaders so as to protect his cover. (Since he then refused to testify against Lilburne and Walwyn, he was kept in jail and ran the gauntlet in Pall Mall.)

Nay, shall such valiant, religious men as Mr. Robert Lockyer[7] be liable to law martial, and be judged by his adversaries, and most unhumanly shot to death? Shall the blood of war be shed in time of peace? Doth not the word of God expressly condemn it? Doth not the Petition of Right declare that no per- son ought to be judged by law martial[8] (except in time of war) and that all commissions[9] given to execute martial law in time of peace are contrary to the laws and statutes of the land? Doth not Sir Edward Coke,[10] in his chapter of murder in the third part of his *Institutes*, hold it for good law (and since owned and published by this Parliament) that for a general or other officers of an army in time of peace to put any man (although a soldier) to death by color[11] of martial law it is absolute murder in that general? And hath it not by this House in the case of the late Earl of Stratford[12] been adjudged high treason? And are we Christians, and shall we sit still and keep at home while such men as have born continual testimony against the injustice of all times and unrighteousness of men, be picked out and be delivered up to the slaughter? And must we show no sense of their sufferings, no tenderness of affections, no bowels of compassion, nor bear any testimony against so abominable cruelty and injustice?

Have such men as these continually hazarded their lives; spent their estates and time; lost their liberties; and thought nothing too precious for defense of us, our lives, and liberties; been as a guard by day and as a watch by night; and when for this they are in trouble and greatest danger, persecuted, and hated even to the death? And should we be so basely ungrateful as to neglect them in the day of their affliction? No, far be it from us. Let it be accounted folly, presumption, madness, or whatsoever in us. Whilst we have life and breath we will never leave them, nor forsake them, nor ever cease to importune you (having yet so much hopes of you as of the unjust judge mentioned, Luke 18 [1–5], to obtain justice—if not for justice sake, yet for importunity), or to use any other means for the enlargement and reparation of those of them that live and for justice against such as have been the cause of Mr. Lockyer's death. Nor will we ever rest until we have prevailed that we, our husbands, children, friends, and servants may not be liable to be thus abused, violated, and butchered at men's wills and pleasures. But if nothing will satisfy but the blood of those just men (those constant, undaunted asserters of the people's freedoms) will satisfy your thirst, drink also and be glutted with our blood, and let us all fall together. Take the blood of one more and take all. Slay one, slay all.

And therefore, again, we entreat you to review our last petition in behalf of our friends above mentioned and not to slight the things therein contained

7. A Leveler supporter and ringleader in 1649 of a mutiny in a London regiment; executed in April 1649.
8. Martial law, military government.
9. Orders.
10. The eminent jurist (1552–1634), author of *The Institutes of the Laws of England*, published in four parts from 1628–1644.
11. Excuse.
12. Thomas Wentworth, the widely hated first earl of Stratford (1593–1641); impeached and executed by the Commons.

because they are presented unto you by the weak hand of women, it being an usual thing with God by weak means to work mighty effects. For we are no whit satisfied with the answer you gave unto our husbands and friends, but do equally with them remain liable to those snares laid in your declaration—which maketh the abetters of the book laid to our friends' charge no less than traitors whenas hardly any discourse can be touching the affairs of the present times but falls within the compass of that book. So that all liberty of discourse is thereby utterly taken away, than which there can be no greater slavery.

Nor shall we be satisfied, however you deal with our friends, except you free them from under their present extrajudicial[13] imprisonment and force upon them and give them full reparations for their forceable attachment, etc. And leave them from first to last to be proceeded against by due process of law, and give them respect from you, answerable to their good and faithful service to the commonwealth.

Our houses being worse than prisons to us, and our lives worse than death; the sight of our husbands and children matter of grief, sorrow, and affliction to us until you grant our desires; and therefore, if ever you intend any good to this miserable nation, harden not your hearts against petitioners nor deny us in things so evidently just and reasonable, as you would not be dishonorable to all posterity. [April 23, 1649]

THE HUMBLE PETITION OF DIVERS WELL-AFFECTED WOMEN INHABITING THE CITIES OF LONDON, WESTMINSTER, THE BOROUGH OF SOUTHWARK, HAMLETS, AND PLACES ADJACENT (AFFECTERS AND APPROVERS OF THE LATE, LARGE PETITION OF THE ELEVENTH OF SEPTEMBER, 1648 IN BEHALF OF LIEUTENANT COLONEL JOHN LILBURNE, MR. WILLIAM WALWYN, MR. THOMAS PRINCE,[14] AND MR. RICHARD OVERTON[15] (NOW PRISONERS IN THE TOWER OF LONDON) AND CAPTAIN WILLIAM BRAY, CLOSE-PRISONER IN WINDSOR CASTLE, AND MR. WILLIAM SAWYER, PRISONER AT WHITEHALL

Unto Every Individual Member of Parliament:

The humble representation of divers afflicted women-petitioners to the Parliament, on the behalf of Mr. John Lilburne

Showeth that we cannot but be much saddened to see our undoubted right of petitioning withheld from us (having attended several days at your House door with an humble petition, desiring the making null of that most unrighteous, illegal act made against Mr. Lilburne by the late Parliament) although it is the

13. Legally unwarranted.
14. A successful London cheese merchant; assistant to Walwyn.
15. A Leveler pamphleteer (fl. 1646); jailed several times.

known duty of Parliaments to receive petitions, and it is ours and the nation's undoubted right to petition, although an act of Parliament were made against it.

Your Honors may please to call to mind the unjust and unrighteous acts made by King Ahasuerus in the case of Mordecai and the Jews. Yet Esther, that righteous woman, being encouraged by the justness of the cause (as we at this time are, through the justness of Mr. Lilburne's cause and the common cause of the whole nation) did adventure her life to petition against so unrighteous acts obtained by Haman, the Jews' enemy.[16]

Your Honors may please to consider whether the late unjust and illegal act against Mr. Lilburne was not obtained by such an enemy as proud Haman was, having no more cause for so doing than Haman had. Neither do we hope that your Honors, upon mature consideration, will have the less regard unto our petition, although women, judging that you will not be worse unto us than that heathen king was to Esther, who did not only hear her petition but reversed that decree or act gone forth against the Jews, and did severely punish the obtainer thereof, as in truth we hope your Honors will judge that man to deserve no less a punishment who obtained the said most unjust and illegal act against Mr. Lilburne (though a favorite, as Haman was). Truly we cannot but judge the said act against Mr. Lilburne, since what is done or intended against him (being against common right and in the face thereof) may be done unto every particular person in the nation.

Your Honors may be pleased to call to mind that never-to-be-forgotten deliverance obtained by the good women of England against the usurping Danes, then in this nation. You may likewise consider the readiness and willingness of the good women of this nation, who did think neither their lives nor their husbands' and servants' lives and estates to be too dear a price for the gaining of yours and the nation's ancient rights and liberties out of the hands of encroachers and oppressors.

And, therefore, we hope that upon second thoughts your Honors will not slight the persons of your humble petitioners, nor withhold from us our undoubted right of petitioning, since God is ever willing and ready to receive the petitions of all, making no difference of persons. The ancient laws of England were not contrary to the will of God: so that we claim it as our right to have our petitions heard, you having promised to govern the nation in righteousness. Therefore, we trust that you will not suffer any further proceedings to be had upon that most unrighteous act against Mr. Lilburne. [July 1649]

John Taylor Describes a Hellish Parliament

John Taylor (1578–1653), called the "Water Poet" because of his job ferrying customers on the Thames River, was a "popular" writer given more to boisterous clown-

---

16. An allusion to the triumph of Esther, Mordecai, and the Jewish people over the machinations of Haman, minister of Ahasuerus. Mordecai directs the Jewish sect, and Esther, married to King Ahasuerus, dares enter his presence unsummoned (Book of Esther).

ing than humanist learning. A royalist Anglican, he had no patience for Catholics and their foreign supporters or for radical Protestants of either sex who undermined clerical, gender, and political hierarchies. The early 1640s, when Britain was torn by civil war, saw a flood of political and religious pamphlets. Some imagined consultations in the underworld—a tradition going back to the Syrian satirist Lucian and exploited in England by such writers as Donne, in *Ignatius His Conclave*, and John Milton, in *Paradise Lost*. Since much national debate was staged in Parliament, satire also took the form of parodic legislative sessions. Here Taylor combines these two satirical methods. Some such satire mocked women who, like others from marginalized or oppressed groups, had upset conservatives by speaking out or joining the frenzy of publication. See, for example, *An Exact Diurnal of the Several Passages in the Parliament of Ladies* (1647) and its sequel *The Ladies a Second time Assembled in Parliament* (1647), or Henry Neville's *News from the New Exchange, or the Commonwealth of Ladies* (1649).

THE HELLISH PARLIAMENT, BEING A COUNTER-PARLIAMENT

His Infernal Majesty, taking into his Hellish consideration the great happiness that now is towards England, and fearing that his dear children, as well those of the Romish faction as of the Brownist sect,[1] should have a terrible fall and their erroneous and seditious practices should be laid open, he resolved, if possibly he could, to trouble the felicious proceedings of the Parliament. And to that end, having long consulted with the subtle judges of his Infernal Empire, he purposed to summon a counter-Parliament against that in England, and gave orders that the most prudent, politic, and impious sectaries within the bounds of his dominions should be assembled to debate, propound, and propound, concerning divers important and very weighty affairs. His mind[2] was quickly fulfilled in such a manner that he was overjoyed to see such an innumerable company of his very diligentest servants of each faction. Therefore his Infernalship, to make it appear how much he [was] pleased therewith, bestowed on them a speech in this ungracious manner:

"Most dearly beloved and adopted children, it is not unknown to your Hellish understandings what great thunderclaps have fallen upon our right trusty and well-beloved servants the Papists in England by that wonder-working Parliament now assembled. I give you now also to understand that if there be not some speedy course taken all will be lost. For as soon as they have done with our dear servants the Papists, they will begin with our best-beloved sons the Brownists. Therefore, as it hath ever been, so now such is our infernal care of the increase of our servants, we have assembled this sinful synod. Rub therefore your Hellish invention and courageously work, striving who shall be forwardest to our

1. "Romish" means Catholic; the "Brownists" belonged to a radical Protestant sect opposing the established church.
2. Desire, request.

(I fear) declining Empire. Let me hear your counsels, and I promise in all your endeavors you shall have my utmost assistance." Then was there a great hubbub between the Papists and Brownists concerning precedence of speech—indeed both are wicked great bawlers. The Papists, being the elder faction, thought [that], of right, priority of speech belonged to them. But though the Brownists were the younger Sir Johns,[3] they were his Infernalship's nursling, most resembling him their father, and his most dearly beloved. Therefore they thought they should speak first. Yet at last, after much squabbling, they yielded. Then, silence being commanded, Guy Fawkes[4] was chosen Speaker for the Papists and, after low obeisance made, he thus began:

"Most Infernal Emperor, we your obedient sons and servants the English Romanists are here prostrate before you, and as dutiful servants do all accord to do you nocturnal and diurnal service. But, Great Emperor, we cannot choose but lament when we remember the disastrous chances that have fallen upon our forward intentions. You may remember with what heroic stomachs[5] we have long plotted for the enlargement of your infernal Empire, as in that fatal year 1588, when with such large sums we negotiated abroad and at home endeavored to conquer for you that same little angle of the world, England. And in that memorable year 1605, when we had hatched such a gigantic stratagem that our bird was almost ready to break the shell. And now in 1639, when we had made a breach between the English and Scottish nations, a more Hellish stratagem than which could not be invented. Behold, then, with a serious eye the grand enterprise of your dear children the Romish Faction. And, profound Emperor, doubt not but, as we have heretofore, so we will stir up all foreign powers now at this last cast against the English Parliament; and if that fail, *Flectere si nequeo superos Acheronta movebo.*"[6] Thus ended bold Guy Fawkes, and for the Brownists who d'ye think was chosen? Samuel How,[7] the most famous and renowned cobbler, who thus began after he had hummed his hoarse voice up:

"Dreadful Emperor, your most zealously affected[8] children the Society of Separatists or non-conformists, alias Brownists, most humble in all reverent and devoted posture, attend your service, and in the name of the whole dispersed tribe I your zealous child and client do pronounce the ardent heat that burns in all our breasts to effect your perpetrations, and whereas Guy Fawkes hath extolled with a wide mouth the endeavors of the Romish faction, as if we never could parallel them, verily, most potent patron, we have exceeded them many ways: for the Brownists (so trimly and slyly) have given such rubs and flaws to your enemies' reputations, that I think verily they'll never recover themselves of the wounds that we have given them. True it is, being backed with foreign

---

3. An old contemptuous term for priests.
4. On November 5, 1605, Fawkes and his confederates were caught trying to blow up Parliament with gunpowder. He was demonized as a symbol of Catholic evil.
5. Courage.
6. "If I cannot bend Heaven, I will stir up Hell," says Juno in *Aeneid* 7.312.
7. Samuel How was notorious for radical speeches and lay sermons.
8. Affectionate, loyal.

princes they have undertook great endeavors, but never to any perfection. But we have not feared (alas, unarmed) to outcry all danger; with what zeal have delivered your commands myself in the Nag's Head Tavern near Coleman Street,[9] some in the fields, some in the country villages, everyone somewhere. Had we been furnished with foreign aid we could have done more than ever they would have done. But what need we desire other power, since your Infernal Majesty doth so stiffly maintain us? And we will requite your love, and will as we use to do in the same sly and slanderous and lying way forge and print any libels and untruths for the furtherance of your ignoble Empire; and had we arms to fight with, we would spritefully[10] and spitefully use them."

After which arose a second fray between either faction, that their Parliament house had like to afire, so hot were they at it; and Pluto thought verily that Hell would have broke loose, but Cerberus hath proclaimed silence.[11] Pluto, with stern and angry look, thus spoke: "What means this noise, what means these angry threatenings? Such looks ye ought to show mine enemies; this is not the way to enlarge but to destroy my Empire. Contention overthrows the greatest states: therefore brethren-like join hands against the common foe. You see how the Parliament of England shakes us so much that if you do not bestir yourselves we shall be quite undone. Then they all embraced mutually: "So this is well done, hence good will doubly redound to us and ours, which is your Kingdom." Then they craved instructions, which they said should be as absolute statutes of that their most Hellish Parliament, to which Pluto most joy-fully accorded.

Then Rhadamanthus[12] presented their hellish worships with these acts following:

1. That there be a strong and perfect league of friendship betwixt His Infernal Majesty's servants the Papists and Brownists.
2. That they should cross, as much as in them lay, all good proceedings of the English Parliament.
3. That the Papists should excite foreign potentates against the said kingdom.
4. That the Brownists should strew all libels about, especially such as tend to the disgrace of learning, His Infernalship being an utter enemy to all sound literature.
5. That the Brownists bear up, relieve, and maintain all contrivers of such libels, such as "Knave," "Reviler," "Hell."
6. John Taylor the Water-poet be declared an open enemy to his Infernalship and both the factions.

9. How did preach at the Nag's Head; see Bernard Cap, *The World of John Taylor the Water Poet* (Oxford: Clarendon, 1994), p. 165.
10. Spiritedly (after all, demons are spirits).
11. Had not Cerberus (Hell's guard-dog) demanded silence.
12. Appointed by Zeus to be judge in Hades.

Thus wicked Satan hath a double way
To work his ends to hinder his decay.
His agents are so many and so wicked bent,
They care not for the truth so they're not shent;[13]
If that the Lion's skin will do no good,
They'll soon put on the cunning Fox's hood.
England, repent, and for this Parliament pray,
Since th'Devil strives to hurt thee every way.

13. Ruined.

19

Margaret Tyler *(fl. 1578)*

Daniel Tuvil *(fl. 1609)*

Margaret Tyler Defends Women's Writings

Margaret Tyler (fl. 1578) is known to us only from her dedicatory letter to a Lord Thomas Howard in her translation of the first part of *The Mirror of Princely Deeds and Knighthood* (1578), a Spanish romance by Diego Ortúñez de Calahorra. Tyler says that she had served Lord Thomas Howard's parents and that she is now old. As Kathryn Coad has shown in *Margaret Tyler* (Aldershot: Scolar, 1996), Tyler's translation marks an important moment in the printing of continental romance in England: it is the first translation of a romance into English directly from Spanish. Its preface constitutes another important first: it contains a sprightly, and for England very early, defense of women's publication of secular material. We reprint this "Epistle Dedicatory" from the 1578 edition.

From *The Mirror of Princely Deeds and Knighthood*
Epistle to the Reader

Thou hast here, gentle reader, the history of Trebatio, an emperor in Greece, whether a true story of him, indeed, or feigned fable I wot[1] not; neither did I

---

1. Know.

greatly seek after it in the translation. But by me it is done into English for thy profit and delight. The chief matter therein contained is of exploit of wars, and the parties therein named are especially renowned for their magnanimity and courage. The author's purpose appeareth to be this: to animate thereby and to set on fire the lusty[2] courages of young gentlemen to the advancement of their line by ensuing[3] such like steps. The first tongue wherein it was penned was the Spanish, in which nation, by common report, the inheritance of all war-like commendation hath to this day rested. The whole discourse in respect of the end not unnecessary, for the variety and continual shift of fresh matter very delightful, in the speeches short and sweet, wise in sentence, and wary in the provision of contrary accidents. For I take the grace thereof to be rather in the reporter's device than in the truth of this report, as I would that I could so well impart with this the delight which myself findeth in reading the Spanish. But seldom is the tale carried clean from another's mouth. Such delivery as I have made, I hope thou wilt friendly accept, the rather for that it is a woman's work, though in a story profane and a matter more manlike than becometh my sex.

But as for the manliness of the matter, thou knowest that it is not necessary for every trumpeter or drumster in the war to be a good fighter. They take wage only to incite others though themselves have privy maims[4] and are thereby recureless.[5] So, gentle reader, if my travail in Englishing this author may bring thee to a liking of the virtues herein commended and by example thereof in thy prince's and country's quarrel to hazard thy person and purchase good name, as for hope of well deserving myself that way I neither bend myself thereto nor yet fear the speech of people if I be found backward. I trust every man holds not the plow which would the ground were tilled, and it is no sin to talk of Robin Hood though you never shot his bow.[6] Or be it that the attempt were bold to intermeddle in arms so as the ancient Amazons[7] did, and in this story Claridiana doth, and in other stories not a few, yet to report of arms is not so odious but that it may be borne withal, not only in you men which yourselves are fighters, but in us women, to whom the benefit in equal part appertaineth of your victories, either for that the matter is so commendable that it carrieth no discredit from the homeliness of the speaker, or for that it is generally known that it fitteth every man to speak thereof, or for that it jumpeth with this common fear on all parts of war and invasion.

The invention, disposition, trimming,[8] and what else in this story is wholly another man's; my part none therein but the translation—as it were only in giving entertainment to a stranger, before this time unacquainted with our country

2. Vigorous.
3. Following.
4. Secret injuries.
5. Incurable.
6. The semi-legendary Robin Hood was an outlaw and archer of medieval England who reputedly stole from the rich to give to the poor.
7. A mythical race of women warriors.
8. Decoration.

guise.[9] Marry,[10] the worst perhaps is this: that among so many strangers as daily come over, some more ancient, and some but new set forth, some penning matters of great weight and sadness[11] in divinity or other studies (the profession whereof more nearly beseemeth my years), other some discoursing of matters more easy and ordinary in common talk wherein a gentlewoman may honestly employ her travail, I have, notwithstanding, made countenance only to this gentleman, whom neither his personage might sufficiently commend itself unto my sex nor his behavior (being light and soldierlike) might in good order acquaint itself with my years. So the question now ariseth of my choice, not of my labor, wherefore I preferred this story before matter of more importance. For answer whereto, gentle reader, the truth is that as the first motion to this kind of labor came not from myself, so was this piece of work put upon me by others, and they which first counselled me to fall to work took upon them also to be my taskmasters and overseers least I should be idle.

And yet, because the refusal was in my power I must stand to answer for my easy yielding and may not be unprovided of excuse. Wherein, if I should allege for myself that matters of less worthiness by as aged years have been taken in hand, and that daily new devices are published in songs, sonnets, interludes, and other discourses and yet are borne out without reproach only to please the humor of some men, I think I should make no good plea therein. For besides that I should find thereby so many known enemies as known men have been authors of such idle conceits,[12] yet would my other adversaries be never the rather quieted; for they would say that as well the one as the other were all naught. And though, peradventure, I might pass unknown amongst a multitude, and not be the only gaze[13] or the odd party in my ill doing, yet because there is less merit of pardon if the fault be excused as common I will not make the defense which cannot help me and doth hinder other men.

But my defense is by example of the best, amongst which many have dedicated their labors—some stories, some of war, some physic, some law, some as concerning government, some divine matters—unto divers ladies and gentlewomen. And if men may and do bestow such of their travails upon gentlewomen, then may we women read such of their works as they dedicate unto us. And if we may read them, why not farther wade in them to the search of a truth? And then, much more, why not deal by translation in such arguments, especially this kind of exercise being a matter of more heed than of deep invention or exquisite learning? And they must needs leave this as confessed: that in their dedications they mind not only to borrow names of worthy personages, but the testimonies also for their further credit which neither the one may demand without ambition nor the other grant without overlightness. If women be excluded from the view of such works as appear in their name, or if glory only be sought in our common

9. Manner, way.
10. An oath.
11. Gravity.
12. Conceptions, opinions.
13. Person or thing stared at.

inscriptions, it mattereth not whether the parties be men or women, whether alive or dead. But to return: whatsoever the truth is, whether that women may not at all discourse in learning (for men lay in their claim to be sole possession-ers of knowledge), or whether they may in some manner (that is by limitation or appointment in some kind of learning), my persuasion hath been thus: that it is all one for a woman to pen a story as for a man to address his story to a woman.

But amongst all my ill-willers, some I hope are not so straight[14] that they would enforce me necessarily either not to write or to write of divinity, whereas neither durst I trust mine own judgment sufficiently, if matter of controversy were handled, nor yet could I find any book in the tongue which would not breed offense to some. But I perceive some may be rather angry to see their Spanish delight turned to an English pastime; they could well allow the story in Spanish, but they may not afford[15] it so cheap or they would have it proper to themselves. What natures such men be of, I list not greatly dispute. But my meaning hath been to make other partners of my liking, as I doubt not, gentle reader, but if it shall please thee after serious matters to sport thyself with this Spaniard, that thou shalt find in him the just reward of malice and cowardice, with the good speed of honesty and courage, being able to furnish thee with sufficient store of foreign example to both purposes. And as in such matters which have been rather devised to beguile time than to breed matter of sad learning he hath ever borne away the prize which could season such delights with some profitable reading, so shalt thou have this stranger an honest man when need serveth, and at other times either a good companion to drive out a weary night or a merry jest at thy board. And thus much as concerning this present story that it is neither unseem-ly for a woman to deal in neither greatly requiring a less staid age than mine is. But of these two points, gentle reader, I thought to give thee warning, least per-haps, understanding of my name and years, thou mightest be carried into a wrong support of my boldness and rashness, from which I would gladly free myself by this plain excuse. And if I may deserve thy good favor by like labor, when the choice is mine own I will have a special regard of thy liking.

So I wish thee well.
Thine to use. M. T.

Daniel Tuvil Defends (Good) Women

Daniel Tuvil (or Toutevile), who wrote in the first half of the seventeenth century, published a number of moral and religious texts; his *Essays Moral and Theological* (1609) seems to have sold well. The book we excerpt, *Asylum Veneris* ("Venus' Sanctuary"), is a defense of women in a tradition going back at least to Plutarch and including Christine de Pisan's *City of Ladies*, one that defends women's capacities and virtues by citing impressive examples of female accomplishments and behavior. Like

14. Rigid.
15. Supply, allow.

others in the tradition, Tuvil is careful to distinguish such women from those he sees as wicked or foolish. To them, this sanctuary is shut, just as Christine's "City of Ladies" is built by and for good women only. Tuvil is at pains to show his own erudition, although many Latin phrases are slightly wrong, perhaps because quoted from memory. We select the preliminary poem refusing entry to women undeserving of protection and the chapter on women's learning, basing our text on the 1609 edition.

FROM *ASYLUM VENERIS, OR A SANCTUARY FOR LADIES, JUSTLY PROTECTING THEM, THEIR VIRTUES, AND SUFFICIENCIES FROM THE FOUL ASPERSIONS AND FORGED IMPUTATIONS OF TRADUCING SPIRITS.*

TO THE LOOSER SORT OF WOMEN

Stand off, you foul adulterate brats of Hell,
Whose lungs exhale a worse than sulph'rous smell;
Do not attempt with your profaner hands
To touch the shrine in which chaste Virtue stands.
Hence Messalina,[1] hence, back to the stew,
And in that cage thy blooded pinions mew.[2]
Hence you that weigh not, so your thoughts be stilled,
Though Naboth's[3] blood be innocently spilled,
And being bankrupt of each native grace,
Think to catch Jehu with a bird-limed face.[4]
Hence frisking fairies, that like Herod's niece,
Esteem of dancing as your chiefest piece,[5]
And with Sempronia[6] care not so your lute
Delight the hearers, though your souls be mute.
Hence you, that seek by philters, drugs, and charms
To bring the curled-head youth into your arms,
And do not fear by poison to remove
A worthy husband for a worthless love.

1. Corrupt and cruel wife of the Emperor Claudius.
2. Hawks, falcons, and eagles periodically mew (shed) their large feathers and, if in captivity, must be caged.
3. Slandered by Queen Jezebel, Naboth was killed by King Ahab (1 Kings 2).
4. Jehu overthrew Jezebel and her sons, becoming king of Israel; birds were caught with nets made sticky by lime.
5. Salome danced for Herod and won John the Baptist's head as a reward.
6. Wife of Junius Brutus (consul in 77 B.C.E.), the accomplished but reputedly immoral Sempronia joined Catiline's conspiracy against the Senate.

Hence you, that practice Aretine's vile shapes,[7]
Yet can so fairly solder up your scapes
That in your nuptial's first assaults the bed
Shall boast the conquest of a maidenhead.
Hence you that strive to have your outsides brave,
Yet are within far fouler than your slave,
And will not let,[8] *being stirred by ranker veins,*
The groom away, to try your stallion's reins.
For women only is this place ordained—
But you are monsters, and their sex have stained.
Hence therefore, hence you base, unhallowed crew;
Hope for no shelter here. All such as you
That hitherwards for help and succor fly,
Plucked from the altar, must abjure,[9] *or die.*

CHAPTER 8: OF THEIR LEARNING.

Learning in the breast of a woman is likened by their Stoical[10] adversaries to a sword in the hands of a madman, which he knoweth not how to rule as reason shall inform him but as the motions and violent fits of his distemper shall enforce him. It doth not ballast their judgments but only addeth more sail to their ambition and like the weapon of Goliath serveth but as an instrument to give the fatal period to their honor's overthrow. And surely this fond imagination hath purchased a free inheritance to itself in the bosoms of some indiscreeter[11] parents, who hereupon will by no means endure that their daughters should be acquainted with any kind of literature at all. The pen must be forbidden them as the tree of good and evil, and upon their blessing[12] they must not handle it. It is a pander to a virgin chastity and betrayeth it by venting forth those amorous passions that are incident to hotter bloods [and] which otherwise, like fire raked up in embers, would peradventure in a little space be utterly consumed. But if this be their fear, let them likewise bar them the use of their needle: with this did Philomela fairly character those foul indignities which had been offered her by Tereus, the incestuous husband of her sister Procne.[13] And why then may not others express their loves and their affections in the like form? Cupid hath wings,

7. Aretino was notorious for pornography, including sonnets on various sexual positions.
8. Stop at, hesitate.
9. Taken from the altar, where traditionally one could claim sanctuary and forswear one's evil.
10. Influenced by the severe thinking of the Stoics.
11. With inadequate judgment.
12. Upon pain of losing their parents' blessing.
13. Tereus raped Philomela, sister of his wife, Procne, and cut out her tongue; she exposed him by making a tapestry describing his actions.

and like another Daedalus,[14] if his passage be stopped by land and water, he will cut through the air but[15] he will be master of his desires. You cannot hinder his pinions from soaring high by depriving him of a quill or two. Affection is ingenious and can imp them[16] as it pleaseth her. Leander will not for a Hellespont be kept from Hero's kisses, nor Danae by a brazen tower from Jupiter's embraces.[17] Be Juno never so jealous, Love hath a Mercury[18] that can at all times delude her spies. *Et quid non fiet, quod voluere duo?*[19]

To converse with the dead, and this is to converse with books, hath been still accounted the readiest way to moralize our harsher natures and to wean them from all inbred barbarism to more humane and civil conversation. And hence it was that Julius Agricola,[20] when he had obtained the government of this our isle that he might abase the fierce and fiery temper of the inhabitants, whose knowledge could demonstrate nothing but by arms, took from the nobler Britons their sons and trained them up in all the liberal sciences, whereby he made them willingly submit themselves to the Roman Empire and not [be] prone to rise so often up in arms as formerly by reason of their rough-hewn dispositions they had accustomed to do. Now I see no hindrance why they should not produce the same effect in them[21] which they do in us, their bodies consisting of the same matter and their minds coming out of the same mold.

But if those prohibitions proceed from a providence in them to prevent a curious desire of searching further into the cabinets of Minerva[22] than is fitting, an error incident to capricious and working wits such as they would have women's for the most part to be, let them show me what men are free from the like weakness. Knowledge is infinite, and admitteth no bounds. It is Jacob's ladder, and reacheth from the lowest part of the earth to the highest place in Heaven. Man's thoughts are like those angels, which were seen by the patriarch in his vision: never at a stand but still going either up or down. And therefore Solomon avoucheth[23] that *Qui addit scientiam, addit et dolorem*: an acquist of learning bringeth with it an increase of labor.[24] For the more a man attaineth unto the more he seeth to be attained, and so not content with any former purchase wearieth out himself in pursuit of that which is behind. *Nil actum credens, cum quid*

14. Legendary builder of the Labyrinth at Crete who escaped prison on wings of wax and feathers.
15. "Unless" or "in order to."
16. To "imp" is to add feathers to a wing.
17. Greek legend says that Leander swam the Hellespont (the Dardanelles, between Thrace and what is now Turkey) to see Hero; Danae's father kept her in a tower but Jove visited her as a shower of gold, begetting the hero Perseus.
18. The god's wing-footed messenger (and trickster god of theft).
19. "And what cannot be done if two wish it?" (cf. Ovid, *Amores* 2.3.16.)
20. Agricola (37–93) was a Roman general, statesman, father-in-law of the historian Tacitus, and governor of Britain from 78–84.
21. In women.
22. Goddess of wisdom and knowledge.
23. Declares.
24. "He who increases knowledge also increases sorrow," from Eccles. 1:18.

sibi cernit agendum.[25] Those that are altogether unfurnished of this diviner complement are as the Italian termeth them "humanate bestie," things that resemble reasonable creatures only in the bark and rind and could not possibly be distinguished from statues made of clay and marble but by their outward sense and motion. These are they which like Aesop's cock spurn at the jewel which they cannot prize, and such were Nero, Domitian, Cleisthenes, who as Tacitus reporteth, *Virtutem ipsam excindere concupientes*, studying as much as in them lay how to bring Virtue herself unto the block, made philosophy a capital offense, and put to death those professors of wisdom and good arts who betimes did not retire themselves from the reach of their infernal rage.[26] And such as these, no doubt are those, or at least not many degrees short of them, who out of an idle supposition of their own addle-brains think learning a thing superfluous in any. For as it is a plain testimony of ignorance itself to know nothing, so is it an ample sign of dullness to rest satisfied with the knowledge of any something. Adam's fingers, notwithstanding God's menaces, will be still itching at the forbidden tree: The Children of Israel, for all the threatening proclamations which Moses doth divulge amongst them from the Lord, will hardly be restrained from advancing forward at the mount of Sinai. The Bethshemites[27] will be peering into the Ark, though the lives of more than fifty thousand of them be made the forfeiture of their presumption.[28] Divine St. Augustine will be diving into the mystery of the Trinity till he see a child become the censurer of his folly; and holy Daniel will trouble himself in searching after the condition of future times till an angel from Heaven will him to stand upright in his place.[29] In a word, it so bewitcheth us that we grow desperate in the chase. Pliny will have no other urn than the mountain Vesuvius for his ashes when he cannot find out the reason of its flames, nor Aristotle any other sepulcher than Euripus when, angling for the hidden causes of its ebbs and flows, he seeth nothing will hang upon his hook.[30] And upon this intemperance of men was grounded peradventure that moral precept of antiquities, *Noli altum sapere*, aim not at things beyond your reach, as likewise that admonition of St. Paul's "Be wise unto sobriety."[31]

From all which premises I gather this conclusion, that meats might as well be forbidden women for fear of surfeiting as the use of learning for fear of over-

---

25. "Thinking nothing done when he sees there is more to do," quoted loosely from Lucan's *Civil War* 2.657.
26. The emperor Nero (37–68), says Tacitus in *Annales* 16.21.2, "wished to extinguish Virtue herself." The despotic emperor Domitian (51–96) was murdered by his wife. Cleisthenes is probably the tyrant of Sicyon, in Greece (ruled ca. 600–570), not his grandson the ruler of Athens.
27. On the city of Beth-shemesh and the Ark of the Covenant see 1 Sam. 6:9–15.
28. Beth-shemesh captured the Ark of the Covenant (1 Sam. 6:9–15).
29. Tuvil may vaguely remember Augustine's *Confessions* 8.12: in the throes of spiritual confusion, Augustine hears a child singing "take and read," consults the Bible, and is transformed. Tuvil may also refer to Dan. 2.
30. Pliny was killed when he got too close to the volcano that buried Pompeii. Euripus was a dangerous strait between Euboea and the Greek mainland.
31. "Do not wish to know the heights" (Rom. 11:20); see also Rom. 16:19.

weening, unless we ourselves will be content to be registered with them as liable to the like miscarrying, in the same role. But I hear our adversaries cry out what a prodigious[32] thing it was counted among the Romans for a woman to speak in public, and when it happened, what speedy recourse they had unto their augurs to know what disastrous fortune so strange an accident might portend to their commonweal.[33] Against which particular custom of a people, which for wit and valor might boast themselves the legitimate children as well of Mercury as of Mars, I will say nothing, though I could easily show with what good success the daughter of Hortensius pleaded the matrons' cause to the freeing of them from the greatest part of that grievous taxation which the Triumvirs had most injuriously imposed upon them.[34] As likewise how Amaesia Sentia, being arraigned before L. Titius, then Praetor, pleaded so stoutly and exactly to every point of her inditements, that she acquitted herself, maugre the power of her enemies, with the general applause of all.[35]

To that wherewith they urge us out of Holy Writ touching the restraint of their teaching and speaking publicly in the Temples, I answer that the blessed Apostle [I Cor. 14:34] alludeth only to some ignorant and prating gossips who, when attention should be given to the dispensers of God's mysteries, are continually asking, to their own hurt and others' hindrance, such frivolous questions as on the instant are begotten in their idle brains. And [1 Tim. 2:12], where he permitteth them not to teach because, as they would have it, *Semel docuit, et omnia subuertit* (she taught but once, and that once brought all things out of order), he doth but utter his own opinion, and howsoever he allow not of it, yet he doth not condemn it. So that his meaning, as I take it there, is only this: They should not, when men of sufficiency are in place, and such as can discharge the duties that appertain to so high a calling, usurp over their authority. For otherwise the Scripture informeth us that Deborah was a prophetess, and that Anna the daughter of Phanuel (Luke 2:37) never stirred out of the Temple but spent therein both day and night in prayer and fasting and speaking fervently of Jesus Christ, the Savior of the world, to all that waited for their deliverance in Jerusalem. And indeed the light of the moon is needless when the sun is in his transcendent, but if he be gone, her beams, though not so pregnant, will afford much comfort. Apollos may be eloquent and mighty in the scriptures, Priscilla yet may take him unto her and expound unto him the ways of God more plainly.[36]

But *scienta inflat*: knowledge puffeth up,[37] and there is nothing, say our opposites, more swelling and imperious, than a woman that seeth she hath the

32. Like a prodigy or an alarming supernatural sight.
33. Augurs foretold the future by studying bird entrails.
34. Hortensia, daughter of the orator and tribune Quintus Hortensius (b. 114 B.C.E.), persuaded the triumvirate ruling Rome to spare wealthy matrons a wartime tax.
35. Amaesia Sentia (active 77 B.C.E.) acted as her own attorney before the praetor (top magistrate); she was called "Androgyne" for having a "male" spirit in a female body. "Maugre" means "despite."
36. In Acts 18:24–26 Aquila and Priscilla are better expounders of God's word than Apollos, an eloquent Jewish convert from Alexandria who was "mighty in the scriptures."
37. 2 Cor. 8:1.

superiority and start of her husband in anything: *"Faciunt grauiora coactae / imperio sexus minimumque libidine peccant."*[38] As if they should conform themselves to men's weaknesses and pattern out their own abilities by [men's] defects. He that is deprived of his bodily sight is content to be led, though by a child: and shall he that is blind in his understanding disdain to be directed by her who by the ordinance of God and the rules of sacred wedlock is allotted him a fellow-helper in all his business? The husband and the wife are the eyes of a family: if the right one be so bleared that it cannot well discern, the guiding of the household must of necessity be left unto the left, or on the sudden all will go to wrack. And surely I see no reason but the hen may be permitted to crow where the cock can do nothing but cackle. So that learning, we see, is an ornament and a decency most expedient for women were it for no other respect than to supply as occasion may require the defects that are in men. And truly some of them, by seconding a natural propensity in themselves to letters with an industrious pursuit, have attained to so high a perfection in them that men, considering how imperiously they challenge a preeminence over them herein, have had just cause to blush at their own ignorance. There are some which Antiquity objecteth to our view whose many rare and profitable inventions made them deserve the names of goddesses here on earth, as Pallas, Ceres and the Sybils, whose mouth it pleased God many times to use as a sacred oracle, whereby to publish unto the world what He purposed in His will.[39] Others again, which have had the tutoring of diverse very famous and worthy persons, as Aspasia, Macrina, and Diotima, who by her prayers and devouter sacrifices, prorogued a certain pestilence, which was then to light upon the Athenians, till ten years after.[40] I could here allege Nicostrata, the mother of Evander, who was the first that taught the Latins what letters were, as likewise Corinna, Sappho, Sulpicia, and the schoolmistress of Pindar the lyric [poet], all of them worthy admiration for their excellency in poesy.[41] But I desire not to travel far for what I may procure near home. A countrywoman of our own, having disguised herself into the habit of a student took her journey to Rome, where in a while she grew so famous for wit and knowledge that from one degree of dig-

---

38. Juvenal, *Satires* 6.134–35, on love-crazed women's resort to sorcery and poisons: "they commit worse crimes, urged by the imperious power of sex, and the sins of lust are the least [of their sins]."

39. One theory ("euhemerism") held that such gods as Pallas Athena, goddess of wisdom, and Ceres, goddess of agriculture, were human beings whose accomplishments won for them a reputation for divinity. The sybils were Apollo's priestesses; one set of their supposed prophecies was widely thought to foretell Christ.

40. Aspasia, sophisticated mistress of the fifth-century B.C.E. Athenian statesman Pericles, made her house a center for literary and philosophical discussion; legend called her Socrates' tutor. St. Macrina, from what is now Turkey, founded a community of holy women and taught her ten orphaned brothers so well that two, Basil and Gregory, became famous saints and theologians. In Plato's *Symposium* the priestess Diotima teaches Socrates about ideal love.

41. Legend says that a few years before the fall of Troy, Evander, son of Mercury and the nymph Nicostrata (also called Themis), led Greek colonists to Italy and taught the natives how to write; Corinna was an early fifth-century B.C.E. Greek lyric poet; Sappho of Lesbos (b. 612 B.C.E.), one of the greatest of Greek poets, wrote love poems to men and women; Sulpicia, a first-century Roman poet and satirist, wrote love-poems to her husband; Pindar (518–438 B.C.E.) is most famous for his heroic odes (we have not identified his teacher).

nity to another, she stepped at length into Saint Peter's chair and had the custody of the keys.[42] And this, if their adversaries like deaf adders stop not their ears when Reason charmeth, may very well suffice to maintain them learned. Their wisdom is the next, which men with their traducements would enviously impeach, but you shall quickly see it uncanopied of those misty clouds which would obscure it and shining out as clear as brightest day.

42. The notorious (and probably legendary) Pope Joan, disguised as a man.

20

Diana Primrose *(fl. 1630)*

William Shakespeare *(1564–1616)*

Diana Primrose Praises Elizabeth Tudor

Although Diana Primrose (fl. 1630) is styled a "noble lady" on the title page of *A Chain of Pearl* (1630), she has not been further identified. Nor has Dorothy Berry, author of a prefatory poem. Primrose lives through her poems on ten of Elizabeth Tudor's virtues, published at a time when to praise Elizabeth could hint at criticism of the Stuart kings. We base our text on the 1630 edition.

A Chain of Pearl
OR A *Memorial of the Peerless Graces and Heroic Virtues*
OF *Queen Elizabeth, of Glorious Memory*

> *To all noble ladies and gentlewomen:*
> *To you, the honor of our noble sex,*
> *I send this chain, with all my best respects.*
> *Which, if you please to wear, for her sweet sake,*
> *For whom I did this slender poem make,*
> *You shall erect a trophy to her name,*
> *And crown yourselves with never-fading fame.*
> > *Devoted to your virtues,*
> > *Diana P.*

TO THE EXCELLENT LADY, THE COMPOSER OF THIS WORK:

Shine forth (Diana), dart thy golden rays
On her blest life and reign, whose noble praise
Deserves a quill plucked from an angel's wing,
And none to write it but a crownèd king.
She, she it was that gave us golden days
And did the English name to heaven raise:
Blest be her name! Blest be her memory!
That England crowned with such felicity.
And thou, the prime-rose of the muses nine,
(In whose sweet verse Eliza's fame doth shine
Like some resplendent star in frosty night)
Hast made thy native splendor far more bright,
Since all thy pearls are peerless-orient,
And to thyself a precious ornament.
  This is my censure of thy royal chain
  Which a far better censure well may claim.
  Dorothy Berry

THE INDUCTION

As golden Phoebus[1] with his radiant face,
Enthroned in his triumphant chair of state,
The twinkling stars and asterisms[2] doth chase
With his imperial scepter, and doth hate
All consorts in his starry monarchy
As prejudicial to his sovereignty,
So great Eliza, England's brightest sun,
The world's renown and everlasting lamp,
Admits not here the least comparison,
Whose glories do the greatest princes damp[3]
  That ever scepter swayed or crown did wear
  Within the verge of either hemisphere.
Thou English goddess, empress of our sex,
O thou whose name still reigns in all our hearts,

---

1. Phoebus Apollo, god of the Sun.
2. Constellations.
3. Dull by comparison.

To whom are due our ever-vowed respects,
How shall I blazon thy most royal parts
    Which in all parts did so divinely shine,
    As they deserve Apollo's quill (not mine).
Yet, since the gods accept the humble vows
Of mortals, deign (O thou star-crownèd queen)
T'accept these ill-composèd pearly-rows
Wherein thy glory chiefly shall be seen
    For by these lines, so black and impolite,[4]
    Thy swan-like luster shall appear more white.
        Thy imperial majesty's eternal votary,
        Diana

The First Pearl: Religion

[Elizabeth's "true religion," says Primrose, showed in her initial tolerance when she "swayed the scepter with a lady's hand" and in her later rigor necessitated by Catholic subversion at home and attacks from abroad.]

The Second Pearl: Chastity

The next fair pearl that comes in order here
Is chastity, wherein she had no peer
'Mongst all the noble princesses which then
In Europe wore the royal anadem.[5]
And though for beauty she an angel was
And all our sex did therein far surpass,
Yet did her pure unspotted chastity
Her heavenly beauty rarely beautify.
How many kings and princes did aspire
To win her love? In whom that vestal fire
Still flaming, never would she condescend
To Hymen's rites,[6] *though much she did commend*
That brave French Monsieur[7] *who did hope to carry*
The golden fleece[8] *and fair Eliza marry.*
Yea Spanish Philip, husband to her sister,[9]

---

4. Unpolished.
5. Wreath.
6. Hymen was god of weddings.
7. François, duc d'Anjou, a prince who wooed Elizabeth in the 1570s and 1580s.
8. Captured by Jason and the Argonauts, with the help of Medea's magic.
9. Mary Tudor (1516–1558), wife of Philip of Spain and daughter of Henry VIII and Catherine of Aragon, reigned from 1553–1558.

Was her first suitor, and the first that missed her.
And though he promised that the pope by the bull
Should license it, she held it but a gull;[10]
For how can pope* with God's own law dispense?
Was it not time such popes to cudgel hence?
Thus her impregnable virginity,
Throughout the world her fame did dignify.
And this may be a document to all,
The pearl of chastity not to let fall
Into the filthy dirt of foul desires
Which Satan kindles with his Hell-bred fires.
For whether it be termed virginal
In virgins, or in wives styled conjugal,
Or vidual in widows,[11] *God respects*
All equally, and all alike affects.

And here I may not silent overpass
That noble lady of the court which was
Solicited by Taxis, that great don,[12]
Ambassador for Spain (when she was gone)**
Who to obtain his will, gave her a chain
Of most rare Orient pearl, hoping to gain
That worthy lady to his lust. But she,
That well perceived his Spanish policy,
His fair chain kept but his foul offer scorned
That sought (thereby) her husband to have horned.
Taxis, repulsed, sent to her for his chain,
But (as a trophy) she did it retain.
Which noble precedent may all excite,
To keep this pearl, which is so Orient bright.***

*Yet his Canonists say *Bene dispensa! Dominus Papa contra Apostolum Extra de Renunc. Ca post translationem.*[13]
**Primo Jacobi[14]
***Related by the honorable knight and baronet, Sir Richard Houghton of Houghton Tower.[15]

10. Deception, trick.
11. Primrose gives the traditional classifications for women: maid, wife, widow.
12. Spanish for "sir" or "lord." Perhaps Juan Bautista de Tassis (or Taxis), c. 1530–1610, a nobleman and diplomat who was the Spanish ambassador to France in the 1580s.
13. Primrose parodies Catholic jurists, claiming that they say the Pope is God, not merely apostolic. The (bad) Latin begins by saying something like "Well dispensed! The Pope is Lord over the Apostle except concerning proclamations." "Ca" is not Latin (unless short for "circa"). The passage ends with the phrase "after translation"—perhaps translation to the papacy.
14. First year of the reign of James I.
15. Possibly Sir *Robert* Houghton of Norwich.

The Third Pearl: Prudence

[Elizabeth's prudence helped her "steer" England through "the most dangerous times that ever were," choosing wise advisers and showing foresight. Such prudence was the more impressive, says Primrose, because "so rarely incident / To our weak sex."]

The Fourth Pearl: Temperance

The golden bridle of Bellerophon[16]
Is Temperance, by which our passion
And appetite we conquer and subdue
To reason's regiment. Else may we rue
Our yielding to men's siren-blandishments
Which are attended with so foul events.
*　　This pearl in her was so conspicuous,*
As that the *King her brother still did use,
To style her his "Sweet Sister Temperance";
By which her much admired self-governance,
Her passions still she checked, and still she made
The world astonished, that so undismayed
She did with equal tenor still proceed
In one fair course—not shaken as a reed—
But built upon the rock of temperance.**
Not dazed with fear; not 'mazed with any chance;
Not with vain hope (as with an empty spoon)
Fed or allured to cast beyond the moon;
Not with rash anger too precipitate;
Not fond to love, nor too, too prone to hate;
Not charmed with parasites' or sirens' songs—
Whose hearts are poisoned though their sugared tongues
Swear, vow, and promise all fidelity
When they are brewing deepest villainy.
Not led to vain or too profuse expense,
Pretending thereby state magnificence;
Not spending on these momentary pleasures
Her precious time, but deeming her best treasures
Her subjects' love, which she so well preserved***
By sweet and mild demeanor as it served

16. Tamer of the winged horse, Pegasus, aided by Athena's golden bridle.

To guard her surer than an army royal:
So true their loves were to her, and so loyal.
O golden age! O blest and happy years!
O music sweeter than that of the spheres![17]
When prince and people mutually agree
In sacred concord and sweet symphony!
*Edward
**Semper eadem[18]
***Omnibus incutiens blandum per pectora amorem[19]

The Fifth Pearl: Clemency

Her royal clemency comes next into view,
The virtue which in her did most renew
The image of her Maker, who in that
Exceeds Himself and doth commiserate
His very rebels, lending them the light
Of sun and moon and all those diamonds bright.
So did Eliza cast her golden rays*
Of clemency on those which many ways
Transgressed her laws and sought to undermine
The church and state, and did with Spain combine.
And though by rigor of the law she might,
Not wronging them, have taken all her right,
Yet her innate and princely clemency
Moved her to pardon their delinquency,
Which sought her gracious mercy and repented
Their misdemeanors and their crimes lamented.
So doth the kingly lion with his foe,
Which once prostrate he scorns to work his woe.
So did this virtue's sacred Auriflame,[20]
Immortalize our great Eliza's name.
*monstra, t[a]eterrima monstra[21]

---

17. Many thought that the universe comprises eight turning concentric spheres, each emitting a particular music and the whole making a harmony audible after death.
18. Semper eadem (always the same) was Elizabeth's motto.
19. Striking soft love into each breast (Lucretius, *De rerum natura*, 1.19).
20. Probably "oriflamme," like the flame-red banner of French kings.
21. Monsters, most hideous monsters.

The Sixth Pearl: Justice

Her Justice next appears, which did support
Her crown and was her kingdom's strongest fort.
For should not laws be executed well
And malefactors curbed, a very hell
Of all confusion and disorder would
Among all states ensue. Here to unfold
The exemplary penalties of those,
Which to the realm were known and mortal foes—
And as some putrid members pared away
Least their transcendent villainy should sway
Others to like disloyalty—would ask
A larger volume and would be a task
Unfit for feminine hands, which rather love
To write of pleasing subjects than approve
The most deservèd slaughtering of any,
Which justly cannot argue tyranny.
For though the pope have lately sent from Rome
Strange books and pictures painting out the doom
Of his pretended martyrs, as that they
Were baited in bears' skins and made a prey
To wild beasts and had boots with boiling lead
Drawn on their legs and horns nailed to their head,
Yet all our British world knows these are fables,
Chimeras, phantasms, dreams, and very baubles
For fools to play with, and right goblin sprites
Wherewith our nurses oft their babes affrights.
His Holiness these martyrdoms may add
To The Golden Legend, for they are as mad
That first invented them, as* he that writ
That brainless book,[22] and yet some credit it.
For cruelty and fond credulity
Are the main pillars of Rome's hierarchy.
*Vappa Voraginosa[23]

---

22. Jacobus Voraginus's hugely popular *Golden Legend* (*Legenda Aurea*).
23. A pun: "vappa," flat or stale wine, was Roman slang for "good-for-nothing." In sum, "A Voraginite good-for-nothing" of "bad voraginous wine."

The Seventh Pearl: Fortitude

[Elizabeth, a "majestic queen" who seemed to awed observers like an angel in her grace, showed fortitude in braving would-be assassins and in the "heroic march" and speech with which she was able to "animate" the troops at Tilbury as the Spanish Armada approached. Her "magnanimity" and "haughty courage" showed her to be a true daughter of "great Henry."]

The Eighth Pearl: Science

Among the virtues intellectual,
The van [24] is led by what we "Science" call:
A pearl more precious than the Egyptian queen
Quaffed off to Anthony, [25] of more esteem
Than Indian gold or more resplendent gems
Which ravish us with their translucent beams.
How many arts and sciences did deck
This heroina who still had at beck [26]
The Muses and the Graces [27] when that she
Gave audience in state and majesty.
Then did the goddess Eloquence [28] inspire
Her royal breast; Apollo with his lyre
Ne'er made such music. On her sacred lips
Angels enthroned, most heavenly manna sips.
Then might you see her nectar-flowing vein [29]
Surround the hearers, in which sugared stream
She able was to drown a world of men,
And drowned, with sweetness to revive again.
Alasco, the Ambassador Polonian,
Who perorated like a mere Slavonian, [30]
And in rude rambling rhetoric did rule,
She did with Attic eloquence control. [31]
Her speeches to our academians
Well showed she knew among Athenians
How to deliver such well-tuned words
As with such places punctually accords.

24. Vanguard.
25. Cleopatra supposedly dissolved a pearl in wine and toasted Antony.
26. At her nod, summons.
27. The Muses inspire the arts; the Graces attend Venus and personify what is harmonious, beautiful, gracious.
28. Eloquence was sometimes personified as a goddess.
29. Her godlike style [vein] of speech.
30. Slav.
31. Outdid others in the Attic Greek (or Ciceronian) manner.

But with what oratory ravishments,
Did she imparadise her parliaments!
Her last, most princely speech doth verify,
How highly she did England dignify.
Her loyal commons how did she embrace
And entertain with a most royal grace![32]

The Ninth Pearl: Patience

Now come we her rare patience to display,
Which, as with purest gold, did pave her way
To England's crown. For when her sister ruled
She was with many great afflictions schooled;[33]
Yet all the while her mot was Tanquam Ovis,[34]
Nor could her enemies prove ought amiss
In her although they thirsted for her blood,
Reputing it once shed, their sovereign good.
Sometime in prison this sweet saint was pent;
Then hastily away she thence was sent
To places more remote; and all her friends
Debarred access; and none but such attends
As ready were with poison, or with knife
To sacrifice this sacred princess' life
At bloody Bonner's[35] *beck or Gardiner's*[36] *nod,*
Had they not been prevented by that God
Who did Susanna from the elders free,[37]
And at the last, gave her, her liberty.
Thus by her patient bearing of the cross,
She reapèd greatest gain from greatest loss.
(For he that loseth his blest liberty
Hath found a very hell of misery.)
By many crosses thus she got the crown,
To England's glory, and her great renown.

32. An allusion to her final, "Golden Speech."
33. Upon the death of Edward VI, the new queen, Mary, restored Catholicism. Daughter of the Protestant Anne Boleyn and hence suspect, Elizabeth was for a time imprisoned, her life in danger.
34. Her motto was "as a sheep." Edward Dering used the phrase in a 1569 sermon preached before Elizabeth that may have irritated her but was much reprinted: "If you have said sometime of your self: *Tanquam ovis*, as a sheep appointed to be slain, take heed you hear not now of the prophet: *tanquam indomita juvenca* ("as an untamed and unruly heifer"). See Ps. 44:22 and Jer. 31:18.
35. Edmund Bonner (1500–1569?), bishop of London, helped prosecute Protestants under Mary.
36. Stephen Gardiner (c. 1497–1555), conservative bishop of Winchester.
37. See the biblical tale of Susanna and the elders.

The Tenth Pearl: Bounty

As rose and lily challenge chiefest place
For milk-white luster and for purple grace,
So England's rose and lily had no peer
For princely bounty shining everywhere.
This made her fame with golden wings to fly
About the world, above the starry sky.
Witness France, Portugal, Virginia,
Germany, Scotland, Ireland, Belgia
Whose provinces and princes found her aid
On all occasions, which sore dismayed
Spain's king whose European monarchy,
Could never thrive during her sovereignty.
So did she beat him with her distaff, so
By *Sea and Land she him did overthrow,
Yea, so that tyrant on his knees she brought,
That of brave England peace he** begged and thought
Himself most happy that by begging so
Preserved all Spain from beggary and woe.[38]
        Here all amazed my muse sets up her rest
        Adoring her was so divinely blest.
*Elisabetha fuit Terrae Regina Marisque[39]
**Primo Jacobi
        At nos horrifico cinefactam TE propre Busto,
        Insatiabiliter deflebimus, aeternumque.[40]

William Shakespeare on Elizabeth I

At the climax of *King Henry VIII*, a pageant-filled history play perhaps written by Shakespeare (1564–1616) jointly with John Fletcher and known also as *All is True*, Thomas Cranmer, Archbishop of Canterbury, celebrates the baptism of Queen Anne Boleyn's baby, Elizabeth. In historical fact, Henry was disappointed. He had, after all, thrown off the Pope's authority because the latter would not annul his marriage to Catherine of Aragon, who had borne no male heir. In this scene, though, the stress is on Elizabeth's future glory. When the play was first staged in 1613, James I was king; despite the impatience many had felt during Elizabeth's later years, a degree of nostalgia for her reign had set in. Recent events may also have affected the first audience: in 1612 the popular Prince Henry had died, and early in 1613 James's daughter

---

38. An allusion to England's defeat of the Armada.
39. Elizabeth was queen of land and sea.
40. Lucretius 3.906: "Yet near your dread-giving tomb we will, and always, insatiably weep thee, thus turned to ashes."

Elizabeth had married the Protestant Elector Palatine. We base our excerpt on the edition by John Margeson (Cambridge University Press, 1990); the introduction notes that the play is less anti-Catholic than many contemporary works.

KING HENRY VIII, ACT 5, SCENE 4

[As the scene opens, Cranmer has survived a conspiracy against him by more conservative statesmen and clergymen. Many in the 1613 audience would know that he had helped establish the reformed Church of England and compiled its prayerbook. Under Mary Tudor he recanted, then withdraw his recantation, and went to the stake in 1556; it was said that he stretched to the fire the hand with which he had temporarily betrayed his beliefs.]

[*Enter trumpets sounding: then* two aldermen, Lord Mayor, Garter,[1] Cranmer, Duke of Norfolk[2] with his marshal's staff, the Duke of Suffolk,[3] two noblemen *bearing great standing bowls for the christening gifts; then* four noblemen *bearing a canopy under which* the Duchess of Norfolk,[4] godmother, *bearing* the child *richly habited in a mantle, etc., train borne by* a lady; *then follows* the Marchioness Dorset,[5] *the* other godmother, *and* ladies. *The troop pass once about the stage, and* Garter *speaks:*]

GARTER: Heaven, from thy endless goodness, send prosperous life, long and
    ever happy, to the high and mighty princess of England, Elizabeth.

Flourish. Enter King [Henry VIII] *and* guard.

CRANMER [*Kneeling*]: And to your royal grace, and the good queen,
    My noble partners and myself thus pray:
    All comfort, joy in this most gracious lady,
    Heaven ever laid up to make parents happy,
    May hourly fall upon ye.

KING: Thank you, good lord archbishop.
    What's her name?

CRANMER: Elizabeth.

KING: Stand up, lord.

[*The king kisses the child*]

With this kiss, take my blessing: God protect thee,
    Into Whose hand I give thy life.

---

1. The Garter Knight at Arms was chief herald and expert on matters relating to genealogy and coats of arms. His title alludes to the Order of the Garter, England's chief chivalric order.
2. Thomas Howard, father of the poet Surrey and third duke of Norfolk.
3. Charles Brandon, husband of Henry's sister Mary.
4. Elizabeth Stafford, the duke of Buckingham's daughter and unhappily married to Thomas Howard.
5. Margaret, daughter of Sir Robert Wotton and widow of Thomas Grey, second Marquis of Dorset; her son, Henry, was the father of Lady Jane Grey.

CRANMER: Amen.

KING: My noble gossips,[6] y'have been too prodigal:
    I thank ye heartily; so shall this lady
    When she has so much English.

CRANMER: Let me speak, sir,
    For Heaven now bids me; and the words I utter
    Let none think flattery, for they'll find 'em truth.
    This royal infant (Heaven still move about her!),
    Though in her cradle, yet now promises
    Upon this land a thousand thousand blessings
    Which time shall bring to ripeness. She shall be
    (But few now living can behold that goodness)
    A pattern to all princes living with her
    And all that shall succeed. Saba[7] was never
    More covetous of wisdom and fair virtue
    Than this pure soul shall be. All princely graces
    That mold up[8] such a mighty piece[9] as this is
    With all the virtues that attend the good
    Shall still[10] be doubled on her. Truth shall nurse her,
    Holy and heavenly thoughts still counsel her;
    She shall be loved and feared. Her own shall bless her,
    Her foes shake like a field of beaten corn
    And hang their heads with sorrow. Good grows with her;
    In her days, every man shall eat in safety
    Under his own vine what he plants, and sing
    The merry songs of peace to all his neighbors.[11]
    God shall be truly known, and those about her
    From her shall read the perfect ways of honor
    And by those claim their greatness, not by blood.
    Nor shall this peace sleep with her, but as when
    The bird of wonder dies, the maiden phoenix,
    Her ashes new create another heir
    As great in admiration as herself,[12]
    So shall she leave her blessedness to one
    (When Heaven shall call her from this cloud of darkness)

6. Colloquially, friends, people to chat with (derived from fellow [god]parents: "godsibs" or "siblings in God").
7. Queen of Sheba who, hearing of his wisdom, visited Solomon (1 Kings 10).
8. Form, add up to, like matter filling a mold.
9. Masterpiece; often applied, with no disrespect, to a lady.
10. Always.
11. Lines echoing 1 Kings 4:25 and Mic. 4:1–4.
12. When the phoenix is old she makes a spicy nest which then burns; arising from her own ashes, she is reborn as herself.

Who from the sacred ashes of her honor
Shall star-like rise, as great in fame as she was,
And so stand fixed. Peace, plenty, love, truth, terror,
That were the servants to this chosen infant,
Shall then be his, and like a vine grow to him.
Wherever the bright sun of Heaven shall shine,
His honor and the greatness of his name
Shall be, and make new nations. He shall flourish,
And like a mountain cedar reach his branches
To all the plains about him: our children's children
Shall see this, and bless Heaven.

KING: Thou speakest wonders.

CRANMER: She shall be, to the happiness of England,
An agèd princess; many days shall see her,
And yet no day without a deed to crown it.
Would I had known no more![13] But she must die;
She must; the saints must have her; yet a virgin,
A most unspotted lily must she pass
To th'ground, and all the world shall mourn her.

KING: O, lord archbishop,
Thou has made me now a man; never before
This happy child did I get[14] anything.
This oracle of comfort has so pleased me
That when I am in Heaven I shall desire
To see what this child does, and praise my Maker.
I thank ye all. To you, my good lord mayor,
And your good brethren, I am much beholding.
I have received much honor by your presence,
And ye shall find me thankful. Lead the way, lords:
Ye must all see the queen, and she must thank ye;
She will be sick else. This day, no man think
'Has business at his house, for all shall stay—
This little one shall make it Holy-day.[15]

13. This shift to dismayed anticipation of loss may be meant to recall Virgil's *Aeneid* VI when Anchises foretells the greatness of Rome and then, reluctantly, the death of young Marcellus; both poets then mention lilies.
14. Beget. In fact, Henry had another daughter, Mary.
15. Doubtless both holy day and holiday.

21

Anne Edgcumbe Dowriche *(before 1560–after 1613)*

Christopher Marlowe *(1564–1593)*

Anne Edgcumbe Dowriche Interprets History

Anne Dowriche (before 1560–after 1613), daughter of Sir Richard Edgcumbe of Mount Edgcumbe, Cornwall, married Hugh Dowriche, a rector, and bore at least three children. Her strongly Protestant *French History* (1589) is a long poem, in poulter's measure (hexameters alternate with fourteeners), with three parts: "The outrage called the winning of St. James his street, 1557," "The constant martyrdom of Annas Buggaius, one of the king's council, 1559," and "The bloody marriage of Margaret, sister to Charles IX, Anno 1572." Dowriche bases her story on Thomas Timme's translation of Jean de Serres's *Commentaries* (1574) and François Hotman's *De furoribus gallicis* (printed in London in both Latin and English, 1573; Marlowe, too, used Hotman's text for his *Massacre at Paris*). Her prefaces confess to her brother, Pearse Edgcumbe, and to the reader that weaknesses in her work show "that it is merely a woman's doing"; but she hopes "to restore again some credit if I can unto poetry": for there is not "in this form anything extant which is more forceable to procure comfort to the afflicted, strength to the weak, courage to the faint hearted, and patience unto them that are persecuted, than this little work, if it be diligently read and well considered." We give portions of Part 3 from the 1589 edition, including its marginal glosses in our notes.

FROM *THE FRENCH HISTORY*
THE BLOODY MARRIAGE OR BUTCHERLY MURDER OF THE ADMIRAL
OF FRANCE AND DIVERS OTHER NOBLE AND EXCELLENT MEN
AT THE MARRIAGE OF MARGARET, THE KING'S OWN SISTER,
UNTO PRINCE HENRY, SON TO THE QUEEN OF NAVARRE,
COMMITTED THE 24 OF AUGUST IN THE CITY OF PARIS, ANNO 1572.

> *Now have you heard before of faggot, fire, and sword*
> *Enhanced by Satan for to quell God's truth and blessèd word.*
> *But now I must begin such treason to unfold*
> *As former times for cruelty and ages new and old*
> *Have never seen the like in Christendom till now,*
> *When sacred faith—by flattery and oath of princely vow—*
> *By treason did contrive to shed the guiltless blood*
> *Of them which now by peace did seek to do their country good.*
> *For when the Lord did send His truth into the land*
> *He raisèd up some noble men to take this cause in hand,*
> *Among the which as chief and sovereign of the field*
> *There was Prince Henry of Navarre[1] with such as would not yield*
> *Unto the Guisian race.[2] The Prince of Condé[3] next;*
> *The Admiral[4] and D'Andelot,[5] with others that were vexed*
> *By bloody Guises' band who daily did invent*
> *How to oppress the word of truth, which Christ had thither sent.*
> *But when as Satan saw by words and dealing plain*
> *That many princes were in arms this truth for to maintain,*
> *It galled him to the heart that where he did devise*
> *To choke the word that even there the more it did arise.*
> *He summons all his mates these matters to debate*
> *How they might choke this springing seed before it were too late.*

1. Henri de Navarre (1553–1610), Protestant son of Antoine de Bourbon and Jeanne d'Albret, married Marguerite, sister of Charles IX, in 1572. The gathering of Huguenots in Paris for the marriage facilitated the St. Bartholomew's Day Massacre. In 1589, on the death of his brother-in-law, Henri III, Navarre became Henri IV, although it took more civil war, English help, and a conversion to Catholicism to confirm his rule.
2. An illustrious and ancient family that led the militantly Catholic faction and later helped found the famous Holy League.
3. Henri I of Condé; the Condés were a junior line of the royal family, prominent as Huguenot leaders.
4. Gaspard de Coligny, Lord Admiral (1519–1572), led the Huguenots; his murder marked the start of the massacre.
5. Gloss: "Gaspard de Coligny Admiral of France. François d'Andelot his brother, captain of the fonterie" [perhaps "foundry," for manufacturing artillery].

Where all within a round they come without delay
To whom this bloody captain then these words began to say:[6]
"There is a subtle vein that feeds this cankered sore,
For now the deeper it is lanced it riseth still the more.
We see that fire and sword cannot at all prevail;
We see that all our bloody broils their courage cannot quail.
We see how noble men their forces daily bend
To counter cross our planted plots, this cause for to defend.
Two civil wars are past; the third is now in hand;
We see how stoutly they are bent our forces to withstand.
Therefore we must devise to play some other part,
Or else in vain we take in hand these princes to subvert.
Now lend your listening ears and mark what I shall say;
A secret thing I have bethought which here I will bewray.[7]
You must make show as though you loved to live at ease,
As weary of these broils you must entreat to have a peace.
The king as chiefest man this play must first begin,
By loving letters, words, and cheer at first to bring them in.
And look what they mislike, the king must rase[8] *it out*
And yield to all things they request to put them out of doubt.
The king must show such face to them above the rest,
As though he did unfeignedly of all men love them best.
The worst of all their band the king must entertain
With such good will that no mistrust in any may remain.
And he must make them know as though of late he felt
Some prick in conscience for the cause against the which he dealt.
And that he will forgive all quarrels that are past
In hope that this their new good will with love might ever last.
And he must make complaint, as though he did of late
Mislike the dealings of the Guise and such as they do hate.
And then the Guises must awhile from court retire,
For thus you shall entrap them all and have your full desire.
The king must yield to all that they request or crave,
And he must grant for to confirm the thing that they would have.
The mother queen[9] *in this must also play her part*
That no suspect of treason may remain within their heart.

---

6. Gloss: "The second oration of the devil to the Queen Mother of France, the Guises, and the rest of the Papists."
7. Reveal. A marginal gloss reads "The devil's ghostly counsel."
8. Erase.
9. Catherine de Medici (1519–1589), widow of Henri II and mother of François II (husband of Mary Stuart), Charles IX (at this point king), and Henri III.

And here you must give out, as though you would employ
Their service in some foreign wars which doth your state annoy,
As if you would not trust the weight of such affairs
To any man but them alone, whose faith and watchful cares
You long have tried, and so you may your plot prepare
By these and such like feignèd things, to trap them in your snare.
If this prevail not then I stand in fearful doubt
What practice next to put in ure[10] to have them rooted out.
Now therefore say your mind if thus it be not best
To cut them off that so again we all may live in rest." . . .

[The Council agrees, and the king offers Coligny an alliance against Spanish power. Half suspecting a plot, the "wise Admiral" comes to court, where the king showers him with favor and seems to offer Protestants protection. Even the Guises feign friendship so as to fool the Huguenots.]

But nothing did prevail to put them out of doubt
So much as one thing, which as now, the king did go about.
Which was that he did wish his sister for to match
Unto Prince Henry of Navarre, by this in hope to catch
Them all within his snare. For this he did conclude
Not for good will but mere deceit the godly to delude.
Which match the king would have consummate out of hand,
That so it might remain, said he, a sure and perfect band
Of that unfeignèd love and inward, hearty care,
Which we to those that love the truth and gospel now do bear.
Which made them all rejoice and quite cast off their fear,
When in the king they did behold such love and friendly cheer.
Yet some did here allege that conscience did restrain
The prince to match with her which yet did seem for to remain
In love with popish rites. To which the king replied
That he to ease those scruples all such order would provide
Which they should not mislike. For he would there dispense
With all such rites and orders as might breed the least offense.
Which courtiers all mislike and openly repined
Much doubting least unto the truth the king had been inclined.
The admiral again was much confirmed besides
By other signs not doubting now their falsehoods and their slides.
The godly did rejoice to see the king so bent
Not thinking of the treachery and treason that they meant.
So matters being past, and parties all agreed,
In Paris town to have them joined by both it was decreed.

10. Use.

The Queen of Navarre[11] *now (a rare and virtuous dame)*
With others to the prince's court in full assurance came.
Where having stayed awhile, she took her leave to ride
To Paris for this solemn feast the better to provide.
The king to like effect by message did request
The admiral that he would go to Paris there to rest,
And see that nothing want for that appointed day,
And that himself would after come and make no long delay.
And that he might not fear the malice and the rage
That Paris men did bear to him, he said he would assuage
The same himself. And so he presently did write
To Marcel,[12] *provost of the town (perceiving well their spite),*
That he should entertain and use in friendly wise
The admiral and all his train, that nothing might arise
Which might offend his mind or burst to any flame,
For if there did he swore he would most fiercely plague the same.
The king and queen also unto the like effect
Unto the Duke of Anjou[13] *did their letters now direct.*
So that the admiral, not doubting any foe,
Resolved himself and did provide to Paris for to go.
Where being come he found the king and all the rest
With friendly welcomes, so as more he could not well request.
    But whilst that every man was busy to provide
Within the court most suddenly the Queen of Navarre died.
Which afterward was known (as some have plainly said)
That by a pair of gloves perfumed this treason was conveyed.
Which lewd and sinful deed was now no sooner done
But that the kingdom of Navarre descended to her son.
Here many did rejoice in hope of perfect rest,
Yet this unequal bloody match the Guises did detest.
That dismal day is come, the marriage must begin,
Where were assembled solemnly the chief of every kin.
And for because the mass their minds might grieve no more,[14]
The marriage was solemnifed before the great church door
Of Paris with such words as both were well content,
Which done, into the church the bride in solemn manner went

11. Jeanne d'Albret, mother of Henri de Navarre.
12. Claude Marcel, provost of Paris and follower of the Guise faction.
13. Henri, brother of Charles IX; he wooed Elizabeth Tudor before his younger brother, duc d'Alençon, took up that cause.
14. Huguenots would not want to attend a Catholic nuptial mass.

To hear a popish mass, both she and all her train,
Her husband walked without the door till she returned again.
Then home at last they go with mirth and passing joy,
They little thought this pleasant day would end with such annoy.
    And now begins the plays, the dancings, and the sport
Which were performed by lusty youths that thither did resort.
The king and nobles all in pleasures are so mad,
That for to talk of great affairs no leisure could be had.
And now the admiral from court had gone his way
Had not some causes of the church enforcèd him to stay.
Now from the wedding night five days are come and past
When as the king and senate were contented at the last
In council for to sit such matter to decide
As best might fit their feignèd wars in Flanders to provide.
Which ended, near about the middle of the day
As every man unto his house did take his ready way,
The admiral himself, with other nobles moe,
Along the streets (not doubting hurt) in pleasant talk do go.
A harquebus[15] *was shot from other side the street*
Which chargèd was with bullets two the admiral to greet.
Which cursèd blow did wound and strike this noble man
That thorough[16] *both his valiant arms the leaden pellets ran.*
Which done, although the wound did touch him somewhat near,
Yet nothing daunted with the stroke, he said with wonted cheer,
"From yonder house it came; go look who is within;
What vile, unworthy treachery is this they do begin?"
And therewithal he sent in haste unto the king
Such as might show unto his grace this bad and shameful thing.
    The message being done, the king as then did play
At tennis with the Duke of Guise. He fiercely threw away
His racket in a rage, as though it grieved his heart
That thus the admiral was hurt, and straight he did depart
Unto his castle, where awhile he did remain
Close with his brother of Navarre till he might hear again
More certain news. But now the matter was too plain
That this assault was surely made by one of Guise's train.
Now whilst these grievous wounds the surgeons had in cure
He sent Téligny[17] *to the king (because he was not sure*

15. A portable artillery piece.
16. Through.
17. Coligny's son-in-law, Charles de Téligny.

Where he should live or die) for to desire his grace
That he would now vouchsafe to come unto that simple place
Where he did lie, for that he had a secret thing
To tell him which did much concern the safety of the king.
Which was no sooner said, the king was well content
And with the man the message came without delay he went.
 They went likewise that sought the Admiral to kill,
The mother queen, with all her mates no doubt for great good will.
Which all no sooner did within the door appear,
But that the king saluted him with sweet and friendly cheer:[18]
"Alas my dearest friend, how cam'st thou to this place,
Where wounded now I see thee lie methinks in heavy case?
What arrant villain wrought this lewd and sinful act?
Would God I knew the wicked wretch that did commit the fact.
For though, my admiral, the hurt be done to thee,
Yet the dishonor of the fact and shame redounds to me.
Both which I will revenge, by death of God I swear,
As like in France was never seen to make such wretches fear."[19]
 Such speeches had the king and questions many more
Concerning judges, health, and grief and how he felt his sore.
To which the admiral, with mild and quiet mind,
Such answer gave as moved them much such patience for to find
In him that had received such cause of deadly ire
Who did request but only that the king would straight inquire
Upon the fact. "Which was, I surely know," said he
"Procurèd by the Duke of Guise for great good will to me.
Which deed the Lord revenge as He shall think it best
For if I die I hope by faith with Christ to be in rest."
The rest he did desire a while to stand away
For that he had some secret thing unto the king to say.
Which done he thus began:[20] *"O, king, this life to save,*
Is not the thing, I thank the Lord, that I do greatly crave.
For this I know is true: we all must pay a death
To God our maker which hath lent this use of lively breath.
But to your Majesty the great good will I bare
Is it which now above the rest doth most increase my care.

---

18. Gloss: "The feigned words of the king to the admiral."
19. Gloss: "This king was a horrible blasphemer and used this and such other like filthy oaths."
20. Gloss: "The secret speeches between the admiral and the king after the admiral was wounded."

To see you now beset with such as wish no good
Unto your health, your crown and life, and such as seek the blood
Of you and of your friends, to spill your noble race
That so they may in future time your princely stock deface,
And so at length engraft[21] *a strange Italian weed*
Which may in France most surely choke the prince's royal seed.
This is the only mark to which they do aspire;
This is the only wood, O king, that doth maintain the fire
Of these your civil wars, although they do pretend
Religion and some other thing, this is the chiefest end
Of all their drift. Therefore, O king, beware by time,
Mark this eclipse whilst yet ye see the moon is in her prime.
I say the less because I know your grace is wise,
You shall in time most plainly see this plot of their device;
Your wisdom doth perceive, I hope, whom I do mean
For of the same with grief before I heard you oft complain.

　　For though that I do lie here wounded as you see,
The chiefest treason they intend is not alone to me
But to your noble grace, whose death they daily crave,
Whose life by treason long ere this and now desire to have.
I know when God shall take this frail and wretched life,
Some will not stick to say that I was cause of all the strife.
But God that is above and you my witness be,
How dear the safeguard of my prince and peace hath been to me.
God grant you so in time your friends from fleering[22] *foe,*
That still in safety you may reign devoid of grief and woe.
Now I can say no more, but God preserve your grace,
And shield you from your feignèd friends which bear a double face.
And this amidst your mirth I pray remember still,
That they that seek to have my life do bear you no good will."

　　Which said the king did give such speech as he thought best,
And then in loud and solemn words, in hearing of the rest,
He did with friendly cheer request the admiral
Unto his court for to remove whatever should befall. . . .

[The king lyingly promises to protect the wounded Admiral.]

　　But here the prologue ends, and here begins the play,
For bloody minds resolvèd quite to use no more delay.[23]

21. Insert a cutting into another plant's stem or trunk ("stock").
22. Scoffing.
23. Gloss: "The Queen Mother leads out the king, the duke of Anjou, Gonzague, Taniques, the Count de Retz (called Gondi) into her gardens, called Tegliers."

The mother queen appears now first upon the stage,
Where like a devilish sorceress with words demure and sage
The king she calls aside, with other trusty mates
Into a close and secret place with whom she now debates
The great desire she had to quit them all from care
In planting long a bloody plot which now she must declare.[24]
   "O, happy light," quoth she, "O, thrice most happy day,
Which thus hath thrust into our hands our long desired prey.
We have them all in hold, we have the chiefest fast,
And those for whom we waited long we have them all at last.
Why should we longer stay? What can we farther crave?
What are not all things come to pass which we do long to have?
Doth not our mightiest foe lie wounded in his bed
Not able now to help himself, which others long hath led?
The captains captive are, the King of Navarre sure,
The Prince of Condé with the rest that mischief did procure
Are close within our walls; we have them in a trap;
Good fortune, lo, hath brought them all, and laid them in our lap.[25]
By force or flight to save their lives it is too late,
If we, to cut off future fear and cause of all debate
Do take the proferred time, which time is only now,
And wisdom matched with policy our dealings doth allow.
We need not fear the spot of any cruel fame
So long as we may feel some ease or profit by the same.[26]
For wisdom doth allow the prince to play the fox
And lion-like to rage, but hates the plainness of an ox.[27]
What though ye do forswear?[28] *What though ye break your faith?*
What though ye promise life and yet repay it with their death?[29]
Is this so great a fault? Nay, nay, no fault at all;
For this we learn we ought to do, if such occasions fall.
Our masters do persuade a king to cog[30] *and lie,*
And never keep his faith, whereas his danger grows thereby.[31]

---

24. Gloss: "The oration of the Queen Mother unto the King and other of his bloody council."
25. Gloss: "The queen mother was a good scholar of that devil of Florence, Machiavel, of whom she learned many bad lessons, as this."
26. Gloss: "1. That a prince must not care to be accounted cruel, so that any profit come by it. Theor. Politico."
27. Gloss: "2. Lesson. A prince must imitate the natures of a fox and a lion: a fox to allure and deceive, a lion to devour without mercy when occasion is offered."
28. Gloss: "3. Lesson that a prince may not doubt to forswear, to deceive, and dissemble."
29. Gloss: "This is a wholesome schoolmistress for a young king."
30. Cheat, deceive.
31. Gloss: "4. Lesson: That a prudent prince is not to keep faith, where any ill may grow by it. These be the pillars and this the fruit of Popish religion."

Cut off therefore the head of this infectious sore
So may you well assure yourselves this bile[32] will rise no more;
The captains being slain, the soldiers will be faint;
So shall we quickly on the rest perform our whole intent.
Pluck up therefore your sp'rits, and play your manly parts,
Let neither fear nor faith prevail to daunt your warlike hearts.
What shame is this that I, a woman by my kind,
Need thus to speak or pass you men in valor of the mind?
For here I do protest, if I had been a man,
I had myself before this time this murder long began.
Why do you doubting stand, and wherefore do you stay?
If that you love your peace or life, procure no more delay.
We have them in our hands, within our castle gates,
Within the walls of Paris town—the masters and their mates.
This is the only time this matter to dispatch,
But being fled these birds are not so easy for to catch.
The town of Paris will most gladly give consent
And three score thousand fighting men provide for this intent.
So shall we quickly see the end of all our strife
And in a moment shall dispatch these rebels of their life.
But if we stand in fear and let them 'scape our hand,
They will procure in time to come great trouble in our land.
For if the admiral his strength receive again
Can any doubt but that he will be mindful of his pain?
It is a simple thing for princes to believe
That new good will an ancient hate from gallèd hearts can drive.[33]
Therefore if we permit these rebels to retire
We soon shall see by wars again our country set on fire.
This is a woman's mind, and thus I think it best;
Now let us likewise hear, I pray, the sentence of the rest."
　　This counsel of them all was likèd passing well,
And in respect of present state all others did excel.
Some doubting musèd long which were the better way:
The King of Navarre and the Prince of Condé for to slay,
Or else to save their lives in hope they would recant
Because the proof of perfect[34] years they both as yet did want.[35]

---

32. A pun on "boil" (then pronounced "bile") and "bile" anger. "Bile" is also acid stomach juice.
33. Gloss: "5. Lesson: That it is a simple thing to think that new benefits can make old miseries to be forgotten."
34. Mature, adult.
35. Gloss: "It was of most thought best partly for age, partly for affinity sake, that the King of Navarre should be saved. And for the Prince of Condé, the opinion of Gonzague took place that he should with fear of death be drawn from religion."

But here they did prevail (as God, no doubt would have)
Who thought it best in this assault these princely youths to save.
Because they were in hope that when those imps[36] should see
Their mates tormented thus they would most willingly agree
To bow where they would bind, to go where they would call,
And to forswear their former faith would make no doubt at all.
But all the rest remain condemnèd for to die,
Which cruel verdict must be put in practice presently.
The night that should ensue then next without delay,
Beginning ere the same were spent long time before the day.[37]
The Duke of Guise was thought the fittest of the train
To take in hand this bloody plot to have the godly slain.
Concluding thus they go, each one unto his place,
The godly doubting nothing less than this so heavy case.

Christopher Marlowe's French History

The Massacre at Paris by Christopher Marlowe (1564–1593) stages scenes from the French civil wars. In 1586 the death of Henri III's brother (Elizabeth I's former suitor, the duc d'Anjou) made Henri, king of Navarre (a small realm southwest of France) the childless king's heir. There ensued a three-sided war among Huguenots (Protestants) led by Navarre, the ultrapapist Holy League led by Henri duc de Guise with Spanish help, and Catholics loyal to Henri III. In 1588 Henri III had Guise murdered; his own assassination, by a supporter of the League, followed the next year. Navarre was now Henri IV, but the war went on. Elizabeth helped him with men and money, while English printers produced pamphlets on his fortunes. Marlowe died before Henri's conversion to Catholicism in July, 1593 (when there is no evidence he ever said "Paris is worth a mass"). *Massacre*, first put on that January or earlier, starts before the St. Bartholomew's Day massacre on August 24, 1572, when thousands of Huguenots were massacred. It ends with the murders of Guise and Henri III. It is unclear if Marlowe is pleasing the crowd and the government by anti-Guise propaganda or treating all sides ironically, a debate not clarified by the inadequate printed text (1602). We excerpt the opening scenes in which Guise arranges the death of Navarre's mother, Jeanne d'Albret, daughter of Antoine de Bourbon and Marguerite de Navarre, who in fact died of natural causes. We adapt the text edited by H. J. Oliver (London: Methuen, 1968).

36. Youths.
37. Gloss: "It was decreed that this murder should begin about midnight of the night next following."

From *The Massacre at Paris* (c. 1593)

Act I, Scene 1

[*Enter* Charles IX of France, Catherine de Medici the Queen Mother, the King of Navarre, Prince of Condé, the Lord Admiral, and Margaret Queen of Navarre, with others]

CHARLES: Prince of Navarre my honorable brother,[1]
    Prince Condé, and my good Lord Admiral:
    I wish this union and religious league,
    Knit in these hands, thus joined in nuptial rites,
    May not dissolve 'til death dissolve our lives,
    And that the native sparks of princely love
    That kindled first this motion in our hearts
    May still be ffuelèd in our progeny.

NAVARRE: The many favors which Your Grace hath shown
    From time to time, but specially in this,
    Shall bind me ever to Your Highness' will
    In what Queen Mother or Your Grace commands.

QUEEN MOTHER: Thanks, son Navarre; you see we love you well,
    That link you in marriage with our daughter here:
    And, as you know, our difference in religion
    Might be a means to cross you in your love.

CHARLES: Well, Madame, let that rest.
    And now, my Lords, the marriage rites performed,
    We think it good to go and consummate
    The rest with hearing of a holy mass.
    Sister, I think yourself will bear us company.

MARGARET: I will, my good Lord.

CHARLES: The rest that will not go, my Lords, may stay.
    Come, Mother,
    Let us go to honor this solemnity.

QUEEN MOTHER [*aside*]: Which I'll dissolve with blood and cruelty.

Exeunt Charles, the Queen Mother, *and* Margaret

---

1. Charles IX was to be succeeded by his brother, Henri III. His mother, the Italian Catherine de Medici, was the widow of Henri II; Protestants often accused this broad-minded and force-ful woman of being a tyrannical murderer skilled in poisons. Navarre was Charles IX's second cousin and his brother-in-law by marriage to Marguerite de France (Marlowe's "Queen of Navarre," later notorious as "Queen Margot"). Although Protestant, Prince Louis de Condé and the Admiral, Gaspard de Coligny, were close to Charles and thus a threat to Catherine and Guise, who engineered their murders.

NAVARRE: Prince Condé and my good Lord Admiral,
    Now Guise may storm but do us little hurt,
    Having the King, Queen Mother on our sides
    To stop the malice of his envious heart
    That seeks to murder all the Protestants.
    Have you not heard of late how he decreed,
    If that the King had given consent thereto,
    That all the Protestants that are in Paris
    Should have been murderèd the other night?

ADMIRAL: My Lord, I marvel that th'aspiring Guise
    Dares once adventure without the king's consent
    To meddle or attempt such dangerous things.

CONDÉ: My Lord, you need not marvel at the Guise,
    For what he doth the Pope will ratify
    In murder, mischief, or in tyranny.

NAVARRE: But He that sits and rules above the clouds
    Doth hear and see the prayers of the just,
    And will revenge the blood of innocents
    That Guise hath slain by treason of his heart
    And brought by murder to their timeless[2] ends.

ADMIRAL: My Lord, but did you mark the Cardinal
    The Guise's brother,[3] and the Duke Dumaine,[4]
    How they did storm at these your nuptial rites
    Because the house of Bourbon now comes in
    And joins your lineage to the crown of France?[5]

NAVARRE: And that's the cause that Guise so frowns at us
    And beats his brains to catch us in his trap
    Which he hath pitched within his deadly toil.[6]
    Come my Lords, let's go to the church and pray
    That God may still defend the right of France
    And make His gospel flourish in this land. [*Exeunt*]

Act I, Scene 2

[*Enter* the Duke of Guise]

GUISE: If ever Hymen[7] lowered at marriage rites
    And had his altars decked with dusky lights:

---

2. Untimely.
3. Marlowe merges Guise's brother Louis, Cardinal of Guise (d. 1588), and his uncle Charles, Cardinal of Lorraine (d. 1574).
4. Henri de Guise's brother, the duc de Mayenne, whom the English regularly (as in Shakespeare's *Love's Labors Lost*) called Dumaine; after Guise's murder he led the League.
5. Henri established the Bourbon dynasty.
6. Net; the trap may be lined with pitch, unless Marlowe means "placed."
7. God of marriage rites.

If ever sun stained Heaven with bloody clouds
And made it look with terror on the world:
If ever day were turned to ugly night
And night made semblance of the hue of Hell,
This day, this hour, this fatal night
Shall fully show the fury of them all.
Apothecary— [*Enter* Apothecary]

APOTHECARY: My Lord.

GUISE: Now shall I prove and guerdon[8] to the full
This love thou bear'st unto the house of Guise.
Where are those perfumed gloves which I sent
To be poisoned? Hast thou done them? Speak.
Will every savor breed a pang of death?

APOTH.: See where they be, my good Lord,
And he that smells but to them, dies.

GUISE: Then thou remainest resolute?

APOTHECARY: I am, my Lord, in what your grace commands 'til death.

GUISE: Thanks, my good friend; I will requite thy love.
Go, then: present them to the Queen Navarre,
For she is that huge blemish in our eye
That makes these upstart heresies in France.
Be gone, my friend, present them to her straight.
Soldier! [*Exit* Apothecary; *enter* a Soldier]

SOLDIER: My Lord.

GUISE: Now come thou forth and play thy tragic part:
Stand in some window opening near the street,
And when thou seest the Admiral ride by,
Discharge thy musket and perform his death.
And then I'll guerdon thee with store of crowns.

SOLDIER: I will my Lord. [*Exit* Soldier]

GUISE: Now, Guise, begins those deep engendered thoughts
To burst abroad those never dying flames
Which cannot be extinguished but by blood.
Oft have I leveled,[9] and at last have learned,
That peril is the chiefest way to happiness,
And resolution honors fairest aim.
What glory is there in a common good
That hangs for every peasant to achieve?
That like I best that flies beyond my reach.
Set me to scale the high Pyramids,

8. I will test and reward.
9. Believed, suspected.

And thereon set the diadem of France:
I'll either rend it with my nails to naught
Or mount the top with my aspiring wings,
Although my downfall be the deepest Hell.
For this I wake when others think I sleep;
For this I wait, that scorns attendance else;
For this my quenchless thirst whereon I build
Hath often pleaded kindred to the king;
For this, this head, this heart, this hand and sword
Contrives, imagines, and fully executes
Matters of import aimèd at by many
Yet understood by none.
For this, hath Heaven engendered me of earth;
For this, this earth sustains my body's weight;
And with this weight I'll counterpoise a crown
Or with seditions weary all the world.
For this, from Spain the stately[10] Catholics
Sends Indian gold to coin me French écus.[11]
For this have I a largesse[12] from the Pope,
A pension, and a dispensation too:
And by that privilege to work upon,
My policy[13] hath framed religion.
Religion—O, Diabole—
Fie, I am ashamed, however that I seem,
To think a word of such a simple sound
Of so great matter should be made the ground.
The gentle King, whose pleasure uncontrolled
Weak'neth his body and will waste his realm
If I repair not what he ruinates,
Him as a child I daily win with words,
So that for proof he barely bears the name.
I execute, and he sustains the blame.
The Mother Queen works wonders for my sake,
And in my love entombs the hope of France,
Rifling the bowels of her treasury
To supply my wants and necessity.
Paris hath full five hundred colleges,[14]
As monasteries, priories, abbeys and halls,
Wherein are thirty thousand able men,
Besides a thousand sturdy student Catholics

10. Proudly powerful.
11. Gold coins. Spanish gold helped support the League.
12. A sum of money.
13. Political cunning and tactics.
14. Schools. Paris sided with the League.

And more: of my knowledge, in one cloister keeps
Five hundred fat Franciscan friars and priests.
All this and more, if more may be comprised,
To bring the will of our desires to end.
Then, Guise,
Since thou hast all the cards within thy hands
To shuffle or cut, take this as surest thing:
That, right or wrong, thou deal thy self a king.
Aye, but Navarre, Navarre. 'Tis but a nook of France,
Sufficient yet for such a petty king
That with a rabblement of his heretics
Blinds Europe's eyes and troubleth our estate.
Him will we— [*Points to his sword*] |
     But first let's follow those in France
That hinder our possession to the crown.
As Caesar to his soldiers, so say I:
Those that hate me, will I learn to loathe.
Give me a look that, when I bend the brows,
Pale death may walk in furrows of my face;
A hand that with a grasp may gripe[15] the world;
An ear to hear what my detractors say;
A royal seat, a scepter, and a crown,
That those which do behold, they may become
As men that stand and gaze against the sun.
The plot is laid, and things shall come to pass
Where resolution strives for victory.[*Exit*]

Act I, Scene 3

[*Enter* Navarre, Margaret, the old Queen of Navarre, Condé, Admiral, *and* Apothecary *with the poisoned gloves*]

APOTHECARY: Madame, I beseech Your Grace to accept this simple gift.

OLD QUEEN: Thanks, my good friend. Hold: take thou this reward.

APOTHECARY: I humbly thank Your Majesty. [*Exit* Apothecary]

OLD QUEEN: Methinks the gloves have a very strong perfume,
     The scent whereof doth make my head to ache.

NAVARRE: Doth not Your Grace know the man that gave them you?

OLD QUEEN: Not well, but do remember such a man.

ADMIRAL: Your Grace was ill advised to take them, then,
     Considering of these dangerous times.

OLD QUEEN: Help, son Navarre!—I am poisoned.

15. Grip and grab.

MARGARET: The heavens forbid Your Highness such mishap.

NAVARRE: The late suspicion of the Duke of Guise
   Might well have moved Your Highness to beware
   How you did meddle with such dangerous gifts.

MARGARET: Too late it is, my lord, if that be true,
   To blame Her Highness; but I hope it be
   Only some natural passion makes her sick.

OLD QUEEN: O no, sweet Margaret, the fatal poison
   Works within my head, my brain pan breaks,
   My heart doth faint, I die. [*She dies*]

22

Mary Fage *(fl. 1637)*

Francis Lenton *(fl. 1630–1640)*

Mary Fage Composes Anagrams

Mary Fage (fl. 1637) was known until recently only as "wife of Robert Fage the younger, Gentleman," as she is called on the title page of her *Fames Roule*. She can now be tentatively identified on the basis of this clue as the wife of Robert Fage and the daughter of Edward Fage in Doddinghurst parish, Essex. If Mary Fage *is* this Fage, then her husband was well connected. This would explain the composition of *Fames Roule*, a series of over four hundred acrostic verses, arranged in order of legally established precedence, each with an anagram and each addressed to one of the noble and powerful of Caroline England. Occasional slips suggest that Fage did not know the persons she addressed, but she knew enough to exclude women, aside from royalty, from her roll of honor.

Anagrams were popular. Noting that Elizabeth I enjoyed anagrams on her name, George Puttenham had in 1589 called them "commendable enough" if "done for pastime and exercise of the wit without superstition" and "a meet study for Ladies."[1] His reference to "superstition" acknowledges that such wordplay appeals to a sense that names have quasi-magical significance. Since Fage's book was entered in the Stationers' Register with the approval of Thomas Herbert, whose imprimatur was required for books on heraldry, it is safe to assume that it

---

1. *The Art of English Poesy*, ed. Gladys D. Willcock and Alice Walker (Cambridge: Cambridge University Press), pp. 108–111. Puttenham had read Estienne Tabourot, *Les Bigarrures* (1588 ed., ed. Francis Goyet [Geneva: Droz, 1986], ff. 102–114).

reflected sentiments agreeable to the powerful. Fage's verses are an extreme example of her age's taste for wordplay. Her very title can be read as either *Fame's Rule* or *Fame's Roll*, and we have therefore not modernized it. We base our selections on the Huntington Library copy of the 1537 edition.

From *Fames Roule*

Certain Rules for the True Discovery of Perfect Anagrams.

Momus,[2] *I know, at this my work will wonder*
And blaming me will belching envy thunder
By blusterous[3] *words out of his mouth, which he*
Shall seconded by Zoilus[4] *likewise be.*
"Tush," say they, "What? A woman this work frame?
Her wit will not attain an anagram.
There many may be false within her book."
Yet Monsieur Critic, notwithstanding, look
I pray thee, on these following rolls and then
Anagrams here according to them scan.[5]
E may most what conclude an English word,
And so a letter at a need afford.[6]
H is an aspiration[7] *and no letter;*
It may be had or left, which we think better.
I may be I, or J, as need require.
Q ever after doth a U desire.
Two V's may be a double V and then
A double V may be two V's again.
X may divided be, and S and C
May by that letter comprehended be.
Z a double S may comprehend.
And lastly, an apostrophe may ease
Sometimes a letter where it doth not please.
Try th'anagrams hereby, and then you'll say
Whether I've usèd all the helps I may.

2. God of mockery.
3. Rough.
4. A grammarian of the time of Philip of Macedon who attacked Homer.
5. Examine.
6. Supply.
7. Breath

And that each one that in the book doth rest
Is framed by mine industry, I protest.
And who will not believe my protestation
I'll hardly lean on their asseveration.[8]
But naught's the verse, 'tis truth: tears so bespotted[9]
The lines in writing, they remain still blotted.
M.F.

(2) To the Most Gracious Majesty of the Great Mary, Maria Stuart

Anagramma: METT RARA AVIS.

Magnanimous great Sol,[10] as he did pace
A RARA AVIS[11] Mett in his true trace:[12]
Regarding of your virtues, gracious queen,
Innated[13] in your breast a rare bird seen.
And Sol's true lively bird, an eagle high,

Striving aloft even unto Sol to fly
The Phoenix[14] rather than the which no more,
Vives[15] on the earth; save one, the only store;[16]
And your unsampled graces so abound,
Rightly proclaim Sol hath this Phoenix found.
This doth your goodness show, truth granteth it,
Ent'ring but this: Sol RARA AVIS METT.

8. Solemn affirmation.
9. Covered with blemishes.
10. Sun.
11. Rare bird.
12. Path.
13. Produced, born.
14. Mythological bird that rises from its own ashes.
15. Endues with life.
16. Stock.

(3) To Their Most Excellent Majesty of Great Britain's Monarchy, Carolus Maria Stuart

Anagramma: AV! VESTA, TRAC SOL, MARRY.

Cheerly[17] *firm Vesta,*[18] *clad in verdant*[19] *green,*
AU! is an emblem of our glorious queen;
Rend'ring[20] *a stable, fast, well-knitted heart*
On our great Sol placed thence not to depart.
Likely an higher goddess cannot be
Vesta-like, ruling in her chastity,
Shining in virtue's gracious increase.

Much glory hath this Vesta, but no peace
A [illeg.] doth to her true soul at all remain,
Returning till she doth her Sol retain
In whom she doth delight; whom in her pace,
Admiring she doth follow in true trace.

So Vesta traceth Sol, and did not tarry,
Till their united graces they did marry,
Virtues conjoinèd thus, Sol in his heat,
And Vesta in her chaste and plenteous great
Rare right increase, doth truly multiply,
Thrusting so forth a great posterity,
Ever to last unto eternity.

17. Blithe, cheerful.
18. A Roman name for Cybele, the Great Mother and goddess of the earth and its surface; also the name of the goddess of the hearth.
19. The green of vegetation.
20. Yielding.

(6) To The High and Mighty Princess Mary, Eldest Daughter of Our Sovereign Lord King Charles, Mary Stuart

Anagramma: A MERRY STATV.

Mirth may with princes very well agree,
A merry statu then, fair Madam, be.
Rightly 'twill fit your age, your virtues, grace,
Yielding a merry statu in your face.

Smile then, high lady, while of mirth write I,
That so my muse may with alacrity
Unto your highness sing without all fear,
And a true statu of your virtues rear.
Reaching whereto, that she may higher flee,
Thus humbly beg I on my bended knee,
Ever a merry statu be to me.

(7) To the High and Mighty Princess Elizabeth, Second Daughter to Our Sovereign King Charles, Elizabeth Stuart.

Anagramma: AH, BEST TY TRU ZEAL.

Elizabeth, *whose highness name declares*
Lively God's oath which he to's[21] *people swears,*
In memory keep great Eliza still,[22]
Zealously running up to virtue's hill.
Ah*! the* Best Ty, Tru Zeal *will always be,*
Best, firmest, fastest that uniteth thee
Either to God, who in a Zeal *most true*
Thy gracious heart honors with service due,
Honoring God by a Tru Zeal, Best Ty,

Suing[23] *the* Best *with His great majesty.*
Then if unto your sovereign parents dear,
Virtuously, a Tru firm Zeal *you bear,*
A great deal better, faster you are tied
Rightly, then by the bands whereby allied
Thou art to them by nature. So, likewise,
Ever Best Ty, Tru Zeal, *thy country cries.*

21. To his.
22. Always.
23. Entreating; or, possibly, following.

(8) To the High and Mighty Princess Anne, Third Daughter of Our Sovereign Lord King Charles

Anagramma: *A NU NEAT STAR.*

A Star *remain you in our firmament,*
Newly *sprung forth, having the luster lent*
Newly *wherewith your excellence doth shine*
(Ah still increase you) from that Sol *of thine.*

Star *doth your birth denote you, and your youth*
Truly averreth you Nu Star *in truth.*
Very much likewise doth your little brow
Actively set you forth A Neat Star *now.*
Reflecting then upon your excellence
That shows your radiant and sweet influence,
Each one doth grant you A Nu Neat Star *hence.*

(292) To the Right Honorable James, Earl of Castlehaven and Lord Audley Baron of Heleigh in England, James Touchet.[24]

Anagramma: *YOU MEET CHAST.*

Joined unto your true nobility,
Advancèd high as noble chastity,
Meet*ing wherewith you show you are a man*
Excellently that moderation can
Show to the life; so you do Chastness meet.

Thus chaste *then is your soul, who married (sweet)*
O to the Lord the world will not retain,
Virtue will ever beat it back again.
Chastity *bears hate to Adult'ry.*
Hatred our soul bears to Idolatry.
Express then to the life, that your chaste *heart*
Truly meets Chastity, *thence will not part.*

24. The son of Mervin Touchet, executed in 1631 for sodomy and for perpetrating a rape of his wife. It was James Touchet himself who brought charges against his father and thus publicized one of the great aristocratic scandals of the time. Fage's verses, with their stress on chastity, afford an instance of the social construction of reality in Caroline England.

Anagrams for Ladies by Francis Lenton

On February 6, 1638, the court saw a masque by Sir William Davenant, *Luminalia: The Queen's Festival of Light*, part of the Shrove Tuesday festivity just before Lent. Featuring figures of light and dark, strange monsters, and a City of Sleep, it presented dances performed by Queen Henrietta Maria and fourteen court ladies. The "Queen's poet," Francis Lenton (fl. 1630–1640), produced fifteen poems in their honor; these were printed separately that same year, arranged according to the rules of social precedence. Lenton wrote other anagrams, "character" sketches, religious verse, and a work rebuking "gallants" who spend time on *Don Quixote*, fencing, and dancing rather than on law books (Lenton had ties to the Inns of Court).

From *Great Britain's Beauties*, or *The Female Glory Epitomized* (1638)

To the Critical Age

Translators and your anagrammatists
(All know) are both confined to narrow lists;[1]
Nor can a rapture or fantastic flame
Fly in its full career upon a name,
'Cause bounded with the letters, where 'tis sin
Not with the name's first letters to begin
Each verse composèd by acrostic art,
Not to run smooth (with sense) in every part.
And for our anagrams, some erst did please
To term them (right) nugae difficiles;[2]
But if you will expect them without blame,
They must reflect o'th' nature, beauty, fame,
Birth, honor, breeding, quality, or wit
Of them whose names your fancy haps to fit:
Which if you rightly construe,[3] *surely then*
You'll find no gross fault in my modest pen.
But if rash censure you will undertake,
I tell you 'tis more ease to mend than make:
Of which, I dare not say you can do neither
'Til you have tried, and faulty prove in either:
Then bandy what you please, this book hath passed,
Approved above, and slights each lower blast.

1. Bounds marked out for horses (to suit "career" two lines later).
2. Difficult trifles.
3. The accent used to go on the first syllable ("conster").

An Anagram upon the Name of our most gracious Queen,

MARIA STUART.

Anagram.

I AM A TRU STAR.

Distich.

A Royal, Sacred, bright, *tru* fixèd *Star*,
In whose compare all others Comets are.

Illustration.

A morning star, *whose roseate blush and smile*
Show's the day's solace and the night's exile;
A radiant Star, *whose luster more divine*
By Charles *(our sun) doth gloriously shine;*
No wand'ring Planet that moves circular,
But a tru, *constant, loyal, fixèd* Star:
A Star *whose influence and sacred light*
Doth beautify the day and bless the night;
Which shining brightly in the highest Sphere
Adorns those smaller Stars *which now appear*
Before her presence, by whose gracious sight
Their numerous[4] feet now pace with rich delight:
O happy they approach unto that Throne
Where virtues are the constellation.
 And let it be proclaimèd, nigh and far,
 That our illustrious Queen *Is a tru Star.*

[There follows a design with an English rose and Scottish thistle flanking a shield with fleurs de lis.]

---

4. Stepping harmoniously in number-based measures.

Her *Grace*'s Acrostic

M INERVA'S Darling, and the Muses' Eye,
A ll Nature's faire Perfection in her Feature,
R are President [5] of virtuous Majesty
I mparalelled by any Mortal Creature,
A strea's Goddess and Diana's joy,
S urpassing both in Grace and Excellence
T hat Sacred Queen which Haman sought to 'stroy,
V asti's Successor of such Eminence,
A Royal Dame of great Magnificence.[6]
R eign, rarest Queen, in Plenty, Pleasure, Peace,
T ill Sol's extinct, and crazy Time shall cease.

An Anagram upon the Name of the beauteous Virgin, the Lady

DOROTHEA SYDNEY.[7]

Anagr. THY EYES DO ADORN.

Distich.

Thy chaste and modest Eyes *so much* adorn,
That Beauty's Queen,[8] *to thee, is but a scorn.*

Illustration.

The Eyes, *they are the beauties of the face,*
And of the feature are the only grace,
The body's light, most pleasant of the sense,
Feeding upon each object's excellence:
The prospect of the soul, which taketh pleasure

---

5. Chief or patroness.
6. When Vasti disobeyed her husband, King Ahasuerus, he replaced her with the Jewish Esther. Esther saved herself and her people from the machinations of the wicked Haman, who was hanged on a gibbet fifty cubits high (events still celebrated at the feast of Purim). In 1537 Lenton wrote an unpublished "Queen Esther's Hallelujahs and Haman's Madrigals."
7. Dorothy Sidney (1617–1684), daughter of the Earl of Leicester, was shortly to make a happy match with Henry, Lord Spencer, future Earl of Sunderland. She had been addressed by the poet Edmund Waller as "Sacharissa" ("Sweetest"). Philip Sidney was her great uncle, Mary Wroth her aunt, and the future republican, Algernon Sidney, whose execution she lived to see, was her brother.
8. Venus.

Thorough these Organs to behold the treasure
Of this large Cosmos, where (as I well ween)
We all delight to see, and to be seen:
So that to have a Body without Eyes
Is like the world sans Phoebus in the skies:
But, not to loose myself, I will return
Unto your Eyes, your Eyes which do adorn.
The baits of Love, from whose enchanting parts
You conquer and enchain the stoutest hearts:
There Love takes fire, and from that train[9] it steals
Down to the heart, which the Report[10] reveals.
Besides these ornaments (chaste Lady fair)
Your roseate Cheek, your coral Lip, and Hair,
Your Person, Presence, Virtues all unite,
In which the greatest Prince may take delight.
In rings by all your Servants, this be worn,
Next to their vanquished hearts: Thy Eyes adorn.
And let her be adorèd to the skies
That is adorned *with such all-conquering* Eyes.

HER ACROSTIC.

D ull world awake, and with thy Dim Eyes look
O 're all the Beauties of Dame Nature's Book,
R ead 'til thy Eyes fall out, thou ne'er wilt find
O ne of so clear a Beauty, clear a Mind.
T ake heed, you flaming Hearts, how you come near
H er fair and princely Presence; for I fear
E ach of you will be taken by her Eye,
A nd led into Love's wished Captivity:

S IDNEY (of Endless Fame) whose rare Compile[11]
I nriched us with sweet Eloquence and Style,
D id not so much all other Pens control[12]
N or to delight the sense, as she the Soul:
E ach Part of her deserves the best of Men
Y mployèd in her Praise beyond my Pen.

9. Line of gunpowder or other inflammable substance.
10. Perhaps a pun on bulletin and explosion.
11. Accumulation (of compositions); Sidney must be Philip.
12. Challenge, dominate.

23

Eleanor Audley Davies [Douglas]
(1590–1652)

A "Digger" Follower of Gerrard Winstanley
(c. 1649)

Eleanor Audley Davies [Douglas] Prophesies

Although the daughter of a baron (George Touchet, later earl of Castlehaven) and wife of two statesmen (Sir John Davies and Sir Archibald Douglas), Lady Eleanor (1590–1652) experienced the literal restraints on woman's public speech endemic in her culture, enduring imprisonments, the public burning of her works, and alienation from her husbands. An idiosyncratic mid-century prophet, she was of her time in her tendency to prophesy and in her elaborate wordplay. A member of no sect, she identified herself with the prophet Daniel, composing an anagram on her name: "Reveale O Daniel" (see below). Her elliptic, occasionally incoherent writings ranged over religious and political matters, while her unpopular, outspoken sentiments earned her the counter-anagram "Never so mad a ladie." She published more than fifty tracts, most printed abroad after 1640, some repeatedly. For the text of *Strange and Wonderful Prophecies*, an early, often reprinted work, we rely on the 1649 edition. As its extended title says, the text appeared with "notes to the said prophecies: how far they are fulfilled and what part remains yet unfulfilled concerning the late king and kingly government and the armies and people of England (and particularly Whitehall); and other wonderful predictions." We print these glosses, with their original sign system, after each stanza. Esther Cope's edition of Davies's writings (Oxford, 1995) does not give this version.

STRANGE AND WONDERFUL PROPHECIES BY THE LADY ELEANOR AUDLEY,
WHO IS YET ALIVE AND LODGETH IN WHITE HALL

> *To a Sion most beloved I sing*
>   b *of Babylon a song,*[1]
> *Concerns you more full well I wot*[2]
>   *than ye do think upon.*
> c *Belshazzar,*[3] *lo, behold the king*
>   *feasting his thousand lords;*
> *Phoebus and Mars*[4] *praised on each string,*
>   *every day records.*

a Those that believe this prophecy.
b So she frequently called the bishops and courtiers of England.
c The late King Charles,[5] whom in all her books she called Belshazzar because the wall of the banqueting house at White Hall, where he feasted, should be terrible to him as a writing on the wall was to Belshazzar, which proved true for there he was beheaded.

> *The temple vessels of God's House,*
>   *boldly in drunk about:*
> *His* d *own ('tis like) were made away,*
>   *bids holy things bring out;*
>   e *Praising of gold and brass, the gods*
>   *of iron, wood, and stone,*
>   f *See, hear, nor know, but now alas,*
>   *praised in court alone.*

d Here she prophesied of his pawning and selling of his plate.
e The pulling down of pictures and organs in churches.
f All did rise against him but the court faction.

> *A* g *hand appears, lo in his sight,*
>   *as he did drink the wine,*
> *Upon the wall against the light*
>   *it wrote about a line*
> *In presence of his numerous peers,*
>   *not set an hour full,*

1. Cf. Ps. 137:2–4.
2. Know.
3. The king in Dan. 5.
4. Phoebus Apollo (sun god) and Mars (god of war), i.e., pagan deities.
5. Charles I (1600–1649), reigned from 1625. Defeated in the English civil wars, he was captured, tried, and beheaded.

> *In loins nor knees had he no might,*
> *changed as a ghastly skull.*

g Here she prophesied of the king's death, which fell out true. For the headman took the hatchet in his hand wherewith he was beheaded on the wall of the banqueting house, after the king had drunk a glass of wine, at one blow or line of blood, in presence of his then equals (for he died as Charles Stuart). After he had been scarce an hour upon the scaffold, he fell down on his knees and so laid his neck on the block with a pale ghastly countenance, without any opposition.

> *Who might it read, alas, the thing,*
> *Belshazzar i loud did shout;*
> *Calls for magicians all with speed*
> *came in, as wife went out.*
> *Chaldeans*[6] *and soothsayers sage*
> *the meaning who so can*
> *Of Mene Mene third realms peer*
> *in scarlet robe the man.*[7]

i Here she speaks of the high court of justice where the king pleaded hard and so did the three lords,[8] but they were sentenced for their treasons, etc., and put to death according to judgment denounced by the lord president in scarlet.

> *His k majesty forgets to sup,*
> *Nobles astonished all;*
> *Musicians may their pipes put up,*
> *stood gazing on the wall.*
> *The l pleasant wine at length as sharp,*
> *too late till thought upon;*
> *Division m of another strain*
> *unfolds the fingers long.*

k The king did eat no supper the night before he died.
l He drank a glass of wine a little before he came to execution.
m His head was divided from his body.

> *When n to the banqueting house so wide,*
> *Where host of lords did ring,*

---

6. A Semitic people, thought to be great astrologers.
7. Dan. 5: "Whosoever shall read this writing, and show me the interpretation thereof, shall be clothed with scarlet, and have a chain of gold about his neck, and shall be the third ruler in the kingdom" (7). "And this is the writing that was written, Mene, Mene, Tekel, Upharsin" (25), meaning "You have been weighed in the balance and found wanting."
8. Presumably Arthur Capel, Lord Capel of Hadham (1610?–1649); James Hamilton, first duke of Hamilton (1606–1649); and Henry Rich, first earl of Holland (1590–1649). All were beheaded in March 1649 after a vote in Parliament. There is no note "h" in the original.

> *So wisely came the grateful queen,*
>   *said, "Ever live, O king.*
> *Needs o trouble, O king, thy thoughts no more,*
>   *forthwith shall it be read;*
> *Daniel there is who heretofore*
>   *like doubts did open spread."*[9]

n Here she names the banqueting house, the very place where he should be executed, and that before the host or army. And this did befall him for being led by his queen.[10]

o This she wrote to persuade the king to believe her prophecy.

> *Could all interpretating show*
>   *which profound man soon brought,*
> *On whom confer the king needs would*
>   *his p orders high unsought.*
> *Needless preferments yours reserve,*
>   *Sir, keep your gifts in store,*
> *High offices let others gain,*
>   *there's given too much afore.*

p The king delivered his George to the bishop of London for Prince Charles, but the parliament, considering his raising forces against them, would not let them have it.[11]

> *Yet unto thee shall here make known,*
>   *resolve this oracle true,*
> *Sure as in q thy banqueting house,*
>   *where all that come may view:*
> *The vessels of my God are brought,*
>   *the palm salutes thee know*
> *Herewith; for these profaned by thee*
>   *threateneth the fatal blow.*

q Here she set down the very place and manner of his execution which was true, for at the banqueting house the king had his head cut off at one fell blow.

> *O king, even thou, the most high God*
>   *unto thy r grandsire bold,*
> *Chaldean land, a nation fell*
>   *gave them to have and hold.*

---

9. Dan. 5:10–12.
10. Henrietta Maria (1609–1649), whose influence on Charles I was powerful.
11. George Villiers, first duke of Buckingham (1592–1628), the favorite first of James I and then of Charles I; widely detested, he was assassinated.

> *The royal scepter and the crown*
> *advanced whom he would have,*
> *And whom he would he pullèd down,*
> *could put to death and save:*

r His grandfather was put to death in Scotland, which she did usually call Chaldean land.[12]

> *Till walking at the twelve months' end,*
> *subject full tides do fall;*
> *Excellent s majesty how gone,*
> *Court exchangèd for the stall.*[13]
> *Thy t grandsire on, as came to pass,*
> *at all yet minded not,*
> *As if a feignèd story but*
> *his miserable lot.*

s Here she prophesied that monarchy should cease in England and White Hall—which was the king's court—be turned into an hold for soldiers.
t She here prophesied that he should as surely be put to death as his grandfather was, though not in the same manner.

> *Expelled was for the words escaped,*
> *memory can speak well,*
> *Hardened in pride, unheard of such,*
> *the wild ass with did dwell:*
> *Sent to the ox, its owner knows,*
> *u undreamt of this his doom:*
> *Fowls their appointed time observe*
> *wots not the night from noon.*

u Here she prophesied of the souls which flew over the king when he was at execution to show his folly that he would not know his time but bring himself to that miserable end.

> *Whose w heart made equal with the beast,*
> *driven out with those that bray,*[14]
> *The diadem as well fits thee,*
> *Ass, go, as much to say.*
> *x Until returned came to himself,*
> *knew Him that rules on high,*

12. Perhaps because Chaldea sounds like "Caledonia," a name for Scotland. Charles's grandfather, Lord Darnley, was murdered, perhaps with the connivance of his wife, Mary Stuart.
13. A place of confinement for animals.
14. Cry out; now often used of the ass.

> *Over the sons of men appoints*
> *what office they supply.*

w Here she prophesied that his entrails should be taken out, and his body be embalmed, which was true.

x She speaks this of his spiritual estate, that God in mercy hath saved his soul.

> y *During which space this Assyrian,*
> *what watch kept night and day,*
> *Thus metamorphosed over him,*
> *lest make himself away.*
> z *Fields, woods as well ring out, as men*
> *for woe, and echoes call*
> *Mercy this savage king upon,*
> *in holy temples all.*

y During the time of the king's imprisonment, there were guards upon him night and day.

z This fell out true, for he was much lamented by those of his own party especially.

> *Bewailed, dejected soul, thus fall'n,*
> *fed now grazing full low,*
> *whilst they bedew the ground with tears*
> *a discerns not friend from foe.*
> *Earth that of late made seem to dawn*
> *with songs of triumph high,*
> *Fleeth each wight*[15] *abased*[16] *as much,*
> *among the herd doth lie.*

a It was grown to a common proverb that the king knew not his friends from his foes, all being abased and none daring to stir or move for him.

> *By b starlight for device who gave,*
> *as graven on his shield,*
> *An eagle mounted on the crest,*
> *a hart in silver field.*
> *Extolled again his God as high,*
> *blessed him all his days:*
> *c Others reputes them as nothing,*
> *alone proclaims His praise.*

b Speaking of her own family.

c She here blames those that would not believe her.

15. Creature.
16. Downcast.

Whose seven d *times it servèd forth,*
 in vain for rest to crave;
Whom devils legions do possess
 a monarch turned a slave.
Deposèd thus thou knowest well
 Belshazzar, d*[sic] O his son,*
And renewed so, e *deliverance is*
 voicèd by every one.

d Here she prophesied of the very time—seven times seven—that is 49th year of his age the king was beheaded.

d Prince Charles. [The original uses note "d" twice.]

e This fell out true, for presently after the king's death the House of Commons voted England a deliverance from monarchy.[17]

A day a f *trumpet made to sound*
 for generations all;
And with a feast solemnizèd,
 that no time might recall
The memory of such an act,
 yet as it had not been
Thy favorites who are more this day,
 or matchèd to thy kin.

f An act was published in all parts against kingly government, notwithstanding the many favorites thereof and lords that the king used to call cousins.

Then they, g *adoring wood and stone,*
 statutes forsake divine;
Meditate carvèd statutes on
 in faction do combine
With enemies of God most high
 to thrust Him from his throne,
And thus hast lifted up thyself
 so facile and so prone.

g This is not yet fulfilled, but it seems to point out that the king's statues and arms shall be broken and pulled down from all public places, as he in his reign had promoted idolatry, liberty on the Lord's day, and other notorious sins against God.

Against the Lord of heaven thy king,
 not humbling of thy heart,
But stiffened hast with pride thy neck
 unto thy future smart.

17. Established England as a commonwealth or republic.

Behold, polluting holy things
*   with Sabbath so divine,*
Idolatry and revels in
*   that day and night made thine.*

But He in whose hand rests thy life,
*   even breath, thy ways, and all,*
Thou hast not glorifièd Him
*   sent this writ on the wall:*
God numberèd thy kingdom hath
*   ended; the hand points here,*
In balance He hath weighed thee too,
*   the set hour drawing near.*

How light soever by thee set,
*   thou as thy weightless God,*
His Image wanting, found much more
*   lighter than can be told.*
b Parted, divided thine estate,
*   given to the Medès[18] is,*
At hand, the hand bids it adieu,
*   i finished thy majesty's.*

h This is in part fulfilled by the king's lands and goods now upon sale.
i She prophesies here that there shall be no more kings in England.

Reveale O Daniel [Anagram] Eleanor Audley

A Follower of Winstanley Bids Diggers Arise

A religious and political radical, Gerrard Winstanley (1609–1676) came to believe that Christ lives in human souls, not in any church, and that a just society would have no private ownership of land. In a trance, he had heard the words, "Work together, eat bread together" (quoted in the preface to *The Works of Gerrard Winstanley*, ed. George H. Sabine [1941; New York: Russell & Russell, 1965]). When some of his few followers tried to take over and cultivate village lands, first at St. George's Hill in Surrey and then elsewhere in England, they acquired the nickname "Diggers." Cromwell and his allies rejected him, but in certain ways Winstanley anticipates such later radicals as Blake. This anonymous song shows the thought and tone of some who hoped to establish God's kingdom in England. We use the text in Sabine's edition.

18. Inhabitants of Media, a kingdom in Western Asia.

A Digger Song (c. 1649)

You noble Diggers all, stand up now, stand up now,
You noble Diggers all, stand up now,
The waste land to maintain,[1] *seeing Cavaliers*[2] *by name*
Your digging does disdain and persons all defame
Stand up now, stand up now.

Your houses they pull down, stand up now, stand up now,
Your houses they pull down, stand up now.
Your houses they pull down to fright poor men in town,
But the gentry[3] *must come down and the poor shall wear the crown.*
Stand up now, Diggers all.

With spades and hoes and plows, stand up now, stand up now,
With spades and hoes and plows stand up now,
Your freedom to uphold, seeing Cavaliers are bold
To kill you if they could, and rights from you to hold.
Stand up now, Diggers all.

Their self-will is their law, stand up now, stand up now,
Their self-will is their law, stand up now.
Since tyranny came in they count it now no sin
To make a jail a gin,[4] *to starve poor men therein.*
Stand up now, stand up now.

The gentry are all round, stand up now, stand up now,
The gentry are all round, stand up now.
The gentry are all round, on each side they are found,
Their wisdoms so profound to cheat us of our ground.
Stand up now, stand up now.

The lawyers they conjoin, stand up now, stand up now,
The lawyers they conjoin, stand up now,
To arrest you they advise, such fury they devise,

1. To farm unused village commons.
2. Gentleman royalists who supported the Church of England and private property.
Traditionally, the two sides in the war are called Cavaliers and (for favoring short hair)
"Roundheads."
3. Those with the right to coats of arms; most lived at least partly on profits from their lands.
4. Snare.

The devil in them lies and hath blinded both their eyes.
Stand up now, stand up now.

The clergy they come in, stand up now, stand up now,
The clergy they come in, stand up now.
The clergy they come in and say it is a sin
That we should now begin our freedom for to win.
Stand up now, Diggers all.

The tithe[5] they yet will have, stand up now, stand up now,
The tithes they yet will have, stand up now.
The tithes they yet will have, and lawyers their fees crave,
And this they say is brave, to make the poor their slave.
Stand up now, Diggers all.

'Gainst lawyers and 'gainst priests, stand up now, stand up now,
'Gainst lawyers and 'gainst priests stand up now.
For tyrants they are both, e'en flat against their oath;
To grant us they are loath, free meat, and drink, and cloth
Stand up now, Diggers all.

The club is all their law, stand up now, stand up now,
The club is all their law, stand up now.
The club is all their law to keep men in awe,
But they no vision saw to maintain such a law.[6]
Stand up now, Diggers all.

The Cavaliers are foes, stand up now, stand up now,
The Cavaliers are foes, stand up now;
The Cavaliers are foes, themselves they do disclose
By verses not in prose to please the singing boys
Stand up now, Diggers all.

---

5. The tenth of one's income owed the church; some called it mere custom, not God's law.
6. God never inspired them to use force ("the club").

24

Elizabeth Sawyer *(d. 1621)* and Henry Goodcole *(1586–1641)*

Thomas Dekker *(c. 1772–1632)*, John Ford *(1586–c. 1639)* and William Rowley *(d. 1626)*

Elizabeth Sawyer Interpreted as a "Witch"

Although the witch craze that gripped much of early modern Europe did not take as strong a hold in Britain, that country was by no means free of such persecution. Accusations and executions for this *crimen exceptum* (exceptional crime) increased after the accession in 1603 of James I, who in 1588 had written *Demonology*, a tract on witchcraft. As on the Continent, most victims were women. The reasons for the rise of the witch craze are complex, and the association of women with witchcraft is equally convoluted, but social historians point to the period's economic upheavals as one cause of this phenomenon. In England traditional forms of poor-relief (such as that tendered by church foundations) had been abolished, and the population of the indigent—particularly of indigent women—was growing as crops failed year after year. Perhaps the increase of beggars made those who were unable or unwilling to assist them feel guilty and the poor themselves feel angry. One possible result, when the relatively privileged experienced something they could interpret as retaliation by the village "witch," was accusations of witchcraft against the offending, ignorant, and helpless poor. With time, the tenuousness of such accusations became clearer. We excerpt portions of *The Wonderful Discovery* (1621), an account of the interrogation of an accused (and eventually executed) "witch," Elizabeth Sawyer (d. 1621), by Henry Goodcole (1586–1641), chaplain of Newgate.

FROM *THE WONDERFUL DISCOVERY*
A TRUE RELATION OF THE CONFESSION OF
ELIZABETH SAWYER SPINSTER, AFTER HER CONVICTION OF WITCHERY,
TAKEN ON TUESDAY THE 17 DAY OF APRIL, ANNO 1621,
IN THE JAIL OF NEWGATE, WHERE SHE WAS PRISONER, . . .
UNTO ME, HENRY GOODCOLE, MINISTER OF THE WORD OF GOD,
ORDINARY AND VISITOR FOR THE JAIL OF NEWGATE[1]

[In this manner was I enforced to speak unto her, because she might understand me and give me answer according to my demands, for she was a very ignorant woman.]

Question: *By what means came you to have acquaintance with the devil, and when was the first time that you saw him, and how did you know that it was the devil?*
Answer: The first time that the devil came unto me was when I was cursing, swearing, and blaspheming. He then rushed in upon me, and never before that time did I see him, or he me. And when he, namely the devil, came to me, the first words that he spake unto me were these: "Oh! have I now found you cursing, swearing, and blaspheming? Now you are mine."

[A wonderful warning to many whose tongues are too frequent in these abominable sins. I pray God, that this her terrible example may deter them to leave and distaste them, to put their tongues to a more holy language than the accursed language of hell. The tongue of man is the glory of man, and it was ordained to glorify God. But worse than brute beasts they are who have a tongue, as well as men, that therewith they at once both bless and curse.]

Question: *What said you to the devil when he came unto you and spake unto you? Were you not afraid of him? If you did fear him, what said the devil then unto you?*
Answer: I was in a very great fear when I saw the devil, but he did bid me not to fear him at all, for he would do me no hurt at all but would do for me whatsoever I should require of him. And as he promised unto me, he always did such mischiefs as I did bid him to do, both on the bodies of Christians and beasts. If I did bid him vex them to death, as oftentimes I did so bid him, it was then presently by him so done.

Question: *Whether[2] would the devil bring unto you word or no what he had done for you, at your command. And if he did bring you word, how long would it be before he would come unto you again to tell you?* **Answer:** He would always bring unto me word what he had done for me within the space of a week. He never failed me at that time, and would likewise do it to creatures and beasts two manner of ways, which was by scratching or pinching of them.

Question: *Of what Christians and beasts, and how many were the number, that you were the cause of their death? And what moved you to prosecute them to the death?*

---

1. Henry Goodcole attended prisoners at Newgate and wrote several accounts intended to edify his readers.
2. A conjunction indicating two possibilities.

Answer: I have been, by the help of the devil, the means of many Christians' and beasts' death. The cause that moved me to do it was malice and envy. For if anybody had angered me in any manner, I would be so revenged of them and of their cattle. And do now further confess that I was the cause of those two nurse-children's death, for the which I was now indicted and acquitted by the jury.[3]

Question: *Whether did you procure the death of Agnes Ratcliefe for which you were found guilty by the jury?* **Answer:** No, I did not by my means procure against her the least hurt.

Question: *How long is it since the devil and you had acquaintance together? And how oftentimes in the week would he come and see you and you company[4] with him?* **Answer:** It is eight years since our first acquaintance, and three times in the week the devil would come and see me after such his acquaintance gotten of me. He would come sometimes in the morning and sometimes in the evening.

Question: *In what shape would the devil come unto you?* **Answer:** Always in the shape of a dog and of two colors, sometimes of black and sometimes of white.

Question: *What talk had the devil and you together when that he appeared to you? And what did he ask of you, and what did you desire of him?* **Answer:** He asked of me, when he came unto me, how I did and what he should do for me, and demanded of me my soul and body, threatening then to tear me in pieces if that I did not grant unto him my soul and my body which he asked of me.

Question: *What did you after such the devil's asking of you to have your soul and body, and after this his threatening of you? Did you for fear grant unto the devil his desire?* **Answer:** Yes, I granted for fear unto the devil his request of my soul and body. And to seal this my promise made unto him, I then gave him leave to suck of my blood, the which he asked of me.

Question: *In what place of your body did the devil suck of your blood? And whether did he himself choose the place, or did you yourself appoint him the place? Tell the truth, I charge you, as your [sic] will answer unto the Almighty God. And tell the reason, if that you can, why he would suck your blood.* **Answer:** The place where the devil sucked my blood was a little above my fundament,[5] and that place chosen by himself. And in that place, by continual drawing, there is a thing in the form of a teat[6] at which the devil would suck me. And I asked the devil why he would suck my blood, and he said it was to nourish him.

Question: *Whether did you pull up your coats[7]* or no when the devil came to suck you? **Answer:** No, I did not. But the devil would put his head under my coats, and I did willingly suffer him to do what he would.

Question: *How long would the time be that the devil would continue sucking of you, and whether did you endure any pain the time that he was sucking of you?* **Answer:** He would be sucking of me the continuance of a quarter of an hour, and when he sucked me I then felt no pain at all.

---

3. The two "nurse-children" are never identified.
4. Cohabit with.
5. Anus.
6. Nipple.
7. Petticoat.

Question: *What was the meaning that the devil when he came unto you would sometimes speak and sometimes bark?* **Answer:** It is thus: When the devil spake to me, then he was ready to do for me what I would bid him to do. And when he came barking to me, he then had done the mischief that I did bid him to do for me.

Question: *By what name did you call the devil, and what promises did he make to you?* **Answer:** I did call the devil by the name of Tom, and he promised to do for me whatsoever I should require of him.

Question: *What were those two ferrets that you were feeding on a form[8] with white bread and milk when divers children came and saw you feeding of them?* **Answer:** I never did any such thing.

Question: *What was the white thing that did run through the thatch of your house? Was it a spirit or devil?* **Answer:** So far as I know, it was nothing else but a white ferret.

Question: *Did anybody else know, but yourself alone, of the devil's coming unto you and of your practices? Speak the truth and tell the reason why you did not reveal it to your husband, or to some other friend?* **Answer:** I did not tell anybody thereof (that the devil came unto me) neither I durst not. For the devil charged me that I should not, and said that if I did tell it to anybody at his next coming to me he then would tear me in pieces.

Question: *Did the devil at any time find you praying when he came unto you? And did not the devil forbid you to pray to Jesus Christ, but to him alone? And did not he bid you pray to him the devil as he taught you?* **Answer:** Yes, he found me once praying, and he asked of me to whom I prayed. And I answered him, "To Jesus Christ." And he charged me then to pray no more to Jesus Christ, but to him the devil. And he the devil taught me this prayer, "*Santibicetur nomen tuum.*[9] Amen."

Question: *Were you ever taught these Latin words before by any person else, or did you ever hear it before of anybody, or can you say any more of it?* **Answer:** No, I was not taught it by anybody else but by the devil alone. Neither do I understand the meaning of these words, nor can speak any more Latin words.

Question: *Did the devil ask of you the next time he came unto you whether that you sued to pray unto him in that manner as he taught you?* **Answer:** Yes, at his next coming to me he asked of me if that I did pray unto him as he had taught me. And I answered him again that sometimes I did and sometimes I did not. And the devil then thus threatened me: it is not good for me to mock him.

Question: *How long is it since you saw the devil last?* **Answer:** It is three weeks since I saw the devil.

Question: *Did the devil never come unto you since you were in prison? Speak the truth as you will answer unto Almighty God.* **Answer:** The devil never came unto me since I was in prison. Nor, I thank God, I have no motion of him in my mind since I came to prison. Neither do I now fear him at all.

8. Box.
9. Shaky Latin for "Hallowed be thy name," a blasphemous borrowing from the Lord's Prayer.

Question: *How came your eye to be put out?* **Answer:** With a stick which one of my children had in the hand. That night my mother did die it was done, for I was stooping by the bedside, and I by chance did hit my eye on the sharp end of the stick.

Question: *Did you ever handle the devil when he came unto you?* **Answer:** Yes, I did stroke him on the back, and then he would beck[10] unto me and wag his tail, as being therewith contented.

Question: *Would the devil come unto you all in one bigness?* **Answer:** No. When he came unto me in the black shape he then was biggest, and in the white the least. And when that I was praying, he then would come unto me in the white color.

Question: *Why did you at your trial forswear all this that you do now confess?* **Answer:** I did it thereby hoping to avoid shame.

Question: *Is all this truth which you have spoken here unto me and that I have now written?* **Answer:** Yes, it is all truth as I shall make answer unto Almighty God.

Question: *What moves you now to make this confession? Did any urge you to it or bid you do it? Is it for any hope of life you do it?* **Answer:** No. I do it to clear my conscience. And now having done it, I am the more quiet and the better prepared, and willing thereby to suffer death. For I have no hope at all of my life, although I must confess I would live longer if I might.

**A Relation What She Said at the Place of Execution,
Which was at Tyburn, on Thursday, the 19 Day of April, 1621.**

All this being by her thus freely confessed after her conviction in the jail of Newgate, on Tuesday, the 17 day of April, I acquainted Master Recorder of London therewith, who thus directed me: To take that her confession with me to the place of execution and to read it to her and to ask of her whether that was truth which she had delivered to me in the prison on Tuesday last concerning what she said. And how she died I will relate unto you.

[**Question:**] *Elizabeth Sawyer, you are now come unto the place of execution. Is that all true which you confessed unto me on Tuesday last, when that you were in prison? I have it here and will now read it unto you as you spake it then unto me out of your own mouth. And if it be true, confess it now to God and to all the people that are here present.*

Answer: This confession which is now read unto me by Master Henry Goodcole, minister, with my own mouth I spake it to him on Tuesday last at Newgate, and I here do acknowledge to all the people that are here present that it is all truth, desiring you all to pray unto Almighty God to forgive me my grievous sins.

Question: *By what means hope you now to be saved?*

Answer: By Jesus Christ alone.

Question: *Will you now pray unto Almighty God to forgive you all your misdeeds?*

Answer: Aye, with all my heart and mind.

10. Nod.

This [thus?] was confirmed in the hearing of many hundreds at her last breath what formerly she in prison confessed to me (and at that time spake more heartily then the day before of her execution), on whose body law was justly inflicted, but mercy in God's power reserved to bestow when and where He pleaseth.

My labor thus ended concerning her to testify and avouch to the world and all opposers hereof this to be true. Those that were present with me in the prison, that heard her confession, I have desired here their testimonies, which is as followeth:

We whose names are here subscribed do thereby testify that Elizabeth Sawyer, late of Edmonton in the County of Middlesex, Spinster, did in our hearings, confess on Tuesday the 17 of April, in the jail of Newgate, to Master Henry Goodcole, Minister of the word of God, the repeated foul crimes, and confirmed it at her death, the 19 of April following, to be true. And if we be thereunto required, will be ready to make faith of the truth thereof, namely that this was her confession being alive and a little before her death.

Conclusion

Dear Christians,

Lay this to heart—namely the cause and first time that the devil came unto her, then, even then when she was cursing, swearing, and blaspheming. The devil rageth, and malice reigneth in the hearts of many. O let it not do so, for here you may see the fruits thereof, that it is a plain way to bring you to the devil, nay that it brings the devil to you. For it seemed that when she so fearfully did swear, her oaths did so conjure him that he must leave then his mansion place and come at this wretch's command and will, which was by her imprecations. Stand on your guard and watch with sobriety to resist him—the devil your adversary—who waiteth on you continually to subvert you, that so you that do detest her abominable words and ways may never taste of the cup nor wages of shame and destruction, of which she did in this life; from which and from whose power, Lord Jesus, save and defend Thy little flock. Amen.

Ford, Rowley, and Dekker Put Mother Sawyer on Stage

Late in 1621, the same year that saw the execution of Elizabeth Sawyer for what the authorities called witchcraft, John Ford (1586–c. 1639), William Rowley (1554–1626), and Thomas Dekker (c. 1572–1632) produced a play that while not denying the reality of witchcraft nevertheless treats old "Mother Sawyer" with more sympathy than is shown by Henry Goodcole in the pamphlet from which we take our paired reading. *The Witch of Edmonton* was done for the popular theater but was also performed at court, where the audience would recall the king's interest in witchcraft. The authors worked in a context that encouraged collaborative authorship and invited the exploitation of notorious "true" cases that appealed to Londoners' thirst for news and scandal. The play's subtitle reads: "A Known True Story, Composed into a Tragi-Comedy by Divers Well-Esteemed Poets." We rely on the edition by Peter Corbin and Douglas Sedge (Manchester: Manchester University Press, 1999).

THE WITCH OF EDMONTON, ACT 4, SCENE 1

[Elizabeth Sawyer has been summoned before a Justice of the Peace for interrogation. Her ironic speech on witches will have touches typical of the tone and paradoxes of Renaissance satire.]

JUSTICE: Here's none now, Mother Sawyer, but this gentleman [Sir Arthur Clarington himself], myself, and you. Let us to some mild questions. Have you mild answers? Tell us honestly, . . . are you a witch or no?

SAWYER: I am none.

JUST: Be not so furious.

SAWY: I am none. None but base curs so bark at me. I am none. Or would I were: if every poor old woman be trod on thus by slaves,[1] reviled, kicked, beaten, as I am daily, she to be revenged had need turn witch.

SIR ARTHUR: And you, to be revenged, have sold your soul to the Devil.

SAWY: Keep thine own from him.

JUST: You are too saucy and too bitter.

SAWY: Saucy? By what commission can he send my soul on the Devil's errand, more than I can his? Is he a landlord of my soul, to thrust it when he list[2] out of doors?

JUST: Know whom you speak to.

SAWY: A man: perhaps no man. Men in gay clothes, whose backs are laden with titles and honors, are within far more crooked than I am and—if I be a witch—more witchlike.

SIR ART: Y'are a base Hell-hound. And now, sir, let me tell you, far and near she's bruited[3] for a woman that maintains a spirit that sucks her.

SAWY: I defy thee.

SIR ART: Go, go. I can if need be bring a hundred voices e'en here in Edmonton that shall loud proclaim thee for a secret and pernicious witch.

SAWY: Ha, ha!

JUST: Do you laugh? Why laugh you?

SAWY: At my name, the brave name this knight gives me: witch.

JUST: Is the name of "witch" so pleasing to thine ear?

SIR ART: Pray, sir, give way, and let her tongue gallop on.

---

1. Low-minded and base people.
2. When he likes.
3. Rumored.

SAWY: A witch? Who is not?
>   Hold not that universal name in scorn, then.
>   What are your painted things in princes' courts,
>   Upon whose eyelids Lust sits blowing fires
>   To burn men's souls in sensual hot desires,
>   Upon whose naked paps[4] a lecher's thought
>   Acts sin in fouler shapes than can be wrought?

JUST: But those work not as you do.

SAWY: No, but far worse:
>   These by enchantments can whole lordships change
>   To trunks of rich attire, turn plows and teams
>   To Flanders mares and coaches, and huge trains
>   Of servitors to a French butterfly[5]
>   Have you not seen City-witches[6] who can turn
>   Their husbands' wares, whole standing shops of wares,
>   To sumptuous tables, gardens of stol'n sin,
>   In one year wasting what scarce twenty win?
>   Are not these witches?

JUST: Yes, yes, but the law
>   Casts not an eye on these.

SAWY: Why then on me,
>   Or any lean old beldame?[7] Reverence once
>   Had wont to wait on age. Now an old woman,
>   Ill-favored grown with years, if she be poor,
>   Must be called "bawd"[8] or "witch." Such so abused
>   Are the coarse witches: t'other are the fine,
>   Spun for the Devil's own wearing.

SIR ART: And so is thine.

SAWY: She on whose tongue a whirlwind sits to blow
>   A man out of himself, from his soft pillow
>   To lean his head on rocks and fighting waves,
>   Is not that scold a witch? The man of law
>   Whose honeyed hopes the credulous client draws
>   (As bees by tinkling basins) to swarm to him
>   From his own hive to work the wax in his—
>   He is no witch, not he.

SIR ART: But these men-witches
>   Are not in trading with Hell's merchandise,

---

4. Nipples, breasts.
5. A common accusation was that courtiers paid for fashionable life by wasting their family lands and resources.
6. Wives of the well-to-do living in the City of London.
7. Old woman.
8. A madam for prostitutes.

Like such as you are, that for a word, a look,
Denial of a coal of fire, kill men,
Children, and cattle.

SAWY: Tell them, sir, that do so:
Am I accused for such a one?

SIR ART: Yes, 'twill be sworn.

SAWY: Dare any swear I ever tempted maiden
With golden hooks flung at her chastity
To come and lose her honor? And being lost
To pay not a denier[9] for't? Some slaves have done it.
Men-witches can, without the fangs of law
Drawing once one drop of blood, put counterfeit pieces
Away for true gold.

---

9. Penny. Sawyer's analogy refers to seduction and pregnancy, language the more significant because Sir Arthur is himself the seducer of a young woman.

25

Mary White Rowlandson *(c. 1635–after 1677)*

Thomas Hariot *(1560–1621)*,
Michael Drayton *(1563–1631)*, and
Robert Hayman *(1575–1629)*

Mary White Rowlandson

Born to wealthy parents in Salem, England, Mary Rowlandson (c. 1635–after 1677) married Joseph Rowlandson, minister of Lancaster, Massachusetts, in 1656 and emigrated to the colonies in 1673. In February 1675, during King Philip's War and while her husband was out of town, the Narragansetts captured her, her children, and some others. Many settlers were killed during this raid. Rowlandson's youngest child, six years old, died soon after; the rest of the family was separated. She and a son were ransomed after eleven weeks; a daughter made her way to freedom.

Rowlandson's account of her captivity, which the preface (perhaps by Increase Mather) calls "a memorandum of God's dealing with her" was published—at the insistence of others—so that "God might have his due glory, and others benefit by it as well as herself." Rowlandson's physical endurance and emotional strength are remarkable. Early in her captivity, one of the Indians gave her a Bible; her citation of apt passages to comfort herself is one of her story's fascinations, as are the objectivity with which she discusses her reactions to Indian fare and the calm with which she describes barbarities. Also noteworthy— if perhaps understandable—is her sharp distinction between kindnesses shown her and her family by the settlers who rescued her (for which she expresses great appreciation) and those shown her by many Indians (for which, although they were sharing the goods of a subsistence group, her appreciation is minimal).

Rowlandson moved to Wethersfield, Connecticut, in 1677, but there are no further traces of her. Her narrative, first published in Boston as *The Sovereignty and Goodness of God* (1682), is the earliest best-seller by an American woman. Our excerpts are from the English edition of 1682.

FROM *A NARRATIVE OF THE CAPTIVITY OF MRS. MARY ROWLANDSON*

On the tenth of February, 1675, came the Indians with great numbers upon Lancaster. Their first coming was about sun rising. Hearing the noise of some guns, we looked out: several houses were burning, and the smoke ascending to heaven. There were five persons taken in one house: the father, and the mother, and a sucking child they knocked on the head; the other two they took and carried away alive. . . . Thus these murderous wretches went on, burning and destroying before them. . . .

Then I took my children (and one of my sisters, hers) to go forth and leave the house, but as soon as we came to the door and appeared the Indians shot so thick that the bullets rattled against the house as if one had taken an handful of stones and threw them, so that we were fain[1] to give back. . . . But out we must go, the fire increasing and coming along behind us roaring, and the Indians gaping before us with their guns, spears, and hatchets to devour us. No sooner were we out of the house, but my brother-in-law[2] (being before wounded in defending the house in or near the throat) fell down dead, whereat the Indians scornfully shouted, and hallowed, and were presently upon him, stripping off his clothes. The bullets flying thick, one went through my side and the same (as would seem) through the bowels and hand of my dear child in my arms. One of my elder sister's children (named William) had then his leg broken, which the Indians perceiving, they knocked him on the head.[3] Thus were we butchered by those merciless heathen, standing amazed with the blood running down to our heels. . . .

I had often before this said that if the Indians should come I should choose rather to be killed by them than taken alive, but when it came to the trial my mind changed. Their glittering weapons so daunted my spirit that I chose rather to go along with those (as I may say) ravenous bears then that moment to end my days. And that I may the better declare what happened to me during that grievous captivity, I shall particularly speak of the several removes we had up and down the wilderness.

The First Remove: Now away we must go with those barbarous creatures, with our bodies wounded and bleeding, and our hearts no less than our bodies. About a mile we went that night, up upon a hill within sight of the town where they intended to lodge.[4] There was hard by a vacant house (deserted by the

1. Forced (willing under the circumstances).
2. John Divoll, husband of Rowlandson's youngest sister, Hannah.
3. William was the son of Rowlandson's sister Elizabeth and Henry Kerley.
4. George Hill.

English before for fear of the Indians). I asked them whether I might not lodge in the house that night, to which they answered, "What, will you love Englishmen still?" This was the dolefullest night that ever my eyes saw. Oh, the roaring, and singing, and dancing, and yelling of those black creatures in the night, which made the place a lively resemblance of hell. And as miserable was the waste that there was made of horses, cattle, sheep, swine, calves, lambs, roasting pigs, and fowls (which they had plundered in the town) some roasting, some lying and burning, and some boiling, to feed our merciless enemies, who were joyful enough though we were disconsolate. To add to the dolefulness of the former day and the dismalness of the present night, my thoughts ran upon my losses and sad bereaved condition. All was gone: my husband gone (at least separated from me, he being in the Bay[5]—and to add to my grief, the Indians told me they would kill him as he came homeward); my children gone; my relations and friends gone; our house and home, and all our comforts within door and without—all was gone (except my life, and I knew not but the next moment that might go, too).

There remained nothing to me but one poor wounded babe, and it seemed at present worse than death that it was in such a pitiful condition, bespeaking[6] compassion. And I had no refreshing[7] for it, nor suitable things to revive it. Little do many think what is the savageness and brutishness of this barbarous enemy— even those that seem to profess[8] more than others among them—when the English have fallen into their hands. . . .

The Third Remove: The morning being come, they prepared to go on their way. One of the Indians got up upon a horse, and they set me up behind him with my poor sick babe in my lap. A very wearisome and tedious day I had of it, what with my own wound and my child's being so exceeding sick and in a lamentable condition with her wound. It may easily be judged what a poor feeble condition we were in, there being not the least crumb of refreshing that came within either of our mouths from Wednesday night to Saturday night, except only a little cold water. This day in the afternoon, about an hour by sun, we came to the place where they intended, viz. an Indian town called Wenimesset,[9] northward of Quabang.[10] When we were come, oh, the number of pagans (now merciless enemies) that there came about me, that I may say, as David (Psalms 27:13): "I had fainted, unless I had believed, etc."

The next day was the Sabbath. I then remembered how careless I had been of God's holy time, how many Sabbaths I had lost and misspent, and how evilly I had walked in God's sight, which lay so close upon my spirit that it was easy for me to see how righteous it was with God to cut off the thread of my life and cast me out of His presence forever. Yet the Lord still showed mercy to me and upheld me, and as He wounded me with one hand, so healed me with the other.

5. Massachusetts Bay, where he had gone for help, anticipating an Indian attack.
6. Calling out for.
7. Food.
8. Declare Christian belief.
9. Menameset on the River Ware; now New Braintree.
10. Now Brookfield.

. . . I sat much alone with a poor wounded child in my lap, which moaned night and day, having nothing to revive the body or cheer the spirits of her. But instead of that, sometimes one Indian would come and tell me, "One hour and your master will quickly knock your child in the head." This was the comfort I had from them; "Miserable comforters are ye all," as he said.[11]

Thus nine days I sat upon my knees with my babe in my lap, till my flesh was raw again. My child being even ready to depart this sorrowful world, they bad me carry it out to another wigwam (I suppose because they would not be troubled with such spectacle). Whither I went with a very heavy heart, and down I sat with the picture of death in my lap. About two hours in the night, my sweet babe, like a lamb, departed this life, on February 18, 1675, it being about six years and five months old. It was nine days (from the first wounding) in this miserable condition, without any refreshing of one nature or other, except a little cold water. I cannot but take notice how at another time I could not bear to be in the room where any dead person was, but now the case is changed: I must and could lie down by my dead babe, side by side, all the night after. I have thought since of the wonderful goodness of God to me in preserving me so in the use of my reason and senses, in that distressed time, that I did not use wicked and violent means to end my own miserable life.

In the morning, when they understood that my child was dead, they sent for me home to my master's wigwam. (By my master in this writing must be understood Quinnapin,[12] who was a sagamore[13] and married King Philip's[14] wife's sister; not that he first took me, but I was sold to him by another Narragansett Indian, who took me when first I came out of the garrison). I went to take up my dead child in my arms to carry it with me, but they bid me let it alone. There was no resisting, but go I must and leave it. When I had been a while at my master's wigwam, I took the first opportunity I could get to go look after my dead child. When I came, I asked them what they had done with it. They told me it was upon the hill. Then they went and showed me where it was, where I saw the ground was newly digged, and there they told me they had buried it. There I left that child in the wilderness, and must commit it and myself also, in this wilderness condition, to Him who is above all.

God having taken away this dear child, I went to see my daughter Mary, who was at this same Indian town, at a wigwam not very far off, though we had little liberty or opportunity to see one another. She was about ten years old and taken from the door at first by a Praying Indian,[15] and afterward sold for a gun. When I came in sight she would fall aweeping, at which they were provoked and would not let me come near her, but bade me be gone which was a heart-cutting word

11. Said by Job (Job 16:2).
12. Quannopin, or Quinnapin, sachem in King Philip's War (1675–1676), who bought Rowlandson in February 1676, was executed that August. He was the husband of Weetamoo, to whom Mary Rowlandson became a servant.
13. A chief of the second rank, similar to sachem.
14. "King Philip" (Metacom), c. 1639–1676, was Wampanoag sachem from 1662.
15. A Christian convert.

to me. I had one child dead, another in the wilderness—I knew not where—the third they would not let me come near to. "Me," as he said, "Have ye bereaved of my children. Joseph is not, and Simeon is not, and ye will take Benjamin also, all these things are against me."[16] I could not sit still in this condition, and that I should have children, and a nation which I knew not ruled over them. Whereupon I earnestly entreated the Lord that He would consider my low estate and show me a token for good and, if it were His blessed will, some sign and hope of some relief.

And indeed quickly the Lord answered in some measure my poor prayer. For as I was going up and down mourning and lamenting my condition, my son came to me and asked me how I did. I had not seen him before since the destruction of the town. And I knew not where he was till I was informed by himself that he was amongst a smaller parcel of Indians, whose place was about six miles off. With tears in his eyes, he asked me whether his sister Sarah was dead, and told me he had seen his sister Mary, and prayed me that I would not be troubled in reference to himself. . . .

The next day, viz. to this, the Indians returned from Medfield[17]. . . . And then, oh, the hideous insulting and triumphing that there was over some Englishmen's scalps. . . . I cannot but take notice of the wonderful mercy of God to me in those afflictions, in sending me a Bible. One of the Indians that came from Medfield fight and had brought some plunder came to me and asked me if I would have a Bible. He had got one in his basket. I was glad of it and asked him whether he thought the Indians would let me read. He answered yes, so I took the Bible, and in that melancholy time it came into my mind to read first the 28 Chapter of Deuteronomy, which I did. And when I had read it, my dark heart wrought on this manner that there was no mercy for me, that the blessings were gone, and the curses came in their room, and that I had lost my opportunity. But the Lord helped me still to go on reading till I came to Chapter 30, the seven first verses, where I found there was mercy promised again if we would return to him by repentance. And though we were scattered from one end of the earth to the other, yet the Lord would gather us together, and turn all those curses upon our enemies. I do not desire to live to forget this scripture and what comfort it was to me.

Now the Indians began to talk of removing from this place, some one way and some another. There were now besides myself nine English captives in this place (all of them children, except one woman). I got an opportunity to go and take my leave of them, they being to go one way and I another. I asked them whether they were earnest with God for deliverance; they all told me they did as they were able. And it was some comfort to me that the Lord stirred up children to look to him. The woman, viz. Goodwife Joslin, told me she should never see me again, and that she could find in her heart to run away. I wished her not to

16. Said by Jacob when his sons take Benjamin to Egypt (Gen. 42:36).
17. Medfield (originally Meadfield), southwest of Boston, was founded in 1650, burnt in 1675, and later rebuilt. The battle took place on February 21.

run away by any means, for we were near thirty miles from any English town and she very big with child and had but one week to reckon, and another child in her arms, two years old. And bad rivers there were to go over, and we were feeble with our poor and coarse entertainment.[18] I had my Bible with me. I pulled it out and asked her whether she would read. We opened the Bible and lighted on Psalm 27, in which psalm we especially took notice of that verse ultimate: "Wait on the Lord; be of good courage, and he shall strengthen thine Heart. Wait I say on the Lord."

The Fourth Remove: And now must I part with that little company that I had. Here I parted from my daughter Mary (whom I never saw again till I saw her in Dorchester,[19] returned from captivity) and from four little cousins and neighbors, some of which I never saw afterward. The Lord only knows the end of them. Amongst them also was that poor woman before mentioned who came to a sad end, as some of the company told me in my travel. She, having much grief upon her spirit about her miserable condition, being so near her time, she would be often asking the Indians to let her go home. They not being willing to that, and yet vexed with her importunity, gathered a great company together about her and stripped her naked and set her in the midst of them. And when they had sung and danced about her (in their hellish manner) as long as they pleased, they knocked her on the head and the child in her arms with her. When they had done that, they made a fire and put them both into it and told the other children that were with them that if they attempted to go home they would serve them in the like manner. The children said she did not shed one tear, but prayed all the while.
. . .

The first week of my being among them, I hardly ate any thing. The second week I found my stomach grow very faint for want of something, and yet 'twas very hard to get down their filthy trash. But the third week, though I could think how formerly my stomach would turn against this or that, and I could starve and die before I could eat such things, yet they were pleasant and savory to my taste. I was at this time knitting a pair of white cotton stockings for my mistress, and I had not wrought upon the Sabbath day. When the Sabbath came they bade me to go to work. I told them it was Sabbath day and desired them to let me rest, and told them I would do as much more tomorrow, to which they answered me they would break my face. . . .

The Twelfth Remove: It was upon a Sabbath day morning that they prepared for their travel. This morning I asked my master whether he would sell me to my husband. He answered, "Nux,"[20] which did much rejoice my spirit. My mistress, before we went, was gone to the burial of a papoose, and returning she found me sitting and reading in the Bible. She snatched it hastily out of my hand and threw it out of doors; I ran out, and catched it up, and put it into my pocket, and never let her see it afterward.

18. Accommodations, provisions.
19. Dorchester, Massachusetts.
20. Yes.

Then they packed up their things to be gone and gave me my load. I complained it was too heavy, whereupon she gave me a slap in the face and bade me go. I lifted up my heart to God, hoping that the redemption was not far off, and the rather because their insolency grew worse and worse. . . .

The Thirteenth Remove: Instead of going toward the Bay (which was that I desired) I must go with them five or six miles down the river into a mighty thicket of brush, where we abode almost a fortnight.[21] Here one asked me to make a shirt for her papoose, for which she gave me a mess of broth which was thickened with meal made of the bark of a tree, and to make it the better she had put into it about a handful of pease and a few roasted ground nuts. I had not seen my son a pretty[22] while, and here was an Indian of whom I made inquiry after him and asked him when he saw him. He answered me that such a time his master roasted him, and that himself did eat a piece of him as big as his two fingers, and that he was very good meat. But the Lord upheld my spirit under his discouragement, and I considered their horrible addictedness to lying and that there is not one of them that makes the least conscience of telling the truth. In this place on a cold night as I lay by the fire, I removed a stick which kept the heat from me. A squaw moved it down again, at which I looked up, and she threw an handful of ashes in my eyes. I thought I should have been quite blinded and have never seen more, but lying down, the water run out of my eyes and carried the dirt with it, that by the morning I recovered my sight again. Yet upon this and the like occasions, I hope it is not too much to say with Job, "Have pity upon me, have pity upon me, Oh ye my friends, for the hand of the Lord has touched me."[23] . . .

The Sixteenth Remove: We began this remove with wading over Baquang River.[24] The water was up to the knees and the stream very swift, and so cold that I thought it would have cut me in sunder. I was so weak and feeble that I reeled as I went along and thought there I must end my days at last, after my bearing and getting through so many difficulties. The Indians stood laughing to see me staggering along, but in my distress the Lord gave me experience of the truth and goodness of that promise (Isaiah 43:2): "When thou passest through the waters I will be with thee, and through the rivers, they shall not overflow thee." Then I sat down to put on my stockings and shoes with the tears running down my eyes and many sorrowful thoughts in my heart, but I got up to go along with them. Quickly there came up to us an Indian who informed them that I must go to Wachuset[25] to my master, for there was a letter come from the council to the sagamores about redeeming the captives, and that there would be another in fourteen days, and that I must be there ready. My heart was so heavy before that I could scarce speak or go in the path, and yet now so light that I could run. My strength seemed to come again and to recruit my feeble knees and aching heart. Yet it pleased them to go but one mile that night, and there we stayed two days.

21. Near the Connecticut River, at Hinsdale, New Hampshire.
22. Considerable.
23. Job 19:21.
24. Miller's River in modern Petersham, Massachusetts.
25. Possibly a mountain in north-central Massachusetts near Fitchburg.

In that time came a company of Indians to us, near thirty, all on horseback. My heart skipped within me, thinking they had been Englishmen at the first sight of them, for they were dressed in English apparel (with hats, white neckcloths, and sashes about their waists, and ribbons upon their shoulders). But when they came near there was a vast difference between the lovely faces of Christians and the foul looks of those heathens which much damped my spirit again. . . .

The Eighteenth Remove: We took up our packs and along we went. But a wearisome day I had of it. As we went along, I saw an Englishman stripped naked and lying dead upon the ground, but knew not who it was. Then we came to another Indian town where we stayed all night. In this town, there were four English children, captives, and one of them my own sister's. I went to see how she did, and she was well, considering her captive condition. I would have tarried that night with her, but they that owned her would not suffer it. Then I went to another wigwam where they were boiling corn and beans, which was a lovely sight to see. But I could not get a taste thereof. Then I went into another wigwam where there were two of the English children. The squaw was boiling horses' feet. Then she cut me off a little piece and gave one of the English children a piece also. Being very hungry, I had quickly eat up mine, but the child could not bite it—it was so tough and sinewy—but lay sucking, gnawing, chewing, and slobbering it in the mouth and hand. Then I took it of the child, and eat it myself, and savory it was to my taste, that I may say as Job (Chapter 6:7): "The things that my soul refused to touch are as my sorrowful meat."

Thus the Lord made that pleasant and refreshing which another time would have been an abomination. Then I went home to my mistress's wigwam, and they told me I disgraced my master with begging, and if I did so any more they would knock me on the head. I told them they had as good knock me on the head as starve me to death.

The Nineteenth Remove: They said, when we went out, that we must travel to Wachuset this day. But a bitter, weary day I had of it; travelling now three days together without resting any day between. . . . Going along, having indeed my life, but little spirit, Philip (who was in the company), came up and took me by the hand and said, "Two weeks more, and you shall be mistress again." I asked him if he speak true. He answered, "Yes. And quickly you shall come to your master again, who had been gone from us three weeks." After many weary steps we came to Wachuset, where he was. And glad I was to see him. He asked me when I washed me. I told him not this month. Then he fetched me some water himself, and bid me wash, and gave me the glass to see how I looked, and bid his squaw give me something to eat. So she gave me a mess of beans and meat and a little ground nut cake. I was wonderfully revived with this favor showed me (Psalms 106:46): "He made them also to be pitied of all those that carried them captives." . . .

On Tuesday morning they called their general court (as they styled it) to consult and determine whether I should go home or no. And they all as one man did seemingly consent to it that I should go home, except Philip, who would not come among them. . . . And now God hath granted me my desire. O, the wonderful power of God that I have seen, and the experiences that I have had! I have been in the midst of those roaring lions and savage bears that feared neither God, nor man, nor the devil by night and day, alone and in company all sorts together. And yet not one of them ever offered the least abuse of unchastity to me, in word or action. Though some are ready to say I speak it for my own credit, but I speak it in the presence of God, and to His Glory. God's power is as great now, and as sufficient to save, as when He preserved Daniel in the lions' den,[26] or the three children in the fiery furnace.[27] I may well say as he (Psalms 107:1–2): "Oh give thanks unto the Lord, for He is good. For His mercy endureth forever. Let the redeemed of the Lord say so, whom He hath redeemed from the hand of the enemy." Especially that I should come away in the midst of so many hundreds of enemies, quietly and peaceably, and not a dog moving his tongue.

So I took my leave of them, and in coming along my heart melted into tears, more than all the while I was with them, and I was almost swallowed up with the thoughts that ever I should go home again. About the sun's going down, Mr. Hoar, and myself, and the two Indians came to Lancaster, and a solemn sight it was to me. There had I lived many comfortable years amongst my relations and neighbors, and now not one Christian to be seen, nor one house left standing. We went on to a farmhouse that was yet standing, where we lay all night, and a comfortable lodging we had, though nothing but straw to lie on. The Lord preserved us in safety that night, and raised us up again in the morning, and carried us along, that before noon we came to Concord.

Now was I full of joy, and yet not without sorrow: joy, to see such a lovely sight, so many Christians together, and some of them my neighbors. There I met with my brother and my brother-in-law who asked me if I knew where his wife was. Poor heart! He had helped to bury her and knew it not; she being shot down by the house, was partly burnt, so that those who were at Boston at the desolation of the town and came back afterward and buried the dead did not know her. Yet I was not without sorrow to think how many were looking and longing, and my own children amongst the rest, to enjoy that deliverance that I had now received. And I did not know whether ever I should see them again.

Being recruited with food and raiment, we went to Boston that day where I met with my dear husband. But the thoughts of our dear children, one being dead and the other we could not tell where, abated our comfort each in other. I was not before so much hemmed in with the merciless and cruel heathen, but now as much with pitiful, tender-hearted, and compassionate Christians. In that poor and distressed and beggarly condition, I was received in; I was kindly entertained in several houses. So much love I received from several (some of whom I knew, and others I knew not) that I am not capable to declare it. But the Lord knows them all by name. The Lord reward them seven-fold into their bosoms of his spirituals for their temporals. The twenty pounds, the price of my redemp-

---

26. Dan. 6:16–24.
27. Dan. 3:9–30 and the often appended "Song of Azariah" (3:24–90).

tion, was raised by some Boston gentlewomen and Mrs. Usher,[28] whose bounty and religious charity I would not forget to make mention of. Then Mr. Thomas Shepherd of Charleston received us into his house, where we continued eleven weeks, and a father and mother they were unto us. And many more tenderhearted friends we met with in that place. We were now in the midst of love, yet not without much and frequent heaviness of heart for our poor children and other relations who were still in affliction. . . .

Before I knew what affliction meant, I was ready sometimes to wish for it. When I lived in prosperity, having the comforts of this world about me, my relations by me, and my heart cheerful, and taking little care for anything, and yet seeing many (whom I preferred before myself) under many trials and afflictions—in sickness, weakness, poverty, losses, crosses, and cares of the world—I should be sometimes jealous least I should have my portion in this life. And that scripture would come to my mind (Hebrews 12:6): "For whom the Lord loveth he chasteneth, and scourgeth every son whom he receiveth." But now I see the Lord had his time to scourge and chasten me. The portion of some is to have their affliction by drops, now one drop and then another. But the dregs of the cup, the wine of astonishment, like a sweeping rain that leaveth no food, did the Lord prepare to be my portion. Affliction I wanted and affliction I had, full measure (I thought) pressed down and running over; yet I see when God calls a person to anything, and through never so many difficulties, yet He is fully able to carry them through and make them see and say they have been gainers thereby. And I hope I can say in some measure, as David did, "It is good for me that I have been afflicted."[29] The Lord hath showed me the vanity of these outward things, that they are the vanity of vanities and vexation of spirit, that they are but a shadow, a blast, a bubble, and things of no continuance, that we must rely on God Himself, and our whole dependence must be upon Him. If trouble from smaller matters begin to arise in me, I have something at hand to check myself with, and say when I am troubled, "It was but the other day, that if I had had the world, I would have given it for my freedom, or to have been a servant to a Christian." I have learned to look beyond present and smaller troubles and to be quieted under them, as Moses said (Exodus 14:13): "Stand still, and see the salvation of the Lord."

Thomas Hariot Reacts to the New World

Hariot on Virginia

Thomas Hariot (1560–1621), a mathematician and astronomer who spent time in Virginia as a surveyor on a 1586 expedition under the leadership of Sir Richard Greville and the auspices of Sir Walter Ralegh, published an account of the place in

28. Wife of Hezekiah Usher, a bookseller and selectman of Boston. Mr. Hoar was John Hoar of Concord.
29. Psalms 119:71.

1588. His views of Virginian religion should be read warily. Like Ralegh, whose *Discovery of Guiana* (1596) is worth reading in conjunction with this text, he had a reputation for heterodoxy. His report shows his age's interest in religious syncretism—in what the earth's peoples, past and present, might agree upon theologically and the esoteric wisdom behind varied traditions. He may also show some skeptical irony by identifying as superstition beliefs and practices with parallels back home. Hariot's work is included in Richard Hakluyt's *Principal Navigations of the English Nation* (1600), available in an Everyman edition (London: Dent, 1907); we follow that version.

OF THE NATURE AND MANNERS OF THE PEOPLE

It resteth I speak a word or two of the natural inhabitants, their natures and manners, leaving large discourse thereof until time more convenient hereafter: now only so far forth, as that you may know how that they, in respect of troubling our inhabiting and planting, are not to be feared, but that they shall have cause both to fear and love us that shall inhabit with them.

They are a people clothed with loose mantles made of deer skins, and aprons of the same round about their middles, all else naked, of such a difference of statures only as we in England, having no edge tools or weapons of iron or steel to offend us withal, neither know they how to make any: those weapons that they have are only bows made of witchhazel and arrows of reeds, flat edged truncheons also of wood about a yard long; neither have they anything to defend themselves but targets[1] made of barks and some armors made of sticks wickered together with thread. Their towns are but small, and near the seacoast but few, some containing but ten or twelve houses, some twenty. The greatest that we have seen hath been but of thirty-six houses; if they be walled, it is only done with barks of trees made fast to stakes, or else with poles only fixed upright, and close one by another. Their houses are made of small poles, made fast at the tops in round form after the manner as is used in many arbors in our gardens of England, in most towns covered with barks, and in some with artificial mats made of long rushes from the tops of the houses down to the ground. The length of them is commonly double to the breadth. In some places they are but twelve and sixteen yards long, and in othersome we have seen of four-and-twenty. In some places of the country one only town belongeth to the government of a Wiroans, or chief lord, in othersome two or three, in some six, eight, and more: the greatest Wiroans that yet we had dealing with had but eighteen towns in his government, and able to make not above seven or eight hundred fighting men at the most. The language of every government is different from any other, and the further they are distant the greater is the difference.

Their manner of wars amongst themselves is either by sudden surprising one another most commonly about the dawning of the day, or moonlight, or else by

---

1. Shields.

ambushes or some subtle devises. Set battles are very rare except it fall out where there are many trees, where either part may have some hope of defense after the delivery of every arrow in leaping behind some or other. If there fall out any wars between us and them, what their fight is likely to be, we having advantages against them so many manner of ways, as by our discipline, our strange weapons and devices else, especially ordnance great and small, it may easily be imagined: by the experience we have had in some places, the turning up of their heels against us in running away was their best defense.

In respect of us they are a people poor, and for want of skill and judgment in the knowledge and use of our things, do esteem our trifles before things of greater value. Notwithstanding, in their proper manner (considering the want of such means as we have), they seem very ingenious. For although they have no such tools, nor any such crafts, sciences and arts as we, yet in those things they do, they show excellence of wit. And by how much they upon due consideration shall find our manner of knowledges and crafts to exceed theirs in perfection, and speed for doing or execution, by so much the more is it probable that they should desire our friendship and love, and have the greater respect for pleasing and obeying us, whereby may be hoped, if means of good government be used, that they may in short time be brought to civility and the embracing of true religion.

Some religion they have already, which although it be far from the truth, yet being as it is, there is hope it may be the easier and sooner reformed. They believe that there are many gods, which they call Mantoac, but of different sorts and degrees, one only chief and great God, which hath been from all eternity. Who, as they affirm, when he purposed to make the world, made first other gods of a principal order, to be as means and instruments to be used in the creation and government to follow, and after the sun, moon, and stars as petty gods, and the instruments of the other order more principal. First, they say, were made waters, out of which by the gods was made all diversity of creatures that are visible or invisible. For mankind, they say a woman was made first, which by the working of one of the gods conceived and brought forth children, and in such sort they say they had their beginning. But how many years or ages have passed since, they say they can make no relation, having no letters nor other such means as we to keep records of the particularities of times past, but only tradition from father to son.

They think that all the gods are of human shape, and therefore they represent them by images in the forms of men, which they call Kewasowok (one alone is called Kewas): them they place in houses appropriate or temples, which they call Machicomuck, where they worship, pray, sing, and make many times offering unto them. In some Machicomuck we have seen but one Kewas, in some two, and in othersome three. The common sort think them to be also gods. They believe also the immortality of the soul, that after this life as soon as the soul is departed from the body, according to the works it hath done, it is either carted to heaven, the habitacle[2] of gods, there to enjoy perpetual bliss and happiness, or

2. Dwelling place, habitation.

else to a great pit or hole, which they think to be in the furthest parts of their part of the world toward the sunset, there to burn continually: the place they call Popogusso.

For the confirmation of this opinion, they told me two stories of two men that had been lately dead and revived again—the one happened but few years before our coming into the country—of a wicked man, which having been dead and buried, the next day the earth of the grave, being seen to move, was taken up again, who made declaration where his soul had been, that is to say, very near entering into Popogusso, had not one of the gods saved him and gave him leave to return again and teach his friends what they should do to avoid that terrible place of torment. The other happened in the same year we were there, but in a town that was sixty miles from us, and it was told me for strange news, that one being dead, buried, and taken up again as the first, showed that although his body had lain dead in the grave yet his soul was alive and had traveled far in a long broad way, on both sides whereof grew most delicate and pleasant trees, bearing more rare and excellent fruits than ever he had seen before or was able to express, and at length came to most brave and fair houses, near which he met his father that had been dead before, who gave him great charge to go back again and show his friends what good they were to do to enjoy the pleasures of that place, which when he had done he should after come again.

What subtlety soever be in the Wiroances and priests, this opinion worketh so much in many of the common and simple sort of people that it maketh them have great respect to their governors, and also great care what they do to avoid torment after death and to enjoy bliss, although notwithstanding there is punishment ordained for malefactors, as stealers, whoremongers, and other sorts of wicked doers, some punished with death, some with forfeitures, some with beating, according to the greatness of the facts. And this is the sum of their religion, which I learned by having special familiarity with some of their priests. Wherein they were not so sure grounded, nor gave such credit to their traditions and stories, but through conversing with us they were brought into great doubts of their own, and no small admiration of ours, with earnest desire in many to learn more than we had means for want of perfect utterance in their language to express.

Most things they saw with us, as mathematical instruments, sea compasses, the virtue of the lodestone in drawing iron, a perspective glass whereby was showed many strange sights, burning glasses, wildfire works, guns, hooks, writing and reading, spring-clocks that seem to go of themselves and many other things that we had, were so strange unto them, and so far exceeded their capacities to comprehend the reason and means how they should be made and done, that they thought they were rather the works of gods then of men, or at the leastwise they had been given and taught us of the gods. Which made many of them to have such opinion of us as that if they knew not the truth of God and religion already, it was rather to be had from us, whom God so specially loved, than from a people that were so simple as they found themselves to be in comparison of us. Whereupon greater credit was given unto what we spoke of concerning such matters.

Many times and in every town where I came, according as I was able, I made declaration of the contents of the Bible, that therein was set forth the true and only God and his mighty works, that therein was contained the true doctrine of salvation through Christ, with many particularities of Miracles and chief points of religion, as I was able then to utter and thought fit for the time. And although I told them the book materially and of itself was not of any such virtue as I thought they did conceive, but only the doctrine therein contained, yet would many be glad to touch it, to embrace it, to kiss it, to hold it to their breasts and heads, and stroke over all their body with it to show their hungry desire of that knowledge which was spoken of.

The Wiroance with whom we dwelt, called Wingina, and many of his people would be glad many times to be with us at our prayers and many times call upon us both in his own town, as also in others whither he sometimes accompanied us, to pray and sing Psalms, hoping thereby to be partaker of the same effects which we by that means also expected. Twice this Wiroans was so grievously sick that he was like to die, and as he lay languishing, doubting of any help by his own priests, and thinking he was in such danger for offending us and thereby our God, sent for some of us to pray and be a means to our God that it would please Him either that he might live or after death dwell with Him in bliss, so likewise were the requests of many others in the like case.

On a time also when their corn began to wither by reason of a drought which happened extraordinarily, fearing that it had come to pass by reason that in something they had displeased us, many would come to us and desire us to pray to our God of England that He would preserve their corn, promising that when it was ripe we also should be partakers of the fruit. There could at no time happen any strange sickness, losses, hurts, or any other cross unto them but that they would impute to us the cause or means thereof, for offending or not pleasing us. One other rare and strange accident, leaving others, will I mention before I end, which moved the whole country that either knew or heard of us, to have us in wonderful admiration.

There was no town where we had any subtle device practiced against us, we leaving it unpunished or not revenged (because we sought by all means possible to win them by gentleness), but that within a few days after our departure from every such town the people began to die very fast, and many in short space, in some towns about twenty, in some forty, and in one six score, which in truth was very many in respect of their numbers. This happened in no place that we could learn, but where we had been where they used some practice against us, and after such time. The disease also was so strange that they neither knew what it was nor how to cure it; the like by report of the oldest men in the country never happened before, time out of mind, a thing specially observed by us, as also by the natural inhabitants themselves. Insomuch that when some of the inhabitants which were our friends, and especially the Wiroans Wingina, had observed such effects in four or five towns to follow their wicked practices, they were persuaded that it was the work of our God through our means, and that we by Him might kill and slay whom we would without weapons and not come near them. And thereupon when it had happened that they had understanding that any of their enemies had abused us in our journeys, hearing that we had wrought no revenge with our weapons, and fearing upon some cause the matter should so rest, did come and entreat us that we would be a means to our God that they as others that had dealt ill with us might in like sort die, alleging how much it would be for our credit and profit, as also theirs, and hoping furthermore that we would do so much at their requests in respect of the friendship we professed them.

Whose entreaties, although we showed that they were ungodly, affirming that our God would not subject Himself to any such prayers and requests of men, that indeed all things have been and were to be done according to His good pleasure as He had ordained, and that we to show our selves His true servants ought rather to make petition for the contrary, that they with them might live together with us, be made partakers of His truth, and serve Him in righteousness, but notwithstanding in such sort that we refer that, as all other things, to be done according to His divine will and pleasure, and as by His wisdom He had ordained to be best. Yet because the effect fell out so suddenly and shortly after according to their desires, they thought nevertheless it came to pass by our means, and that we in using such speeches unto them, did but dissemble the matter, and therefore came unto us to give us thanks in their manner, that although we satisfied them not in promise, yet in deeds and effect we had fulfilled their desires.

This marvelous accident in all the country wrought so strange opinions of us that some people could not tell whether to think us gods or men, and the rather because that all the space of their sickness there was no man of ours known to die, or that was specially sick. They noted also that we had no women amongst us, neither that we did care for any of theirs. Some therefore were of opinion that we were not born of women, and therefore not mortal, but that we were men of an old generation many years past, then risen again to immortality. Some would likewise seem to prophesy that there were more of our generation yet to come to kill theirs and take their places, as some thought the purpose was, by that which was already done. Those that were immediately to come after us they imagined to be in the air, yet invisible and without bodies, and that they by our entreaty and for the love of us did make the people to die in that sort as they did, by shooting invisible bullets into them.

To confirm this opinion, their physicians (to excuse their ignorance in curing the disease) would not be ashamed to say but earnestly make the simple people believe that the strings of blood that they sucked out of the sick bodies were the strings wherewith the invisible bullets were tied and cast. Some also thought that we shot them ourselves out of our pieces[3] from the place where we dwelt and killed the people, in any town that had offended us, as we listed,[4] how far distant from us soever it were. And othersome said that it was the special work of God for our sakes, as we ourselves have cause in some sort to think no less, whatsoever some do or may imagine to the contrary, specially some astrologers, knowing

3. Guns.
4. As it pleased us.

of the eclipse of the sun which we saw the same year before in our voyage thitherward, which unto them appeared very terrible. And also of a comet which began to appear but a few days before the beginning of the said sickness. But to exclude them from being the special causes of so special an accident, there are further reasons then I think fit at this present to be alleged. These opinions I have set down the more at large that it may appear unto you that there is good hope they may be brought through discreet dealing and government to the embracing of the truth, and consequently to honor, obey, fear and love us. And although some of our company towards the end of the year showed themselves too fierce in slaying some of the people in some towns upon causes that on our part might easily enough have been borne withal, yet notwithstanding because it was on their part justly deserved, the alteration of their opinions generally and for the most part concerning us is the less to be doubted.[5] And whatsoever else they may be, by carefulness of ourselves need nothing at all to be feared.

Michael Drayton Praises Voyagers to Virginia

Michael Drayton (1563–1631) wrote in nearly every poetic genre popular in the Renaissance, including the ode in the heroic manner. He first published this celebration of British adventure abroad in *Poems Lyric and Pastoral* (1606). Although patriotic, and perhaps meant to encourage an often reluctant government to support such enterprises, the poem inscribes intriguing ambiguities: Virginia is a "paradise," yet the English ship has cannon. We modernize the standard edition by J. William Hebel (Oxford: Shakespeare Head Press, 1961).

TO THE VIRGINIAN VOYAGE

You brave heroic minds,
Worthy your country's name,
   That honor still pursue,
   Go, and subdue,
Whilst loit'ring hinds[6]
Lurk here at home, with shame.

Britons, you stay too long:
Quickly aboard bestow you,
   And with a merry gale
   Swell your stretched sail,
With vows as strong
As the winds that blow you.

5. Feared.
6. Rustic men of base birth.

Your course securely steer,
West and by south forth keep;
   Rocks, lee-shores, nor shoals,
   When Aeolus[7] scowls,
You need not fear,
So absolute the deep.[8]

And cheerfully at sea,
Success you still entice,
   To get the pearl and gold,
   And ours to hold,
Virginia,
Earth's only paradise.

Where nature hath in store
Fowl, venison, and fish,
   And the fruitfull'st soil,
   Without your toil,
Three harvests more,
All greater then you wish.

And the ambitious vine[9]
Crowns with his purple mass,
   The cedar reaching high
   To kiss the sky,
The cypress, pine
And useful sassafras.[10]

To whose, the golden age[11]
Still Nature's laws doth give,
   No other cares that tend,
   But them to defend
From winter's age,
That long there doth not live.

When as the luscious smell
Of that delicious land,

7. God of winds.
8. The sea is too deep for dangerous sands, reefs, or rocks.
9. Here the grape vine.
10. A small tree with often mitten-shaped and savory leaves used in cooking.
11. The benign reign of Saturn, before human corruption set in.

Above the seas that flows,
The clear wind throws,
Your hearts to swell
Approaching the dear strand.

In kenning[12] *of the shore*
(Thanks to God first given),
  O you the happi'st men,
  Be frolic then,
Let cannons roar,
Frighting the wide heaven.

And in regions far
Such heroes bring ye forth
  As those from whom we came,
  And plant our name
Under that star[13]
Not known unto our north.

And as there plenty grows
Of laurel every where,
  Apollo's sacred tree,
  You it may see,
A poet's brows
To crown, that may sing there.

Thy Voyages *attend,*
Industrious Hakluyt,[14]
  Whose reading shall inflame
  Men to seek fame,
And much commend
To aftertimes thy wit.

12. Knowing.
13. Which one is unclear.
14. Richard Hakluyt (1553–1616), a cleric who never went to sea but collected and edited many accounts of English voyages; Drayton apparently read about Virginia in his *Principal Navigations* (1st ed. 1589).

Robert Hayman Encourages Settlement in Newfoundland

In 1628 Robert Hayman (1575–1629), home in England after some years as governor of the Harbor Grace colony in Newfoundland, published his epigrams. Many are to friends such as John Donne, others to fellow colonists, and some to women. Although Hayman's own settlement had prospered, investors found economic returns chancy. *Quodlibets* means to encourage them, praising Canadian weather, fertility, and fauna while arguing for the legitimacy of settling on what was, in this part of Newfoundland, fairly empty land ("Yours is a holy, *just* plantation," he tells Lord Baltimore, "And not a *just*ling [jostling] supplantation"). In late 1628 Hayman returned to the Americas, dying of fever while tracing the Amazon upstream.

From *Quodlibets*

II 80: TO ALL THOSE WORTHY WOMEN WHO HAVE ANY DESIRE TO LIVE IN NEWFOUNDLAND, ESPECIALLY TO THE MODEST AND DISCREET GENTLEWOMAN, MISTRESS MASON, WIFE TO CAPTAIN MASON, WHO LIVED THERE DIVERS YEARS.[15]

> *Sweet creatures, did you truly understand*
> *The pleasant life you'd live in Newfoundland,*
> *You would with tears desire to be brought thither.*
> *I wish you, when you go, fair wind, fair weather:*
> *For if you with the passage can dispense,*[16]
> *When you are there, I know you'll ne'er come thence.*

15. John Mason (1586–1635), author of *A Brief Discourse* on Newfoundland (1620), was the Newfoundland Company's second governor and founder of New Hampshire; Anne Greene, a London goldsmith's daughter, married him in 1606, bore a daughter, and died in 1655.
16. Overlook the trip across the ocean.

II.94: To my very good Friend, Mr. John Poyntz, Esquire, one of the Planters of Newfoundland in Doctor Vaughan's Plantation.

'Tis said, wise Socrates looked like an ass,
Yet he with wondrous sapience fillèd was;
So, though our Newfoundland look wild, savage,
She hath much wealth penned in her rustic cage.
So have I seen a lean-cheeks, bare and raggèd,
Who of his private thousands could have braggèd.
Indeed, she now looks rude, untowardly:
She must be deckèd with neat husbandry.
So have I seen a plain, swart, sluttish Joan
Look pretty, pert, and neat with good clothes on.

III.84: To the Queen (Henrietta Maria).

When wise Columbus offered his New-land
To wise men, they him held vain, foolish, fond;
Yet a wise woman, of a happy wit,
With good success adventurèd upon it.
Then the wise men their wisdoms did repent,
And their heirs since their follies do lament.
My New-land, Madam, is already known:
The way, the air, the earth, all therein grown.
It only wants a woman of your spirit
To make't a land fit for your heirs t'inherit.
Sweet dreaded Queen, your help here will do well:
Be here a famous second Isabel.

LOVE AND

SEXUALITY

26

Mary Sidney Wroth *(1587?–1653?)*

Robert Sidney *(1563–1626)* and Philip Sidney *(1554–1586)*

Mary Sidney Wroth Writes on Love

In addition to the poems interspersed throughout her prose romance, *The Countess of Montgomery's Urania* (1621), Mary Wroth (1587?–1653?) appended a series of poems, "Pamphilia to Amphilanthus," that includes a corona, or "Crown of Sonnets." In a corona, the first and last lines of each sonnet are repeated, and the first and last lines of the sequence are the same, making a circular "crown." Wroth's corona is a conscious literary expression by a woman poet of the voice of a woman in love, a provocative counterpoint to the incomplete corona of sonnets by her father, Sir Robert Sidney (see below). Here we rely on the late Josephine A. Roberts's edition: *The Poems of Lady Mary Wroth* (Louisiana State University Press, 1992).

A Crown of Sonnets Dedicated to Love

1.

In this strange labyrinth how shall I turn?
Ways are on all sides while the way I miss.
If to the right hand, there in love I burn;
Let me go forward, therein danger is.

If to the left, suspicion hinders bliss;
Let me turn back, shame cries I ought return
Nor faint though crosses with my fortunes kiss.
Stand still is harder, although sure to mourn.

Thus let me take the right or left hand way;
Go forward, or stand still, or back retire;
I must these doubts endure without allay[1]
Or help, but travail[2] *find for my best hire.*[3]

Yet that which most my troubled sense doth move[4]
Is to leave all and take the thread of love.[5]
2.
Is to leave all and take the thread of love,
Which line straight leads unto the soul's content,
Where choice delights with pleasure's wings do move,
And idle fancy never room had lent.

When chaste thoughts guide us, then our minds are bent
To take that good which ills from us remove.
Light of true love brings fruit which none repent
But constant lovers seek and wish to prove.

Love is the shining star of blessings light,
The fervent fire of zeal, the root of peace,
The lasting lamp fed with the oil of right,
Image of faith, and womb for joy's increase.

Love is true virtue, and his ends delight;
His flames are joys, his bands[6] *true lovers' might.*
3.
His flames are joys, his bands true lovers' might,
No stain is there but pure as purest white
Where no cloud can appear to dim his light
Nor spot defile, but shame will soon requite.[7]

---

1. Abatement, dilution.
2. Exertion, hardship.
3. Recompense.
4. Stir.
5. An allusion to the thread Ariadne gave Theseus to help him find his way out of the Minotaur's labyrinth. Theseus later betrayed her.
6. Bonds, chains.
7. Repay.

Here are affections, tried by Love's just might
As gold by fire, and black discerned by white,
Error by truth, and darkness known by light,
Where faith is valued for Love to requite.

Please him and serve him, glory in his might,
And firm he'll be as innocency white,
Clear as the air, warm as sun beams, as daylight,
Just as truth, constant as fate, joyed to requite.

Then Love obey, strive to observe his might,
And be in his brave court a glorious light.
4.
And be in his brave court a glorious light,
Shine in the eyes of faith and constancy,
Maintain the fires of Love still burning bright
Not slightly sparkling but light flaming be,

Never to slack till earth no stars can see,
Till sun, and moon do leave to us dark night,
And second chaos[8] once again do free
Us, and the world, from all divisions' spite.

Till then, affections which his followers are
Govern our hearts, and prove his powers gain
To taste this pleasing sting seek with all care
For happy smarting is it with small pain

Such as although it pierce your tender heart
And burn, yet burning you will love the smart.
5.
And burn, yet burning you will love the smart,
When you shall feel the weight of true desire,
So pleasing, as you would not wish your part
Of burden should be missing from that fire.

But faithful and unfeignèd heat aspire
Which sin abolisheth, and doth impart
Salves[9] to all fear, with virtues which inspire
Souls with divine love, which shows his chaste art.

8. A return of the chaos described in Gen. 1:2.
9. Healing ointments.

And guide he is to joyings;[10] *open eyes*
He hath to happiness, and best can learn
Us means how to deserve. This he descries,
Who blind yet doth our hiddenest thoughts discern.

Thus we may gain since living in blest love
He may our prophet, and our tutor prove.
6.
He may our prophet and our tutor prove
In whom alone we do this power find:
To join two hearts as in one frame to move;
Two bodies, but one soul to rule the mind;

Eyes which must care to one dear object bind;
Ears to each other's speech as if above
All else they sweet and learnèd were; this kind
Content of lovers witnesseth true love.

It doth enrich the wits and make you see
That in yourself which you knew not before;
Forcing you to admire such gifts should be
Hid from your knowledge, yet in you the store.

Millions of these adorn the throne of Love,
How blest be they, then, who his favors prove.
7.
How blest be they, then, who his favors prove
A life whereof the birth is just desire,
Breeding sweet flame which hearts invite to move
In these loved eyes which kindle Cupid's fire

And nurse his longings with his thoughts entire;
Fixed on the heat of wishes formed by Love,
Yet whereas fire destroys this doth aspire,
Increase, and foster all delights above.

Love will a painter make you, such as you
Shall able be to draw your only dear
More lively, perfect, lasting, and more true
Than rarest workman, and to you more near.

10. Enjoyments.

These be the least, then all must needs confess
He that shuns Love doth love himself the less.
8.
He that shuns Love doth love himself the less
And cursèd he whose spirit not admires
The worth of Love, where endless blessedness
Reigns, and commands, maintained by heavenly fires,

Made of virtue, joined by truth, blown by desires,
Strengthened by worth, renewed by carefulness,
Flaming in never-changing thoughts. Briars
Of jealousy shall here miss welcomeness.

Nor coldly pass in the pursuits of Love
Like one long frozen in a sea of ice.
And yet but chastely let your passions move;
No thought from virtuous love your minds entice.

Never to other ends your fancies place,
But where they may return with honor's grace.
9.
But where they may return with honor's grace
Where Venus'[11] follies can no harbor win
But chasèd are as worthless of the face
Or style of Love who hath lascivious been.

Our hearts are subject to her son,[12] where sin
Never did dwell or rest one minute's space.
What faults he hath, in her did still[13] begin,
And from her breast he sucked his fleeting pace.

If lust be counted love, 'tis falsely named
By wickedness a fairer gloss to set
Upon that vice which else makes men ashamed
In the own[14] phrase to warrant but beget

This child for love, who ought like monster borne
Be from the court of Love and reason torn.

11. Goddess of love.
12. Cupid.
13. Always.
14. Its own.

10.
Be from the court of Love and reason torn
For Love in reason now doth put his trust,
Desert and liking are together born
Children of Love and Reason, parents just.

Reason adviser is, Love ruler must
Be of the state which crown he long hath worn.
Yet so as neither will in least mistrust
The government where no fear is of scorn,

Then reverence both their mights thus made of one,
But wantonness and all those errors shun
Which wrongers be, impostures, and alone
Maintainers of all follies ill-begun,

Fruit of a sour and unwholesome ground
Unprofitably pleasing and unsound.
11.
Unprofitably pleasing and unsound
When heaven gave liberty to frail, dull earth
To bring forth plenty that in ills abound
Which ripest yet do bring a certain dearth.

A timeless and unseasonable birth
Planted in ill, in worse time springing found,
Which hemlock-like might feed a sick-wit's mirth
Where unruled vapors swim in endless round.

Then joy we not in what we ought to shun
Where shady pleasures show, but true-born fires
Are quite quenched out, or by poor ashes won
Awhile to keep those cool and wan desires.

O no, let Love his glory have and might
Be given to him who triumphs in his right.
12.
Be given to him who triumphs in his right
Nor fading be, but like those blossoms fair
Which fall for good, and lose their colors bright
Yet die not, but with fruit their loss repair.

So may Love make you pale with loving care
When sweet enjoying shall restore that light
More clear in beauty than we can compare
If not to Venus in her chosen night,

And who so give themselves in this dear kind
These happinesses shall attend them still:
To be supplied with joys, enriched in mind
With treasures of content, and pleasures fill.

Thus Love to be divine doth here appear
Free from all fogs but shining fair and clear.
13.
Free from all fogs but shining fair and clear
Wise in all good, and innocent in ill
Where holy friendship is esteemèd dear
With truth in love, and justice in our will,

In love these titles only have their fill
Of happy life maintainer, and the mere
Defense of right, the punisher of skill
And fraud from whence directions doth appear.

To thee, then, lord commander of all hearts,
Ruler of our affections, kind and just,
Great King of Love, my soul from feignèd smarts
Or thought of change, I offer to your trust

This crown, my self, and all that I have more,
Except my heart which you bestowed before.
14.
Except my heart which you bestowed before,
And for a sign of conquest gave away
As worthless to be kept in your choice store.
Yet one more spotless with you doth not stay.

The tribute which my heart doth truly pay
Is faith untouched; pure thoughts discharge the score
Of debts for me, where constancy bears sway,
And rules as lord, unharmed by envy's sore,

Yet other mischiefs fail not to attend;
As enemies to you, my foes must be;
Curs'd jealousy doth all her forces bend
To my undoing; thus my harms I see.

So though in love I fervently do burn,
In this strange labyrinth, how shall I turn?

Love Poetry by Robert and Philip Sidney

Although Robert Sidney (1563–1626), brother of Lady Mary and Sir Philip Sidney, was an Elizabethan diplomat, governor of Flushing (in the Netherlands), and eventually earl of Leicester, he never won the royal favor he expected. Around 1597 he compiled a volume of sonnets, elegies, pastorals, and songs; most voice the anguished frustration typical of Petrarchan tradition and relevant to political discouragement.[1] The manuscript, which came to public notice in 1974, has an unfinished "corona" of sonnets wreathed together by repeated lines. The lady in these poems is unidentified, but since Sidney was happily married to his "sweetheart," Barbara Gammage, perhaps he wrote some for her pleasure. We rely on transcriptions in the edition by J. P. Croft (Oxford: Clarendon Press, 1984). Since the syntax can be obscure, we note some variants. And, for further comparison with Mary Wroth's, we append two sonnets from Philip Sidney's *Astrophil and Stella* (1591), written in the 1580s.

SONNET 4

These purest flames, kindled by beauties rare,
Strengthened by Love, assured by Destiny,
In whom I live, which in me cannot die,
Which are what I am, and I what they are,
True vestal-like,[2] which with most holy care
Preserve the sacred fires, religiously
I do maintain, and that no end they try
Of my best parts their subject[3] I prepare.
And with a mind free from all false desires,
Untouched of other loves, of vows untrue,[4]
I worship her that shineth in those fires—

---

1. Millicent V. Hay, *Life of Robert Sidney* (Washington: Folger Books, 1984).
2. Tending a holy flame like a Roman priest or priestess (Vesta was goddess of hearths and altars). There was a long tradition of imagining the lover at a lady's altar.
3. Replaces "fuel."
4. Unstained by loving others or by untrue vows.

Thinking it shame, nay sin, if that in me
Those fairest beams (of Heaven the image true)
With powers of meaner worth should matchèd be.

SONNET 10

She whom I serve to write did not despise:[5]
Few words, but which with wonder filled my sprite
How from dark ink, as from springs of delight,
Beauty, sweetness, grace, joy and love should rise.
Till I remembered, that those fairest eyes,
Whose beams are joys and love, did lend their light;
That happy hand those blessèd words did write
Which, where it[6] *toucheth, marks of beauty ties;*
Those ruby lips, full of nectar divine,
A rosy breath did on the words bestow;
That heavenly face did on the paper shine
From whose least motion thousand graces flow;
And that fair mind the subject did approve,
Which is itself all other praise above.

"A CROWN OF SONNETS, BUT UNFINISHED" (SONNETS 11–15)

1.

Though the most perfect style[7] *cannot attain*
The praise to praise enough the meanest part
Of you—the ornament of Nature's art,
Worth of this world, of all joys the sovereign;
And though I know I labor shall in vain
To paint in words the deadly wounds the dart
Of your fair eyes doth give, since mine own heart
Knows not the measure of my love and pain;
Yet since your will the charge on me doth lay
(Your will, the law I only reverence),[8]

---

5. Did not disdain to write me.
6. Her hand.
7. "Style" retained something of Latin "stylus," a tool for impressing wax and thus by extension writing itself.
8. Your will is the only law I revere.

Skilless and praiseless I do you obey.
Nor merit seek but pity, if thus I
Do folly show to prove obedience.[9]
Who gives himself, may ill his words deny.
2.
Who gives himself may ill his words deny.
My words gave me to you, my word I gave
Still to be yours; you speech and speaker have:
Me to my word, my word to you, I tie:
Long ere I was,[10] *I was by destiny*
Unto your love ordained a free bound slave—
Destiny, which me to mine own choice drave,[11]
And to my ends made me my will apply.
For ere on earth in you true Beauty came,[12]
My first breath I had drawn, upon the day
Sacred to you, blessèd in your fair name;
And all the days and hours I since do spend
Are but the fatal, wishèd time[13] *to slay*
To seal the bands of service without end.
3.
To seal the bands of service without end,
In which myself I from myself do give,
No force but yours my thoughts could ever drive,
For in my choice Love did your right defend.
I know there are which title do pretend[14]
As in their service having vowed to live,
But Reason fatal faults wills to forgive:
Love gave me not to them, he did but lend.
Not but their beauties, were of power[15] *to move*
The proudest heart to fall down at their feet,
Or that I was so enemy to Love,
But those fair lights[16] *which do all for the best*
And rule our works below thought it most meet
That so great love to you should be addressed.

9. Cf. Petrarch's *Rime* 1 that hopes to find pity for his folly.
10. Before I was born.
11. Drove; "choice replaces "liking" in the MS.
12. Before true beauty came to earth in the form of you.
13. The destined wished-for time. "Time" replaces "hour" in the MS.
14. "Which" means "who." Sidney's feudal conceit is that Love defended the lady's right to be the lover's choice above all other claimants.
15. "Of power" replaces the canceled "enough."
16. Stars, destiny (with perhaps an overtone of Providence).

4.

That so great love to you should be addressed,
Than which the sun nothing doth see more pure,
Your matchless worth your judgment may assure,
Since rarest beauties like[17] faith have possessed.
Yet would on me no note of change did rest
Which in your sight my truth's light may obscure;
Ah, let not me for changing blame endure,
Who only changed, by change to find the best.
For now in you I rest, in you I find
Destiny's foresight, Love's justice,[18] Will's end,
Beauty's true[19] wonders, joy and rest of mind.
Let me be then to you accounted true;
Defend you then who for you does offend:
Who for you is unjust, is just to you.
5.
Who for you is unjust, is just to you.
O you, the fair excuse of faults in love;
Who for you errs, his errors praises prove,
O you, to me honor, wisdom, virtue.

[The rest of the thirteen sonnets doth want.]

SONNET 31

Forsaken woods, trees with sharp storms oppressed,
Whose leaves once hid the sun, now strew the ground,
Once bred delight, now scorn,[20] late used to sound
Of sweetest birds, now of hoarse crows the nest;
Gardens, which once in thousand colors dressed
Showed Nature's pride, now in dead sticks abound,
In whom proud summer's treasure late was found
Now but the rags of winter's torn coat rest;
Meadows, whose sides late fair brooks kissed, now slime
Embracèd holds; fields, whose youth green and brave
Promised long life, now frosts lay in the grave:
Say all, and I with them, "What doth not Time!"

17. Similar.
18. Substituted for "strength, my" in the MS.
19. Substituted for "great" in the MS.
20. That used to produce delight but now raise scorn.

But they, who knew Time, Time will find again;
I, that fair times lost, on Time call in vain.

APPENDED TO ELEGY 16

Once to my lips my boiling heart did rise
At heaven-dew of her lips refreshed to be;
When, with short sighs, swollen breast, and dazzled eyes,
I prayed one kiss might press joy's wine to me,
With those lips, where the soul of kissing lies,
"A parting kiss," said she, "I will give thee!"
She kissed, I parted, parting in that kiss
    With taste of love's rich feast, first cup of bliss.

Astrophil and Stella, a sonnet sequence with interspersed songs by Sir Philip Sidney (1554–1586), was published posthumously in 1591. It was an open secret that "Stella" was modeled on Penelope Rich, sister of the earl of Essex. "Astrophil" is a fictional creation, but his name ("star-lover") plays on related Greek elements in the name *Phil*ip *Sid*ney ("lover" of a "star"). We base our text on the edition of his poems by William Ringler (Oxford: Clarendon, 1962).

FROM PHILIP SIDNEY'S *ASTROPHIL AND STELLA*

41

Having this day my horse, my hand, my lance
    Guided so well, that I obtained the prize,
    Both by the judgment of the English eyes,
And of some sent from that sweet enemy, France:
Horsemen my skill in horsemanship advance,[21]
    Townfolks my strength; a daintier judge applies
    His praise to sleight,[22] *which from good use doth rise;*
Some lucky wits[23] *impute it but to chance;*
    Others, because of both sides I do take
    My blood from them who did excel in this,

21. Praise.
22. Canny use of deceptions, feints; the context probably discourages an otherwise inviting pun on "too slight."
23. Fortune-minded observers.

Think Nature me a man of arms did make.
How far they shoot awry! The true cause is,
Stella looked on, and from her heav'nly face
Sent forth the beams which made so fair my race.

63

O grammar rules, O now your virtues show:
So children still read you with awful[24] eyes,
As my young dove may in your precepts wise
Her grant to me, by her own virtue know.
For late, with heart most high, with eyes most low,
I craved the thing which ever she denies:
She lightning Love, displaying Venus' skies,
Lest once should not be heard, twice said, "No, no."
Sing then my Muse, now "Io Paean" sing,
Heav'ns envy not at my high triumphing,
But Grammar's force with sweet success confirm,
For Grammar says (O this, dear Stella, weigh),
For Grammar says (to Grammar who says nay?)
That "in one speech two negatives affirm."

24. Awe-filled.

27

Katherine Fowler Philips *(1632–1664)*

Richard Barnfield *(b. 1574)* and
William Shakespeare *(1564–1616)*

Katherine Fowler Philips on Friendship

Many of the poems of Katherine Philips (1632–1664) celebrate female friendship, and critics debate their possibly lesbian cast. The earliest of these attachments, a friendship with Mary Aubrey, a cousin of John Aubrey whom Philips styled "Rosania," began in Philips's schooldays, cooled after Aubrey's marriage to Sir William Montagu in 1652, but was taken up again before Philips's death. Another was that with Anne Lewis Owen of Orielton ("Lucasia"), who lived in Llandshipping, about twenty-five miles from Philips's home in Cardigan, Wales. It was during an extended visit with Lucasia in Dublin, after Owen's remarriage in 1662, that Philips's translation of Corneille's *Pompée* was translated and produced on stage as *Pompey*. Members of the "Sacred Society of Friendship" all bore pseudonyms: Philips was "Orinda." Others in the circle included Sir Charles Cotterell, later Philips's literary executor, or "Poliarchus"; Francis Finch ("Palaemon"); and Sir Edward Dering ("Silvander"). In the poems below, "Antenor" is Philips's husband and the "C. P." whose marriage is celebrated is Philips's sister-in-law, Cicely Philips. We have relied on the edition by Patrick Thomas (Stump Cross Books, 1982). Elizabeth Hageman and Andrea Sununu are preparing an edition for Oxford University Press.

To my dearest Antenor on his parting[1]

Though it be just to grieve when I must part
With him that is the guardian of my heart,
Yet, by a happy change, the loss of mine
Is with advantage paid in having thine.
And I (by that dear guest instructed) find
Absence can do no hurt to souls combined.
And we were born to love, brought to agree
By the impressions of divine decree.
So when united nearer we became,
It did not weaken, but increase, our flame,
Unlike to those who distant joys admire
But slight them when possessed of their desire,
Each of our souls did its own temper fit,
And in the other's mold so fashioned it
That now our inclinations both are grown,
Like to our interests and persons, one.
And souls whom such an union fortifies
Passion can ne'er betray, nor fate surprise.
     Now as in watches, though we do not know
When the hand moves we find it still doth go:
So I, by secret sympathy inclined,
Will absent meet and understand thy mind.
And thou, at thy return, shalt find thy heart
Still safe with all the love thou didst impart.
For though that treasure I have ne'er deserved,
It shall with strong religion be preserved.
But besides this thou shalt in me survey
Thy self reflected while thou art away.
For what some forward arts do undertake,
The images of absent friends to make
And represent their actions in a glass,
Friendship itself can only bring to pass.
That magic which both fate and time beguiles
And in a moment runs a thousand miles,

1. Sometimes styled "To Antenor parting." Philips's poems bear alternate titles in seventeenth-century manuscript and printed versions.

So in my breast thy picture drawn shall be,
My guide, life, object, friend, and destiny.
And none shall know, though they employ their wit,
Which is the right Antenor, thou, or it.

TO MY DEAR SISTER MRS. C. P. ON HER NUPTIALS[2]

We will not like those men our offerings pay
Who crown the cup, then think they crown the day.
We'll make no garlands, nor an altar build
Which help not joy but ostentation yield.
Where mirth is justly grounded, these wild toys
Do but disturb and not adorn our joys.
2
But these shall be my great solemnities,
Orinda's wishes for Cassandra's bliss:
May her content be as unmixed and pure
As my affection, and like that endure.
And that strong happiness may she still find
Not owing to her fortune, but her mind.
3
May her content and duty be the same,
And may she know no grief but in the name.
May his and her pleasure and love be so
Involved and growing, that we may not know
Who most affection or most peace engrossed,
Whose love is strongest, or whose bliss is most.
4
May nothing accidental e're appear
But what shall with new bands their souls endear.
And may they count the hours as they do pass
By their own joys, and not by sun or glass,
While every day like this may sacred prove
To friendship, duty, gratitude, and love.

---

2. Variably titled "To My Dear Sister Mrs. C. P. on Her Marriage."

FRIENDSHIP IN EMBLEM, OR THE SEAL, TO MY DEAREST LUCASIA[3]

The hearts thus intermixèd speak
A love that no bold shock can break;
For joined and growing, both in one,
Neither can be disturbed alone.

2

That means a mutual knowledge, too;
For what is't either heart can do
Which by its panting sentinel
It does not to the other tell?

3

That friendship hearts so much refines
It nothing but itself designs;
The hearts are free from lower ends,
For each point to the other tends.

4

They flame, 'tis true, and several ways,
But still those flames do so much raise
That while to either they incline
They yet are noble and divine.

5

From smoke or hurt those flames are free,
From grossness or mortality.
The hearts—like Moses'[4] bush presumed—
Warmed and enlightened, not consumed.

6

The compasses that stand above
Express this great immortal love.
For friends, like them, can prove this true,
They are, and yet they are not, two.

7

And in their posture is expressed
Friendship's exalted interest.
Each follows where the other leans
And what each does, the other means.

---

3. Also titled, "To my dearest Lucasia, friendship in emblem or the seal." This poem is useful-ly compared to John Donne's "Valediction Concerning Mourning," from which much of its imagery and wording seems to derive.
4. Alluding to the unconsumed burning bush seen by Moses (Exod. 3:1–5).

8

And as when one foot does stand fast,
And t'other circles seeks to cast,
The steady part does regulate
And make the wanderer's motion straight;

9

So friends are only two in this—
T'reclaim each other when they miss,
For whosoe're will grossly fall
Can never be a friend at all.

10

And as that useful instrument
For even lines was ever meant;
So friendship from good angels springs,
To teach the world heroic things.

11

As these are found out in design
To rule and measure every line,
So friendship governs actions best,
Prescribing law to all the rest.

12

And as in nature nothing's set
So just as lines and numbers met,
So compasses for these being made,
Do friendship's harmony persuade.

13

And like to them so friends may own
Extension, not division;
Their points—like bodies—separate,
But head, like souls, knows no such fate.

14

And as each part so well is knit,
That their embraces ever fit,
So friends are such by destiny,
And no third can the place supply.

15

There needs no motto to the seal.
But that we may the mine[5] reveal
To the dull eye, it was thought fit
That friendship only should be writ.

---

5. Source of abundant supply.

16
But as there is degrees of bliss,
So there's no friendship meant by this,
But such as will transmit to fame
Lucasia's and Orinda's name.

FRIENDSHIP

Let the dull brutish world that know not love
Continue heretics and disapprove
That noble flame, but the refinèd know
'Tis all the heaven we have here below.
Nature subsists by love, and they tie
Things to their causes but by sympathy.
Love chains the differing elements in one
Great harmony, linked to the heavenly throne,
And as on earth so the blest choir above
Of saints and angels are maintained by love.
That is their business and felicity,
And will be so to all eternity.
That is the ocean. Our affections here
Are but streams borrowed from the fountain there,
And 'tis the noblest argument to prove
A beauteous mind that it knows how to love.
Those kind impressions which fate can't control,
Are heaven's mintage on a worthy soul.
For love is all the arts' epitome,
And is the sum of all divinity.
He's worse than beast that cannot love, and yet
It is not bought by money, pains, or wit.
So no chance nor design can spirits move,
But the eternal destiny of love.
For when two souls are changed and mixèd so,
It is what they and none but they can do.
And this is friendship, that abstracted flame
Which creeping mortals know not how to name.
All love is sacred, and the marriage tie
Hath much of honor and divinity.
But lust, design, or some unworthy ends
May mingle there, which are despised by friends.

Passion hath violent extremes, and thus
All oppositions are contiguous.
So when the end is served the love will hate,
If friendship make it not more fortunate.
Friendship! that love's elixir, that pure fire,
Which burns the clearer 'cause it burns the higher.
For love, like earthy fires (which will decay
If the material fuel be away)
Is with offensive smoke accompanied,
And by resistance only is supplied.
But friendship, like the fiery element,
With its own heat and nourishment content,
(Where neither hurt, nor smoke, nor noise is made)
Scorns the assistance of a foreign aid.
Friendship (like heraldry) is hereby known:
Richest when plainest, bravest when alone,
Calm as a virgin, and more innocent
Than sleeping doves are, and as much content
As saints in visions, quiet as the night,
But clear and open as the summer's light.
United more than spirits' faculties,
Higher in thoughts then are the eagle's eyes.
Free as first agents are true friends, and kind,
As but themselves I can no likeness find.

To My Excellent Lucasia, on Our Friendship[6]

I did not live until this time
    Crowned my felicity.
When I could say without a crime,
    I am not thine, but thee.
This carcass breathed, and walked, and slept,
    So that the world believed
There was a soul the motions kept—
    But they were all deceived.
For as a watch by art is wound
    To motion, such was mine;
But never had Orinda found
    A soul till she found thine.

6. Also titled "To the Excellent Lucasia, on our mutuall friendship promisd."

Which now inspires, cures, and supplies,
    And guides my darkened breast;
For thou art all that I can prize,
    My joy, my life, my rest.
No bridegroom's nor crown-conqueror's mirth
    To mine compared can be;
They have but pieces of this earth,
    I've all the world in thee.
Then let our flame still light and shine,
    And no bold fear control,
As innocent as our design,
    Immortal as our soul.

PARTING WITH LUCASIA, A SONG[7]

Well, we will do that rigid thing
    Which makes spectàtors think we part,
Though absence hath for none a sting
    But those who keep each other's heart.
2
And when our sense is dispossessed
    Our laboring souls will heave and pant,
And gasp for one another's breast,
    Since their conveyances they want.
3
Nay, we have felt the tedious smart
    Of absent friendship, and do know
That when we die we can but part,
    And who knows what we shall do now?
4
Yet since I must go, we'll submit,
    And so our own disposers be;
For while we nobly suffer it,
    We triumph o'er necessity.
5
By this we shall be truly great,
    If having other things o'ercome,
To make our victory complete
    We can be conquerors at home.

7. Alternately titled "Parting" or "A Parting."

6

Nay then to meet we may conclude,
And all obstructions overthrow,
Since we our passion have subdued,
Which is the strongest thing I know.

ON ROSANIA'S APOSTASY, AND LUCASIA'S FRIENDSHIP

Great soul of friendship, whither art thou fled?
Where dost thou now choose to repose thy head?
Or art thou nothing but voice, air, and name
Found out to put souls in pursuit of fame?
Thy flames being thought immortal, we may doubt
Whether they e'er did burn that see them out.

Go weary soul, find out thy wonted rest
In the safe harbor of Orinda's breast.
There all unknown adventures thou hast found
In thy late transmigrations[8] *expound*
That so Rosania's darkness may be known
To be her want of luster, not thy own.

Then to the great Lucasia have recourse,
There gather up new excellence and force,
Till by a free, unbiased, clear commerce,
Endearments which no tongue can e'er rehearse,
Lucasia and Orinda shall thee give
Eternity, and make even friendship live.

Hail, great Lucasia, thou shalt doubly shine,
What was Rosania's own is now twice thine.
Thou saw'st Rosania's chariot and her flight,
And so the double portion is thy right.
Though 'twas Rosania's spirit, be content
Since 'twas at first from thy Orinda sent.

8. Removals.

Richard Barnfield Sighs for a Young Man; William Shakespeare is Ambiguous

Born in 1574 to a prosperous family in Staffordshire and graduating from Oxford in 1592, Richard Barnfield dedicated works to such luminaries as Lady Penelope Rich (Sidney's "Stella"). Dying young, although exactly when is unclear, he seems to have become estranged from his family, perhaps because his lines so often praise a young man. His preface to *Cynthia, with Certain Sonnets and the Legend of Cassandra* (1595) claims that his homoerotic pastorals had merely imitated Virgil's second eclogue, but this implausible denial is followed by the sequence of twenty love sonnets to "Ganymede," from which we take our selections. Barnfield's sighs for another male long troubled the few who wrote about him—Elizabethans in his circle were less disconcerted—and he has only recently received his due. We rely on George Klawitter's edition (Selinsgrove, Penn.: Susquehanna University Press, 1990).

SONNETS FROM CYNTHIA

SONNET 4

> *Two stars there are in one fair firmament*
>   *(Of some, entitled Ganymede's[1] sweet face),*
>   *Which other stars in brightness do disgrace,*
> *As much as Po in clearness passeth Trent.[2]*
> *Nor are they common-natured stars: for why,*
>   *These stars when other shine veil[3] their pure light,*
>   *And when all others vanish out of sight,*
> *They add a glory to the world's great eye.[4]*
> *By these two stars my life is only led,*
>   *In them I place my joy, in them my pleasure,*
>   *Love's piercing darts, and Nature's precious treasure;*
> *With their sweet food my fainting soul is fed.*
>   *Then when my sun is absent from my sight,*
>   *How can it choose with me but be dark night?*

1. Desiring Ganymede, son of King Tros of Troy, Jove disguised himself as an eagle and flew the boy to Olympus, making him his cupbearer. Although some allegorized this as contemplative rapture, "Ganymede" was a common synonym for a young male object of male sexual desire.
2. The Po flows east through northern Italy into the Adriatic; the Trent passes through Staffordshire, joining the Humber on its way to the North Sea.
3. "Vaile" may pun on "veil" and "vail" (let go slack).
4. The sun.

SONNET 6

Sweet coral lips, where Nature's treasure lies,
  The balm of bliss, the sovereign salve of sorrow,
  The secret touch of Love's heart-burning arrow,
Come quench my thirst or else poor Daphnis dies.
One night I dreamed (alas, 'twas but a dream)
  That I did feel the sweetness of the same,
  Wherewith inspired, I young again became,
And from my heart a spring of blood did stream;
But when I waked, I found it nothing so,
  Save that my limbs, methought, did wax more strong
  And I more lusty far, and far more young.
This gift on him rich Nature did bestow.
  Then, if in dreaming so, I so did speed,
  What should I do, if I did so indeed?[5]

SONNET 8

Sometimes I wish that I his pillow were,
  So might I steal a kiss, and yet not seen,[6]
  So might I gaze upon his sleeping eyne,
Although I did it with a panting fear:
But when I well consider how vain my wish is,
  Ah foolish bees (think I) that do not suck
  His lips for honey, but poor flowers do pluck
Which have no sweet in them, when his sole kisses
Are able to revive a dying soul.
  Kiss him, but sting him not, for if you do,
  His angry voice your flying will pursue.
But when they hear his tongue, what can control
  Their back return? For then they plain may see,
  How honey-combs from his lips dropping be.

5. If kissing him in a dream made me feel younger and stronger, what might an actual kiss do?
6. While I am unseen.

SONNET 10

Thus was my love, thus was my Ganymede
    (Heaven's joy, world's wonder, Nature's fairest work,
    In whose aspèct Hope and Despair do lurk),
Made of pure blood in whitest snow yshed,[7]
And for sweet Venus only formed his face,
    And his each member delicately framed,
    And last of all faire "Ganymede" him named,
His limbs (as their Creatrix) her embrace;
But for his pure, spotless, virtuous mind,
    Because it sprung of chaste Diana's blood
    (Goddess of maids, directress of all good),
It wholly is to chastity inclined.
    And thus it is: as far as I can prove,[8]
    He loves to be beloved, but not to love.

SONNET 11

Sighing, and sadly sitting by my love,
    He asked the cause of my heart's sorrowing,
    Conjuring me by Heaven's eternal King
To tell the cause which me so much did move.
Compelled, quoth I: "To thee will I confess,
    Love is the cause, and only love it is
    That doth deprive me of my heavenly bliss;
Love is the pain that doth my heart oppress."
"And what is she," quoth he, "whom thou dost love?"
    "Look in this glass," quoth I "there shalt thou see
    The perfect form of my felicity."
When, thinking that it would strange magic prove,
    He opened it, and taking off the cover,
    He straight perceived himself to be my lover.

7. Past participle of "shed," typical of Barnfield's Spenserian diction.
8. Determine through experience.

SONNET 12

Some talk of Ganymede th'Idalian boy,[9]
    And some of fair Adonis[10] make their boast;
    Some talk of him whom lovely Leda lost,[11]
And some of Echo's love[12] that was so coy.
They speak by hearsay; I of perfect truth.
    They partially[13] commend the persons named,
    And for them sweet encomiums have framed;
I only t'him have sacrificed my youth.
As for those wonders of antiquity,
    And those whom later ages have enjoyed
    (But, ah, what hath not cruel Death destroyed—
Death, that envies this world's felicity?),
    They were, perhaps, less fair than poets write.
    But he is fairer than I can indite.[14]

SONNET 14

Here, hold this glove, this milk-white cheveril[15] glove,
    Not quaintly[16] overwrought with curious knots,
    Not decked with golden spangs[17] nor silver spots,
Yet wholesome for thy hand, as thou shalt prove.
Ah no, sweet boy: place this glove near thy heart.
    Wear it and lodge it still within thy breast;
    So shalt thou make me (most unhappy) blessed.
So shalt thou rid my pain and ease my smart.
"How can that be?" perhaps thou wilt reply,
    "A glove is for the hand, not for the heart,
    Nor can it well be proved by common art
Nor reason's rule." To this, thus answer I:
    "If thou from glove dost take away the 'g,'
    Then 'glove' is 'love': and so I send it thee."

9. Ganymede was on Mount Ida (hence "Idalian") near Troy when Zeus noticed him.
10. A youth beloved by Venus; killed while hunting a boar, he was often read by mythographers as the annually dying and returning sun.
11. Desiring Leda, Zeus became a swan and mated with her; Castor, her son by her husband, King Tyndarus, was killed while sailing with the Argonauts and was made immortal by the gods. Whom Leda "lost" is unclear.
12. Narcissus, who preferred his reflection to the nymph Echo.
13. With partiality.
14. Put in writing.
15. Kidskin.
16. Curiously, fancifully.
17. Spangles.

SONNET 17

Cherry-lipped Adonis in his snowy shape
  Might not compare with his pure ivory white,
  On whose fair front a poet's pen may write,
Whose roseate red excels the crimson grape;
His love-enticing delicate soft limbs
  Are rarely[18] framed t'entrap poor gazing eyes;
  His cheeks the lily and carnation dyes
With lovely tincture which Apollo's dims.
His lips ripe strawberries in nectar wet,
  His mouth a hive, his tongue a honeycomb,
  Where Muses (like bees) make their mansiòn;
His teeth pure pearl in blushing coral set.
  Oh, how can such a body, sin-procuring,
  Be slow to love, and quick to hate enduring?

William Shakespeare (1564–1616) began writing sonnets in the 1590s, but *Sonnets* did not appear until 1609 (whether authorized or not is unknown). Most scholars agree that the first 126 sonnets address a young man, often with intense feeling. The nature of this feeling is debated. Is it what we would call homosexual? Is it homoerotic with little or no hint of actual sex? Is it profoundly loving but nonerotic? The following sonnet denies that the love is "homosexual" but its puns and ambiguities, for some readers, imply the reverse. We adapt the 1609 text, consulting the edition by Stephen Booth (New Haven: Yale University Press, 1977).

FROM *SONNETS*

SONNET 20

A woman's face with Nature's own hand painted
Has thou, the master-mistress of my passion;
A woman's gentle heart, but not acquainted
With shifting change, as is false women's fashion;
An eye more bright than theirs, less false in rolling,
Gilding the object whereupon it gazeth;[19]

---

18. In a rare fashion, exceptionally.
19. Many once believed that sight entails a beam emitted from the eye.

A man in hue,[20] *all hues in his controling,*[21]
Which steals men's eyes and women's souls amazeth.
And for a woman wert thou first created,
Till Nature, as she wrought thee, fell a-doting,
And by addition me of thee defeated[22]
By adding one thing to my purpose nothing.[23]
　　But since she pricked thee out[24] *for women's pleasure,*
　　Mine be thy love, and thy love's use[25] *their treasure.*

20. Complexion (color and mixture of elements) and form.
21. "Control" then meant dominate but also outdo, transcend.
22. Deprived.
23. "Thing" is of course a penis, but "nothing" was also, thanks to its circular shape as zero ("naught"), slang for vagina. That Shakespeare could pun on "nothing," (probably in his day pronounced "noting"), "no thing," and "naught" is shown by the title of *Much Ado About Nothing*. Note the witty arithmetical impossibility: "adding" a "thing" that is also "nothing."
24. To "prick" was to mark a name or item on a list so as to indicate selection; as a verb "prick" also meant "to spur" and as a noun it meant penis.
25. "Use" here probably puns on "use" to mean earning interest, the sense behind "usury." By "using" his "one thing" the friend can give women babies as earned interest and hence increase their stock. Shakespeare may also play, seriously or not, with an Augustinian distinction: we should "use" ("utor") the things of this world but "enjoy" ("fruor") the divine.

28

Isabella Whitney *(fl. 1566–1573)*

Edmund Spenser *(1552?–1599)*, Thomas Campion *(1567–1620)*, and John Donne *(1572–1631)*

Isabella Whitney on False Lovers

Although Isabella Whitney (fl. 1566–1573) is the first Englishwoman known to have written original secular poetry in English for publication, we know little about her. Comments in her *Copy of a Letter* (1567?) and *Sweet Nosegay* (1573) supply some facts: she was of gentle rank (*Copy*, title page); was strapped financially (*Nosegay*, sig. A5ᵛ); was able to write because she was single (*Nosegay*, sig. D2); and came from a large family to whom she addressed "Familiar Epistles and Friendly Letters" (*Nosegay*, sigs. C6ʳ–Eᵛ). Some think her the sister of Geoffrey Whitney (1548?–1601?), author of *A Choice of Emblems* (1586), but she calls herself London "bred" (*Nosegay*, sig. E2ᵛ) and Geoffrey was from Cheshire. Nor is she named in his will—unless by 1600 she had become, through marriage, his "Sister Eldershae" or "Sister Evans."

Whitney is most memorable for effervescent poetry in the spirit of her London's literary world. The earlier anthology, from which we take our excerpts, has four poems written in the personae of persons jilted in love; the "Admonition" appended to the title poem is, like *Copy*, in a sprightly female voice. The tone suggests that these love complaints are fictional, as does the statement by the printer, Richard Jones, who specialized in popular ephemera: *Copy*, he says, is "both false and also true." The same jaunty spirit characterizes the two final poems in the collection, both voiced—and conceivably written—by a man. The second anthology, also printed by Jones, contains both prose and poetry. At both beginning and end are substantial poems: the *Sweet Nosegay* of quatrains much indebted to Hugh Platt's *Flowers of Philosophy* (1572) and a "Will and Testament" to the city of London (pp. xii–xiii): a frolic, in the form of a mock testament, through an engagingly described city.

From *Copy of a Letter*

I. W. to Her Unconstant Lover

As close[1] as you your wedding kept
  yet now the truth I hear,
Which you (yet now) might me have told,
  what need you nay to swear?

You know I always wished you well,
  so will I during life;
But sith[2] you shall a husband be
  God send you a good wife.

And this, where so you shall become,
  full boldly may you boast:
That once you had as true a love,
  as dwelt in any coast.

Whose constantness had never quailed
  if you had not begun,
And yet it is not so far past,
  but might again be won.

If you so would, yea and not change
  so long as life should last.
But if that needs you marry must
  then farewell, hope is past.

And if you cannot be content
  to lead a single life,
Although the same right quiet be,
  then take me to your wife.

1. Secret.
2. Since.

So shall the promises be kept,
   that you so firmly made,
Now choose whether ye will be true,
   or be of Sinon's[3] trade.

Whose trade if that you long shall use,
   it shall your kindred stain
Example take by many a one
   whose falsehood now is plain.

As by Aeneas[4] first of all,
   Who did poor Dido leave,
Causing the queen by his untruth
   with sword her heart to cleave.

Also I find that Theseus[5] did
   his faithful love forsake,
Stealing away within the night
   before she did awake.

Jason[6] that came of noble race,
   two ladies did beguile;
I muse how he durst show his face
   to them that knew his wile.

For when he by Medea's art
   had got the fleece of gold
And also had of her that time
   all kind of things he would.

He took his ship and fled away
   regarding not the vows
That he did make so faithfully
   unto his loving spouse.

How durst he trust the surging seas
   knowing himself forsworn?

3. The Greek who convinced Troy to admit the Trojan Horse into the city.
4. In Virgil's *Aeneid*, Aeneas deserts the love-stricken Dido, who then kills herself, because his destiny requires him to reach Latium. Whitney's criticism of him, although not unique, remains remarkable.
5. Although Ariadne had saved his life, Theseus abandoned her on the island of Naxos.
6. Although Medea helped Jason win the golden fleece, he betrayed her.

Why did he 'scape safe to the land
before the ship was torn?

I think King Aeolus[7] stayed the winds
and Neptune[8] ruled the sea,
Then might he boldly pass the waves;
no perils could him flee.

But if his falsehood had to them
been manifest before,
They would have rent his ship as soon
as he had gone from shore.

Now may you hear how falseness is
made manifest in time,
Although they that commit the same
think it a venial[9] crime.

For they for their unfaithfulness
did get perpetual fame.
Fame? Wherefore did I term it so?
I should have called it shame.

Let Theseus be, let Jason pass,
let Paris[10] also 'scape
That brought destruction unto Troy
all through the Grecian rape.

And unto me a Troilus[11] be;
if not, you may compare
With any of these persons that
above expressèd are.

But if I cannot please your mind
for wants that rest in me,
Wed whom you list; I am content
your refuse for to be.

7. Ruler of the winds.
8. God of the sea.
9. Pardonable.
10. Son of Priam, king of Troy, who abducted Helen, wife of Menelaus and thereby started the Trojan War.
11. Son of Priam and lover of Cressida, who betrayed him.

It shall suffice me, simple[12] soul,
  of thee to be forsaken:
And it may chance, although not yet,
  you wish you had me taken.

But rather then you should have cause
  to wish this through your wife,
I wish to her, ere you her have,
  no more but love of life.

For she that shall so happy be
  of thee to be elect[13]
I wish her virtues to be such
  She need not be suspect.

I rather wish her Helen's face[14]
  than one of Helen's trade,
With chasteness of Penelope[15]
  the which did never fade.

A Lucres[16] for her constancy,
  and Thisbe[17] for her truth;
If such thou have, then Peto[18] be
  not Paris, that were ruth.[19]

Perchance ye will think this thing rare
  in one woman to find:
Save Helen's beauty, all the rest
  the gods have me assigned.

These words I do not speak thinking
  from thy new love to turn thee;

---

12. Open, guileless.
13. Chosen.
14. Helen of Troy, of whom Marlowe's Dr. Faustus asks: "Is this the face that launched a thousand ships?"
15. Wife of Ulysses, who remained faithful during the twenty years he spent besieging Troy and then journeying home.
16. Lucretia, chaste wife of Collatinus was raped by Tarquin and killed herself because of the dishonor; the scandal led to a revolt against the Tarquin dynasty and the start of the Roman Republic.
17. Beloved of Pyramus who killed herself on finding his body.
18. We cannot identify Peto.
19. A pity.

Thou know'st by proof what I deserve,
I need not to inform thee.

But let that pass. Would God I had
Cassandra's gift[20] *me sent.*
Then either thy ill chance[21] *or mine*
my foresight might prevent.

But all in vain. For this I seek
wishes may not attain it;
Therefore may hap[22] *to me what shall*
and I cannot refrain it.

Wherefore I pray God be my guide
and also thee defend,
No worser then I wish myself
until thy life shall end.

Which life I pray God may again
King Nestor's life[23] *renew,*
And after that your soul may rest
amongst the heavenly crew.

Thereto I wish King Xerxes'[24] *wealth*
or else King Croesus' gold,[25]
With as much rest and quietness
as man may have on mold.[26]

And when you shall this letter have
let it be kept in store:
For she that sent the same hath sworn
as yet to send no more.

---

20. Daughter of Priam to whom Apollo gave the gift of prophesy—although it was fated that nobody would believe her.
21. Fortune.
22. Happen.
23. The long-lived King of Pylos, renowned for garrulity, eloquence, knowledge of war and justice.
24. King of Persia (485–465 B.C.E.).
25. Last king of Lydia, famed for wealth, who reigned 560–546 B.C.E.
26. On earth.

And now farewell. For why? At large
   my mind I here expressed.
The which you may perceive if that
   you do peruse the rest.
      Finis Is. W.

THE ADMONITION BY THE AUTHOR TO ALL YOUNG GENTLEWOMEN AND TO ALL OTHER MAIDS BEING IN LOVE

Ye virgins that from Cupid's[27] tents
   do bear away the foil[28]
Whose hearts as yet with raging love
   most painfully do boil,

To you I speak. For you be they
   that good advice do lack.
Oh, if I could good counsel give
   my tongue should not be slack.

But such as I can give I will
   here in few words express,
Which if you do observe, it will
   some of your care redress.

Beware of fair and painted talk,
   beware of flattering tongues;
The mermaids do pretend no good
   for all their pleasant songs.

Some use the tears of crocodiles,
   contrary to their heart;
And if they cannot always weep
   they wet their cheeks by art.

Ovid[29] within his Art of Love
   doth teach them this same knack:

27. God of love.
28. Obscure: probably a defeat, fall, or disgrace.
29. Roman poet (43 B.C.E.–18 C.E.), best known for his *Ars Amatoria* (or *Art of Love)*, *Metamorphoses*, and *Heroides*.

To wet their hand and touch their eyes
　　so oft as tears they lack.

Why have ye such deceit in store?
　　have you such crafty wile?
Less craft then this, God knows, would soon
　　us simple souls beguile.

And will ye not leave off, but still
　　delude us in this wise?
Sith it is so, we trust we shall
　　take heed to feignèd lies.

Trust not a man at the first sight,
　　but try him well before.
I wish all maids within their breasts
　　to keep this thing in store.

For trial shall declare his truth,
　　and show what he doth think:
Whether he be a lover true,
　　or do intend to shrink.

If Scylla[30] had not trust too much
　　before that she did try
She could not have been clean forsake
　　when she for help did cry.

Or if she had had good advice
　　Nisus had livèd long;
How durst she trust a stranger and
　　do her dear father wrong?

King Nisus had a hair by fate,
　　which hair while he did keep,
He never should be overcome,
　　neither on land nor deep.[31]

---

30. Daughter of King Nisus of Megara who killed her father to help Minos get his kingdom. The gods punished her by making her into barking dogs from the waist down.
31. Ocean.

The stranger that that daughter loved
       did war against the king,
And always sought how that he might
       them in subjection bring.

This Scylla stole away the hair
       for to obtain her will,
And gave it to the stranger that
       did straight her father kill.

Then she, who thought herself most sure
       to have her whole desire,
Was clean reject and left behind
       when he did home retire.

Or if such falsehood had been once
       unto Oenone[32] known,
About the fields of Ida wood
       Paris had walked alone.

Or if Demophoön's deceit
       to Phyllis had been told,
She had not been transformèd so
       as poets tell of old.[33]

Hero[34] did try Leander's truth
       before that she did trust,
Therefore she found him unto her
       both constant, true, and just.

For he always did swim the sea
       when stars in sky did glide
Till he was drownèd by the way
       near hand unto the side.

She scratched her face, she tore her hair
       (it grieveth me to tell),

32. Daughter of a sea god who killed herself after Paris died.
33. King of Athens, son of Theseus, and engaged to Phyllis, daughter of the king of Thrace. When he was late in arriving, she hanged herself, becoming a tree that put out leaves when a repentant Demophoön embraced it.
34. Hero killed herself after her lover Leander drowned in the Hellespont.

When she did know the end of him,
that she did love so well.

But like Leander there be few,
therefore in time take heed
And always try before ye trust,
so shall you better speed.

The little fish that careless is
within the water clear,
How glad is he, when he doth see
A bait for to appear.

He thinks his hap right good to be
that he the same could spy
And so the simple fool doth trust
too much before he try.

Oh, little fish, what hap hadst thou
to have such spiteful fate?
To come into one's cruel hands
out of so happy state?

Thou didst suspect no harm when thou
upon the bait didst look.
Oh, that thou hadst had Linceus' eyes[35]
for to have seen the hook.

Then hadst thou with thy pretty mates
been playing in the streams
Whereas Sir Phoebus[36] *daily doth*
show forth his golden beams.

But sith thy fortune is so ill
to end thy life on shore
Of this thy most unhappy end
I mind to speak no more,

35. An Argonaut renowned for sharp sight.
36. The sun.

> But of thy fellow's chance that late
>   such pretty shift [37] did make,
> That he from fisher's hook did sprint
>   before he could him take.
>
> And now he pries on every bait
>   suspecting still that prick
> For to lie hid in everything
>   wherewith the fisher's strike.
>
> And since the fish that reason lacks
>   once warnèd doth beware,
> Why should not we take heed to that
>   that turneth us to care?
>
> And I who was deceivèd late
>   by one's unfaithful tears,
> Trust now for to beware if that
>   I live this hundreth years.
>   FINIS. Is. W.

Spenser, Campion, and Donne Imagine Female Lovers

Like Isabella Whitney, all three of the poets in this group experimented with various tones and voices. We have chosen poems in which those voices are female, although one by Campion ("If thou long'st") could be by a man to a boy.

Edmund Spenser's Britomart Addresses the Waves

In 1590 Edmund Spenser (c. 1552–1599) published the first three books of his epic romance, *The Faerie Queene*. The heroine of Book III, Britomart, represents chastity—not abstinence but a dynamic channeling of *eros* first into virginity and then, as foretold by the prophet Merlin, into fruitful marriage. Disguised as a doughty knight, Britomart sets forth to find her destined mate, Artegall (the knight of Justice), whom she has seen only in a magic mirror. In a version of the old Petrarchan ship metaphor, she addresses the ocean. To retain Spenser's wordplay and the archaic style that sustains his fantasy world, few editors modernize his verse. We have used the *Norton Critical Edition of Spenser* by Hugh Maclean and Anne Lake Prescott (New York: Norton, 1993).

37. Astute stratagem.

THE FAERIE QUEENE III.IV.7–11

There she alighted from her light-foot beast,
And sitting downe upon the rocky shore,
Bad her old Squire[1] unlace her lofty creast;
Tho[2] having vewd a while the surges hore,[3]
That gainst the craggy clifts did loudly rore,
And in their raging surquedry[4] disdaynd,
That the fast[5] earth affronted them so sore,
And their devouring covetize[6] restraynd,
Thereat she sighed deepe, and after thus complaynd.

"Huge sea of sorrow, and tempestuous griefe,
Wherein my feeble barke is tossed long,
Far from the hoped haven of reliefe,
Why do thy cruell billowes beat so strong,
And thy moyst mountaines each on others throng,
Threatning to swallow up my fearefull life?
O do thy cruell wrath and spightfull wrong
At length allay,[7] and stint[8] thy stormy strife,
Which in these troubled bowels raignes, and rageth rife.

"For else my feeble vessell crazd, and crackt
Through thy strong buffets and outrageous blowes,
Cannot endure, but needs it must be wrackt
On the rough rocks, or on the sandy shallowes,
The whiles that love it steres, and fortune rowes;[9]
Love my lewd[10] Pilot hath a restlesse mind
And fortune Boteswaine no assurance knows,
But saile withouten starres gainst tide and wind:
How can they other do, sith[11] both are bold and blind?

1. Her nurse, Glauce (Greek for "gray"), disguised as her squire.
2. Then.
3. The hoary (gray-white) waves.
4. Proud excess.
5. Unmoving.
6. Envious desire; greed.
7. Moderate.
8. Cease.
9. Love (Cupid) steers her boat while Fortune rows it.
10. "Lewd" could have its modern meaning; it often meant uncouth ignorance.
11. Since, for.

"Thou God of winds,[12] *that raignest in the seas,*
   That raignest also in the Continent,[13]
   At last blow up some gentle gale of ease,
   The which may bring my ship, ere it be rent,
   Unto the gladsome port of her intent:
   Then when I shall my selfe in safety see,
   A table[14] *for eternall moniment*[15]
   Of thy great grace, and my great jeopardee,
Great Neptune,[16] *I avow to hallow*[17] *unto thee."*

Then sighing softly sore, and inly deepe,
   She shut up all her plaint in privy[18] *griefe;*
   For her great courage would not let her weepe,
   Till that old Glauce[19] *gan with sharpe repriefe,*[20]
   Her to restraine, and give her good reliefe,
   Through hope of those,[21] *which Merlin had her told,*
   Should of her name and nation be chiefe,
   And fetch their being from the sacred mould[22]
Of her immortall wombe, to be in heaven enrold.

Thomas Campion Plays the Female Lover

Thomas Campion (1567–1620) was born in London, attended Cambridge University, studied law at Gray's Inn, fought in the forces sent to help Henri IV become king of France, and in 1605 took a degree in medicine. He also wrote masques and a number of lyrics, many published with music by the lutanist Philip Rosseter. Campion preferred the air to the madrigal: written for single voices, airs allow the listener to hear the subtleties of tone and rhythm. Such songs, says the preface to his *Book of Airs* (1601), are like the Roman epigram: "short and well seasoned." Most, he adds, concern love ("and why not amorous songs, as well as amorous attires?"). We have used *The Works of Thomas Campion*, ed. Walter R. Davis (London: Faber and Faber, 1969).

12. Aeolus, who kept the winds in his cave.
13. On land.
14. An image, portrait.
15. Monument (sometimes with an overtone of "admonition").
16. God of the ocean.
17. Dedicate and make holy.
18. Private, secret, inward.
19. Her nurse, disguised as her squire.
20. Reproof.
21. Those descendants (including the Tudor kings).
22. Mold, but also matter, matrix.

A BOOK OF AIRS (1601) PART ONE, NO. 5

My love hath vowed he will forsake me,
And I am already sped.[23]
Far other promise he did make me
When he had my maidenhead.
If such danger be in playing,
And sport must to earnest turn,
I will go no more a-maying.[24]

Had I foreseen what is ensued,
And what now with pain I prove,[25]
Unhappy then I had eschewed
This unkind event[26] *of love:*
Maids foreknow their own undoing,
But fear naught till all is done,
When a man alone is wooing.

Dissembling wretch, to gain thy pleasure
What did'st thou not vow and swear?
So did'st thou rob me of the treasure
Which so long I held so dear.
Now thou prov'st to me a stranger,
Such is the vile guise of men
When a woman is in danger.

That heart is nearest to misfortune
That will trust a feignèd tongue;
When flatt'ring men our loves importune
They intend us deepest wrong.
If this shame of love's betraying
But this once I cleanly shun,[27]
I will go no more a-maying.

23. Undone.
24. It was traditional on the first of May to gather greenery, play games, and sometimes misbehave. Stricter "Puritans" thought such traditions "pagan."
25. Feel and show.
26. Result; "unkind" may retain the sense of "unnatural."
27. Escape, presumably with no pregnancy and with reputation intact.

FROM *THE SECOND BOOK OF AIRS* (1613?) NO.15

So many loves have I neglected
    Whose good parts might move me
That now I live of all rejected:
    There is none will love me.
Why is maiden heat so coy?[28]
    It freezeth when it burneth,
Loseth what it might enjoy
    And, having lost it, mourneth.

Should I then woo, that have been wooed,
    Seeking them that fly me?
When I my faith with tears have vowed,
    And when all deny me,
Who will pity my disgrace,
    Which love might have prevented?
There is no submission base
    Where error is repented.

O happy men, whose hopes are licensed
    To discourse[29] *of their passion,*
While women are confined to silence,
    Losing wished occasion.
Yet our tongues than theirs, men say,
    Are apter to be moving:
Women are more dumb than they,
    But in their thoughts more roving.

When I compare my former strangeness[30]
    With my present doting,
I pity men that speak in plainness
    Their true hearts' devoting
While we with repentance jest
    At their submissive passion;
Maids, I see, are never blessed
    That strange be but for fashion.[31]

28. Reluctant.
29. Speak of; the accent is on the first syllable.
30. Cool distance.
31. That is, who are stand-offish only to seem modish.

FROM *THE THIRD BOOK OF AIRS* (1617?) NO. 16[32]

If thou long'st so much to learn, sweet boy, what 'tis to love,
Do but fix thy thought on me, and thou shalt quickly prove.
  Little suit at first shall win
    Way to thy abashed[33] desire,
  But then will I hedge thee in,
    Salamander-like,[34] with fire.

With thee dance I will, and sing, and thy fond dalliance bear;
We the grovey hills will climb and play the wantons[35] there;
  Other whiles we'll gather flowers,
    Lying dallying on the grass,
  And thus our delightful hours
    Full of waking dreams shall pass.

When thy joys were thus at height, my love should turn from thee;
Old acquaintance then should grow as strange as strange might be:
  Twenty rivals thou should'st find
    Breaking their hearts for me,
  When to all I'll prove more kind
    And more forward[36] than to thee.

Thus thy silly youth, enraged, would soon my love defy,
But, alas, poor soul, too late: clipped wings can never fly.
  Those sweet hours which we had passed,
    Called to mind, thy hart would burn;
  And, could'st thou fly ne'er so fast,
    They would make thee straight return.

32. This song recalls Marlowe's "Come live with me," itself modeled on Virgil's homoerotic second eclogue. The lover's gender is unspecified.
33. Modest.
34. Salamanders were said to be able to live in fire.
35. Act in a sensual, loose manner.
36. Forthcoming.

FROM *THE FOURTH BOOK OF AIRS* (1617?) NO. 24

Fain would I wed a fair young man that day and night could please me,
When my mind or body grieved that had the power to ease me.[37]
Maids are full of longing thoughts that breed a bloodless sickness,[38]
And that, oft I hear men say, is only cured by quickness.[39]
Oft have I been wooed and prayed, but never could be movèd:
Many for a day or so I have most dearly lovèd,
But this foolish mind of mine straight loathes the thing resolvèd.[40]
If to love be sin in me, that sin is soon absolvèd.
Sure, I think I shall at last fly to some holy order;[41]
When I once am settled there, then can I fly no farther.
Yet I would not die a maid, because I had a mother:
As I was by one brought forth, I would bring forth another.

John Donne Imagines Being Sappho

Sappho was one of the great poets of Greek antiquity, although most of her work is lost. Married and the mother of a daughter, she lived on the isle of Lesbos in c. 600 B.C.E., offering love and poetry to both sexes. This poem by John Donne (1572–1631), which imagines her writing a young woman with a name meaning "friend" (and recalling a courtesan in dialogues by the ancient satirist, Lucian), suits a fashion for lovers' epistles in the style of Ovid's *Heroides* (Ovid, however, makes Sappho heterosexual). With precedents in French poems by Pontus de Tyard and Pierre de Ronsard, it is probably the first "lesbian" poem in English. Its authorship has been questioned (Helen Gardner placed it among the "dubia" in her 1965 edition of Donne's *Elegies* and *Songs and Sonnets*), but there is no reason to doubt Donne's ability to envision perspectives other than his own. It was printed with his first collected poetry in 1633. Manuscripts vary somewhat; we follow the choices in Donne's *Complete English Poems*, ed. C. A. Patrides (New York: Knopf, 1991).

37. Give me relief.
38. Also called "green-sickness": a pallor once blamed on lack of sex but probably due to the onset of menstruation. The standard cure was marriage.
39. Vitality—presumably of a sexual nature.
40. Presumably the resolution to marry one of her suitors.
41. Become a nun.

SAPPHO TO PHILÆNIS

Where is that holy fire which verse is said
  To have? Is that enchanting force decayed?
Verse, that draws Nature's works from Nature's law,
  Thee, her best work, to her work cannot draw.
Have my tears quenched my old poetic fire?
  Why quenched they not as well that of desire?
Thoughts, my mind's creatures, often are with thee,
  But I, their maker, want[42] their liberty.
Only thine image, in my heart, doth sit;
  But that is wax, and fires environ it.
My fires have driven, thine have drawn, it hence;
  And I am robbed of picture, heart, and sense.
Dwells with me still mine irksome memory,
  Which both to keep and lose grieves equally.
That tells me how fair thou art: thou art so fair
  As gods, when gods to thee I do compare,
Are graced thereby.[43] And to make blind men see
  What things gods are, I say they're like to thee.
For if we justly call each silly[44] man
  A little world, what shall we call thee, then?
Thou art not soft, and clear, and straight, and fair,
  As down, as stars, cedars, and lilies are,
But thy right hand, and cheek, and eye, only
  Are like thy other hand, and cheek, and eye.
Such was my Phao[45] awhile, but shall be never
  As thou wast, art, and, oh, mayst be ever.[46]
Here lovers swear, in their idolatry
  That I am such; but grief discolors me.
And yet I grieve the less, lest grief remove
  My beauty, and make me unworthy of thy love.
Plays some soft boy with thee? Oh, there wants yet[47]
  A mutual feeling which should sweeten it.

42. Lack (but also, perhaps, desire).
43. You are as lovely as the gods are when they are graced by my comparing them to you.
44. Insignificant, frail.
45. Phaon was a young ferryman, the legend goes, whom Sappho loved when older, leaping off a cliff when he left her.
46. Probably in the sense of "may you ever be."
47. There is still lacking.

His chin a thorny hairy unevenness
  Doth threaten and some daily change possess.
Thy body is a natural paradise
  In whose self, unmanured,[48] all pleasure lies
Nor needs perfection; why shouldst thou then
  Admit the tillage[49] of a harsh, rough man?
Men leave behind them that which their sin shows,
  And are as thieves traced which rob when it snows.[50]
But of our dalliance no more signs there are
  Than fishes leave in streams, or birds in air.
And between us all sweetness may be had:
  All, all that Nature yields or Art can add.
My two lips, eyes, thighs, differ from thy two
  But so as thine from one another do,
And, oh, no more; the likeness being such,
  Why should they not alike in all parts touch?
Hand to strange hand, lip to lip none denies:
  Why should they breast to breast, or thighs to thighs?
Likeness begets such strange self-flattery
  That touching myself, all seems done to thee.
My self I embrace, and my own hands I kiss,
  And amorously thank my self for this.
Me, in my glass, I call thee; but alas,
  When I would kiss, tears dim mine eyes and glass.
O cure this loving madness, and restore
  Me to me; thee, my half, my all, my more.
So may thy cheeks' red outwear scarlet dye,
  And their white, whiteness of the galaxy;[51]
So may thy mighty amazing beauty move
  Envy in all women and, in all men, love;
And so be change and sickness far from thee,
  As thou, by coming near, keep'st them from me.

48. Uncultivated, unworked, untilled.
49. Allow cultivation, plowing.
50. Men leave proof of sin, like robbers who make tracks in snow.
51. The Milky Way ("galaxy" comes from the Greek word for milky).

29

Mary Sidney Wroth *(1587?–1653?)*

Philip Sidney *(1554–1586)*

Mary Sidney Wroth Writes a Romance

Niece of Sir Philip Sidney and of Mary Sidney Herbert, Countess of Pembroke, and daughter of their brother, Sir Robert Sidney, Mary Sidney Wroth (1587?–1653?) participated in the literary creativity of a remarkable early modern family. Her arranged marriage to Sir Robert Wroth in 1604 was not wholly successful, but her husband was a favorite of the king, and Lady Wroth participated in some Jacobean court activities, appearing in the *Masque of Blackness* and *The Masque of Beauty*. On Wroth's early death in 1614, she was left deeply in debt and with an infant son whose death in 1616 left her in even worse financial straits. Lady Wroth began writing while married, and there are many allusions to courtly entertainments in the work for which she is best known, *The Countess of Montgomery's Urania* (1621). She modeled this long prose romance on her uncle's *Arcadia*, but with a female hero and an emphasis on such qualities as constancy in love that are less central to romances by men. We base our selection of the opening of *Urania* on the 1621 edition; see also the modern edition by Josephine A. Roberts (Tempe: Medieval and Renaissance Texts and Studies 140, 1995, for the Renaissance English Text Society).

From *The Countess of Montgomery's Urania*

When the spring began to appear like the welcome messenger of summer, one sweet (and in that more sweet) morning, after Aurora[1] had called all careful eyes to attend the day, forth came the fair shepherdess Urania (fair indeed; yet that far too mean a title for her who for beauty deserved the highest style could be given by best knowing judgments). Into the mead[2] she came, where usually she drove her flocks to feed, whose leaping and wantonness[3] showed they were proud of such a guide. But she, whose sad thoughts led her to another manner of spending her time, made her soon leave them and follow her late begun custom, which was (while they delighted themselves) to sit under some shade bewailing her misfortune; while they fed to feed upon her own sorrow and tears, which at this time she began again to summon, sitting down under the shade of a well-spread beech, the ground (then blest) and the tree with full and fine leaved branches, growing proud to bear and shadow such perfections. But she regarding nothing in comparison of her woe, thus proceeded in her grief: "Alas, Urania," said she (the true servant to misfortune), "of any misery that can befall woman, is not this the most and greatest which thou art fallen into? Can there be any near the unhappiness of being ignorant, and that in the highest kind, not being certain of mine own estate or birth? Why was I not still continued in the belief I was, as I appear, a shepherdess and daughter to a shepherd? My ambition then went no higher than this estate; now flies it to a knowledge. Then was I contented, now perplexed. O ignorance, can thy dullness yet procure so sharp a pain? And that such a thought as makes me now aspire unto knowledge? How did I joy in this poor life being quiet? Blest in the love of those I took for parents, but now by them I know the contrary, and by that knowledge not to know myself. Miserable Urania, worse art thou now than these thy lambs, for they know their dams, while thou live unknown of any."

By this were others come into that mead with their flocks, but she, esteeming her sorrowing thoughts her best and choicest company, left that place, taking a little path which brought her to the further side of the plain to the foot of the rocks, speaking as she went these lines, her eyes fixed upon the ground, her very soul turned into mourning:

> *Unseen, unknown, I here alone complain*
> *To rocks, to hills, to meadows, and to springs,*
> *Which can no help return to ease my pain,*
> *But back my sorrows the sad echo brings.*

---

1. Goddess of dawn.
2. Meadow.
3. Pleasure-seeking.

Thus still increasing are my woes to me,
    Doubly resounded by that moanful voice,
Which seems to second me in misery,
    And answer gives like friend of mine own choice.
Thus only she doth my companion prove,
    The others silently do offer ease:
But those that grieve, a grieving note do love;
    Pleasures to dying eyes bring but disease:
And such am I, who daily ending live,
    Wailing a state which can no comfort give.

In this passion she went on till she came to the foot of a great rock. She, thinking of nothing less than ease, sought how she might ascend it, hoping there to pass away her time more peaceably with loneliness, though not to find least respite from her sorrow, which so dearly she did value as by no means she would impart it to any. The way was hard, though by some windings making the ascent pleasing. Having attained the top, she saw under some hollow trees the entry into the rock. She, fearing nothing but the continuance of her ignorance, went in where she found a pretty room, as if that stony place had yet in pity given leave for such perfections to come into the heart as chiefest and most beloved place, because most loving. The place was not unlike the ancient (or the descriptions of ancient) hermitages: instead of hangings, covered and lined with ivy, disdaining ought else should come there, that being in such perfection. This richness in Nature's plenty made her stay to behold it and almost grudge the pleasant full-ness of content that place might have—if sensible—while she must know to taste of torments.

As she was thus in passion mixed with pain, throwing her eyes as wildly as timorous lovers do for fear of discovery, she perceived a little light, and such a one as a chink doth oft discover to our sights. She, curious to see what this was, with her delicate hands put the natural ornament aside, discerning a little door which she, putting from her, passed through it onto another room like the first in all proportion. But in the midst there was a square stone, like to a pretty table, and on it a wax-candle burning, and by that a paper which had suffered itself patiently to receive the discovering of so much of it as presented this sonnet (as it seemed newly written) to her sight:

Here all alone in silence might I mourn,
    But how can silence be where sorrows flow?
    Sighs with complaints have poorer pains outworn,
    But broken hearts can only true grief show.
Drops of my dearest blood shall let love know
    Such tears for her I shed, yet still do burn
    As no spring can quench least part of my woe,
    Till this live earth, again to earth do turn.

> *Hateful all thought of comforts is to me,*
> *Despisèd day, let me still night possess;*
> *Let me all torments feel in their excess,*
> *And but this light allow my state to see.*
> *Which still doth waste, and wasting as this light,*
> *Are my sad days unto eternal night.*

"Alas, Urania," sighed she, "How well do these words, this place, and all agree with thy fortune? Sure, poor soul, thou wert here appointed to spend thy days, and these rooms ordained to keep thy tortures in, none being assuredly so matchlessly unfortunate."

Turning from the table, she discerned in the room a bed of boughs, and on it a man lying, deprived of outward sense, as she thought, and of life, as she at first did fear, which struck her into a great amazement. Yet, having a brave spirit, though shadowed under a mean habit, she stepped unto him, whom she found not dead but laid upon his back, his head a little to her-wards, his arms folded on his breast, hair long, and beard disordered, manifesting all care. But care itself had left him: curiousness thus far afforded him[4] as to be perfectly discerned the most exact piece of misery. Apparel he had suitable to the habitation, which was a long gray robe. This grieveful spectacle did much amaze the sweet and tender-hearted shepherdess, especially when she perceived (as she might by the help of the candle) the tears which distilled from his eyes who, seeming the image of death, yet had this sign of worldly sorrow: the drops falling in that abundance as if there were a kind strife among them to rid their master first of that burdenous carriage, or else—meaning to make a flood and so drown their woeful patient in his own sorrow—who yet lay still.

But then, fetching a deep groan from the profoundest part of his soul, he said, "Miserable Perissus, canst thou thus live knowing she that gave thee life is gone? Gone! O, me! And with her all my joy departed. Wilt thou (unblessed creature) lie here complaining for her death and know she died for thee? Let truth and shame make thee do something worthy of such a love, ending thy days like thyself and one fit to be her servant. But that I must not do. Then thus remain and foster storms still to torment thy wretched soul withal, since all are little and too, too little for such a loss. O, dear Limena, loving Limena, worthy Limena, and more rare—constant Limena. Perfections delicately feigned to be in women were verified in thee. Was such worthiness framed only to be wondered at by the best, but given as a prey to base and unworthy jealousy? When were all worthy parts joined in one but in thee (my best Limena)? Yet all these grown subject to a creature ignorant of all but ill, like unto a fool who, in a dark cave that hath but one way to get out, having a candle but not the understanding what good it doth him, puts it out. This ignorant wretch, not being able to comprehend thy virtues, did so by thee in thy murder, putting out the world's light and men's admiration. Limena, Limena. O, my Limena."

---

4. Strangeness thus allowed him.

With that he fell from complaining into such a passion as weeping and crying were never in so woeful a perfection as now in him, which brought as deserved a compassion from the excellent shepherdess, who already had her heart so tempered with grief, as that it was apt to take any impression that it would come to seal[5] withal. Yet taking a brave courage to her, she stepped unto him. Kneeling down by his side and gently pulling him by the arm, she thus spake.

"Sir," said she, "having heard some part of your sorrows, they have not only made me truly pity you but wonder at you, since if you have lost so great a treasure you should not lie thus leaving her and your love unrevenged, suffering her murderers to live while you lie here complaining. And if such perfections be dead in her, why make you not the phoenix[6] of your deeds? Live again, as to new life raised out of the revenge you should take on them! Then were her end satisfied, and you deservedly accounted worthy of her favor, if she were so worthy as you say." "If she were? O God!" cried out Perissus. "What devilish spirit art thou that thus dost come to torture me? But now I see you are a woman, and therefore not much to be marked and less resisted. But if you know charity, I pray now practice it and leave me who am afflicted sufficiently without your company. Or if you will stay, discourse not to me." "Neither of these will I do," said she. "If you be then," said he, "some fury, of purpose sent to vex me, use your force to the uttermost in martyring me. For never was there a fitter subject than the heart of poor Perissus is." "I am no fury," replied the divine Urania, "nor hither come to trouble you, but by accident lighted on this place, my cruel hap being such as only the like can give me content, while the solitariness of this like cave might give me quiet—though not ease—seeing for such a one I happened hither. And this is the true cause of my being here, though now I would use it to a better end if I might. Wherefore, favor me with the knowledge of your grief, which heard it may be I shall give you some counsel and comfort in your sorrow."

"Cursed may I be," cried he, "if ever I take comfort, having such cause of mourning. But because you are, or seem to be, afflicted I will not refuse to satisfy your demand, but tell you the saddest story that ever was rehearsed by dying man to living woman, and such a one as I fear will fasten too much sadness in you. Yet, should I deny it I were to blame, being so well known to these senseless places as, were they sensible of sorrow, they would condole, or else, amazed at such cruelty, stand dumb as they do to find that man should be so inhumane.

"Then, fair shepherdess, hear myself say my name is Perissus. Nephew I am to the King of Sicily, a place fruitful and plentiful of all things, only niggardly[7] of good nature to a great man in that country, whom I am sure you have heard me blame in my complaints. Heir I am as yet to this king, mine uncle, and truly may I say so, for a more unfortunate prince never lived, so as I inherit his crosses, howsoever I shall his estate. There was in this country (as the only blessing it

5. Seals were used to make an impression on warm wax, which, when hardened, would serve to secure an envelope, ratify a document, etc.
6. A mythical bird periodically reborn from its own ashes.
7. Parsimonious, grudging.

enjoyed) a lady (or rather a goddess for incomparable beauty and matchless virtues) called Limena, daughter to a duke but princess of all hearts. This star coming to the court to honor it with such light, it was in that my blessed destiny to see her and be made her servant, or better to say, a slave to her perfections. Thus long was I happy, but now begins the tragedy, for wars falling out between the people and the gentlemen, the king was by the people (imagining he took the other part) brought into some danger, and so great an one as rudeness joined with ill nature could bring him into. Being at last besieged in a stronghold of his, all of us (his servants and gentle subjects) striving for his good and safety, in this time nothing appearing but danger and but wise force to preserve men's lives and estates unto them, everyone taking the best means to attain unto their good desires.

"The duke (father to the best and truest beauty) would yet bestow that upon a great lord in the country, truly for powerful command and means a fit match for any but the wonder of women, since none could without much flattery to himself think he might aspire to the blessing of being accounted worthy to be her servant, much less her husband. She, seeing it was her father's will, esteeming obedience beyond all passions how worthily soever suffered, most dutifully though unwillingly said she would obey, her tongue faintly delivering what her heart so much detested, loathing almost itself for consenting in show to that which was most contrary to itself. Yet thus it was concluded, and with as much speed as any man would make to an eternal happiness."

Sir Philip Sidney's Arcadian Pastoral

In the early 1580s the courtier, diplomat, soldier, and poet Sir Philip Sidney (1554–1586) wrote a five-part romance that he then revised so as to make it more heroic. He never finished his revision, probably because he died fighting for the Dutch against the Spanish at the battle of Zutphen. The revised part was printed in 1590, and in 1593 his sister Mary Herbert, countess of Pembroke (author of the "Dolefull Lay" included in this volume), produced an edition that joined the last part of the "Old Arcadia" to what she had of the "New." Soon popular with readers of both sexes, *The Arcadia* combines pastoral, romance, drama, poetry, heroics, and commentary on politics and religion in a leisurely ornate style that pauses for metaphors of startling complexity and with sentences that suit Elizabethan, but not our own more rigid, syntax. Our selection—the opening of the "New Arcadia"—is based on the old-spelling edition by A. Feuillerat; we have also consulted the modernized edition by Victor Skretkowicz (Oxford: Clarendon Press, 1987).

FROM *THE COUNTESS OF PEMBROKE'S ARCADIA* (1590)

It was in the time that the earth begins to put on her new apparel against the approach of her lover,[1] and that the sun, running a most even course becomes an indifferent arbiter between the night and the day, when the hopeless shepherd Strephon was come to the sands which lie against the island of Cythera,[2] where viewing the place with a heavy kind of delight, and sometimes casting his eyes to the isleward, he called his friendly rival the pastor Claius unto him, and setting first down in his darkened countenance a doleful copy of what he would speak, "O my Claius," said he, "hither we are now come to pay the rent, for which we are so called unto by overbusy Remembrance, Remembrance, restless Remembrance, which claims not only this duty of us, but for it will have us forget ourselves. I pray you, when we were amid our flock, and that of other shepherds, some were running after their sheep strayed beyond their bounds, some delighting their eyes with seeing them nibble upon the short and sweet grass, some medicining their sick ewes, some setting a bell for an ensign of a sheepish squadron, some with more leisure inventing new games of exercising their bodies and sporting their wits: did Remembrance grant us any holiday either for pastime or devotion, nay either for necessary food or natural rest, but that still it forced our thoughts to work upon this place where we last (alas that the word 'last' should so long last) did gaze[3] our eyes upon her ever-flourishing beauty? Did it not still cry within us, 'Ah you base-minded wretches, are your thoughts so deeply bemired in the trade of ordinary worldlings as, for respect of gain some paltry wool may yield you, to let so much time pass without knowing perfectly her estate, especially in so troublesome a season? To leave that shore unsaluted from whence you may see to the island where she dwelleth? To leave those steps unkissed wherein Urania printed the farewell of all beauty?' Well, then: Remembrance commanded, we obeyed, and here we find that as our remembrance came ever clothed unto us in the form of this place, so this place gives new heat to the fever of our languishing remembrance.

"Yonder my Claius, Urania lighted; the very horse methought bewailed to be so disburdened. And as for thee, poor Claius, when thou wentest to help her down I saw reverence and desire so divide thee that thou didst at one instant both blush and quake, and instead of bearing her wert ready to fall down thyself. There she sat vouchsafing my cloak (then most gorgeous) under her. At yonder rising of the ground she turned herself, looking back toward her wonted abode, and because of her parting bearing much sorrow in her eyes, the lightsomeness whereof had yet so natural a cheerfulness as it made even sorrow seem to smile. At that turning she spoke unto us all, opening the cherry of her lips, and Lord how greedily mine ears did feed upon the sweet words she uttered! And here she

1. The sun; it is the spring equinox.
2. Near which Venus emerged from the sea.
3. Skretkowicz reads "grace."

laid her hand over thine eyes when she saw the tears springing in them as if she would conceal them from others and yet herself feel some of thy sorrow. But, woe is me, yonder, yonder did she put her foot into the boat, at that instant as it were dividing her heavenly beauty between the earth and the sea. But when she was embarked did you not mark how the winds whistled and the seas danced for joy, how the sails did swell with pride, and all because they had Urania? O Urania, blessed be thou Urania, the sweetest fairness and fairest sweetness."

With that word his voice broke so with sobbing that he could say no further, and Claius thus answered: "Alas my Strephon," said he, "what needs this score to reckon up only our losses? What doubt is there, but that the light of this place doth call our thoughts to appear at the court of Affection, held by that racking[4] steward Remembrance? As well may sheep forget to fear when they spy wolves as we can miss such fancies when we see any place made happy by her treading. Who can choose, that saw her, but think where she stayed, where she walked, where she turned, where she spoke? But what is all this? Truly no more but, as this place served us to think of those things, so those things serve as places to call to memory more excellent matters. No, no, let us think with consideration, and consider with acknowledging, and acknowledge with admiration, and admire with love, and love with joy in the midst of all woes: let us in such sort think, I say, that our poor eyes were so enriched as to behold, and our low hearts so exalted as to love, a maid who is such that as the greatest thing the world can show is her beauty, so the least thing that may be praised in her is her beauty.

"Certainly, as her eyelids are more pleasant to behold than two white kids climbing up a fair tree and browsing on his tenderest branches, and yet are nothing compared to the day-shining stars contained in them; and as her breath is more sweet then a gentle southwest wind which comes creeping over flowery fields and shadowed waters in the extreme heat of summer, and yet is nothing compared to the honey-flowing speech that breath doth carry: no more all that our eyes can see of her (though when they have seen her, what else they shall ever see is but dry stubble after clover grass) is to be matched with the flock of unspeakable virtues laid up delightfully in that best-builded fold. But indeed as we can better consider the sun's beauty by marking how he gilds these waters and mountains than by looking upon his own face, too glorious for our weak eyes, so it may be our conceits (not able to bear her sun-staining excellence) will better weigh it by her works upon some meaner subject employed. And alas, who can better witness than we, whose experience is grounded upon feeling? Hath not the only love of her made us, being silly ignorant shepherds, raise up our thoughts above the ordinary level of the world so as great clerks[5] do not disdain our conference? Hath not the desire to seem worthy in her eyes made us when others were sleeping to sit viewing the course of heavens? When others were running at base, to run over learned writings? When other mark their sheep, we to mark ourselves? Hath not she thrown reason upon our desires and as it were given eyes

4. The "rack" was a stretching device used for torture.
5. Scholars, savants.

unto Cupid? Hath in any, but in her, love-fellowship maintained friendship between rivals and beauty taught the beholders chastity?"

[The shepherds see a naked and handsome shipwrecked youth clutching a casket. "Lifting his feet above his head, making a great deal of salt water to come out of his mouth," they lay him on some of their own garments and rub him until he recovers. The young man, Musidorus, thinking his friend Pyrocles has drowned, tries to throw himself back to the sea and objects when the shepherds stop him.] They, hearing him speak in Greek, which was their natural language, became the more tender-hearted towards him and, considering by his calling and looking that the loss of some dear friend was great cause of his sorrow, told him they were poor men that were bound by course of humanity to prevent so great a mischief and that they wished him, if opinion of somebody's perishing bred such desperate anguish in him, that he should be comforted by his own proof, who had lately escaped as apparent danger as any might be. "No, no," said he, "it is not for me to attend so high a blissfulness: but since you take care of me,[6] I pray you find means that some bark may be provided that will go out of the haven, that if it be possible we may find the body, far, far too precious a food for fishes; and for the hire,"[7] said he, "I have within this casket of value sufficient to content them."

Claius presently[8] went to a fisherman, and having agreed with him and provided some apparel for the naked stranger, he embarked, and the shepherds with him, and were no sooner gone beyond the mouth of the haven but that some way into the sea they might discern, as it were, a stain of the water's color, and by times some sparks and smoke mounting thereout. But the young man no sooner saw it but that, beating his breast, he cried that there was the beginning of his ruin, entreating them to bend their course as near unto it as they could, telling how that smoke was but a small relic of a great fire which had driven both him and his friend rather to commit themselves to the cold mercy of the sea than to abide the hot cruelty of the fire, and that therefore, though they both had abandoned the ship, that he was, if anywhere, in that course to be met with.[9] They steered, therefore, as near thitherward as they could; but when they came so near as their eyes were full masters of the object, they saw a sight full of piteous strangeness: a ship, or rather the carcass of the ship, or rather some few bones of the carcass, hulling there, part broken, part burned, part drowned, death having used more than one dart to that destruction. About it floated great store of very rich things, and many chests which might promise no less. And amidst the precious things were a number of dead bodies, which likewise did not only testify both elements'[10] violence, but that the chief violence was grown of human inhumanity: for their bodies were full of grisly wounds and their blood had, as it were, filled the wrinkles of the sea's visage, which it seemed the sea would not wash

6. Are concerned about me.
7. Reward, payment.
8. At once.
9. Pyrocles may be, if anywhere, near the burned ship.
10. Fire and water.

away, that it might witness it is not always his fault when we condemn his cruelty—in sum, a defeat where the conquered kept both field and spoil, a shipwreck without storm or ill footing, and a waste of fire in the midst of water.

But a little way off they saw the mast, whose proud height now lay along, like a widow having lost her mate of whom she held her honor; but upon the mast they saw a young man (at least if he were a man) bearing show of about eighteen years of age, who sat as on horseback, having nothing upon him but his shirt, which being wrought with blue silk and gold had a kind of resemblance to the sea: on which the sun, then near his western home, did shoot some of his beams. His hair, which the young men of Greece used to wear very long, was stirred up and down with the wind, which seemed to have a sport to play with it, as the sea had to kiss his feet, himself full of admirable beauty set forth by the strangeness both of his seat and gesture: for, holding his head up full of unmoved majesty, he held a sword aloft with his fair arm which often he waved about his crown as though he would threaten the world in that extremity. But the fishermen, when they came so near him that it was time to throw out a rope by which hold they might draw him, their simplicity bred such amazement and their amazement such a superstition, that (assuredly thinking it was some god begotten between Neptune and Venus that had made all this terrible slaughter) as they went under sail by him held up their hands and made their prayers. Which when Musidorus saw, though he were almost as much ravished with joy as they with astonishment, he leaped to the mariner and took the rope out of his hand, and saying, "Dost thou live, and art well?" (who answered, "Thou canst tell best, since most of my well-being stands in thee"), threw it out. But already the ship was passed beyond Pyrocles, and therefore Musidorus could do no more but persuade the mariners to cast about again, assuring them that he was but a man, although of most divine excellencies, and promising great rewards for their pain.

[A pirate ship sails by, and the terrified mariners abandon Pyrocles despite the pleas of Musidorus, who helplessly watches his friend captured. Another ship attacks the pirates but Pyrocles loses sight of the battle; the shepherds tell him to keep hoping and to seek help from a wise Arcadian gentleman, Kalander. They all set out, and Musidorus comes to "marvel at such wit in shepherds" and to enjoy their company. Soon they come to Arcadia.]

There were hills, which garnished their proud heights with stately trees; humble valleys, whose base estate seemed comforted with refreshing of silver rivers; meadows, enameled with all sorts of eye-pleasing flowers; thickets, which being lined with most pleasant shade were witnessed so to by the cheerful deposition of many well-tuned birds; each pasture stored with sheep feeding with sober security while the pretty lambs with bleating oratory craved the dams' comfort: here a shepherd's boy piping as though he should never be old, there a young shepherdess knitting, and withal singing, and it seemed that her voice comforted her hands to work and her hands kept time to her voice's music. As for the houses of the country (for many houses came under their eye), they were all scattered, no two being one by the other and yet not so far off as that it barred mutual succor: a show, as it were, of an accompanable solitariness and of a civil wildness. "I pray you," said Musidorus, then first unsealing his long-silent lips, "what countries be these we pass through, which are so divers in show: the one wanting no store, th'other having no store but of want?"

"The country," answered Claius, "where you were cast ashore and now are passed through, is Laconia, not so poor by the barrenness of the soil (though in itself not passing fertile) as by a civil war, which being these two years within the bowels of that state between a gentleman and the peasants (by them named "helots") hath in this sort as it were disfigured the face of Nature and made it so inhospitable as now you have found it: the towns neither of the one side nor the other willingly opening their gates to strangers, nor strangers willingly entering for fear of being mistaken. But this country where now you set your foot is Arcadia, and even hard by is the house of Kalander whither we lead you, this country being thus decked with peace, and the child of peace, good husbandry. These houses you see so scattered are of men, as we two are, that live upon the commodity of their sheep: and therefore in the division of the Arcadian state are termed shepherds—a happy people, wanting little because they desire not much."

30

Mary Moders Carleton (d. 1673)
Thomas Whythorne (1528–1598)
Robert Spencer (fl. 1687–1689)

Mary Moders Carleton on Trial

We have few facts about Mary Moders Carleton (d. 1673) with the notable exception of her death by hanging as a felon. She was apparently a con-woman who found herself at several times in conflict with the law. Although she claimed foreign birth as a "German princess," her enemies said that she was of lower-class British origin. The subject of close to a dozen narratives, her tale is the type of rogue biography that constitutes one basis for the early novels of the next century. While Carleton cannot be shown to have composed any of these pamphlets completely, her voice is heard in several, including the one we excerpt: an account of her arraignment for bigamy, printed by N. Brook in 1663. Her voice is confident and her arguments quick and resourceful. The indictment was brought by her father-in-law, and the trial provoked charges and countercharges among Mary Carleton, her husband, and his father. While early modern justice was executed swiftly, the court seems to have been fairly careful here in evaluating evidence that could have condemned Carleton to death. Nevertheless, women were disadvantaged under early modern law: they had no "clergy" (see below), and although in this case Carleton is judged innocent, she is left, as a "feme covert," with no recourse for regaining property her husband and father-in-law had taken from her since that property is not hers under the law. Our excerpts are from the 1663 text of *The Arraignment, Trial, and Examination of Mary Moders*. To preserve the original flavor, we have retained variations in the spelling of "Carleton."

FROM *THE ARRAIGNMENT, TRIAL, AND EXAMINATION OF MARY MODERS*

At Justice-Hall in the Old Bailey,[1] the court being sat, a bill of indictment was drawn up against Mary Moders, alias Stedman, for having two husbands now alive, viz. Thomas Stedman and John Carleton. The grand jury found the bill,[2] and was to the effect following, viz., that she, the said Mary Moders, late of London, spinster, otherwise Mary Stedman, the wife of Thomas Stedman . . . did take to husband the aforesaid Thomas Stedman, and him the said Thomas Stedman then and there had to husband. And that the said Mary Moders . . . feloniously did take to husband one John Carleton, and to him was married, the said Thomas Stedman her former husband then being alive, and in full life. . . . . Afterwards the said Mary Moders, alias Stedman, was called to the bar and appearing was commanded to hold up her hand, which she accordingly did. And her indictment was read to her as followeth.

CLERK OF THE PEACE "Mary Moders, alias Stedman, thou standest indicted in London by the name of Mary Moders, late of London, spinster, otherwise Mary Stedman, the wife of, etc." (And here the indictment was read as above.) "How sayst thou? Art thou guilty of the felony whereof thou standest indicted, or not guilty?"

MARY MODERS "Not guilty, my lord."

CLERK OF THE PEACE "How wilt thou be tried?"

PRISONER "By God and the country."[3]

CLERK OF THE PEACE "God send thee a good deliverance."[4]

And afterwards, she being set to the bar in order to her trial she prayed time till the morrow for her trial, which was granted, and all persons concerned were ordered to attend them at nine of the clock in the forenoon

. . . .

The court was sat. Proclamation was made: "*Oyes*,[5] all manner of persons that have anything more to do, etc. Set Mary Moders to the bar," where she accordingly stood.

CLERK OF THE PEACE "Mary Moders, alias Stedman, hold up thy hand," which she did. "Those men that you shall hear called and personally appear are to pass between our sovereign lord the king and you for your life. If you will challenge them or any of them you must do it when they come to the book to be sworn, before they are sworn." . . . And she challenged none, but were severally sworn by the oath following, "Look upon the prisoner. You shall well and truly try, and true deliverance make, between our sovereign lord the king and the prisoner at the bar whom you shall have in charge, according to your evidence, so help you God."

1. A famous criminal court in London.
2. Decided that the evidence warranted hearing a case.
3. A legal formula signifying an agreement to be tried by jury.
4. Another legal formula.
5. Law French for "Hear ye"; hence a demand for silence.

CLERK OF THE PEACE "Cryer, make proclamation, oyes, if any one can inform . . . before this inquest be taken between our sovereign lord the king and the prisoner at the bar, let them come forth and they shall be heard. For now the prisoner stands at the bar upon her deliverance, and all others that are bound by recognizance[6] to give evidence against the prisoner at the bar come forth and give evidence, or else you'll forfeit your recognizance." . . .

After some stay the witnesses came into the court and the prisoner set to the bar and silence being commanded, the indictment was again read.

CLERK OF THE PEACE "Upon this indictment she has pleaded 'Not Guilty' and for her trial has put herself upon God and the country, which country you are. Your charge is to inquire whether she be guilty of the said felony or not guilty. If you find her guilty, you shall inquire what goods and chattels she had at the time of the felony committed or at any time since.[7] If you find her not guilty, you shall inquire whether she did flee for it.[8] If you find that she fled for it, you shall inquire of her goods, etc., as if she had been guilty. If you find she be not guilty, nor that she did flee for it, say so and no more and hear your evidence."

Several witnesses were sworn by the oath following: "The evidence that you shall swear between our sovereign lord the king and the prisoner at the bar shall be the truth, the whole truth, and nothing but the truth, so help you God."

JAMES KNOT "My lord and gentlemen of the jury, I gave this woman in marriage to one Thomas Stedman, which is now alive in Dover, and I saw him last week."

COURT "Where was she married?"

KNOT "In Canterbury."

COURT "Where there?"

KNOT "In St. Mildred's, by one parson man who is now dead."

COURT "How long since were they married?"

KNOT "About nine years ago."

COURT "Did they live together afterwards?"

KNOT "Yes, about four years, and had two children."

COURT "You gave her in marriage, but did the minister give her to her husband then?"

KNOT "Yes, and they lived together."

JURY "Friend, did you give this very woman?"

KNOT "Yes."

COURT "What company was there?"

KNOT "There was the married couple, her sister, myself, the parson and the

6. Notice.
7. These would be forfeit if the accused were found guilty.
8. Flight also would render goods forfeit if the accused were convicted.

sexton."

COURT "Where is that sexton?"

KNOT "I know not, my lord."

COURT "You are sure they were married in the church, and this is the woman?"

KNOT "Yes, I am sure of it."

COURT "How long ago?"

KNOT "About nine years ago." . . .

COURT "Where is this man her husband? Hearsay must condemn no man. What do you know of your own knowledge?"

CARLETON THE ELDER "I know the man is alive."

COURT "Do you know he was married to her?"

CARLETON "Not I, my lord."

SARAH WILLIAMS "My lord, this woman was bound for Barbados, to go along with my husband, and she desired to lodge at our house for some time and did so. And when the ship was ready to go, she went into Kent to receive her means, and said she would meet the ship in the Downs, and missing the ship, took boat and went to the ship. After several days remaining there, there came her husband with an order and fetched her ashore, and carried her to Dover Castle."

COURT "What was his name that had an order to bring her on shore again?"

SARAH WILLIAMS "His name was Thomas Stedman."

COURT "Have you any more to prove the first marriage?"

CHARLTON THE ELDER "No, none but Knot. There was none but three: the minister dead, the sexton not to be found, and this Knot who has given evidence."

COURT "What became of the two children, Knot?"

KNOT "They both died."

CHARLTON THE ELDER "Stedman said in my hearing that he had lived four years together, had two children by her, and both dead. Five years ago last Easter since she left him."

COURT "Mr. Charlton, what have you heard this woman say?"

CHARLTON "My lord, she will confess nothing that pleases him."

COURT "Mr. Charlton, did you look in the church register for the first marriage?"

CHARLTON "I did look in the book, and he that is now clerk was then sexton (just now not to be found). He told me that marriages being then very numerous, preceding the act before-mentioned, the then clerk had neglected the registry[9] of this marriage. If she intended this trade, she likewise knew how to make the clerk mistake registering the marriage."

YOUNG CHARLTON'S BROTHER SWORN, WHO SAID, "My lord and gentlemen of the

9. Registration.

jury, I was present at the marriage of my brother with this gentlewoman, which was on or about 25 April 1662. They were married at Great St. Bartholomew's by one Mr. Smith, a Minister here in court, by license."

MR. SMITH, THE PARSON, SWORN. "My lord, all that I can say is this. That Mr. Charlton, the younger, told me of such a business, and desired me to marry them. They came to church, and I did marry them by the Book of Common Prayer."

COURT "Mr. Smith, are you sure that is the woman?"

PARSON "Yes, my lord, it is. I believe she will not deny it."

PRISONER "Yes, my lord, I confess I am the woman."

COURT "Have you any more witnesses." . . .

PRISONER "May it please your honors, and gentlemen of the jury, you have heard the several witnesses, and I think this whole country cannot but plainly see the malice of my husband's father against me, how he causelessly hunts after my life. When his son, my husband, came and addressed himself to me, pretending himself a person of honor, and upon first sight pressed me to marriage, I told him, 'Sir,' said I, 'I am a stranger, have no acquaintance here, and desire you to desist your suit.' I could not speak my mind, but he (having borrowed some threadbare compliments) replied, 'Madam, your seeming virtues, your amiable person, and noble deportment, renders you so excellent that were I in the least interested in you, I cannot doubt of happiness.' And so with many words to the like purpose courted me. I told him, and indeed could not but much wonder, that at so small a glance he could be so presumptuous with a stranger to hint this to me, but all I could say would not beat him off. And presently afterwards, he having intercepted my letter by which he understood how my affairs stood and how considerable my means were, he still urged me to marry him. And immediately by the contrivance of his friends, gaping at my fortune, I was hurried to church to be married which the parson at first did without license, to secure me to my husband, and sometime after had a license.

"And my husband's father afterwards considering I had a considerable fortune pressed me that in respect I had no relations here. 'And because,' says he, 'We are mortal, you would do well to make over your estate to my son, your husband. It will be much for your honor, satisfaction of the world, and for which you will be chronicled for a rare woman.' And perceiving he had not baited his hook sufficient (with some fair pretenses) to catch me then, he and his son (who were both willing to make up some of their former losses in circumventing me of what I had) they robbed me of my jewels and clothes of great value, and afterwards pretended they were counterfeit jewels and declared that I had formerly been married to one at Canterbury which place I know not. And this grounded on a letter (of their own framing) sent from Dover, with a description of me, that I was a young fat woman, full breasted, that I spoke several languages. And therefore they imagined me the person and so violently carried me from my lodging before a justice of peace only to affright me that I might make my estate over to them.

"The justice, having heard their several allegations, could not commit me unless they would be bound to prosecute me, which my husband being unwilling to, the justice demanded of his father whether he would prosecute me, saying they must not make a fool of him. And so, after some whisperings, the father and his son were both bound to prosecute and thereupon I was committed to prison. And since that, these people have been up and down the country and finding none there that could justify anything of this matter they get here an unknown fellow, unless in a prison and from thence borrowed you cannot but all judge, to swear against me.

"My lord, were there any such marriage as this fellow pretends, methinks there might be a certificate from the minister or place. Certainly if married it must be registered. But there is no registry of it and so can be no certificate, no minister, nor clerk to be found. And if I should own a marriage then you see that great witness cannot tell you whether I was lawfully married or how, but it is enough for him (if such a paltry fellow may be believed) to say I was married. I was never yet married to any but John Charlton the late pretended lord. But these persons have sought always to take away my life, bring persons to swear against me, one hired with five pounds and another old fellow persuaded to own me for his wife, who came to the prison and seeing another woman owned her, and afterwards my self, and indeed anybody. If such an old inconsiderable fellow had heretofore wooed me, it must have been for want of discretion, as Charleton did for want of money, but I know of no such thing. Several scandals have been laid upon me, but no mortal flesh can truly touch the least hair of my head for any such like offense. They have framed this of themselves. My lord, I am a stranger and a foreigner, and being informed there is a matter of law in this trial for my life, my innocence shall be my counselor, and your lordships my judges, to whom I wholly refer my cause.

"Since I have been in prison, several from Canterbury have been to see me pretending themselves (if I were the person as was related) to be my schoolmates. And when they came to me, the keeper can justify[10] they all declared they did not know me."

COURT "Knot, you said she lived near you at Canterbury. What woman or man there have you to prove she lived there? Have you none in that whole city, neither for love, nor justice, nor right will come to say she lived there?"

KNOT "I believe I could fetch one."

COURT "Well said. Are they to fetch still?"

PRISONER "My lord, I desire some witnesses may be heard in my behalf."

ELIZABETH COLLIER EXAMINED. "My lord, my husband being a prisoner in the

10. Testify, prove.

Gatehouse[11] I came there to see my husband and did work there adays. And where came in an old man, his name was Billing, he said he had a wife there. Says Mr. Baley, 'Go in and find her out.' And he said I was his wife, turned my hood, and put on his spectacles, looks upon me, and said I was the same woman his wife, and afterwards said I was not, and so to others. I can say no more."

JANE FINCH EXAMINED. "My lord, there came a man and woman one night and knocked at my door. I came down, they asked to speak with one Jane Finch. 'I am the person,' said I. 'We understand,' said they, 'You know Mrs. Charleton now in prison.' 'Not I,' said I, 'I only went to see her there.' Said they, 'Be not scrupulous. If you will go and justify anything against her, we will give you five pounds.' "

COURT "Who are those two?"

FINCH "I do not know them, my lord."

MR. BALEY EXAMINED. "My lord, there has been at least 500 people have viewed her, several from Canterbury, 40 at least that said they lived there, and when they went up to her, she hid not her face at all, but not one of them knew her."

COURT "What country woman are you?"

PRISONER "I was born in Cologne in Germany."

COURT "Mr. Charlton, how came you to understand she was married formerly?"

CHARLTON ELDER "I received a letter from the recorder of Canterbury to that purpose."

PRISONER "They that can offer 5 pounds to swear against me, can also frame a letter against me. They say I was 19 years of age about 9 years ago, and am now but 21."

COURT "Mr. Charlton, you heard what Knot said. He said she lived near him 4 years a wife. Why did not you get somebody else from thence to testify this?"

CHARLETON "Here was one Davis that was at her father's house, and spoke with him—"

COURT "Where is he?"

CHARLTON "I know not. He was here."

COURT "You were telling the court of a former indictment against her. What was that for?"

CHARLTON "She was indicted for having two husbands, Stedman of Canterbury her first husband, and Day of Dover, surgeon, her second husband. The indictment was traversed[12] the year before His Majesty came to England. She was found not guilty."

11. The prison at Westminster Gatehouse.

COURT "Who was at that trial?"

CHARLTON "One here in court was of the jury. But that party said there was such a trial, but knows not that this is the woman."

JUDGE HOWEL "Gentlemen of the jury, you see this indictment is against Mary Moders, otherwise Stedman, and it is for having two husbands, both at one time alive, the first Stedman, afterwards married to Charlton, her former husband being alive. You have heard the proof of the first marriage, and the proof does depend upon one witness, that is Knot. And he indeed does say he was at the marriage, gave her, and he names one Man the parson that married her, that he is dead. None present there but the married couple that must needs be there, the parson, this witness, her sister, and the sexton, that he knows not what is become of the sexton. All the evidence given on that side to prove her guilty of this indictment depends upon his single testimony. It is true, he says she was married at Canterbury, but the particulars or the manner of the marriage he does not so well remember, whether by the Book of Common Prayer or otherwise, but they lived together for four years, had two children. If she were born there, married there, had two children there, and lived there so long, it were easy to have brought somebody to prove this. That is all that is material for the first marriage. For the second, there is little proof necessary. She confesses her self married to Charlton and owns him. The question is whether she was married to Stedman, or not?

"You have heard what defense she has made for herself, some witnesses on her behalf. If you believe that Knot, the single witness, speaks the truth so far forth to satisfy your conscience that that was a marriage, she is guilty. You see what the circumstances are: it is penal. If guilty, she must die; a woman has no clergy;[13] she is to die by the law, if guilty. You heard she was indicted at Dover for having two husbands, Stedman the first and Day the second. There it seems by that which they have said, she was acquitted; none can say this was the woman. That there was a trial may be believed, but whether this be the woman tried or acquitted does not appear. One here that was of that jury says there was a trial but knows not that this is the woman. So that upon the whole it is left to you to consider of the evidence you have heard and so to give your evidence."

The jury went forth and after some short consultation returned to their places. Their names were called and all answered.

CLERK OF THE PEACE "Are you all agreed of your verdict?"

JURY "Yes."

CLERK "Who shall say for you?"

JURY "The Foreman."

12. Contradicted formally.
13. Defense of clergy was a legal loophole by which men, but not women, were able to escape hanging if they could qualify as clergy by reading the passage that came to be called the "neck verse."

CLERK "Mary Moders, alias Stedman, hold up thy hand. Look upon her, gentlemen, what say you? Is she guilty of the felony whereof she stands indicted or not guilty?"

FOREMAN "Not guilty."

And thereupon a great number of people being in and about the court kissed
and clapped their hands.

CLERK "Did she flee for it?"

FOREMAN "Not that we know."

Afterwards she desired that her jewels and clothes taken from her might be
restored to her. The court acquainted her that they were her husband's and that
if any detained them from her he might have his remedy at law.[14] She, charging
Old Mr. Charlton with them, he declared they were already in the custody of his
son, her husband.

Thomas Whythorne Goes A'Wooing

Thomas Whythorne (1528–1596), born to a moderately prosperous family, was
trained as a chorister in Cambridge and briefly attended the university. Attached later
to several important households, he saw a range of social worlds from the inside, serving John Heywood (poet and collector of proverbs), Ambrose Dudley (later Earl of
Warwick), Matthew Parker (Archbishop of Canterbury), and William Bromfield (a
London merchant). He wrote several books of songs, his story of when and why he
composed them being the first secular autobiography in English. He wrote it in a
reformed spelling derived, says his modern editor, from John Hart's *Orthography*
(1569); perhaps he thought it would help poets deal better with meter. He was
unlucky in love. Some women paid him unwelcome attention, one leaving notes
tucked in his guitar and another scoffing that he "lacked audacity." Sometimes he was
the disappointed suitor, as in the following account. James M. Osborn edited the
manuscript (Oxford: Clarendon Press, 1961) and made a modern-spelling version
(New Haven: Yale University Press, 1961) that we adapt.

FROM THE AUTOBIOGRAPHY OF THOMAS WHYTHORNE (C. 1576).

[A friend has offered to arrange a marriage for Whythorne with a well-to-do
childless young widow. After visiting her, Whythorne gives his reaction.] I told
him that as yet I misliked her not, and if it should please God that we should join
in marriage, I may not, nor I hope I should not, refuse what He hath appointed.
Quoth my friend, "I have told you her estate, and beside that which I have told
you I dare warrant her to be worth a hundred marks;[1] and therefore she is not
only worthy to be liked, but also to have such a one by whom her wealth may be

14. Under law, a married woman could not own property.

rather increased than impaired." Quoth I to him, "If I have her, I will not only increase her wealth as much as you say hers is, but also after the decease of my mother I will leave her during her natural life as much of yearly rents as shall amount to ten pounds a year. And for the performance thereof I will enter into such a reasonable bond as shall be thought meet by your and my learned counsel in law." Quoth he, "You have made me such an answer as I am very well content and satisfied with. I would wish," quoth he, "that you would see her either tomorrow or the next day. I would go with you, but I have such business for three or four days that I cannot be in the city." (Here ye shall understand that this widow was a Londoner.) "But in five days if ye will come to my lodging," quoth he, "you shall understand what she thinketh of you and what is like to become of your suit to her." Quoth I, "I am content to do as you will have me in the matter." And thereupon we parted company. . . .

[The widow tells the friend that she likes Whythorne and the settlement he has agreed to make her in his will. She has, the friend reports, "determined to forsake all her other suitors."]

When I came at my widow, after due salutation and ceremonies belonging to a wooer's function, I told her that I came presently from my said friend. And then I recounted to her what he told me of her promise to him concerning the knitting up of our marriage. Whereunto she said that such a promise she made to him and was willing to perform it, upon which words I gave to her a token of good will and she received it. Then she and I grew into talk of such things as we thought meet and convenient for our marriage (for I looked for no other assurance of her at that time than that promise which she made then). And among the circumstances of my talk I told her that, seeing she had referred the day of our marriage to my assignment, I would have it to be the next term[2] (which was the term after Christmas and not much above three weeks after the time that we had this talk). "Because," quoth I, "I have a brother-in-law that is a lawyer, who cometh to London at that term, and I would be glad to have him at my marriage."

These words of mine my widow seemed not to gainsay otherwise than thus (and yet that was so colorably[3] done as I understood not her meaning therein): she said she would marry within that year or else she would never marry, by which words I thought that she meant to marry within a year after she had spoken those words or else she would never marry. But by the sequel it appeared that she meant to marry before that old year went out or the new year should begin, which was within a fortnight after her words so spoken. Also, she seemed somewhat to mislike that I came no oftener to her because I came but once in three days. To which I answered her that my business had been such that I could come no oftener, but I would afterward amend that fault. After this I took my leave of her.

And the second day after, I came to her again, at what time I found my

1. A mark was about fourteen shillings.
2. A period during which law courts are in session.
3. Plausibly, with fair show.

widow so strange[4] as though she had never made me any such faithful promise as is before spoken of. Whereat I was suddenly cast into a dump,[5] in which while I remained I considered with myself what should be the cause of this sudden revolt and strangeness. And when I had mused a little while on the matter I, as one that had had some experience in such cases before that time, plucked up my spirits and began to say to my widow, "Gentlewoman, I do marvel at this your sudden change of countenance toward me. I hope that whatsoever you do outwardly show yourself toward me, you do mean the same inwardly as ye before professed to your friend and me outwardly." Quoth she, "And if you had taken me at my word and not prolonged the time with me, I would have performed my promise, the which promise was no such contract but that may be broken again." "Indeed," quoth I, "it was no such contract in matrimony as should farther bind your conscience than a friendly promise without the plighting of our troths one to the other; and yet I for my part thought that I should not need to have done it till we had met at the church together for that purpose. But," quoth I, "I think ye do this but to try me; and if it be so, I am contented therewith and will willingly tarry your pleasure and will perform the premises."[6] "Nay," quoth she, "I am fully resolved in that matter. And if I should have you, what should I be enriched by the having of you?" Quoth I, "As for my riches, I am assured they be nothing inferior to yours, if ye be no richer than your friend told me of." . . . And when I was gone from her, I wrote this sonnet following:

> *I have ere this time heard many one say,*
> *Take time while time is, for time will away.*
> *Whoso that great affairs have to be done*
> *Which, at their own will, they may dispatch soon,*
> *Let no deferring of time be usèd,*
> *Lest they be far off when they would be sped.[7]*
> *Among the loving worms,[8] this thwarting word*
> *Is oftimes blown out, in earnest or bourd:[9]*
> *"When that ye might have had, then would ye not,*
> *Therefore when that ye would, then shall ye not."*
> *Many in sundry sorts have found this true,*
> *Which were too long (each way) here for to show.*
> *Wherefore remember what now hath been said,*
> *And let all things with time be richly weighed.*

[Torn between desire and suspicion, Whythorne writes more poetry.]
  When I had thus somewhat eased my mind, I then bestirred my stumps like

---

4. Remote and stand-offish.
5. A fit of melancholy.
6. The previously mentioned agreements on, e.g., property transfers.
7. When they hope to succeed.
8. Amorous fancies that gnaw heart and mind.
9. Jest.

a nettled hen till I found out my friend. And then I showed him the whole circumstance of the jar between the widow and me; he, seeming to marvel much thereof, was in a doubt lest my ill demeanor toward her had given her the cause. Quoth I to him, "If she took any new occasion to break her hest[10] toward me, it was because I came not to see her every day. I thought that once seeing of her in two days would have contented her, or else peradventure she liked not to tarry so long unmarried now as until the beginning of the next term, because it is so long hence. She saith that she shall not benefit by marrying me, and I told her that she should have more benefit by marrying me than I should have by wedding her."
. . .

[According to the friend, the widow claims that Whythorne should have married her at once, that there had been no firm contract, and that she would never marry.] "After this," quoth he, "I told her brother" (for she then did lie in a brother's house of hers) "of your offer to her, of her promise to you and of her breach thereof; whereupon he went to her and taunted her a little. Yea, even the servants of the house spoke to her on your behalf, reprehending her for her inconstancy and breach of promise, which hath brought her into a quandary; notwithstanding, she keeps her to her hold, which is that she will never marry. By which you may see," quoth he to me, "what tracting[11] of the time doth in this case. If you had given credit to my report of her at the first and not prolonged the time of marriage, this matter had not been so far back as it is now." Quoth I to him, "I ensure that I did not delay the day of marriage for any other cause than that I would have had my brother-in-law at it, who might have reported the same to my mother and sisters when he had returned to the West Country again.

"Now I do perceive some great likelihood that these proverbs and old sayings be true which have been devised upon this sort of wooing. One of which is thus: 'Blessed be the wooing that is not long a-doing.' And if I had followed this proverb then my wooing had been at an end by this time. Also another saith that he who doth woo a maid shall not be the worse welcome though he come but now and then to her, as in three or four days; but he that wooeth a widow must ply her daily. Also another saith that he that wooeth a maid must go trick and trim and in fine apparel; but he that wooeth a widow must go stiff before.[12] I promise you so was I stiff. But yet, considering that the time was not likely to be long to the wedding day; and also that the market was likely to last all the year long; and I, loving her, meant not to attempt any dishonesty unto her, for a sinful fact it had been, till we had been married, and we should have provoked God's heavy displeasure and wrath to light upon us for our wickedness. And if those be the causes of her revolt, then do I count her as good lost as found." . . .

[The next day Whythorne goes to her brother's house and explains that he is worried; the brother reassures him.] And so growing into other talk, at length the gentleman called for a piece of brawn[13] and a Christmas pie for us to break our fasts therewith, which being brought to a table prepared for the purpose, we

10. Promise.
11. Drawing out.
12. Boldly, resolutely.

went to breakfast. And before we should sit down thereat, the gentleman sent to the widow his sister to know whether she would break her fast with us or not. But the widow being in bed (as her custom was to keep her bed in the morning till ten o'clock) would none at that time. Wherefore, shortly after our answer, we went to breakfast. The gentleman, not being satisfied with her answer, sent to her again and desired her to make her ready and to come to him. And so, with much ado, she came at length.

When she was come, after a few salutations without embracings and busses,[14] she sat down at the table, where there was such friendly talk and drinking to with slender pledgings,[15] as are commonly used between such between whom there is but ordinary friendship. And when breakfast was done we fell into talk of divers matters, in the end whereof the gentleman slunk away and left the widow and me alone. To whom I then renewed my old suit, and charged her with inconstancy and with breach of her promise; wherewith she laid for[16] herself that if I had not delayed the time and [had] taken her at her word, she would not have gone from it. "But," quoth she, "I am fully determined now never to marry." And therewithal she seemed to be much troubled in her mind and sighed often. . . . [Whythorne goes home discouraged, but his friend urges him on. The widow, although making no promises, now asks for a ring and offers gold with which to have it made "after the manner of a wedding ring."] I thereupon imagining that she meant some marriage, and that she would not have requested me to get the ring to be made in that fashion except I should be privy of the marriage, I, in hope to put the ring on her finger, seemed (as I was indeed) to be very glad that she would commit such a matter to be done by me. And then I told her that I hoped that with that ring I should wed her; and, as for the day of wedding, seeing that it pleased her not as I did set it, I would now resign that appointment to her assignment. Whereunto she said little that made for my purpose. Notwithstanding, I meant now to follow daily my enterprise till the ring was made. And then if I liked not the sequel, I meant to know off or on,[17] and so lose no more time.

When she and I had passed the time away a pretty while, she went to her chest and fetched out of it as much old gold as was worth nigh about a mark, which she said that she would have bestowed in the ring. And then she, looking on certain rings that I wear on my little finger, seemed to like one of them and said that she would wear it a while for my sake. Whereupon I offered to give it to her, but she would not take it of gift, which made me suspect by and by that she mistrusted that I would not restore her gold to her again, and if her imagination fell out right[18] yet she, having my ring, should not lose all. Notwithstanding my suspicion, I did mean not now to leave this matter thus

13. Muscle meat, especially pork.
14. Kisses.
15. Scanty toasts.
16. Claimed as an excuse.
17. Know whether or not the marriage would happen.

rawly, and when my widow and I had passed away the time in this said manner I took a lover's leave and so parted from her company.

The next day I went to a goldsmith, to whom I delivered the gold and told him of what fashion I would have the ring made, and also gave this sentence to grave in it: "The eye doth find, the heart doth choose, and love doth bind till death doth loose." I do write this sentence in this sort because it is not of my making; yet so well liked of me as, if I should make another wedding ring, it should have the same sentence. But to my matter: when I had given order to my goldsmith for the making of the ring, with the bigness of her finger, and had received of him a counterpane[19] or weight of the gold, I agreed with him to have the ring made by the fourth day after, in which four days I did ply my widow for life. And to make her the more coming, or at least more tractable and merry, I caused one of my lutes to be brought to her brother's house, on which I would sometimes play when I was there to pass the time away with.

And when I had thus passed away the four days, in which time I missed not to visit her every day once, I went to my goldsmith's for the ring. For the making whereof when I had paid him, and saw that the weight thereof agreed with my counterpane and weight aforesaid, I brought the ring to my widow, which when she did see she grew therewithal into a great melancholy and said that it was not of the newest and best fashion. Quoth I, "It is of the best fashion that I do know." And therewithal I ministered further talk to appease her anger; but all my words prevailed nothing, for still her melancholy increased, which brought her quickly into glumming, pouting and sighing. When I did see her in that perplexity, I sought with all the fair persuasions that I could devise to content her, showing her that if I might see the fashion that she liked I would cause it to be made anew in that fashion—and I would pay for the making thereof myself. "No," quoth she," it shall not need. I must content me with it as it is, seeing it is my fortune." These last words of hers made me to doubt that she had practiced[20] before that time with some astrologer or soothsayer to know of what credit her husband should be, which astrologer or soothsayer willed her to cause this ring to be made, and as the fashion of that chanced to like her,[21] so should her husband like her.

[Whythorne visits his friend, playing the lute and discussing books; next day they revisit the widow.] And when the meat was set on the table and every one of us set thereat according to our degree, occasions of talk were moved diversely, wherewith we passed away the dinnertime. The end whereof being come, my friend, remembering the cause of our meeting there at the time, began to rehearse the same to us and then turned himself to the widow and did her in mind of my suit to her, showing her also that I desired now to have a determinate and final answer and end thereof. Whereupon she, using but few words, in the end of them said that she was determined never to marry; with which words

18. If what she feared took place.
19. An object of equal value used as a guarantee.
20. Fear that she had had dealings with.
21. Please her.

her brother and my friend, not being willing to be so answered, took the widow aside and fell anew to persuading of her. And while these persuasions were a-making, her brother left her and my friend together and came to me, seeming to be sorry that my suit took no better effect; adding thereunto that whereas he was contented that she should live in his house for a time till God would send her such a mate or husband as by whom she might live in a house of her own, he perceived that she meant to trouble his house still by refusing such a one as was well to be thought of.

And by that time that her brother and I had talked a while, my friend came from the window to me and would needs have me prove her again. The which I did, and told her also what her brother had said to me concerning her with promise that, if I might obtain my suit of her, the first thing that I went about should be to get a handsome house. And in the meanwhile, rather than she should lie out of the doors, she should lie in my chamber. For which she gave me thanks, but yet she would none of my offer. And in the end of her words she said that one of the causes why she would not marry was because she was many times troubled and oppressed with a melancholy humor, at which time she should peradventure displease her husband. And then, if he could not bear with her and put it up quietly, it would be some disquietness between them. Quoth I to her, "If you would not misuse me too much, I could bear with you well enough in that case." "Well," quoth she, "because I know what I shall say in that case and what will fall out thereof, I do mean to prevent the worst. . . ." By the time I came to my lodging I remembered that I had as yet the widow's ring and that she had mine (of which I [had] thought to have made an exchange with her). But she, not minding[22] such a change, sent her maid to my lodging the next day, who on her behalf requested me to come to her mistress and to speak with her. Whereupon, mistrusting that it was to have her ring, I told her maid that I would be with her mistress the next day in the morning. And against that time I wrote in a piece of paper the verses that I caused to be graven in her ring, somewhat altered as thus:

> *The eye did find,*
> *The heart did choose,*
> *And love did bind*
> *Till death should loose.*

To which verses I added these four verses following:

> *For reason now*
> *Hath broke the band,*
> *Since to your vow*
> *Ye would not stand.*

The next day in the morning I went to my widow, of whom once more I

---

22. Wishing for.

demanded whether she was willing to perform her first promise made to me and my friend or not. To which she made answer that the promise was none such but she might break well enough with safe conscience; and harping on her old string, she said that she would never marry. "Well then," quoth I, "here I have brought you your ring; and if you will pay me for the making thereof and will also redeliver to me the tokens which ye received of me, you shall have your ring." Immediately after my words so spoken, she paid me the money for the making of the ring and delivered me my tokens again. Upon the receipt whereof I delivered her her ring and therewithal gave to her a kiss; and saying that, when it should please God to send her a husband, I wished she might have one with whom she might live no worse than she might have done with me. For which words she thanked me, and so we parted.

[Wondering if the widow rejected him before he, tired of her "melancholy" moods, could do the same to her, Whythorne tells of a priest who, out bird-catching, mistakes a toad for a bird and is poisoned; he then explains his allegory.] For ye shall understand that it is said that the love of a woman's first husband goeth to her heart, where it so warmeth the same that she hath a care not to change him. And if she chance to bury him and marry another husband, then the love that she beareth to her second husband, finding a way already made to her heart, pierceth through her heart and therewith inflameth the same in such sort that she hath the like care to change as she had before. But if she chance to bury her second husband and love also, then afterward, if she chance to have never so many lovers, the loss of them will grieve her but a little; for when she hath a hole through her heart she can never love so hotly and constantly as she did before, neither will the loss of her lover grieve her inwardly very much.

Now sir, even as the state standeth with the widow that hath had two husbands, so it hath been with me in wooing of divers women, as partly ye may perceive by that which I have before written in wooing matters. Which women have for a short time given me such cause to think that they have loved me that I have thought that the sun would have lost his light before they would have changed; and their inconstancy hath grieved me somewhat also. But yet I am not only alive, but also then I did both eat my meat and drink my drink and sleep well enough. By that which I do gather and have learned touching my nativity, if there be any credit to be given to astrology, I do think now that at the hour of my birth the sign Virgo was in the horoscope and ascendant, the lord of whose house is Mercury: wherefore he was the lord of my birth. Then do I read in our ancient poet Sir Geoffrey Chaucer that Mercury and Venus be contrary in their working and disposition, and therefore one of them falleth in the other's exaltation.[23] Yet do I imagine that although Venus was retrograde at the hour of my birth, she was favorably aspected with benevolent planets or signs towards me, which made me to receive some commodity[24] by some women, although their great good will

---

23. Whythorne wrongly makes Chaucer a knight; the Wife of Bath, in the *Canterbury Tales*, says that since Mercury (god of rhetoric) can oppose Venus's planetary influence, scholars are misogynists and inept lovers.

toward me did soon vanish away by the means of her retrogradation.

[Whythorne vows to give up women.] I will be shortly like unto a good fellow who, being somewhat stepped in years and past the snares of Venus' darlings and babes, came by chance into a secret place where he found a young man and a young woman embracing and kissing together. Wherewith he stood still a little, and then he made a cross on his forehead with thumb, and then with hand he made as it were a penthouse[25] over his eyes as one doth whose sight is troubled by the brightness of the sunlight if he look toward it. The which being done, he said, "Jesus! Doth this world last yet?"—as [one] who would have said, "Doth this embracing and kissing continue still?" Because all such kind of actions were past with him, he thought that they had been done with by everybody else. And yet I will not swear that I will do so, for when one doth swear that he will or will not do a thing, then will the Devil be ever tempting him to break his oath. But as I am thus advised,[26] I will not alter nor change my mind in that case. I have stayed you too long in this loving. Howbeit, if you do mark well all the actions and speeches therein it may be for your good, if ye chance to have the like happen to you.

And now, seeing that it is like to be the last that I do intend to trouble you with after this time, bear with me and I will conclude this matter thus: not long after my widow and I parted as is aforesaid, she being hot in the sear[27] and of the spur could tarry no longer without a mate; therefore in haste she stumbled under an ostler[28] who now doth lubber-leap her. For he, with rubbing horseheels and greasing them in the roofs of their mouths, got so much money as therewith he so bleared the widow's eyes that she, thinking all had been gold that shined, took him to be her wedded spouse. So that the dor,[29] having flown all the day about among herbs and flowers, hath now shrouded[30] her under a horseturd. And to say the truth, he is sweet enough for such a sweet piece as she is.

Robert Spencer Sues a Rich Widow

In 1686–87, Robert Spencer, Esquire (fl. 1686–89), a relation of Robert Spencer, second earl of Sunderland, was one of many who wooed Lady Elizabeth Wiseman (c. 1647–1730), daughter of Dudley North, fourth baron North (1602–1677). Her first husband, Sir Robert Wiseman, had died in 1684, leaving her attractively wealthy. Spencer's suit was supported by Wiseman's oldest brother, Charles, and his wife, Lady Katharine North. North family documents, however, including letters and narratives penned by Wiseman and her three sympathetic brothers—Sir Dudley North, Commissioner for Customs; Roger North, Attorney General for the queen; and

---

24. Advantage, gain.
25. An overhanging storey.
26. Alerted.
27. Readily made to fire, like a canon.
28. A horse-groom.
29. A dungbeetle.
30. Sheltered, hidden. Several years later Whythorne got married.

Montague North, a London merchant—show Wiseman's efforts to evade Spencer's unwelcome overtures. She even tried relocating to the home of her sister, Christina Wenyeve, in Suffolk. Apparently organized by Roger in anticipation of Spencer's complaint (for breach of promise) before London's Consistory Court, the papers illuminate late seventeenth-century social practice and support Wiseman's contention that she never encouraged Spencer. They contrast starkly with Spencer's riveting statements in the record from which we take our extracts. In March 1687, Wiseman married William Paston, second earl of Yarmouth (1652–1732), who took the case to the Court of Arches. Spencer eventually renounced his legal claim, but in 1689 he sent a challenge to Paston; the outcome is unknown.

Spencer's pursuit of Wiseman is described in Mary Chan's edition of North family documents about the imbroglio (*Life into Story* [Scolar Press, 1998]). The manuscript of his complaint is in the London Metropolitan Archives (DL/C/144); we modernize the longer of two versions, dropping some Latin legal tags, because it includes marginal comments. We thank Professor Chan for a transcription of photocopies furnished her by Timothy Wales. We thank the Bishop of London, the Rt. Revd. and Rt. Hon. Dr. Richard Chartres, for his kindness in allowing us to reproduce these excerpts.

FROM THE COMPLAINT OF ROBERT SPENCER

1. *Imprimis*[1] That in or about the month of August 1686 the said Robert Spencer, Esquire, was and had conference with Dame Elizabeth Wiseman, the . . . widow of Sir Robert Wiseman deceased, at her house in Kings Square in Soho, . . . where he continued with her for an hour or two or thereabouts, and was kindly received by her. And she did then particularly view his person and took particular notice of him and of his carriage, demeanor, and discourse, and did like the same very well and so appeared to do.

2. *Item* That the said Robert Spencer was and is a person of good blood and extraction, viz. he was and is the son of William Spencer and Elizabeth his wife, which William Spencer was and is the son of the . . . baron of Worme Leighton in the county of Warwick, and that Elizabeth was and is the daughter of Charles, Lord Gerard baron of Bromley in the county of Stafford, deceased.

3. *Item* That the said Robert Spencer was and is a bachelor, young, ruddy, and handsome, of a comely visage, straight limbs and proportion, of a lovely countenance, of a civil life and conversation, of a gentle and fair carriage, of a sweet and complaisant nature, and a person every way acceptable, fit, and capable to make his addresses to the said Lady Wiseman in the way of marriage, and so he was by herself looked upon and taken to be.

4. *Item* That the said Lady Wiseman in or about the month of August 1686 [was] by some of her relations commended to be a fit wife for him the said Robert Spencer and that some discourses happened thereupon, to which she was privy

---

1. First.

and had knowledge thereof.

5. *Item* That the said Lady Wiseman, having seen the said Mr. Robert Spencer as is before alleged, did express that she was well pleased with and did like his person, and she was contented and so expressed herself that he should be admitted to make his addresses to her in the way of marriage.

6. *Item* That the said Lady Wiseman, in order to take and accept of the said Robert Spencer to a near and more familiar discourse with her in the way of marriage, whose person she had liked as aforesaid, did come in her own coach to some of her near relations and did acquaint them that she liked the person of the said Mr. Robert Spencer, but desired that inquiry be made into his life and conversation, which accordingly was done.

7. *Item* That the said Lady Wiseman, after the premises[2] was and appeared to be very well satisfied, and contented with the said character which she had reviewed of the said Mr. Robert Spencer, and did freely and of her own accord inquire where the said Mr. Robert Spencer was in order to speak and converse about marriage to be had between them, and then appeared by her talk and by her carriage and discourse that she had great love and affection for him; and being acquainted that he was gone into the country, the Lady Wiseman, seeming impatient of his absence, asked when he would return again to Town, and whether it would not be by Tuesday next (the said discourse happening the Saturday next before, or thereabouts); and the said Lady Wiseman being then informed that it was believed the said Mr. Spencer would be in Town by that Tuesday, she, the said Lady Wiseman, said she would come and sup the evening of that day at the house of the Lord North and Grey her brother[3] and that she then expected to meet there, and would see and meet with, the said Mr. Spencer, at supper.

8. *Item* That upon the said Tuesday, which happened in August or September 1686, the Lady Wiseman, out of the great affection she had to the said Mr. Robert Spencer and desire to see him, did come to the house of the said Lord North . . . in expectation to see and find the said Mr. Spencer there, being about two hours before Mr. Spencer came thither, his coming thither being about six of the clock, of the same day.

9. *Item* That the said Mr. Spencer being come to the said house, where he found the said Lady Wiseman, the said Mr. Spencer and the said lady had communication and discourse together in a very kind and familiar manner, and the said Mr. Robert Spencer did then court the said Lady Wiseman as a suitor in the way of marriage, which she received with great love and kindness, and then he did very often kiss and embrace her, which she very freely and kindly received.

10. *Item* That after the premises, supper time being near, or it being then supper time, the said Robert Spencer and the Lady Wiseman went down to supper and did sup together in the said house, and all the while they were at supper

2. A legal term for "the aforesaid matter."
3. Charles, oldest son of Dudley North (fourth baron North), who succeeded as fifth baron North and was later made Lord Grey of Rolleston.

the said Lady Wiseman and the said Mr. Robert Spencer sat next together, and all the while they were at supper the said lady did treat, carry, and demean herself to the said Mr. Spencer in an amorous, free, kind, and loving manner, and as being a person whom she had admitted and did admit as a suitor in the way or marriage, and whom she intended to be her husband, and he did then carry, treat, and demean himself towards her in a very free and loving manner, as and being a suitor to her in the way of marriage, and by their several and respective carriage each to other, they were known and looked upon to be lovers, and such persons who had a kindness each for other, and did intend to marry together.

11. *Item* That after supper was ended, the said Mr. Spencer and the said Lady Wiseman continued in company together in the house aforesaid, and then he courted her in the way of marriage, desiring of her that she would accept of him for her husband, and used many words of love and affection to her to that purpose and he did then often embrace and kiss her in a very familiar way several times, and did hug and hold her about the waist, and did handle her naked neck with his naked hand, all which she received with great love and kindness to him in a most engaging and obliging manner, and so much was taken notice of and observed by some person or persons of the acquaintance of the said Lady Wiseman and the said Robert Spencer.

12. *Item* That the said Lady Wiseman was so well pleased with the company and conversation of the said Mr. Robert Spencer, and his courting of her and addresses in the way of marriage, as that she did desire to go with the said Mr. Spencer to the house of the Lord North at Tooting and that accordingly in the afternoon of the next day, being the time appointed for the going the said journey, which happened in August or September 1686, the said Lady Wiseman came to the house of the Lord North in Leicester Fields, where, by appointment aforesaid, the said Mr. Spencer and the said Lady Wiseman were to meet, and that after some discourse of love and affection in the way of marriage which then happened between them, the said Mr. Spencer and the said Lady Wiseman, the said Mr. Spencer did again make his addresses to her in the way of marriage, which she kindly received, and he then took the Lady Wiseman by the hand, which she freely gave him, and he saluted her several times, and then and there used much familiar and amorous discourse to her, and moved and requested her to accept of him for her husband, or to that effect, and they then had and did discourse and treat together of marriage to be had between them, and he then in a very loving and familiar manner continued to kiss and embrace her in his arms, and did lay his naked hand or hands upon her naked breasts and handled the same, which she with great love and kindness received and was very well pleased with the same, and so showed and expressed herself to be, and so was observed to be. . . .

14. *Item* That presently after the said Mr. Robert Spencer and the Lady Wiseman were come to the said house with some other company that came thither, there being a garden or gardens belonging to the said house, the said Lady Wiseman and the said Mr. Spencer walked there very familiarly and lovingly together for some time, and he then often embraced and kissed her there, and locked his arms in hers and she hers in his, and she was very exceedingly

pleased therewith, and received the same with great kindness and love; and the time and place aforesaid, the said Mr. Spencer took the said lady, with her good-will and liking, into his arms, and lifted her from the ground, and he, having her in his arms, closely hugged her to him, and kissed her again and again, all which she did kindly and lovingly accept of, and was and appeared to be very well pleased therewith, and so was looked upon and observed to be.

15. *Item* That the said Lady Wiseman, after the premises, still more and more increased her love and kindness to the said Mr. Spencer, and making demonstrations thereof, used these or the like words unto him, viz. "Come, let us go into the house," which accordingly he did with her; and being come into the house into an entry or passage there, the Lady Wiseman used these words or the like, viz. "Come, let us go upstairs," which accordingly they did; and being come upstairs together, there was a balcony adjoining to the said house into which they both went, and being there the said Mr. Spencer and the Lady Wiseman did carry themselves with great kindness, love, and affection each to other, and made great demonstrations thereof, and the said Mr. Spencer, with her good liking, who freely accepted thereof, did with his naked hands handle her breasts and often kissed and embraced her, and she was so affectionate and kind to him as that with her naked hand she did do and act such kindness and affection to him as was and is unusual to be done by any person but such as intend to be married together, being persons of ingenious education and quality as they were, viz. [she did handle his privy member which then was standing and erected, and continued her hand thereon for some time, and did feel the same, and took delight and was pleased therewith,][4] and that the said Mr. Spencer and the said Lady Wiseman did then kiss and embrace each other several times, and particularly she kissed him and she was seen and observed to kiss him.

16. *Item* That after the premises, the same day, the said Mr. Spencer and the Lady Wiseman went downstairs into the parlor of the said house, where they continued for some time, during which time the said Mr. Robert Spencer and the Lady Wiseman did discourse of love and affection which they had for each other, and she, the said Lady Wiseman, was and appeared to be very much pleased and so much appeared by her gesture and looks, and the said Mr. Robert Spencer often kissed the said lady and embraced her, and so much was observed and taken notice of.

17. *Item* That afterwards the same day, the said Mr. Robert Spencer and the Lady Wiseman returning home from Tooting to the said house of the said Lord North and Grey in Leicester Fields, in the same coach in which they went thither, all the way homeward the said Mr. Spencer and the said Lady Wiseman did carry and demean themselves with singular love and affection each to other, and he did almost all the way homeward kiss and embrace her and handle her naked breasts with his hands which she lovingly accepted and showed so much being very pleasant and merry, and did sing several love songs, and she was looked upon and taken to be exceedingly affected to and taken with the said Mr. Spencer, and

---

4. The bracketed words are underlined in the manuscript and marked "Rejected" in the margin.

she did show such favors and admitted him to such intimate familiarities with her that she was not looked upon to be fit to have any man for her husband but the said Mr. Robert Spencer.

18. *Item* That the day aforesaid, the said Mr. Robert Spencer and the said Lady Wiseman being then in company together, and that they might the more endear themselves each to other, and to show the entire affection they had each for other, did admit each other to the most intimate, and endearing arts that lovers in the way of marriage can be admitted to, viz. [the said Lady Wiseman did lay her naked hand, or at least the same was laid with her good liking upon the privy]⁵ member of the said Mr. Robert Spencer, where the same did lie and continue for some considerable time, and she was well pleased therewith, and did handle the same, and the said lady did the time aforesaid freely and willingly suffer the said Mr. Spencer so to do, and in token of her great affection which being in the way of marriage, did freely and voluntarily admit him to take, and he did with his hands take her by the privates through her petticoat and continue the same there for some time, handling the same, with which she was very well pleased, and before he did the same, by way of inviting him thereunto, she herself of her own accord did pull up one or two of her upper petticoats, under which he conveyed his hand.

19. *Item* That a day or two after the premises, being on or about the twenty-fourth day of September 1686, the said Mr. Spencer and the said Lady Wiseman, being in the Lord North and Grey's house in Leicester Fields, they did there in a most familiar, loving, and kind manner carry and demean themselves and were very well pleased therewith, each to other, as and being such persons who were looked upon to be such persons who were to marry each other, and they, the said Mr. Spencer and the said Lady Wiseman, then had amorous and obliging discourses touching love and marriage between them, and the said Mr. Spencer did then and there often kiss and embrace the said lady and with his naked hands handle her naked breasts, which she freely admitted him to do, and was very pleased therewith [and then did freely suffer the said Mr. Spencer to lay his hands upon her thighs, and to feel her privates through her petticoat, which favor of hers caused]⁶ an erection of Mr. Spencer's privy member, who thereupon lay the Lady Wiseman's bare hand upon his bare privy member, which she willingly and freely permitted, and handled the same, bare, with her bare hand, which she had done several times before the same day freely and of her own accord.

20. *Item* That when the said Lady Wiseman did handle the said Mr. Spencer's privy member as aforesaid in the next precedent article, he the said Mr. Spencer did ask the said Lady Wiseman how she liked it, to which the Lady Wiseman answered, "Very well," and thereupon took him about the neck and kissed him several times, and then said that she never had done so much by any but her late husband, Sir Robert Wiseman, and the said Mr. Spencer, being rav-

---

5. The passage in brackets is marked "Rejected to the end."
6. The passage in brackets is marked "Rejected to the end."

ished with her kindness, said, "Oh, Madam, what shall I do?" To which she, in an amorous and kind manner replied, "Do? Do what you will," and then said, "I will not, or cannot, be unkind to you," or words to that effect.[7]

21. *Item* That amongst some of the passages and discourses which then happened between the said Mr. Spencer and the Lady Wiseman and the discourses they then had, one of the passages was as follows: viz. [the said Lady Wiseman then having the said Mr. Spencer's naked privy member in][8] her bare hand, and being very well pleased therewith, in a smiling and pleasant manner used these familiar and kind words to the said Mr. Spencer, "Fie, fie, naughty Mr. Spencer," and the said words were overheard by some person or persons, who were of her familiar acquaintance, and did and do know her manner and tone of speaking, and were and are well acquainted with the same.

22. *Item* That after the premises, viz. on or about the 25th of September 1686, the said Mr. Robert Spencer and the said Lady Wiseman, having had treaty and communication concerning marriage between them as is before alleged, and then being free from marriage and matrimonial contracts with any other, did by the mutual consent of each other, and with an intent and mind to contract themselves in marriage together by the words of the present expressing their mutual consent therein, seriously and in a solemn manner contract themselves in marriage together, in the words following or words to the same effect, viz. the said Mr. Robert Spencer then holding the said Lady Wiseman by the hands, used these or the like words, viz. "I, Robert Spencer, take thee, Elizabeth, to my wedded wife," and she, the said Lady Wiseman, used these or the like words: "I, Elizabeth, take thee, Robert, to my wedded husband," and there contracted together, in marriage as aforesaid by their mutual consent, and the same was freely done by them, the said Robert and Elizabeth, and that ever since the said contract of marriage, the said Mr. Robert Spencer and the said Lady Wiseman were and are man and wife, and so are and ought to be accounted, and that the said contract was had and made in the presence of credible witnesses, some of which did then and there wish much joy and happiness to them, the said Mr. Robert Spencer and the said (Dame Elizabeth) Lady Wiseman, and wished God to bless them, which they kindly accepted and thanked them for their good wishes or to that effect.[9]

23. *Item* That before and . . . at the time the said Mr. Robert Spencer and the said Lady Wiseman were contracting themselves in marriage, as aforesaid, and after the same was done the time aforesaid, the said Lady Wiseman was very cheerful and pleasant, and was very well pleased and contented with what was done therein.

24. *Item* That presently, after the said Mr. Robert Spencer and the Lady

---

7. A marginal note says, "This article wholly rejected."
8. The passage in brackets is marked "Rejected to the end." Indeed, says Professor Chan, the entire paragraph is marked by a vertical line and annotated "Wholly rejected."
9. Had Spencer and Wiseman actually made these vows in the present tense, and before witnesses, they would have been legally bound to each other. This, even more than the alleged sexual flirting and fondling, would prove Spencer's claim.

Wiseman were contracted together as aforesaid, the said Robert, with the free will and good liking of the said Lady Wiseman, did take her into his arms and embraced and kissed her, with which she was very exceedingly pleased, and then they went hand in hand together in the said house, as and being contracted in marriage together. . . .

26. *Item* That the said Lady Wiseman, well knowing that she and said Mr. Robert Spencer were contracted in marriage together, and that there had passed great and endearing words and actions between them, did acquaint the Lord North and Grey and his lady with many of the familiar passages of love and kindness between her and the said Mr. Spencer which are before alleged.

27. *Item* That the said Mr. Robert Spencer and the Lady Wiseman being so contracted together in marriage as aforesaid, the said Mr. Robert Spencer did wait upon her at her house aforesaid, and there had speech and communication with her and was with great love and kindnesses received by her, and a license being obtained for the solemnization of the said marriage,[10] the same was intimated to the said Lady Wiseman at her said house, upon or about the Sunday following, in discourse about the day for the said marriage, and then the Thursday next following, the said Sunday was by consent of the Lady Wiseman appointed to be the day for the solemnization of the said marriage. . . .

29. *Item* That at the time and place aforesaid, the said Lady Wiseman, in confirmation of the said contract of marriage between her and the said Mr. Spencer, and to give him all possible assurance she could of her entire love and affection towards him, did admit him to the most near and familiar acts of love and affection that could be desired or expected by him from her [and particularly, he did, with her consent, after some passages of love and dalliance between them, lay the Lady Wiseman's naked hand upon his naked privy member which was then erected, which she then for some time handled, and then she, being in a great chair and he being right before her, she did in an amorous, loving, and inviting posture throw herself backward in the said chair, still holding in her naked hand the naked privy member of the said Mr. Spencer, but the said Mr. Spencer did not then proceed any further, being interrupted by servants passing to and fro][11] . . . but put the Lady Wiseman in mind of the day appointed for the marriage, to which she replied she would not forget it, and this was and is true.

30. *Item* That the said Lady Wiseman did still persist and continue in her love and affection towards the said Mr. Spencer and her resolution to solemnize the said marriage, nor had nor would be drawn from the same, but that Sir Dudley North and Mr. Roger North, her brothers, both or one of them being informed or hearing that the said Mr. Robert Spencer and the said lady were contracted in marriage together, and that a day was appointed for the solemnization of the same, did come to the said Lady Wiseman and did cast false aspersions and calumnies upon Mr. Spencer and his family, and did vilify him to her, and there-

10. The religious rite that would complete and bless the marriage.
11. The passage in brackets is marked in the margin "Rejected to the end"; the entire section is marked by a vertical line and the words "Wholly rejected."

by, and by threats used to her, they, having an aversion to the said Mr. Spencer and the said marriage, did persuade and prevail with her not to solemnize the said marriage, and not to admit the said Mr. Spencer to come to her nor see her.

31. *Item* That after the premises in the next precedent article, the said Sir Dudley North was informed, after inquiries being made touching the said contract of marriage before alleged between the said Mr. Spencer and the said Lady Wiseman, that the said lady was contracted to the said Mr. Spencer, and that there had passed so much between the Lady Wiseman and him that she was not fit to be a wife for any man but him.

32. *Item* That the said Sir Dudley North, having received credible information that the said Lady Wiseman and Mr. Spencer were contracted together in marriage, and being satisfied and convinced of the truth thereof, did not long after go to the Lord North and Grey, and endeavored to induce and persuade him to speak to Mr. Spencer and to prevail with him, if he could, to give his sister the Lady Wiseman a release from the said contract of marriage.

(signed) Robert Spencer